PACIFIC
ALAMO

PACIFIC ALAMO

THE BATTLE FOR WAKE ISLAND

John Wukovits

NEW AMERICAN LIBRARY

New American Library
Published by New American Library, a division of
Penguin Group (USA) Inc., 375 Hudson Street,
New York, New York 10014, U.S.A.
Penguin Books Ltd, 80 Strand,
London WC2R 0RL, England
Penguin Books Australia Ltd, 250 Camberwell Road,
Camberwell, Victoria 3124, Australia
Penguin Books Canada Ltd, 10 Alcorn Avenue,
Toronto, Ontario, Canada M4V 3B2
Penguin Books (N.Z.) Ltd, Cnr Rosedale and Airborne Roads,
Albany, Auckland 1310, New Zealand

Penguin Books Ltd, Registered Offices:
80 Strand, London WC2R 0RL, England

First published by New American Library, a division of Penguin Group (USA) Inc.

First Printing, July 2003
10 9 8 7 6 5 4 3 2 1

 REGISTERED TRADEMARK—MARCA REGISTRADA

LIBRARY OF CONGRESS CATALOGING-IN-PUBLICATION DATA:
Wukovits, John F., 1944–
Pacific Alamo : the battle for Wake Island / John Wukovits.
p. cm.
Includes bibliographical references and index.
ISBN 0-451-20873-0 (alk. paper)
1. Wake Island, Battle of, Wake Island, 1941. I. Title.

D767.99.W3W84 2003
940.54'26—dc21   2003044174

Set in Eldorado Text Light
Designed by Ginger Legato

Printed in the United States of America

To Matthew Dickerman,
my first grandson—
may he
and the other members of
his generation
never forget the sacrifices made for them
by the men of Wake Island
and by the other individuals
who gave so much in wartime

Contents

Preface

In my role as World War II historian, I have long been familiar with the story surrounding Wake Island. The heroics exhibited by the men, civilian and military, stirred my soul, just as tales of courage under fire from Guadalcanal, Tarawa, Iwo Jima, and other Pacific Theater locales captivated me.

My interest in Wake intensified in 1989, when I had the opportunity to meet a handful of Wake veterans at a reunion. Their remarkable stories moved me, and I left the gathering grateful to have had a chance to speak with such an extraordinary collection of men who meant so much to the nation in the bleak early days of World War II. The only fact that dampened my enthusiasm was that the nation, now busy with other matters, no longer showed much interest in these gallant warriors.

Little more occurred until 2001 when my agent, Jim Hornfischer, mentioned the possibility of my writing a book about the 1941 battle. I jumped at the chance, for I knew that I would have a subject matter that not only deserved public notice, but could once again move people as it had sixty years ago.

Since then I have embarked upon a remarkable odyssey. Research has taken me to all points of the nation, introduced me to heroes who scoff at the notion that they are heroes, and immersed me in a saga that has rarely been equaled in the annals of military lore. I came away feeling fortunate to have met men who, while achieving nobility so long ago, yet retain simple humility and decency.

Many individuals aided me along the way: My multitalented agent, Jim Hornfischer, not only arranged the book contract, but also offered valued suggestions throughout the writing process. At New American Library, my editor Doug Grad and production editor Adrian Wood provided assistance at every step of the process and proved that professionalism certainly exists in the publishing industry. Jeffrey Ward added the splendid maps that accompany the text.

Barry Zirby guided me through the labyrinthine paths at the National Archives, Alex Rankin lent his expertise at the Special Collections of the Boston University Library, and Dr. James Ginther directed me to the superb material stored at the Marine Corps Research Center in Quantico, Virginia. In Washington, D.C., Fred Allison, Charles Melson, and Robert Aquilina made my visit to the Marine Historical Center a useful one.

I could never have produced the volume that emerged without the assistance of the Wake Island veterans, who readily gave me their time for interviews, their help in locating other individuals, and the use of their photograph collections. Franklin Gross, who publishes the newsletter *Wake Island Wig-Wag*, freely offered his assistance in numerous ways. Ewing Laporte, Kenneth Marvin, Martin Gatewood, John S. Johnson, and James King, among others, shared lengthy oral reminiscences. Cathy Sanders, the daughter of deceased Marine veteran Jacob Sanders, kindly e-mailed her father's written account of his time on Wake and in prison camp.

A few others deserve special mention, for they gave me the information that provided the backbone to this narrative. I spent hours, sometimes spread out over a period of days, interviewing these men, occasionally over the telephone, but most often in their homes. I came to know them like newfound relatives; I granted them the same respect I reserve for only those few who have earned it. Col. Robert M. Hanna, USMC (Ret.) and Ralph Holewinski yielded the material for the gripping battle around Hanna's gun and demonstrated that noble warriors can be humble, unassuming next-door neighbors. Colonel Hanna also illustrated the enduring love that binds a man, first to his beautiful wife and then to his beloved Marine Corps. Joe Goicoechea, Murray Kidd, and George Rosendick, as much fun as when I spoke with them as they were in their youth, fascinated me with their gaiety, spirit of adventure, and their fondness for one another. Their information helped me grasp what life for the civilians was like. J. O. Young not only talked about his experiences, but also shared his written account and that of his uncle, Forrest Read. Along with Colonel Hanna, Young and his wife, Pearl Ann, show that romance and love last long beyond youth.

Two influences on my historical career merit credit. My college adviser in my student days and now professor emeritus of history at the University of Notre Dame, Bernard Norling, has long offered assistance whenever asked. An established World War II historian in his own right, with a list of books to his credit, Dr. Norling has provided suggestions and advice since the earliest days of my writing career. He is the image of what a teacher-adviser should be.

The other individual is an esteemed author of World War II material, whose biographies of Adms. Ernest J. King and Raymond A. Spruance stand as examples of solid research and powerful writing. For more than a decade Tom Buell, who sadly passed away in 2002, provided guidance and friendship, and I could never have attained any success without his help. He and his wife, Marilyn, are two of the finest people I have come to know, and I shall dearly miss Tom.

As always in my life, members of my family also helped me along the way. My older brother, Tom, a former naval aviator, lent inspiration and support. My three lovely daughters, Amy, Julie, and Karen, made the process easier with their cheerful encouragement and with their own pride-inducing accomplishments. My fiancée, Terri Faitel, a powerful force in her own field of mathematics, never failed to take time from her own busy schedule as a teacher and conference presenter to boost my morale and to read my different versions of the manuscript. Matt Gajda's valued suggestions and comments about the manuscript helped make the book better.

Finally, three other people who are no longer with us helped inspire me along the way. My parents, Tom and Grace, never gave up on me, and the memory of my younger brother, Fred, who left us all too soon, prodded me to do the best I could.

"Wake Island Marine on Deck!"

The aged man appeared to be in his early eighties, but *graying* and *frail* were not the first words you would use to describe him. The bounce in his step was still there, and energy shone in his eyes, carrying more than a hint of what a force he once was. He stood amidst the large gathering of naval and Marine officers, relaxing after a long day's schedule of reunion meetings. They sipped coffee and told tales of their service histories.

Suddenly, someone spotted him, and a deep voice barked out above the din, "Attention! Wake Island Marine on deck!"

"Everyone stopped talking," said a naval officer who witnessed the incident. "We stood at attention, faced the Marine, and saluted. Those guys are legendary in the Navy and Marines for what they did, and whenever one is around, you pay him the highest respect."[1]

No wonder. Sixty years ago, the old man was one of a tiny band of Marines who staged one of history's most dramatic battles. In the bleak early days of the Pacific War, while America could only watch as Japan rolled to victory from Oahu to the South China Sea, a handful of America's soldiers and civilians on Wake redeemed the nation's honor and handed the United States a blueprint for its eventual victory.

Two and a half years before the "citizen soldiers" at Normandy began the drive to reclaim Europe, the island outpost of Wake stood alone, like a cavalry fort in some oceanic version of the Western frontier. Most of America's Pacific battle fleet, the backbone of the nation's power in the hemisphere, rested on Pearl Harbor's muddy bottom along with almost two thousand young American sailors. Marines on Guam and British infantry in Malaya were fighting futile holding actions against swarms of enemy troops. In the Philippines, Japanese bombers demolished Gen. Douglas MacArthur's air force before it lifted from the ground, and Japanese infantry shoved his troops into a disastrous retreat toward the Bataan Peninsula. Hong Kong and Singapore were poised to fall, and the destruction of two British warships, the HMS *Prince of Wales* and the HMS *Repulse*, at the hands of Japanese planes off Malaya, caused British prime minister Winston Churchill to lament the numerous deficiencies of Allied power in the Pacific.

Barely six hundred miles—less than two days' steaming time or four hours' flying time—from the closest Japanese base, Wake stood next on the Japanese timetable. There was little reason to believe the island would offer anything but the feeblest resistance to invasion. Pearl Harbor, the nearest American base that could offer assistance, lay a distant two thousand miles to the east, and it was a smoking ruin.

Wake, a coral atoll comprising three islands whose highest point was barely twenty feet above sea level and whose vegetation consisted of scrubby trees and brush, covered three square miles of total land area. Yet even this tiny real estate, with ten miles of beach, offered too much territory for the tiny garrison to cover. Should the Japanese crash ashore in one of the numerous gaps between gun emplacements, the Americans would be swiftly overrun.

How the "Devil Dog Defenders of Wake Island" battled long odds is one of the great stories in the annals of military lore. The exploits of the Marines and civilian construction workers rank with those of the Spartans at Thermopylae, with the British who fought thousands of Zulu at Rorke's Drift in 1879, and with the Texans at the Alamo.

CHAPTER 1

★

"An Ordinary Group of Americans"

"Last Night the Japanese Attacked Wake Island"

President Franklin D. Roosevelt sat in the White House study on December 7, 1941, an aging leader suddenly appearing older and wearier. The man who infused life and vitality into a depressed country for much of the 1930s, who brought hope to those who had little, now struggled with his own form of shock and despair. Only moments ago he had been enjoying a leisurely lunch in the Oval Office with aide and close friend, Harry Hopkins, during which they amiably chatted about lighthearted topics.

That suddenly changed at 1:40 P.M. when Roosevelt's military commanders at the sprawling American naval base at Pearl Harbor, Hawaii, sent a message that electrified the world—AIR RAID, PEARL HARBOR—THIS IS NO DRILL. The nation of Japan, which had been casting covetous eyes across the Pacific for almost a decade, had bombed the Hawaiian bastion and inflicted major damage to the U. S. Pacific Fleet. The Navy Roosevelt had loved since youth, when he had sailed the bays of New York, and since World War I, when he served as assistant secretary of the Navy, lay in smoldering ruins at the bottom of Pearl Harbor.

Hopkins glanced at Roosevelt and muttered that the news had to be mistaken. He could not believe that the Japanese could strike so quickly and with such devastating results at the most important military arsenal in the Pacific. But the news reports did not lie.

Aides rushed in and out of the office with the latest updates. With each bulletin, Roosevelt's secretary, Grace Tully, thought that Roosevelt looked more nervous and tense. One by one, additional Pacific targets had either fallen or were about to be overwhelmed. Roosevelt, feeling much like a cornered boxer staggering under a flurry of blows, listened to a litany of disasters—Japanese aircraft bombed Guam and Midway Islands; the Japanese invaded the Philippines, Shanghai, and Hong Kong; Japanese soldiers poured into North Borneo and the Dutch East Indies; the Japanese overwhelmed Malaya and Thailand. The attacks unfolded on such a grand scale that they unbelievably encompassed seven time zones and covered almost seven thousand miles.

As Grace Tully typed new reports telephoned to her from Chief of Naval Operations Adm. Harold Stark, presidential aides huddled behind her to read each word as it appeared on the paper. Every sentence contained fresher evidence of the debacle, causing experienced political advisers to tighten their jaws in anger and mutter expletives under their breath. When Tully handed the bulletins to Roosevelt, he repeatedly shook his head in dismay. Tully claimed that the president took the naval catastrophe so hard that to Roosevelt, the loss of each ship was "like the losing of a friend."[1]

Hoping to learn fresher information from a firsthand source, Roosevelt contacted Gov. Joseph B. Poindexter in Honolulu. The governor of the Territory of Hawaii was calmly describing the damage caused by the first air raid when he suddenly started shouting. Roosevelt turned to his aides and said, "My God, there's another wave of Jap planes over Hawaii right this minute."[2] Still reeling from the initial raid, from halfway around the globe Roosevelt now had to listen helplessly as a second attack caused more havoc. He and the other silent men congregating in the White House could only wonder what further devastation lay ahead on this horrific day.

At 8:40 P.M., Cabinet members entered his study to be briefed about the day's events. Most had been out of town on business and had been quickly called back to Washington by White House operators, so they knew little of the day's events. When Labor Secretary Frances Perkins arrived, she noticed that the president's typical warm greeting had been replaced with a perfunctory hello.

Roosevelt started by labeling the meeting the most serious Cabinet session since Abraham Lincoln assembled his advisers in the dark early days of the Civil War. In a subdued voice Roosevelt explained that the only certain information they had was that serious losses had been absorbed and that the Navy had suffered the worst defeat in its history.

"His pride in the Navy was so terrific," wrote Perkins later, "that he was having actual physical difficulty in getting out the words that put him on record as knowing that the Navy was caught unawares, that bombs dropped on ships that were not in fighting shape and not prepared to move, but were just tied up. I remember that he said twice to [Secretary of the Navy W. Franklin] Knox, 'Find out, for God's sake, why those ships were tied up in rows.'"

Perkins later added, "It was obvious to me that Roosevelt was having a dreadful time just accepting the idea that the Navy could be caught unawares."[3]

One hour later, congressional leaders, including Majority Leader Alben W. Barkley, House Speaker Sam Rayburn, and the chairmen of important committees, joined the Cabinet. The chairman of the Senate Foreign Relations Committee, Texas's Thomas B. Connally, angrily jumped to his feet and banged on the president's desk. "Hell's fire, didn't we do anything!" shouted the irate Connally.

"That's about it," replied a sullen Roosevelt.

Turning his glare toward Secretary Knox, Connally asked the question that every American, from the president to the newest citizen, wanted answered, "Didn't you say last month that we could lick the Japs in two weeks? Didn't you say that our Navy was so well prepared and located that the Japanese couldn't hope to hurt us at all?"

When Knox could not offer a reply, Connally continued his tirade, inquiring why all the ships at Pearl Harbor were crowded together, many in neat rows. "I am amazed by the attack by Japan, but I am still more astounded at what happened to our Navy. They were all asleep. Where were our patrols?"[4]

People in all corners of the nation asked that question and others as the day unfolded. Their faith in the ability of their military to keep them out of harm's way had been badly shaken, so much so that one of the most respected publications of the country, *Time* magazine, bluntly stated, "The U.S. Navy was caught with its pants down. Within one tragic hour—before the war had really begun—the U.S. appeared to have suffered greater naval losses than in the whole of World War I."[5] A nationally syndicated journalist wrote that people believed the United States would not hit the Japanese because it could not.

Aggravating the situation was that the losses came at the hands of a nation most Americans had dismissed as backwards and unable to contend with the strength of the United States. If a supposedly second-rate power inflicted such damage on the United States, what other mayhem might it commit? Fear and uncertainty created fertile grounds for rumors that made an already nervous citizenry more susceptible to panic. Reports circulated that a group of Japanese aircraft had flown over San Jose, California. In Hawaii, residents made plans to leave for the mainland because they feared that an inevitable Japanese invasion could not be repelled by the weakened military. Politicians urged the president to consider the West Coast indefensible and to pull back the military to fortified positions in the Rocky Mountains. Roosevelt's son, Elliott, even called him from Texas to explain that he had heard the Japanese were about to launch an attack from Mexico against Texas or California.

As night fell on Washington, D.C., on December 7, groups of citizens collected outside the White House fence, as if their presence near the nation's leaders could at the same time breathe wisdom into their proceedings and deliver reassurance to themselves. A hushed crowd silently stared at the presidential mansion, then started singing, "God Bless America."

After his Cabinet and congressional leaders departed, Roosevelt kept an appointment with renowned newsman Edward R. Murrow, whose radio broadcasts from London had moved a world. The two shared beer and sandwiches while the president discussed the last twenty-four hours. Finally, he erupted in an angry tone that American aircraft had been destroyed "on the ground, by God, on the ground!"[6]

The next day a more determined president, leaning for support on the arms of his son, Marine Corps Capt. James Roosevelt, shuffled to the rostrum of the House of Representatives to ask Congress to declare war on Japan. Accompanying him were his wife, Eleanor, and Mrs. Woodrow Wilson, whose husband had once appeared before Congress to ask for a similar declaration.

In measured tones, the president began his speech to the hushed crowd. "Yesterday, December 7, 1941—a date which will live in infamy— the United States of America was suddenly and deliberately attacked by naval and air forces of the Empire of Japan."

Roosevelt then listed the places that had been attacked along with Pearl Harbor. "Yesterday the Japanese government also launched an attack against Malaya.

"Last night Japanese forces attacked Hong Kong.

"Last night Japanese forces attacked Guam.

"Last night Japanese forces attacked the Philippine Islands.

"Last night the Japanese attacked Wake Island."

He added that "Japan has, therefore, undertaken a surprise offensive extending throughout the Pacific area. The facts of yesterday and today speak for themselves. The people of the United States have already formed their opinions and will understand the implications to the very life and safety of our nation."

He warned Japan that the American people, stunned as they were, would never forget such a heinous deed. "With confidence in our armed forces—with the unbounding determination of our people—we will gain the inevitable triumph—so help us God."[7]

At a press conference the next day with reporters, Roosevelt continued his efforts to be realistic in his assessments of the situation, yet encouraging to the people. He warned of bad times ahead and asked the country to pull together:

"We are now in this war. We are all in it—all the way. Every single man, woman, and child is a partner in the most tremendous undertaking of our American history. We must share together the bad news and the good news, the defeats and the victories—the changing fortunes of war.

"So far, the news has been all bad. We have suffered a serious setback in Hawaii. Our forces in the Philippines, which include the brave people of that commonwealth, are taking punishment, but are vigorously defending themselves. The reports from Guam and Wake and Midway Islands are still confused, but we must be prepared for the announcement that all these three outposts have been seized."[8]

Amidst the gloom and the demoralizing details, a beacon of hope emerged from the unlikeliest of sources. On desolate Wake, an atoll 7,500 miles southwest of the White House, a handful of Marines, Navy, and Army personnel, buttressed by a few hundred hardy civilians—the first "citizen soldiers" of the war—were poised to mount one of history's grandest spectacles—a valiant defense against superior forces. From their efforts would reemerge the hope that Pearl Harbor had shattered; from the actions of an ordinary group of Americans a depressed nation would learn how to hold its head high once again and to believe their side could prevail.

"I Wanted to Travel"

They came to Wake from all parts of the country and from all backgrounds, as if drawn by an immense magnet, each bearing his own reason for being on the island when the war started. Some journeyed to the Pacific isle for money, some for adventure. Others headed to Wake because orders sent them there or to escape trouble back home. Yet at the sound of the first bombs, military and civilians alike discarded previous notions about their futures and forged an effective fighting force. In the process, they turned Wake into the nation's initial victory, gave birth to emotional war slogans, created the first, and possibly the noblest, of World War II's handful of epic actions, and handed Hollywood the makings for an emotional movie.

As in any gripping drama, unique characters abound, bringing varied experiences and backgrounds to the stage. Most of the Marines eventually landed on Wake for the same reason—they followed orders. Their differences lie in why they joined the Marines in the first place.

Robert M. Hanna would never have been selected as the Marine on the recruiting poster, although he seemed predestined to a military life. His ancestors served in the Revolutionary War and on both sides of the Civil War, and Hanna would be joined in World War II by twenty-five other members of his extended family. An undersize individual born in the desolate countryside of what is now Riverside, Texas, on April 29, 1914, Hanna spent a great deal of time on his own, preferring solitude to the fast-paced activities of school chums. While other boys played sports and fought one another, he loved to sneak into the family country store and grab some candy while no one was looking, or slump into a comfortable chair to read his favorite books—westerns and crime stories. The soft-spoken individual rarely confided in anyone and counted few close friends.

In the early 1930s, Hanna joined the military. Six years in the Army, where the enlisted man saw officers repeatedly treat the men with disdain, disillusioned the young Hanna. One time he received verbal permission from his commanding officer for two days' leave. While Hanna was away, every man was ordered back to camp for a surprise maneuver, but Hanna never learned of the event. When he returned, the camp commandant confined Hanna to his quarters for being absent without leave. Hanna's commanding officer, who had forgotten to report Hanna's absence, failed to back the young man to avoid receiving a reprimand.

Hanna learned from this incident. He believed a leader should not only treat his men with respect, but should also join in their labors and lead by example. Without these ingredients, Hanna felt an officer would never gain the trust of his men.

Hanna's six years in the Army ended in 1939. Still seeking a military career, he turned to the Marines, where he thought a rigid insistence on loyalty to the unit and Corps offered a better alternative. As a young lieutenant, he tried to remember the lessons about leadership he had observed and formulated while in the Army—to be fair and honest, to take care of all the small details, and to put the men first. For instance, during the post's dinner celebration every November 10, the birthday of the Marine Corps, Hanna made sure his men passed through the food line before he did.

If a man landed in trouble, Hanna took the time to check his story and interrogate witnesses before passing judgment. In that manner, even if Hanna delivered a harsh punishment, the Marine knew his commanding officer was willing to go the extra mile for him. Hanna hoped that as a result, in a tough situation like combat, his men would be willing to exert more effort for him.

Hanna was not all business. Though he rarely frequented local bars or chased women like some men, he did enjoy himself on occasion. On January 7, 1937, in exchange for the use of Hanna's car, a fellow officer set him up on a blind date with Vera Edith Bryant, an attractive, serene brunette. The two seemed made for each other—they both loved quiet pastimes and avoided loudmouthed individuals—but two months passed before the shy officer called and asked for a second date. After that the two were almost inseparable, often driving around the countryside in Hanna's car, talking to each other and enjoying nature.

The couple wed on Christmas Day 1938, in Fort Worth, Texas. Unlike many men, who seem to forget the romantic element once marriage happens, Hanna delivered almost-daily reminders to Vera of his love for her. On the way home from the base he would purchase a single rose or some other small gift to let her know she was never out of his thoughts. For her part, Vera always cooked the meals that her husband most loved.

By March 1941, Hanna—after training in Quantico, Virginia, and San Diego, California—received new orders. With other members of a freshly formed unit called the First Marine Defense Battalion, Hanna boarded a troop transport and headed to the Pacific. Final destination—Wake Island.

All his life, Ralph Holewinski has called Gaylord, Michigan, his home. Nestled in the luscious forests and pine trees of northern Michigan, Gaylord offered year-round activities—hunting and golf in the summer and skiing and skating in the winter. While Holewinski enjoyed those hobbies, he spent most of his time on the family farm, where his parents needed his help in harvesting the crops that brought the family through the Depression.

Holewinski's educational training at Saint Mary's Catholic School in Gaylord fashioned a firm foundation, both educational and religious. The Dominican nuns that taught classes instilled basic values in Holewinski, such as loyalty and devotion. He especially recalled one mathematics teacher, a nun who ran her class in military style and demanded strict attention, who warned the students in the 1930s that the world was headed toward a general war in the 1940s.

Two years after graduating from high school, Holewinski enlisted in the Marine Corps, drawn by the lure of a steady job and travel to distant places. He immediately headed to San Diego for boot camp and training on a .30-caliber machine gun. Like Hanna, he was assigned to the First Defense Battalion and ordered to a place about which he knew nothing— Wake Island.

Twenty-year-old Corp. Franklin Gross, the tenth of twelve children born in Dewitt, Missouri, experienced early wanderlust, and as a teenager often hopped freight trains to travel about the western portion of the nation. "In the 1930s, the Depression years, I don't care what freight train went by, it had dozens and dozens of hoboes. Nobody had work." Gross headed from Dewitt to Kansas City, swung north to Minnesota to harvest wheat, and then traveled to South Dakota for a brief stint working for the railroad.

He later hitchhiked to Wyoming, where he hopped another train going to California.

Gross enlisted with the Marines in January 1939, before friction with the Japanese grabbed so many headlines. As for most Wake Marines, a possible Pacific war was not a factor in Gross's decision. He said he joined because "I wanted to travel"9 and to see other parts of the world.

While Gross journeyed about the country, another Missouri native, eighteen-year-old Ewing E. Laporte, bounced around the Midwest. Because of the Depression, he and his father moved to wherever their carpentry skills were needed. In the harsh economic conditions, Laporte—like many other healthy young men—eventually looked to the military to solve his employment difficulties. He joined the Marines because he saw an opportunity to better his condition, not because he felt a sense of duty in the face of distant war rumblings.

"The lack of work knocked out any ambition for civilian life. I joined the Marines on December 7, 1940, one year to the day before Pearl Harbor."10

"We Were All Hell-raisers Then"

Marines and civilian construction workers on Wake should have forged a firm friendship, since the men shared common backgrounds. The rough-hewn, hard-living construction workers, Depression-era sons just like Gross and Laporte, feared few challenges, at least in construction. Many had worked on the massive Grand Coulee and Boulder Dam projects, but unlike the Marines, they had willingly traveled to Wake for an opportunity to earn fantastic amounts of money. The men ranged in age from seventeen to seventy-two, and they included a handful of father-and-son combinations. Forerunners of the citizen-soldier armies that would so ably augment the regular armed forces and fuel the American military to victory in World War II, the civilian construction workers played a key role in the Wake story.

While the Hannas embarked on their new lives together, and Holewinski, Gross, and Laporte started on their paths to Wake, the fun-loving trio of Joe Goicoechea, Murray Kidd, and George Rosendick enjoyed life to the fullest in Boise, Idaho. The teenagers had been friends since grade school, and as they advanced through their senior year at Boise High and beyond, they became almost inseparable. Everyone knew of their reputation—if you wanted to laugh and have a good time, hook up with Joe, Murray, and George. The three, sometimes joined by Murray's girlfriend, Lena, pocketed what little change they had and headed to the movies at the Ada Theater or grabbed milk shakes at the local hamburger joint after Friday-night high school football games. After all, the Depression's effects lingered, so they could not waste money, but they were young, single, and ready for everything life had to offer—except marriage. "Hell, we couldn't take care of ourselves let alone having someone else around,"[11] said Goicoechea.

Boise, a small town, with a population of twenty thousand, could have been a model for a Norman Rockwell painting. Neighbors said hello to each other and never locked their doors at night. Winters brought skiing and ice skating, while summers provided ample opportunity for baseball and other outdoor activities. Since the town was nestled in the Rockies, hunting and fishing were year-round options. Every summer since they were kids, the three remembered racing down to the Boise River to watch workers pitch a series of circus tents for the annual county fair. The carnies, with their air of independence, travel, and mystique, fascinated the trio.

"Boise was a perfect place to grow up in," said the rambunctious Goicoechea. "You knew everybody. We had baseball and softball, and guys headed for the hills for fishing and hunting. We'd hunt everything—deer, elk, bear. It was a great place to be."[12]

Like most Boise youth in those days, they came from immigrant families. Born July 31, 1921, to Basque immigrants from Spain, Goicoechea was the eldest of four siblings. He worked in a grocery store to help provide money for the family, which because of financial problems moved four times before Goicoechea entered high school. "We had to stay a jump ahead of the house collectors. It was the Depression."[13]

Kidd's family traveled to Boise because of farming and logging, the town's two major industries. The serious-minded Kidd awoke at 3:30 A.M. each day to deliver newspapers to his huge route of two hundred customers, carefully placing each paper in a newspaper slot or setting it on the porch instead of casually tossing it anywhere on the front yard. Knowing his parents lacked the money to send him to college, Kidd studied bookkeeping in high school so he could work for a business after graduation. He eventually became the bookkeeper for a Boise stationery store.

Of the three, George Rosendick most appealed to the girls. Good-looking and affable, Rosendick felt as comfortable in the presence of females as he did with Joe and Murray. Like the other two, Rosendick appreciated fun but also realized the value of hard work, a trait cultivated by his parents, immigrants from Croatia.

Despite their tribulations, the three never lacked for fun. Goicoechea played baseball with such a flourish that the Cincinnati Reds sent a scout to look him over. The scrappy Kidd joined Boise High's track and basketball teams, even though he stood only five feet tall and weighed less than one hundred pounds as a freshman.

Sometimes their fun almost landed the boys in trouble with the Boise police, most of whom they knew by name. Joe, Murray, and George became adept at sliding lead slugs into pinball machines, which rewarded them by paying off in real nickels. The ploy, profitable for them but a financial bust for the businessmen, had its drawbacks: The trio could pull the scam only so many times before the owner caught on. "We had to be careful about going back into some of those places. We were all hell-raisers then."[14]

Fun can carry a person only so far before responsibility and maturity—and a serious need for money—wedge their way in. Boise offered few exciting job prospects to the adventurous youth, but one industry seemed promising. The giant construction firm, Morrison-Knudsen, had developed a reputation building bridges, roads, and dams all over the world, including Hoover Dam and the San Francisco Bay Bridge. In May 1941, word spread through town that they needed laborers to construct military facilities on some obscure Pacific outpost. In exchange for what was then the incredible amount of $125 a month plus expenses, workers agreed to travel to the Pacific—at company expense—and work for nine months, at which time they would receive a bonus and could either return to the mainland or accept a second nine-month hitch.

Morrison-Knudsen was one of a group of eight huge construction firms hired by the government to develop Pacific bases. To reduce costs, the Navy merged the eight into an immense organization called the Contractors Pacific Naval Air Bases (CPNAB). Morrison-Knudsen received the contracts to complete Wake.

The opportunity seemed tailor-made for the boys, less than one year removed from high school. They would travel to an exotic Pacific isle, accumulate some money, and learn a trade—all in the space of nine short months. If they liked what they were doing, they could always remain in the Pacific. If not, they were free to return to Boise, stocked with fresh cash and new skills. It seemed a no-lose situation.

Obstacles quickly developed. Joe's parents tried to talk him out of it by arguing they needed their oldest child helping out at home rather than roaming about a distant beach. George failed the physical because of flat feet, and a manager told Murray he was too young. The boys refused to give in.

"I was only eighteen at the time, and you had to be at least nineteen, but I really wanted to go," explained Kidd. "I went home and told my mom about it, and she could see how serious I was about it. She got on the phone and called somebody she knew at Morrison-Knudsen, and all of us were signed up. She knew the right people."[15] Barely out of high school and hardly more than kids having fun, Goicoechea, Kidd, and Rosendick signed the appropriate forms and prepared to go to Wake Island.

More than anything, J. O. Young loved to spend time with his fiancée, Pearl Ann Sparks. For less than a dollar, the couple could attend a movie at the Majestic or the Adelaide, then get hamburgers and milk shakes at either of their two favorites on Main Street, the Blue Bird or Saxton's. It was a perfect evening for a pair deeply in love.

Theirs was not the wild, passionate style of affair in which some teenagers indulge. Their relationship started innocently enough—walks through town with a friend of theirs, another girl who caught Young's eye. "She was a cute little button," explained Young years later, "and Pearl and I would walk with her every noon. I had a bad case of puppy love for that other girl. Then she moved, and Pearl and I just kept on walking."

Quiet pastimes, such as trips to nearby lakes, suited the young couple. "With Pearl Ann, it was all milk shakes, movies, and walks," said Young. "We used to get kidded a little once in a while. Pearl's last name was Sparks, and the kids in school used to say, 'Pearl Sparks, doesn't she?' "[16]

Pearl Ann claimed her romance with J. O. was not love at first sight, but that it developed over time. He made her laugh, he took her places, and the two fit comfortably together. "He was easy to be around and a lot of fun, always telling jokes and wisecracking. I was bashful and timid. I guess he made up for that."[17] The couple, high school sweethearts, planned to wed in October 1941.

The nineteen-year-old Young worked as a carpenter in the Boise area, but he never passed on an opportunity to improve the prospects for Pearl and himself. One day he and another carpenter took shelter from a rainstorm in a shed, and as they idled the time, they chatted about Morrison-Knudsen's project. Young's uncle, Forrest Read, had been on Wake since May, and from his letters Young knew the benefits and drawbacks. The thought of earning a significant sum of money in nine months proved too strong a motivation, however. Later that day, without telling Pearl Ann, Young headed to Morrison-Knudsen's offices and signed a contract to work at Wake Island. The move meant that when he returned they would have enough money to purchase their own home, but it also required postponing the wedding. He did not relish the thought of breaking the news to Pearl Ann.

After work, Young drove to nearby Nampa to pick up his fiancée, nervous over what he figured could be an explosive reaction to his decision to leave. Pearl Ann climbed into the car and, as always, immediately slid closer to Young so she could snuggle up to him as he drove them into Boise.

As the car bounded through the countryside, an apprehensive Young finally built the courage to mention what he had done earlier in the day. Not surprisingly, Pearl Ann reacted with hurt and bewilderment. Tears welled in her eyes as she unleashed a flurry of questions. Why had he not first discussed the matter with her? Did he love her any less? What about the wedding plans, now set for less than two months away?

Young tried in vain to explain what he had done. His words met only a cold stare, even after he promised that in nine short months he would return, two thousand dollars richer, and they would be immediately married. "The announcement was not received with enthusiasm or cheering me on," recalled Young, "but she scooted to the far side of the seat against the passenger door and remained there for most of the evening."[18] Pearl Ann, angry and disappointed with the man she thought she would soon marry, did not want Young to board an ocean transport and head to a speck of land in the middle of the Pacific.

"He never did persuade me that what he did was right," explained Pearl Ann. "I guess I felt he's already signed up, and there wasn't much I could do about it. Even up to when he left, I was still upset, but he was going to do that, and that was it. I had no idea where Wake was."[19]

Like Ewing Laporte, the Comstocks—Iowans raised in the heartland of America—futilely scoured the Midwest and West in search of carpentry work. They briefly repaired repossessed homes for an insurance company, but they could never land a job that paid well. In early 1941, the struggling pair read an ad in an Omaha newspaper seeking construction workers for Pacific island military projects. The ad's promise of two hundred dollars per month plus overtime enticed the Comstocks to sign a standard nine-month contract, even though it meant they would have to leave the United States.

Hans Whitney's path also led to Wake. Born in 1911, like Franklin Gross he hopped trains as a teenager to see the United States. He eventually married, had a son, and then signed the same nine-month contract offered to the Comstocks. He had long dreamed of controlling a business that would comfortably provide for his family, and he saw the relatively brief stint at Wake, with its attractive wages, as the vehicle for achieving his hopes.

"I dreamed of being an independent citizen, depending on the whims of no man for a job," claimed Whitney. "I had visions of a young businessman driving to work. Saw his wife and kids in a good home, well dressed and well fed, enjoying life to the full."[20] Wake would be his ticket to the great American dream.

*   *   *

Thus Goicoechea, Whitney, and the other civilians joined Hanna, Holewinski, and the military personnel and headed toward Wake, where they would engage in one of the most gripping battles of the coming war. These men were not superheroes. They were just ordinary men—kids, really—with ordinary dreams, the kind of dreams that have long fueled progress and life in America. The men represented all that was good about the United States—family, hopes, home, loyalty, patriotism, fun, adventure. This group of young men would stand up for those ideals at Wake when the rest of the nation could not, would put aside their own dreams and families so that others could enjoy the chance to have theirs.

A Fort in the Pacific

It is one of the Pacific war's ironies that such a significant military action should occur on such an insignificant plot of land. The first Westerner to sight it, Spain's Álvaro de Mendaña de Neira in 1567, quickly sailed away because Wake, lacking both drinkable water and a viable food source, proved too desolate for his needs. A mere speck on the immense ocean, Wake is a V-shaped atoll of three islets with the open end pointing northwest. Each arm stretches about five miles in length, but channels at the tips of the arms sever the atoll into its three parts. Wake Island, the largest ("Wake" refers to the entire atoll; "Wake Island" to the islet), forms the vertex, with Peale Island to the right and Wilkes Island to the left. The atoll's total land area equals three square miles.

The atoll rests in the middle of the Pacific Ocean along the nineteen degrees north latitude line, equidistant between Tokyo (two thousand miles to its northwest) and Hawaii (two thousand miles to its east). The Philippine Islands stand 2,800 miles to Wake's west. Coarse white sand thinly covers a jagged coral base, making walking a difficult maneuver, while humid, moist air suffocates the island and transforms breathing into an arduous task.

Any man who has ever been there will tell you the sea dominates Wake. The continuous crash of waves against a coral reef surrounding the islands produces such a booming noise that people cannot be heard outside of short distances. The terrain, which supports little more than scrubby bushes and short trees, nestles so low in the water—the highest elevation on the atoll rises hardly more than twenty feet above sea level—that in the strongest typhoons the ocean completely engulfs the land.

Surprisingly, the atoll teemed with animal life, although not always of the most desirable sort. Rats scampered about in droves, while millions of tiny crabs so heavily blanketed the beaches that when they moved around, the whole beach seemed to shift. The beautiful lagoon that nestled inside the V-shaped atoll contained such clear water that a person in a rowboat could peer down and see a variety of aquatic life, from octopuses and eels to all sorts of multicolored exotic fish. Sunrises and sunsets, unrivaled anywhere else on earth, offered breathtaking arrays of soft hues. Wake lacked only palm trees to fit the storybook image of a tropical paradise.

After de Neira's hasty visit, few ships from Europe or America halted at the location. In 1796, British Capt. Samuel Wake gave the atoll and islet their names when he anchored offshore. Forty-five years later, Lt. Charles Wilkes of the United States Navy stopped at Wake as part of his mission to explore and map Pacific islands. After a hasty inspection, he declared the atoll unfit for habitation, but before he departed he named one of the islets to honor a famous naturalist who accompanied the expedition, Titian Peale, and the other, with a touch of arrogance, after himself.

The atoll lay unnoticed by any Western power until July 4, 1898, when the commanding officer of a large force of American troops headed toward the Philippines during the Spanish-American War claimed Wake for the United States. He, too, concluded the forlorn spot could be used for little beyond providing a temporary shelter for ships plying Pacific waters.

For years this was all Wake proved to be. That changed drastically in the 1930s when two nations turned their gazes toward the placid atoll. Resting on the western side of the Pacific, Japan had long intended to join the ranks of the world's top powers. In the eyes of many Japanese, a leading position guaranteed the nation's survival, while to accept an inferior status would relegate her forever to the backwaters of world esteem.

Unlike the United States, whose population enjoyed spacious land, Japan occupied a tiny mountainous area framed by water. The more her population increased, the less space became available. Approximately 80 million people lived in Japan in the 1920s. Japan's total area equaled the state of Montana. If she were to grow, Japan, the most crowded nation on earth, had to seek land beyond her borders.

As an island nation, Japan had to import much of her raw materials and food products. Her people could cultivate only a certain percentage of the national need, and to fill the rest the nation's leaders had to look elsewhere. Almost 70 percent of the country's supply of zinc and tin came from outside, as did 90 percent of its lead, and all its cotton, wool, aluminum, and rubber. When expansionists studied the nearby areas, most eyes turned west toward the Asian mainland and China.

When they sought raw materials from Asia, however, Japanese leaders collided with European interests. She needed rubber, tin, and bauxite from Burma and Malaya, but Great Britain controlled those nations. Indochina's vast rubber plantations contained valuable material, but France held sway in that country. The most eagerly sought product, oil, stood in bountiful amounts in the East Indies, but the Dutch maintained a stranglehold on the region. Everywhere Japan turned, a European nation blocked the path to her future.

Japanese militants who urged immediate expansion onto the Asian mainland were held in check by more moderate forces and by the fact that the Japanese economy depended heavily on the United States for products. The stock market crash of 1929, which ushered in the Great Depression, altered the situation. Military extremists castigated moderates for aligning Japan too closely to the United States. They clamored for a new policy that emphasized conquest and expansion.

An alarmed American ambassador to Japan, Joseph Grew, warned Washington that the Japanese militarists gained strength every day and that they intended to expand to China and other areas of the Pacific. He told his superiors that the military controlled the government and that no step could be taken by civilian politicians without its approval.

As a ten-year-old Joe Goicoechea entered the fifth grade in Boise, Idaho, and a seventeen-year-old Robert Hanna started his final year in high school, the Japanese kicked off the first in a series of events that eventually culminated in World War II. On September 18, 1931, the Japanese Army launched an invasion of China in retaliation for a bomb explosion along a railway they controlled. The United States, then led by President Herbert Hoover, condemned the invasion, but the nation was so embroiled in economic problems of its own that it could do little to affect an event unfolding halfway around the world.

When Franklin Roosevelt took office in 1933, foreign affairs assumed a more important, though still subordinate, role in government. He wanted to strengthen the military and place forces on a string of American-controlled Pacific atolls, but two concerns stopped him—the Depression and isolationism. As long as millions of United States citizens wrestled with unemployment, as long as families went hungry and children went homeless, Roosevelt could do nothing but concentrate his efforts on alleviating the economic stagnation that gripped the country.

Even without the Depression's demands, Roosevelt would have experienced a difficult time in pushing his concerns through an isolationist-controlled Congress: increased spending for the military and more aggressive policies toward Japan. Isolationism flourished in the aftermath of World War I, when many leading politicians and civilians contended that the United States had sent overseas too many of its youth to die on European battlefields for what they believed were European causes. A more rational policy, according to isolationists, was to shun European and Pacific affairs, allow the two oceans to provide a natural barrier against aggression, and take care of domestic matters.

Roosevelt faced formidable opponents in the isolationist movement, including some of the most revered, powerful people in American political and industrial history. Henry Ford lent his name to the cause, as did Theodore Roosevelt's daughter, Alice Roosevelt Longworth, actress Lillian Gish, and aviation icon Charles Lindbergh.

Hamstrung politically, Roosevelt resorted to subterfuge to insert at least a semblance of an American presence on Pacific isles. One move came on December 29, 1934, when he issued Executive Order 6935, which designated Wake as a bird sanctuary under the Navy's control. This action alerted the Japanese that the United States considered Wake an integral part of its territory, yet it did so without alarming the isolationists. At this time Roosevelt could go no further than this simple step, but he intended to militarily fortify the island as soon as conditions warranted.

The following spring, Roosevelt received welcome assistance from the commercial sector when Pan American Airways announced the introduction of its new transpacific route. In one journey taking less than a week, travelers could fly from the West Coast to the Philippines by way of flying boats dubbed China Clippers. The aircraft hopped across the Pacific along a string of stations located on Pacific islands held by the United States, including Guam and Wake.

Roosevelt jumped at the chance to help Pan Am develop the needed fuel and rest stops. He ordered his then Secretary of the Navy, Claude A. Swanson, to issue permission for Pan Am to construct a facility at Wake that would service its clippers; then he had his director of war plans, Rear Adm. William S. Pye, work closely with the company in designing facilities that could easily be switched from commercial to military use. Roosevelt diverted whatever funds he could to helping Pan Am erect a seaplane base and housing quarters.

Instead of openly announcing the importance of Wake as a military base and building adequate facilities, Roosevelt had to proceed at a snail's pace and in the shadows, where his moves would not be subjected to scrutiny. This tactic prevailed for much of the decade, which frustrated Roosevelt and his military advisers, who wanted to place men and weapons on the atoll.

Japan, which considered the Pacific its personal realm, nervously noted Roosevelt's feeble moves. Wake might not have posed a threat in 1935, but the location lay astride Japanese possessions in the Marshall and Caroline Islands. Any American military presence on Wake could hinder future Japanese operations on and from those two spots. American bombers operating out of Wake could hit Japanese targets in her island possessions or could attack Japanese forces advancing toward Wake long before the Japanese ships reached their destinations. American aircraft could support a Navy drive against Japanese islands, and they could conduct surveillance hundreds of miles out to sea. In Japan's hands, Wake not only sheltered Japanese possessions to the west, but it also turned into a dangerous staging area for an assault on Hawaii. Wake's importance to both the United States and Japan grew as the tension mounted, transforming the tiny atoll from a lonely outpost into a likely scene of combat.

Relations between the United States and Japan worsened in December 1937, when Japanese aircraft attacked the U.S. gunboat, *Panay*, in Chinese waters. Two American sailors and one Italian journalist were killed in the attack, which was filmed by a news reporter.

Politicians and citizens in the United States reacted angrily, and for a moment the two nations appeared on the verge of warfare. Hamstrung by the isolationist sentiments, Franklin Roosevelt knew that he could do little to assert American power in China. The Japanese government, already embroiled in military action in China, wanted to avoid conflict with the United States, from which it received valuable shipments of scrap iron and oil. With neither side eager for fighting, a peaceful solution emerged. Roosevelt demanded that Japan offer a public apology and pay more than two million dollars in damages. Tokyo agreed, and Roosevelt accepted the explanation that the Japanese pilots had incorrectly identified the *Panay* as a Chinese boat. Though both sides avoided war at this time, the affair soured relations between Japan and the United States.

The *Panay* incident handed Roosevelt justification for increasing his military efforts, though. One month after the gunboat sank, Roosevelt asked for and received from Congress a 20 percent increase in funds for the Navy so it could build enough ships to station a fleet in both the Atlantic and Pacific Oceans. At the same time, he requested that American munitions and aircraft manufacturers stop bargaining with Japan, and he reduced the amount of important products sent to Japan from the United States, such as scrap iron, oil, and cotton.

In May 1938, Roosevelt directed the Navy to conduct an investigation of possible naval bases in the Pacific. Led by Rear Adm. Arthur J. Hepburn, the committee ranked the top three bases as Pearl Harbor, Midway, and Wake, and urged that defense facilities on Wake, such as a patrol plane base, should be constructed as quickly as possible.

The United States Navy wanted Wake and its other Pacific possessions, including Johnston Island, Palmyra Atoll, Samoa, and Midway, to be the nation's early-warning system should the Japanese adopt aggressive moves. Patrol craft sent from Wake and other places would detect Japanese moves hundreds if not thousands of miles before they reached their intended targets. In that manner, they would guard the approaches to Pearl Harbor and the West Coast. Wake thus took its place among the storied Western frontier bastions, such as Fort Apache, except that its field of operations extended over water instead of land.

"They were intended to form a screen against Japan much as blockhouses strung across the western plains formed a screen against hostile tribes in the days of our Indian wars,"[21] wrote a man who would gain fame at Wake, Marine Maj. James P. S. Devereux. When in October 1939, Roosevelt changed the Pacific Fleet's home base from San Diego, California, to Pearl Harbor, Hawaii, in an effort to send a message to the Japanese that the United States opposed their actions in Asia and would react even more strongly in the future, Wake took on more importance.

Wake could serve another purpose. Naval strategists studied different ways in which they could draw the Japanese Navy into a decisive battle should war erupt. To do so, they needed a lure with which to entice the Japanese. A strengthened Wake might be the answer. Could the Japanese allow an American military presence so close to their bases in the Marshalls without responding?

Completely unaware of the looming dangers, Goicoechea, Hanna, and the men bound for Wake headed directly toward a fight. Making matters more precarious was that their destination rested barely 650 miles from Japanese bases, less than a third of the distance Wake stood from possible American assistance at Pearl Harbor.

"Suckers! Suckers!"

Joe Goicoechea, Murray Kidd, and George Rosendick knew little and cared even less about the distant Pacific war rumblings. The only sound they heard was the wind past their windows as their Greyhound bus bounded about the countryside toward California. They were having too much fun to be bothered by anything happening thousands of miles away. Along with seventy other construction workers, the three had boarded two Greyhound buses chartered by Morrison-Knudsen to take the workers to San Francisco. Goicoechea, realizing that the buses would drive directly though some of Nevada's gambling towns, had his hickeys ready.

"I had a whole sack full of those slugs, and they worked in the slot machines," Goicochea explained. "Then when we saw the slugs started coming up on the machines, we took off! We didn't have to spend any of our money for anything for a while."[22]

Goicoechea and his buddies lived it up in San Francisco, as well, even though they were there only a few days. They made so much noise on one of the city's famed trolley cars that the conductor halted the vehicle and booted them off.

So far, the trip to Wake resembled a fraternity vacation more than a bus ride to work, and this was only the beginning. Morrison-Knudsen, possibly feeling guilty over sending the men to such an isolated outpost, landed berths on luxury liners bound for Hawaii for most of the workers. The men ate food they had rarely tasted, slept in soft beds in suites, and mingled with wealthy patrons also along for the voyage. When they arrived in Honolulu, the Royal Hawaiian Band serenaded them with native music while beautiful girls in grass skirts placed leis around their necks.

Five days of sight-seeing greeted the construction workers. "This is the life!" said twenty-one-year-old Hans Whitney of Minnesota, eager to apply the money earned at Wake to that dream home for his family. When he and the other workers heard that Wake's hot, rainy climate taxed the endurance of most men, Whitney dismissed the negative chatter. "I figured I could stand nine months of it. Then, a little business of my own and maybe get filthy rich."[23]

Though none of the men recognized them as such, hints appeared during the two thousand mile journey from Hawaii to Wake that what some considered a golden opportunity might be otherwise. The ship itself, the Navy vessel *William Ward Burrows*, had none of the allure offered by one of the luxury liners that rushed the men across the Pacific to Hawaii. Instead of superb cuisine and relaxation, the men ate beans for breakfast, then according to naval tradition labored at any one of the numerous tasks that awaited them, such as washing dishes or swabbing the decks. Without air-conditioning, the workers sweated belowdecks and slept in cramped quarters.

Up to now, the CPNAB men had dismissed the possibility of war with Japan as a remote likelihood, but the eleven-day trip to Wake reminded them that every mile they traveled west placed them farther outside the control of the United States. Some of the men participated in gun drills aboard the ship, and Goicoechea noticed that the *Burrows* zigzagged its way to Wake as a precaution against torpedo attacks.

The end of the weary journey offered both relief and surprise. The men were delighted to be free from the tedious routine aboard the *Burrows*, but when they took their first look at Wake—the spot of land containing their dreams of excitement and fortune—their eyes widened in astonishment. The dismal-looking island featured little of the enchantment provided by

Pacific isles of lore, with their sandy beaches, enticing palm trees, and exotic birds. Wake offered beaches—stretches of gritty coral sand—but instead of exotic birds the island resounded to the movement of thousands of land crabs, gooney birds, and rats. Instead of majestic palm trees, scrawny scrub trees rose no more than twenty feet high. Suffocating heat and thick humidity greeted the men with an oppressive stickiness.

As many as sixty of the construction workers—already demoralized by the unexpectedly harsh voyage from Hawaii to Wake and affected by homesickness—took one look at Wake and decided to remain aboard ship, return to Hawaii, and head for home. They preferred to renege on their contract and forgo the attractive wages rather than endure nine months at such a desolate location. Twenty-three-year-old James Allen of Missouri stayed, but recalled that in the group that landed on shore, "There's plenty of the fellows that wish they never seen this place."[24]

Their initial footsteps on Wake did not offer any solace, either. Hans Whitney's group landed to hear the jeers of "Suckers! Suckers! Suckers!" shouted by workers who had arrived before them, and every man paused briefly when he read a huge sign shaped like a wheel warning, "War is imminent . . . keep the wheel turning."[25] Despite the suggestions that paradise may have eluded them, enough workers stuck it out so that by November 1941, 1,145 men inhabited the atoll, constructing barracks and roads, runways and sheds.

There they joined the other men led by forty-year-old Nathaniel Daniel "Dan" Teters, who fashioned a reputation as one of the most organized, demanding foremen for Morrison-Knudsen. Born in Ohio in 1900, Teters joined the Army in World War I and helped build airstrips. After the war, he earned an engineering degree from Washington State College in 1922, then embarked upon a career that lasted until 1960. Among the projects in which he participated were the construction of the Boulder and Grand Coulee Dams in the 1930s.

The man was accustomed to giant challenges in out-of-the-way places, and Wake qualified on both counts. Using a combination of firmness and common sense, Teters quickly had the 1,145-man civilian force on Wake humming with efficiency. The workers knew he could be tough—"His word was law," said one—but they also saw instances where Teters took extraordinary measures to make their lives on Wake more bearable. He could be a stern taskmaster, but he cared enough to know every man by name. He demanded accountability, but made sure that everyone received overtime bonuses, even the cooks and mess attendants. Teters so impressed the Marines that one officer claimed Teters was "a tough, hard man who would be good to have along in a fight."[26]

They needed a tough guy, for the task before them was immense. The government contract called for Morrison-Knudsen to dredge a channel for small boats and seaplanes and create a five-thousand-foot runway for Marine aircraft on Wake Island, a submarine base off Wilkes Island, and a seaplane base on Peale Island. The contractors were to construct streets, build barracks, dig water and sewage systems, and connect the three islands with bridges. To complete the work, Teters placed the men on an exhausting schedule—they labored ten hours a day, seven days a week, with one day off every other week.

"We Flipped a Coin, and the Loser Got Wake"

Until August 1941, Teters and his men had Wake to themselves. In that month, however, the first in a series of Marine, Navy, and Army personnel arrived. Goicoechea, Kidd, Rosendick, and the other civilians signed on with the CPNAB to complete new projects, while Lieutenant Hanna, Corp. Holewinski, and Corp. Johnson stepped on Wake with the thought of defending and fighting for what was there.

Like the civilians, each Marine stopped first in Hawaii. While Hanna and his family enjoyed the relatively tame pastimes of sightseeing and strolling on the beaches, most Marines indulged in more raucous endeavors. Pvt. Ewing Laporte compared the scene in Hawaii to the typical image conveyed by Hollywood—bars, women, and fights. Officers or those who could afford it visited the Royal Hawaiian Hotel or the Moana for drinks and conversation, while most Marine privates and corporals headed to the dives that catered to the military, such as the Black Cat on Hotel Street or the Pantheon on Nuuanu Street. Whorehouses, like the Anchor, the Ritz, and the New Senator on River Street, sported long lines of military men waiting to get in, while tattoo parlors, shooting galleries where men could take aim at stationary targets, and souvenir stands enjoyed record business.

"That's about the way it was! It was even worse," said Laporte. "There were miles upon miles of sailors in white off battleship row, and we had a good time. There were lots of fights between Navy and the Marines. The YMCA lawn in Honolulu had nothin' but sailors and Marines fighting."[27]

Cpl. John S. Johnson used to patronize a bar run by Japanese where he ordered rum and Cokes for twenty cents apiece. When off duty, he and his buddies loved to jump in an old Model T Ford with a few cases of beer, then drive to the leeward side of the island for an afternoon of diving and drinking. "Most of us were young, single, and we had a lot of fun in Hawaii,"[28] said Johnson.

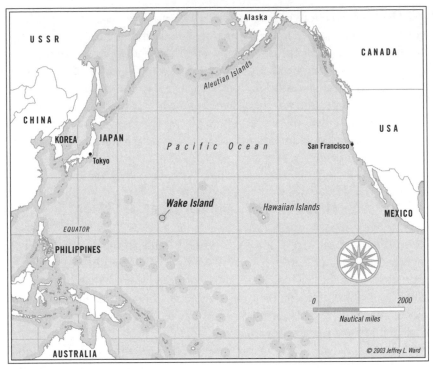

Wake and its position in the Pacific Ocean relative to other major locations.

Those brief days provided the Marines with their last moments of gaiety for a long time. Like their civilian counterparts, most Marines noticed the difference with their first sight of Wake. First Lieutenant Woodrow M. Kessler figured the atoll would not compare to Hawaii's beauties, but he at least expected a decent spot. As he wrote in his memoirs, he erred in this assumption. "It was somewhat as it must have been for a replacement troop of cavalry after having traveled across plains and desert of the Southwest to finally come upon the isolated fort set up in Apache country."[29]

While still in Hawaii, Corporal Gross and another Marine flipped a coin to determine their eventual posting. "The Marines had an opening on Palmyra Island, and I wanted it and so did the other guy. No one knew anything about Wake, but guys had already been on Palmyra and I thought it would be the better place. We flipped a coin, and the loser got Wake. That was me."[30] Gross's wish to see more of the world materialized, but not in quite the manner he hoped.

When Laporte took his first look at the flat, uninviting place, he muttered, "Oh, God!" He recalled, "It didn't strike our eyes as being very nice. The worst thing was the first sergeant who greeted us told us, 'We've been working seven days a week, and you will, too!' "[31]

The initial group of military arrived on August 18, 1941, when five officers and 170 men under Maj. Lewis A. Hohn and his executive, Capt. Wesley M. Platt, disembarked. Marines immediately began building their living quarters in Camp 1—rows of pyramid-shaped tents with wooden floors located on the southern arm of Wake Island. As they worked, they looked across the lagoon toward the civilian area, Camp 2, at the extreme northern tip of Wake.

Once the tents had been erected, Hohn and Platt turned to the primary task—fortifying Wake's defenses. Wearing shorts and T-shirts in the blazing sun, the men had to dig gun emplacements and foxholes, string communications wire, and fill sandbags to protect machine gun and artillery positions.

Other groups of military poured into Wake through the next few months, including eleven naval personnel charged with establishing the naval air station to be situated on Wake and six Army personnel sent to man a communications station for the Army's B-17 bombers. Gradually, the First Defense Battalion's numbers increased until, by November, they stood at 378 Marines, fewer than half the full complement of 859 men allotted for such a unit.

★

CHAPTER 2

"It Would Be Nice to Have Six Months More"

"We Were Sure Happy"

Despite Wake's forlorn appearance, life ranged from the relatively decent to the outstanding. No one lacked food or medical supplies, and thoughts of war hardly entered the men's minds. The difference in living conditions depended upon which group you belonged to. Civilians and military lived within a few miles of each other, but they may as well have occupied different planets.

Numerous amenities made existence for the civilians quite pleasant. They worked long hours at tough tasks—after all, they had come to Wake for that reason—but should any man have an especially difficult day paving roads or blasting coral in the lagoon, he had only to think of what awaited him afterwards. Goicoechea labored with the steel crew, Kidd ferried men across the channel separating Wake from Wilkes, and Rosendick served food at the mess hall, but they returned at night to spacious accommodations. The barracks, which housed eighty men, boasted items that some men could not claim back home—indoor plumbing and showers. Five-foot partitions separated the beds into pairs, and each man had his own locker storage.

The civilians also enjoyed the use of a thousand-man mess hall, a hospital stocked with the latest in medicines, a recreation hall, a laundry, post office, general store, and a canteen that freely dispensed ice cream sodas. In the evenings, the men watched the latest Hollywood films at Wake's outdoor theater, then on their way back to the barracks swerved by the mess hall where cooks placed freshly baked pies on the windowsills for their consumption.

Ask a construction worker what he most remembers about life on Wake before the war, and he will tell you about the mess hall, where a man could eat as much as he wanted from a varied menu. The food, served up by Chinese and Guamanian mess boys, included steaks, hams, potatoes, vegetables, fresh bread, doughnuts, and ice cream. Men boasted of the sumptuous fare in letters to family back home, and despite working ten hours each day, most civilians gained weight during their stay on Wake.

When they had time off, the men could select from among a wide range of activities. Fishermen rushed to the lagoon, where they speared or caught lobster, moray eels, octopuses, turtles, marlin, flying fish, goldfish, and tuna. Barracks battled each other in baseball games on a makeshift field, while other men engaged in tennis and volleyball matches, sunbathed at the beach or the swimming pool, or read books and magazines from the camp library. J. O. Young took time to write his weekly letter to Pearl Ann back in Nampa.

For those who preferred more "active" pastimes, alcohol and gambling offered attractive alternatives. Morrison-Knudsen made it clear to each worker that both items were banned, but short of Draconian measures, there was no way the company could keep some version of alcohol, poker, and dice away from more than 1,100 construction workers confined on an out-of-the-way atoll. After all, they had agreed to do without women. What more could be asked of healthy, vibrant males? They needed something to let off steam.

For five dollars a gallon, a civilian walked away with the island's version of alcohol distilled from fruit in illegal stills located in hidden spots in the brush. One still, operated by Guamanian laborers who worked for Pan Am, churned out alcohol from pineapple they took from their galley. Civilian worker John Rogge claimed, "God, it would really tear you apart! Some of the guys were happy to have it. They were willing to drink anything."[1] If the men wanted the real stuff, they waited for the next Army B-17 bomber, which invariably disgorged crew members eager to part with bottles of bourbon or Johnnie Walker scotch—for ten dollars a bottle.

Poker games flourished most every night. With 1,145 men packed together, some knew more than others about playing cards, and they freely used that knowledge to advantage. As a result, a handful of men made a fortune. "A guy named Shorty Markam was quite a gambler," recalled Rogge. "We had quite a few of 'em from Wake like that—they were not there for construction work or for salaries—they were there to play poker. There's always a bunch of idiots around, and these guys didn't even have to cheat. One guy, a foreman, supposedly shipped home something like twenty thousand dollars before the war started. The guys got a monthly allowance, and some had a lot of money before the war."[2]

Practical jokes seemed to be almost as popular as gambling. One of the favorites was the bed-and-bottle trick. A man filled a bottle with cold water, then carefully placed it in someone else's bed with the stopper slightly ajar. When the target climbed in the bed, he usually jarred loose the stopper and soaked his sheets.

Some men chopped bars of soap so they resembled potato salad, then placed the offending substance on the unsuspecting victim's plate, or soaked vegetables in a chlorine solution to give them a ghastly taste. Rogge fell to both pranks, as did others, but everyone laughed off the incidents. After all, it was another way to break the monotony. Jim Allen so enjoyed his life that he wrote his mother on October 1, "Well, mother, [I] am the luckiest guy in the world, I do believe. I have had nothing but the best of it. I sure hope it holds out."[3]

A camp newsletter, *The Wake Wig Wag*, kept everyone informed of world events. Published almost daily by editor Louis M. Cormier, the paper contained news clips gathered from West Coast radio broadcasts and schedules of coming events. The Thursday, November 6, 1941, issue, for instance, reported results of the fall's political elections, news of the fighting between Germany and the Soviet Union, information that mail was due to arrive on the weekend, and an item that the week's movie was *The Battle of Broadway*, starring Victor McLaglen. According to the paper, meetings to be held that week included a gospel service, the American Legion, the Glee Club, the Veterans of Foreign Wars, and a Bible Class.

Goicoechea, Kidd, and Rosendick loved their time on Wake. They worked hard, but they knew it would last only nine months. In the meantime, they could save almost every dollar they earned—what, after all, could they spend it on at Wake?—and look forward to a bright future back in Idaho. "Boy, we were sure happy," said Goicoechea. "We made lots of money and learned a trade at the same time."[4]

Fortunately for Goicoechea and his friends, they worked and played at Wake completely oblivious of events unfolding elsewhere in the Pacific. Those actions would soon have dramatic consequences for them.

"Digging Holes and Filling Sandbags"

Life on Wake for the Marines carried little of the excitement that was enjoyed by the civilians. Their job was to transform Wake from a placid atoll into an arsenal bristling with weaponry. On each of the three islands they were to emplace two 5-inch guns used against naval targets and four 3-inch antiaircraft guns. In between these larger guns, they had to prepare positions for thirty .30-caliber and eighteen .50-caliber machine guns to repel an enemy land assault or pepper low-flying aircraft. Once everything stood in place, Wake would pack enough bite to make an invader wary, but until then the atoll offered little with which to combat an attack.

Each day brought the military closer to its goal of fortifying the islands. A typical machine gun pit stretched about six feet in diameter, room enough for two or three men. The Marines dug down four feet, then stacked sandbags on the insides for support and two layers of sandbags at ground level around the edges of the pit for protection from enemy bullets. Private Laporte, who served on a .50-caliber machine gun, started his routine the day after he arrived on Wake. "Everybody was digging holes and filling sandbags. That's what it was day in and day out."[5]

Sent out to begin work on the defensive installations, Major Hohn hoped that when his men were not setting up guns and filling sandbags, they could assemble at their positions and practice firing live ammunition. He knew that would enhance team unity and precision, but unfortunately other pressing needs denied him the opportunity. Army B-17 bombers, heading to the Philippines from the mainland, poured into Wake on an almost-daily basis to be refueled for their long trek across the Pacific. Since the Army had detailed no aviation ground crew to Wake, the Marines had to fill in and hand-pump three thousand gallons of gasoline to each bomber that arrived. This sometimes required the Marines to work through the night, seriously impeding the time to fortify their gun positions and eliminating the opportunity for precious gunnery practice.

As if that were not enough, the Marines also had to unload each ship that brought supplies to the island. Since a channel had not yet been widened sufficiently to allow vessels into the lagoon, the ships anchored offshore. In large work parties, the Marines piled the cargo onto barges, ferried the material ashore, and unloaded it into trucks for dispersal to storage areas.

The civilians worked long days, too, but at least they could look forward to relaxing in a comfortable mess hall with the finest foods. The Marines had no such luxury. The fare usually consisted of nothing more than hard-to-digest bully beef, potatoes, or salami—which the Marines derisively called "horse cock." While they choked on their chow, the Marines gazed across the lagoon toward the civilian camp, where they knew their civilian counterparts ate like kings. The thought of so much enticing food so close by tormented the men, but they had orders to stay away from the civilian mess hall.

Not that fighting erupted or jealousies lingered between military and civilian. The two groups blended together relatively well, for after all, as Gross said, "We were Marines and we were disciplined and knew what we were supposed to do and what not to do." But each day the Marines emerged from their Spartan tents and chafed at the obvious differences.

"The civilians were eating like kings," Corporal Gross explained. "We were eating lousy. It wasn't that our food was so bad; there just wasn't enough. Maybe one bowl of potatoes and something else. We hardly ever got any meat. The civilians had pies and cakes and ice cream. I ate over there one time, and it was just like sitting down to Thanksgiving dinner, and they fed them civilians like that three times a day!"[6]

When they could, the men supplemented their diet by fishing or by sneaking over to the civilian mess hall for a decent meal. Cpl. Kenneth Marvin recalled that they could not head over too often, because it meant a three-mile hike, but they sure feasted when they did. "Hell, they had steaks and everything."[7]

Marvin and the Marines enjoyed their revenge, however, for they had something the civilians wanted—beer. Since all forms of alcohol were banned in the civilian camp, while beer was permitted in the Marine camp, the Marines purchased the beverage for $2.40 a case, and then surreptitiously resold it to the civilians for as much as $20 a case. Though the black marketeering did not make the food in the military mess hall taste any better, the Marines at least enjoyed the fact they had one item the civilians lacked.

The military had a few characters who easily matched Goicoechea and his buddies for fun or Teters for efficiency and leadership. Along with Hanna, Holewinski, Johnson, Gross, and Laporte, the men forged the backbone to Wake's fighting force and handed the First Defense Battalion its personality.

Born in Dorchester, South Carolina, on May 26, 1914, Hohn's executive, Capt. Wesley M. Platt, gained the respect of every Marine. The studious Platt graduated from Clemson University, where he specialized in chemistry and gained varsity letters in both boxing and football. He then joined the Marine Corps and received an appointment as a second lieutenant in July 1935.

Platt could be tough as nails in a crisis, but he hated reprimanding his men. Corporal Johnson recalled a private who had once committed a minor infraction. When the Marine came back after being disciplined by Platt, the man explained that Platt had spoken so apologetically to him that "That's the first time I'd been chewed out by an officer and I felt sorry for the officer."

The real reason why the men so loved Platt was that he never handed out an assignment he was not prepared to first do himself. "Platt would pick up a shovel and work with the men," explained Johnson. "Familiarity breeds contempt, but he was the exception to that rule because the more you were around the man, the more you respected him."[8]

Lt. John A. McAlister and Gunners Clarence B. McKinstry and John A. Hamas formed a military trio to rival that of Goicoechea, Kidd, and Rosendick. When off duty, the three lived to joke, fight, or tease. The blond-haired, blue-eyed McAlister, nicknamed "Johnny Mac," stood only five feet nine inches and barely weighed 150 pounds, but no one raised hell like he did. With his quick hands around, no drink, poker game, or assailant was safe—but the men respected his fierce loyalty. A fellow officer, Lt. Woodrow M. Kessler, later wrote that McAlister was "Not big enough to overwhelm the opposition in a barroom brawl, yet tenacious enough to make them decide to call it quits. You could respect him and be glad he was on your side."9

McKinstry, called "Big Mac" to differentiate him from McAlister, rarely took advantage of his 260-pound frame in a fight or to order people around. Recognized from afar by his flowing red beard and bushy mustache, he preferred the more low-key approach of talking things out or using humor to defuse an argument. An expert cardsharp, McKinstry could take a deck shuffled by someone else and still deal out whatever hand he wanted. Despite the obvious talent, the men trusted Big Mac so much that they never banned him from any poker game. He still won, not because he cheated but because he also knew how to count the cards and simply played the odds.

The six-foot-four-inch, 260-pound Hamas, called "Big John," astounded fellow Marines with his dexterity, which included the ability to walk through an open doorway, then kick backwards and touch the lintel with his foot. The men loved Hamas, who occupied such a tender role that Lieutenant Kessler described him as "something of a father figure, a great burly Santa Claus without the beard."10 A soldier in World War I, when he fought in the Austro-Hungarian Army, Hamas immigrated to the United States and enlisted in the Marines. A veteran of action in China, Santo Domingo, and Nicaragua, where he won the Marines' second highest honor for valor, the Navy Cross, Hamas spoke six different languages, often so thoroughly mixing them together that listeners did not know which language he was using.

No one may have been more colorful than G. Sgt. Johnalson Wright. A veteran of the Nicaraguan fighting, Wright was known for his fearlessness. Possibly it had something to do with his being six feet six inches tall and weighing 350 pounds. According to his friends, Wright (nicknamed "Bustgut" because of the size of his enormous belly) could easily drink a case of beer and consume three whole chickens without batting an eye. Other men contended his courage had more to do with the lucky dollar he always carried in his pocket. Wright claimed that he could never be harmed in battle as long as he had that coin with him.

Other Marines brought varied backgrounds. Cpl. Terrence T. McAmis worked as a carnie in a traveling circus. Cpl. Robert M. Brown rushed into the Marine recruiting office, signed enlistment papers, and then asked to be sent as far from the United States as possible so he could avoid an embarrassing paternity suit that had been erroneously filed against him. Sgt. Robert S. Box Jr. sought solace in the military when the girl he loved became engaged to someone else.

Like the civilians, the Marines and other personnel had time to relax after their workdays ended. Once a week, a truck took them over to the civilian camp for a movie. Marvin especially loved the westerns they showed, even though rain frequently interrupted the showings. "We'd sit out in the open and watch the movie, and if a rainstorm came over, we'd run into a building, wait half an hour, and go back."[11]

Some men fished or played cards, wrote letters home, or chewed the fat with buddies. Cpl. Bernard E. Richardson worked on a novel he hoped to have published after the war. He'd titled it *Another Locust Came*, and had 25,000 words completed by November. Captain Platt and Navy Lt. (jg) G. Mason Kahn, a dermatologist in civilian life and now the unit's military officer, enjoyed classical records, while the men in Holewinski's tent listened to Tommy Dorsey and other swing hits of the day. Kahn also spent many hours studying an anatomy book, since he knew he might one day have to perform emergency surgery on one of the men. The strategy paid off on December 1, when an American submarine, *Triton*, put ashore CEM Harold R. Thompson for an emergency appendectomy.

Pranks abounded in the military camp, as well. McKinstry and McAlister, aided by Kessler, once pulled a fast one on Hamas. Convinced that rumors about buried treasure on Wake were true, Hamas spent many of his spare moments scouring the beaches and brush in hopes of unearthing a fortune. McAlister obtained a piece of browned parchment paper from a civilian draftsman, had Kessler draw a map of Wake containing a huge *X* on it, and then handed it to McKinstry. Big Mac wrapped the treasure map in oilskin, then gave it to a collaborator, who buried it under a piece of coral near the location of Hamas's next search. When the map was found, an ecstatic Hamas was sure he had struck it rich. The three secretly enjoyed watching Hamas make preparations for how he would use his newfound wealth, until one of Big John's friends broke the news to him. Though at first angry, Hamas later laughed over the prank.

Lieutenant Hanna cherished his spare time, for it was the one part of the day he could be alone, and when he was, he thought of Vera. Instead of enjoying beer or bull sessions, he headed to the jagged coral reef and to the beaches, where he searched for some of the luminous black shells that dotted the isle. When he collected enough, he planned to string them together and send them to his wife as a reminder of how beautiful he thought she was.

* * *

More than anything, the presence of a beautiful woman made Wake tolerable. Morrison-Knudsen sent men of all ages to Wake, from teenagers to one man in his seventies, and most Marines had barely entered their twenties, so the thought of females was never far from everybody's minds. Fifteen hundred young men with raging hormones faced nine months on an isolated island without women, but at least they had Florence.

Dan Teters's wife, Florence, was a shapely blonde who received permission from company executives to travel with her husband. As the only female on Wake, she acted as the island's hostess whenever important people flew into Wake aboard the weekly Pan Am Clipper. The highlight came when celebrated author Ernest Hemingway arrived and took her deep-sea fishing.

To the Marines and civilians, however, she represented other things. She reminded the married men of their own wives back home, and to the younger, unmarried Marines and civilians—or to those who simply possessed a roving eye—she served as the object of their lust. To all the men, she served notice that while they sweated under a blistering sun on a godforsaken land, decency and civility and normalcy existed. As long as she remained on Wake, the men figured nothing bad could happen. After all, Morrison-Knudsen and the military would never allow a female to stay if it placed her in danger. Before that happened, they would surely evacuate her. Each day they spotted Florence Teters sunbathing or walking about the atoll meant another day that all was well.

The remarkable woman, who collected quite an audience when she headed to the lagoon in her enticing swimsuit for her daily swim, reveled in the attention the men gave her. In return, she adopted them as her boys. She helped arrange baseball games and boxing matches among the civilians and military, and after some of the Navy personnel designed an elaborate barbecue for her use, she hosted parties for the young naval officers.

Florence Teters's stunning looks gained men's initial attention, but when they got to know her better, they were even more impressed with her toughness. Her husband used a small room in which he confined men who committed minor offenses. When some workers complained about the unfairness of being placed in such a tiny room in Wake's heat and humidity, Mrs. Teters locked herself in for an entire day to prove she could take it. No man, especially a hardy construction worker, could object from then on.

While the civilians and Marines settled into their lives on Wake, events in the distant western Pacific threatened to disturb the region's stability. The first occurred when President Roosevelt learned of Japan's advance into French Indochina, south of China. Since Hitler had defeated France and the Netherlands, and appeared ready to knock Great Britain out of the war, Japan saw an opportunity to seize European possessions in the Pacific and gain control of their valuable resources. In September 1940, the Japanese signed the Tripartite Pact with Germany and Italy. The agreement bound each party to declare war on any nation that joined the war against one of the three. The three hoped this alliance would deter the United States from entering the conflict.

Japan then applied pressure on a weakened France into allowing it to place troops in Indochina. While the Japanese claimed that the forces were necessary to protect their southern flank in China, Japan was actually more interested in obtaining Indochina's vast natural resources and possessing a base from which to push southward against British-held Burma and Malaya.

From the White House, President Roosevelt viewed these movements with alarm. When Japanese troops moved into Indochina in July 1941, President Roosevelt cut off all trade with Japan, including the crucial flow of oil that kept the Japanese military machine in motion. He promised to maintain the embargo until Japan withdrew from both China and Indochina and renounced the Tripartite Pact.

In light of Roosevelt's orders curtailing the oil, Japanese leaders could follow one of two paths. They could reach a settlement with the United States and reopen the supply line from that nation, or they could continue their present policy of overseas expansion and risk war with the United States. The leaders had to determine which course to adopt and how best to implement it.

As the Japanese continued to threaten the peace, Roosevelt tried to better prepare his forces. Among the steps was one possibility that no one liked to consider, but it had to be confronted because of the serious manpower shortage at Wake. On August 26, 1941, shortly after the arrival of Hohn's group of Marines, the commander in chief of the Pacific Fleet at Pearl Harbor, Adm. Husband E. Kimmel, wrote to Secretary Stark of his relief that at last, a military presence had been established at Wake. Recognizing the meagerness of this force, however, Kimmel suggested that should the need for more men arise due to a Japanese attack, Hohn might consider using the civilian workers, whose roster included a number of ex–service men.

Four months before war opened, the shorthanded military had already started including the unaware civilians in their plans. Goicoechea, Kidd, Rosendick, and the Marines had little time remaining to enjoy peacetime life.

"All Hell Broke Loose!"

A jarring notice that conditions in the Pacific had changed occurred on October 9, 1941, when thirty-eight-year-old Maj. James P. S. Devereux stepped onto the island as the new Marine commanding officer to replace the departing Hohn. With him came a disturbing sense of urgency.

Devereux traced his roots back to the Norman Conquest of England, when his French ancestors fought for the conquering Norman side. After being attracted to the Marine Corps by its flashy uniforms, Devereux enlisted as a private in 1923. Because he exhibited command potential during boot camp, Devereux entered officer candidate's school and earned a commission as second lieutenant on February 19, 1925. Stints in Nicaragua, Cuba, and China alternated with domestic assignments and gave Devereux superb training in command.

Before leaving Pearl Harbor to take up his post at Wake, Devereux talked with Lt. Col. Omar T. Pfeiffer, Assistant Operations Officer on Adm. Husband E. Kimmel's staff, and Col. Harry Pickett, coordinator of the defense battalions being posted to the Pacific. The discussion bothered Devereux, for it suggested that Wake would be seriously undermanned and short of essential equipment for the immediate future. The staff officers admitted that the men on Wake were not strong enough to repel any significant invasion attempt, but they also disclosed that apart from a few more Marines and some extra supplies, Devereux should expect little additional help for a few months. When Devereux asked what he was supposed to do with inadequate men and supplies should a Japanese assault force suddenly appear, Pfeiffer and Pickett answered that he and his men "were expected to do the best we could."[12]

Sent off with those discomforting words, Devereux recalled the last conversation he had with his brother, Ashton, before heading to the Pacific. When Ashton asked what might happen to Devereux, the officer replied, "Your guess is as good as mine—but I'll probably wind up eating fish and rice."[13]

Devereux's apprehensions deepened when he landed at Wake and saw how poorly his men and the gun positions were prepared for war. Few of the 3-inch or 5-inch guns had been completely emplaced, and he had barely one machine gun with which to defend each quarter mile of beach. Even worse, until additional Marines poured in from Hawaii, he could not even man every gun. Finally, he exploded when he learned that because his Marines had to unload ships and take fuel to Army bombers, they had no time to practice on their guns. "Frankly, it did not make sense to me," he wrote in his memoirs. "None of my men was ground crew personnel. We were artillerymen—that was why we were on Wake Island—but the gasoline business did not leave us much time to work at our trade."[14]

The major, racing the clock to finish his island defenses before the Japanese attacked, quickly altered life for his Marines. Where the construction workers had Teters, the Marines turned to Devereux. The wiry major, who so meticulously planned details that a fellow officer said, "He's the kind of guy who would put all the mechanized aircraft detectors into operation and then station a man with a spyglass in a tall tree"[15] in case the detectors failed, quickly had his men laboring twelve-hour days, seven days a week to complete the defenses on Wake.

Devereux turned to his task with a fury, intending to transform this first line of defense in the Pacific into a bastion that could punish any approaching force. "When Devereux came out there, all hell broke loose!" mentioned Corporal Gross. "He evidently had orders to get those guns in, so we worked seven days a week. Before that, I'm not sure we even worked on Saturday."[16]

His style alienated many Marines. Corporal Holewinski encountered Devereux back in San Diego. The major spotted Holewinski and another Marine walking along without their hats. Normally the infraction would not bother anyone, but Devereux was not one to let a small detail escape notice. He stopped the pair and ordered them to put their hats on.

More than a few recalled Devereux's tendency in previous posts to use a white glove during Saturday morning inspections to search for dust on top of their lockers, or his attempts to catch men gambling. He believed parades and other military traditions built discipline, while his men contended it created animosity. Devereux could be so stringent on military conformity that the Marines contended that his initials—JPS—stood for "Just Plain Shit."

But the man could run an outfit. He might be detested by his men, but their hatred was tinged with reluctant admiration that Devereux commanded things the way an officer was supposed to. Corporal Gross claimed Devereux was "a good leader. He was strict, he kept us in line, and he wasn't going to let any guys resort to anything below being a Marine. He ran a tight ship."[17]

Intentions are noble, but they must be backed with men, weapons, and supplies, and here Devereux suffered. In addition to lacking enough men and equipment, bomb shelters to protect promised aircraft lay incomplete, and Wake's airstrip, meant to house a squadron of Marine fighters, stood empty. Instead of radar to give the defenders advance warning of attack, the island's early-warning system consisted of a man with a pair of binoculars standing on an observation post atop a water tower. World War I–vintage communications wires connected the different outposts, and no one knew how long the frayed and outdated material would last. Usually, when all else failed in the Marines, the men could always count on using their rifles. Not at Wake. At least seventy-five men lacked weapons because the military had yet to ship enough to the outpost.

The situation improved a bit by the end of October, when another contingent of 203 Marines, under Maj. George H. Potter Jr., joined their cohorts on Wake. Shortly after that, six Army enlisted personnel under Sgt. Ernest G. Rogers arrived to man a radio station to help guide the B-17 bombers flying in.

Though the men on Wake did not realize it, they were running out of time. Tension between Japan and the United States heightened on October 15, when a cabinet led by Gen. Hideki Tojo replaced the more moderate government of Prince Fumimaro Konoye. With a more militaristic group of men in Tokyo, Roosevelt knew his chances of avoiding war had sharply diminished.

Two days later Rear Admiral Claude C. Bloch, the military officer supervising the construction on Wake, fired off a message stating that because of the serious international situation with Japan, the island should go on alert status. Devereux contacted Teters about the procedure they would follow in the event of war, and the two agreed that the civilians would handle transportation and feeding of the military to free every possible member of the military for defense tasks.

Japanese military leaders wasted little time. They agreed that if diplomats could not convince President Roosevelt to lift the embargo on oil and other products by the first week in November, they would start their operations against the United States and the European powers. They had only enough oil reserves to last about one year, and poorer weather after December would impede proposed landings on the Malay Peninsula and in the Philippines. While negotiations continued through the month of November, the military would quietly prepare for war.

Japanese diplomats informed their American counterparts that if Roosevelt resumed oil shipments to Japan, the nation would halt her military action in Indochina. Alerted by decoded intercepts that Japanese troops were already embarking on transports for shipment to the Dutch East Indies and Southeast Asia, Roosevelt spurned the proposal. In late November, Secretary of State Cordell Hull informed Roosevelt and his cabinet that diplomacy could not settle the issue and that military action would probably be required.

With their attempt to negotiate failing, the Japanese turned to their military as the only way to seize the needed resources and avoid being economically strangled.

*   *   *

Back on Wake, Devereux instituted more steps to strengthen Wake. He ordered ammunition sent to every gun position and had two cases of rifle ammunition placed in each tent in case his men had to fight their way out to their positions.

To help ease their manpower shortage, the military turned to the civilian workforce. Rear Adm. Claude C. Bloch, commandant of the Fourteenth Naval District out of Pearl Harbor, had earlier sent Major Hohn a notice that, "If we should be so unfortunate as to become involved in hostilities and your island is attacked, it will call for the combined efforts of everybody to beat off the attack."[18]

This thinly veiled suggestion that the undermanned Marines might have to rely on the untrained civilians made an impression on Hohn, who posted a bulletin in Camp 2 asking for volunteers to train with the Marines. When 165 men gathered, including Joe Goicoechea and George Rosendick, Platoon Sergeant Wright and Gunner Hamas showed the men how to fire .30-caliber machine guns, belt ammunition, and other basic military tasks. Most civilians treated the experience as a pleasant diversion from their construction work and as an opportunity to obtain some precious Marine beer. Few, if any, believed they would ever have to use the skills in actual combat.

"We had fun learning how to use the weapons," stated Goicoechea. "Corporal Gross, who taught us how to use a machine gun, kept saying he hoped he had a chance to use it on the Japanese soon. I reminded him of that later on."[19]

Devereux continued the practice when he assumed command. In November, more than two hundred civilians appeared for the training, an increase that pleased the major but hardly reassured him of the value of their contribution should fighting erupt. The volunteers committed the mistakes any neophyte could be expected to make, and those occurred in calm conditions without an enemy rushing toward them. How would they react in actual combat? He was concerned, too, that only 17 percent of the civilians bothered to volunteer. Why didn't more show up?

After another alert in November, Devereux inquired whether he should immediately institute the plan he and Teters developed. He waited for two days before hearing from Bloch that he need not put any civilians into defensive positions. This response, plus the slowness with which he received it, convinced Devereux war was not likely to break out anytime soon.

The pace of events quickened as the days went by. In the second week of November, Devereux hosted special Japanese envoy Saburo Kurusu, then on his way to Washington to meet with Roosevelt over the current situation. *The Wake Wig Wag* reported that Kurusu's mission might de-

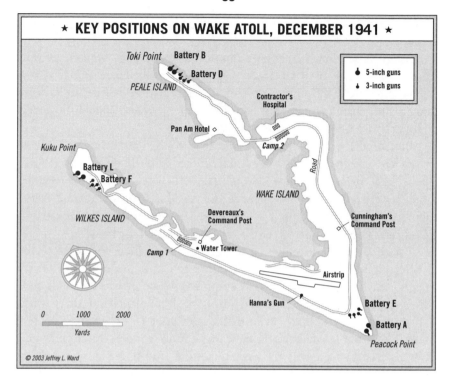

★ KEY POSITIONS ON WAKE ATOLL, DECEMBER 1941 ★

Toki Point   Battery B
Battery D
PEALE ISLAND

5-inch guns
3-inch guns

Contractor's Hospital

Pan Am Hotel
Camp 2

Kuku Point

Battery L
Battery F

Road

WAKE ISLAND

WILKES ISLAND

Devereaux's Command Post

Cunningham's Command Post

Camp 1   Water Tower

Airstrip

Hanna's Gun   Battery E

Battery A

0   1000   2000

Yards

Peacock Point

© 2003 Jeffrey L. Ward

termine whether they soon went to war or enjoyed more peaceful days on Wake.

The envoy agreed with that declaration. Before boarding the Clipper to fly across the Pacific, he told his son that should he not return from the mission, he was to take over family affairs.

When Kurusu arrived and met Devereux, he wondered if he had to remain in the Pan Am hotel to maintain secrecy of the military facilities. A properly formal Devereux responded, "No, sir, but you understand how these things are. None of the passengers may leave the vicinity of the hotel without special permission."[20]

They then adjourned to the hotel, where Kurusu shared drinks for over an hour with Devereux and other military officers. The envoy paid for every drink and told Devereux that he intended to do what he could to prevent a war. The Americans gradually warmed to the Japanese envoy, who was married to an American, and hoped he could achieve success in Washington.

Should Kurusu fail, the Japanese military intended to be ready. On November 17, as Kurusu winged his way across the Pacific to Washington, Japanese carriers weighed anchor and headed toward a secret rendezvous.

Actions had been set in motion for the start of war, both in Hawaii and on Wake.

As hostilities drew closer, the military and construction workers lived in blissful ignorance of what awaited them. Many believed the Japanese would not dare come so far eastward. Others boasted that the U.S. Navy would sink any Japanese ship that left Japanese waters. Most, however, shrugged and went about their daily schedules.

Both civilians and military received an unsettling indication in November, when Secretary of the Navy Knox ordered Mrs. Teters to leave Wake. Dan Teters tried to convince Devereux that his wife should remain on the atoll, but the Marine officer agreed with Knox that the situation demanded her removal. In the middle of November, Mrs. Teters kissed her husband good-bye, stepped aboard the Clipper, and departed for Hawaii.

For the Wake personnel watching from a distance, the sight of the comely blonde disappearing into the airplane was comparable to a thirsty man seeing his final drops of water evaporate. Not only was their sole connection to beauty and womanhood now gone, but the reality of war loomed larger, as well. Dan Teters, who had always gone out of his way to help make life bearable on Wake for the construction workers, would never allow his wife to remain if she were imperiled, and here she was, leaving Wake. Mrs. Teters later said, "I think they realized then that they were in for it. They figured that as long as I was allowed to stay on the island things couldn't be so bad."[21]

Back in Pearl Harbor, another man prepared to take his post at Wake Island. Since Wake's primary function was to provide a seaplane base and a naval airfield, as soon as enough facilities had been built, a naval commander was to be placed in charge. Comdr. Winfield S. Cunningham, a graduate of the Naval Academy Class of 1921 and an aviator, received orders to take over on Wake, with Major Devereux reverting to handling the Marines.

The orders surprised Cunningham, who had been previously told he was headed for another Pacific outpost, Johnston Island. He told a friend he did not mind the move, because "It beats Johnston. Wake has trees." The friend agreed, but reminded Cunningham "it's also about fifteen hundred miles closer to Japan."[22] Even so, his discussions with superiors in Pearl Harbor went so routinely—the possibility of war was never even mentioned—that Cunningham packed his golf clubs in case he could squeeze in some practice.

The modest man arrived so quietly on Wake on November 28 that many Marines had no idea he was there. Cunningham met with Devereux and Navy Lt. Comdr. Elmer B. Greey, the officer in charge of military construction, then unpacked in one of the three cottages for officers and dignitaries that stood near the beach at Camp 2. Afterwards, he intended to make an inspection of the island's defenses.

While Cunningham headed toward Wake, events in the Pacific intensified. Kurusu's mission failed to alleviate the growing crisis, and on November 27, negotiations had so stalemated that Chief of Naval Operations Stark sent a war warning to the commander in chief of the Pacific Fleet, Admiral Kimmel. NEGOTIATIONS WITH JAPAN LOOKING TOWARD STABILIZATION OF CONDITIONS IN THE PACIFIC HAVE CEASED AND AN AGGRESSIVE MOVE BY JAPAN IS EXPECTED WITHIN THE NEXT FEW DAYS.[23] Stark added that the deployment of Japanese forces indicated that action would likely occur in either the Philippines, against Borneo, or in the Far East. No mention of Wake appeared in the communication.

The final military group to reach the atoll flew in on December 4. Led by thirty-eight-year-old Iowa native Maj. Paul A. Putnam, Marine squadron VMF-211 consisted of twelve F4F-3 Wildcat fighters. Their task was to conduct searches of the sea approaches surrounding Wake and provide air defense against a possible enemy assault.

Major Putnam, an ardent golfer and hunter who others claimed exhibited the tenacity of a bulldog, liked to lead through example. After enlisting in the Marine Corps in 1923 as a private, Putnam earned a lieutenant's commission in 1926. He first exhibited his potential during the 1931 Marine expedition to Nicaragua, where his coolness and quiet manner proved to be a source of strength for those under him. He especially impressed other Marines with his aerial attack on a Nicaraguan stronghold, an action that won him a letter of commendation from the Secretary of the Navy.

"I flew with him for two years in Nicaragua," mentioned another officer, "and I never saw him get excited. He is calm, quiet, soft-spoken—a determined sort of fellow."[24]

Ferried from Pearl Harbor into flying range of Wake by the American aircraft carrier *Enterprise*, Putnam and his men picked up disturbing signs that their time on Wake might be difficult. Every aircraft mechanic aboard the *Enterprise* checked and rechecked the twelve fighters with meticulousness, and the carrier's commander, Adm. William F. Halsey, ordered that the men of VMF-211 were to receive whatever supplies they desired. Not used to such attention, Putnam later wrote, "I feel a bit like the fatted calf being groomed for whatever it is that happens to fatted calves, but it surely is nice while it lasts and the airplanes are pretty sleek and fat too."[25]

He may have felt more like a sacrificial lamb following a discussion with an *Enterprise* aviator. When the man learned Putnam was headed toward Wake with only a dozen fighters, he commented that Putnam and his men were probably gifted aviators, but "a dozen seems kind of light to take on the whole Jap air force."[26]

Marines and other military personnel on Wake enthusiastically welcomed VMF-211 on December 4. Now, instead of relying only on the fighting abilities of the ground forces, Wake possessed an air force. Though small, it could reach out hundreds of miles at sea and strike invaders long before they set foot on the island, in effect increasing the range of Wake's offensive capabilities and creating a buffer zone around the atoll. Before an enemy could strike Wake, it first had to contend with Putnam's fighters. The sight of twelve gleaming Wildcats landing on Wake's partially completed airstrip lent a feeling of invincibility to the garrison, which rarely lacked self-assurance or worried over a possible attack anyway.

Unfortunately, the aviators of VMF-211 did not have the same confidence when they surveyed the air facilities at Wake. Putnam and the others found that while one runway was long enough for operations, the soft coral sand base made it impossible for more than one or two aircraft to taxi at a time. Putnam worried about the small pieces of coral that dotted the runway, any one of which could be kicked up during takeoffs and landings and disable the aircraft. Gasoline supplies stood in unsheltered tanks that made tempting targets for an enemy pilot, and not one hangar or revetment had been built to house his twelve aircraft.

Since the ground crews and aviators had been training with biplanes instead of the newer fighters, they were unfamiliar with the capabilities of the aircraft. Mechanics rummaged through the crates of supplies that accompanied the planes for instruction manuals, but could find none—someone at Pearl Harbor had forgotten to pack them. Spare parts for the aircraft were practically nonexistent, which meant that even minor damage could knock them out of the fighting, and the bombs sent to Wake did not fit the bomb racks attached to the fighters. Putnam hoped his aviators and ground personnel, including the squadron mechanics, had enough time to correct the deficiencies. Putnam had no way of knowing that he and the twelve F4F-3 fighters had arrived on Wake a mere four days before the opening of hostilities.

Two of the men who quickly started their assignments were 2d Lt. Robert J. Conderman and thirty-six-year-old Capt. Henry T. Elrod. They shared the same love of flying, but that was as close as the two came in personalities. A graduate of the University of North Carolina, Conderman had a serious, intelligent side belied by his looks—his burning red hair and freckled face reminded fellow aviators of a small-town country boy in the mold of Mark Twain's Huck Finn and Tom Sawyer. "He was a good man," stated Lieutenant Kinney after the war. "Conderman was very friendly, very young looking. He had red hair, and that is where he got his nickname 'Strawberry.' "[27]

On the other hand Elrod, who studied architecture and medicine at both Georgia and Yale, was a hard-drinking career officer with thirteen years' experience who irritated superiors with his reckless manner of flying. In aerial gunnery practice, Elrod flew so close to the target being pulled by other aircraft that observers on the ground thought he had no chance to avoid crashing into it. He always did, usually mere seconds from a collision, but not before leaving behind a shredded target. Though frustrating to commanders, Elrod developed the reputation of being someone a man could count on when the real bullets started flying.

While exhibiting a tough crust when with his men, Elrod showed a tender side when writing to his wife. Frequent lengthy letters ended in similar fashion, with Elrod signing each with his middle name, Talmadge.

"A Bastard-Type Unit"

As the first week in December waned, Cunningham, Devereux, and Putnam faced critical shortages in many areas. Each of the three conducted inspection tours and inventoried their arsenals, and they concluded that deficiency was the norm on each island of Wake.

On Peale Island, off Wake's northern arm, where Joe Goicoechea would spend part of the battle, Capt. Bryghte D. Godbold's position at Toki Point stood in the best shape. Battery B's two 5-inch naval guns, designed for use against enemy ships approaching the island and commanded by 1st Lt. Woodrow M. Kessler, and Battery D's four 3-inch antiaircraft guns, under Godbold's supervision, had been completely emplaced and sandbagged. In addition, four .50-caliber machine guns (one manned by Private Laporte) and four .30-caliber machine guns protected Godbold's position. His had only enough Marines to man three of the 3-inch guns, but he was still better off than his compatriots on both Wilkes and Wake Islands.

The other two main gun positions—the places that would see most of the fighting in the days to come—faced critical shortages. At Corporal Gross's station at Peacock Point on Wake Island's southeast corner, Lt. Clarence A. Barninger could also call on four .50-caliber and four .30-caliber machine guns to guard the approaches to his position, but he had only partially sandbagged and sheltered Battery E's four 3-inch guns, commanded by Lt. William W. Lewis. The four—only three of which could be manned— stood in the open, subject to attack, as did both of Barninger's 5-inch guns.

Barninger's men worked when they could to complete the camouflaging and dig dugouts, but constant interruptions for aircraft refueling made the task difficult at best. A more critical handicap was that none of the 3-inch guns sported height finders, automatic devices used to accurately determine an aircraft's altitude. In an attack, Barninger would have to estimate the altitude by eyesight.

Across the channel separating Wake Island from Wilkes Island, Capt. Wesley M. Platt had to improvise at Kuku Point, as well. His two 5-inch guns, under 2d Lt. John A. McAlister, were fully manned and camouflaged, but a lack of personnel meant that none of his four 3-inch guns could be manned. He did the best he could with his four .50-caliber and two .30-caliber machine guns, scattering them along Wilkes's ocean shore and the lagoon beach.

Lieutenant Hanna and Lieutenant Poindexter spread the rest of their eighteen .50-caliber machine guns and thirty .30-caliber machine guns throughout the atoll, some near the airstrip and the others where the officers felt they could do the most good. Like their counterparts behind the 5-inch and 3-inch guns, Hanna and Poindexter were forced to improvise and guess which gun positions to man and which to leave empty. They could not possibly cover Wake's twenty miles of shoreline with the available personnel, so they tried to think like the enemy and predict where an attack might come. They concluded that the southern shore of Wake Island, where the reef jutted in close to land, and the southern coast of Wilkes were the most probable spots. The two officers posted men along those beaches and hoped that, in the hands of determined Marines, the few guns could inflict serious damage on an invading force. They tried not to dwell on the fact that fewer than six machine gun positions waited to greet the enemy on such an important portion of the atoll.

Cunningham and Devereux faced other critical gaps. Many of the 5-inch guns suffered from a lack of spare parts. The Marine garrison lacked enough rifles to give to the Army and Navy personnel stationed with them. In an attack, those men would have to rely on whatever they brought along, usually a sidearm, or wait until the fighting started and take a rifle from a Marine who had been killed.

Especially frustrating was the lack of radar. The recent invention would have allowed defenders to spot enemy aircraft long before they reached Wake, but Wake had no such advantages. Every time a transport from Hawaii arrived, Devereux and Cunningham prayed it contained the promised radar, but they were disappointed each time. They knew the equipment had been earmarked for the island, for one of the men had seen Wake's radar equipment on the docks of Pearl Harbor, waiting shipment. Would they receive it in time?

In the absence of radar, Devereux had to make do with what he had. He placed two men with binoculars at the atoll's highest spot—the water tower—but this arrangement hardly guaranteed success. The guards could not even rely on sound to help them in detecting enemy aircraft since Wake's booming surf drowned out all such noise.

Fifty years later, Lieutenant Poindexter accurately conveyed the feeling of the time. He called the defenders of Wake "a bastard-type unit equipped with hand-me-down weapons, which were mostly of World War I vintage, and assigned a bastard-type mission. It is, therefore, somewhat ironic that this unlikely aggregation of the prewar military establishment would give the nation its first victory of the Second World War."[28]

"We Were Just Kids"

Even though the pressing duties left little training time for his Marines, in the first week of December, Devereux decided to test the battle readiness of his men. On Saturday morning, December 6, he staged a mock alert. The drill proved to be the first, and only, time that the gun crews worked together in manning their guns. The outcome so pleased Devereux—all the men quickly reported to their stations and appeared ready for battle—that he gave his men that afternoon and all the next day off. Teters followed suit and declared a holiday for his men, as well.

Only Putnam's squad worked on December 6, since many items needed to be done at the airstrip. Chief among them was to fill huge 25,000-gallon gasoline tanks set up along the airstrip. As he helped pump aviation fuel into the tanks, Kinney thought to himself "what juicy targets these would make to enemy bombers."[29]

The rest of the men took full advantage of their free time. On December 7 (December 6 in Pearl Harbor, which stood on the other side of the international date line) many slept in, then headed to the lagoon for some leisurely fishing on a bright, sunny afternoon. With only a few days left until his discharge and a trip to the United States, Sgt. Alton J. Bertels of Battery B organized his personal belongings. Finally, he would be getting off this miserable atoll. Commander Cunningham battled Ens. George Henshaw in tennis, while Lieutenant Barninger and Lieutenant Lewis went sailboating in the lagoon. Kessler and McAlister packed some sardines, crackers, and beer and rowed a boat to the reef northwest of Kuku Point, where they spent the day observing the aquatic life that scurried and swam about. The giant clams, which slowly clamped together their shells whenever Kessler's or McAlister's shadow loomed over them, fascinated the pair.

If you have enough healthy Americans in one spot, sooner or later a baseball game is likely to break out. In a bit of friendly rivalry, the Marines challenged their civilian counterparts to a contest. In front of a large crowd of enthusiastic supporters, who passed around bets and insults in equal measure, the Marines won a hard-fought game, 2 to 1, earning bragging rights.

That December 7, which would be their final day of rest for the next forty-five months, provided a boost in morale to a bunch of men who had worked long days for months at a time. "We hadn't had a day off for two months," said Corporal Marvin. "This was the first time since Devereux came out there that we got any time off. We had a ball!"[30]

One Marine battled mixed emotions over calling the day off a reward, for it terminated recent hopes of heading home. On December 5, Lieutenant Poindexter had inspected his gun position and found it lacking. The officer called the work "slipshod," turned to Holewinski, and angrily promised, "I don't think that people like you should be that far away from the United States, so I'm gonna see if you can get sent back." Rather than being insulted, Holewinski greeted his prospects with enthusiasm. December in the United States had to be better than December on Wake.

Before Poindexter could follow through on his claim, Devereux and Cunningham came by on their Saturday-morning inspection. "Boy, this is nice," exclaimed Commander Cunningham when he surveyed Holewinski's work. "Who's in charge here?"[31] Holewinski reluctantly raised his hand, realizing that Cunningham's praise canceled Poindexter's criticism and effectively ended his chances of seeing the mainland for the foreseeable future.

In Washington, President Roosevelt faced troubles of his own. On December 6, while the men at Wake enjoyed their last carefree day, Roosevelt learned the Japanese would present a fourteen-part ultimatum the next day. "This means war," Roosevelt mentioned to his trusted adviser, Harry Hopkins. When Hopkins stated it was too bad the United States could not launch a first strike, Roosevelt added, "No, we can't do that. We are a democracy and a peaceful people. But we have a good record."[32] He could do nothing but wait for the Japanese to strike.

While the festivities unfolded elsewhere on Wake, two men preferred to spend the moments in more contemplative ways. Since he had been on the island only a few days, Lieutenant Kinney decided to take a stroll around the atoll. What he saw shocked him—partially completed gun positions, undermanned machine-gun posts, shortages in equipment. He headed over to Pan Am's facilities at Peale Island and talked to one of its crew members, an old friend named Ed Barnett. Barnett handed Kinney some shocking news—Pan Am was evacuating all its civilian dependents from the Philippines in anticipation of war.

Kinney returned to his quarters in a gloomy mood. "I sure hoped that the war would wait a little longer before it got to Wake," he wrote after the war. "None of us in VMF-211 had ever even fired the machine guns in the Wildcats yet."[33] Kinney relaxed when he recalled that the next day, December 8, he and the other aviators were scheduled to start aerial gunnery practice. He would finally get his chance to fire the fighter's machine guns.

After being with other Marines almost around the clock, Lieutenant Hanna appreciated the chance to escape somewhere by himself. Not surprisingly, he strolled to one of the beaches along the lagoon to find more shells for Vera. He needed only a few more to have enough for the necklace; then he could string them together and mail them to his wife. Most men, civilian and military, wanted to be with their friends and have a few laughs, but Hanna was happy to be alone, on a Pacific beach thinking of Vera, family, and home.

As war inched closer to Wake, that final peacetime day closed with much work remaining, but most men shoved that thought aside for the moment. The island boasted a population of 1,145 civilian workers, 72 Pan Am employees, and 524 military personnel, including 6 Army, 69 Navy, and 449 Marines. Not included in the count were the passengers aboard the weekly Clipper, which landed in the lagoon that day. Among its numbers was Herman P. Hevenor, a government auditor sent to Wake to check Morrison-Knudsen's bookkeeping. As soon as he finished the task, he intended to leave Wake as quickly as possible.

December 7 provided a tonic for the men. Thoughts of war, not that they had ever bothered them, receded. Even the most pessimistic among them refused to worry about war with Japan. "We didn't even think about war," said Corporal Marvin. "There were so many rumors, but we were too busy working. We were just kids."[34]

Should war come, they were optimistic the Japanese would be no match for the militarily superior Americans. After all, on December 7 newspapers quoted Secretary Knox as stating the United States Navy had no superior in the world. "I am proud to report that the American people may feel fully confident in their Navy. . . . On any comparable basis, the United States Navy is second to none."[35]

As Kinney related, many dismissed the Japanese as "short bandy-legged men with prominent front teeth and very thick eyeglasses. We were convinced that even if the Japanese planes were mechanically adequate, it would be all the pilots could do to fly them in straight lines. They would be no match for American aerobatic maneuvers."[36]

Joe Goicoechea faced the future with confidence also. He and his buddies believed that should the Japanese be foolish enough to start a war with the United States, it would be over in a few months. "Hell, we thought that Uncle Sam was invincible. We figured our military would beat the hell out of them and that would be it,"[37] he explained.

Nothing indicated that Wake would be one of Japan's first targets, but Cunningham and Devereux still wished they had more time to prepare. When an Englishman and his wife stopped at Wake with the *Clipper,* Devereux drove them around the island. He pointed to his Marines working at the guns and said they were moving as fast as they could. The wife replied, "Yes, it would be nice to have six months more, wouldn't it?"[38]

CHAPTER 3

"The Marines Will Show Them a Thing or Two"

"This Is No Drill! Pass the Word!"

Wake Island civilians and military awoke on Monday, December 8 (Sunday, December 7, in Pearl Harbor), refreshed from the break of the past twenty-four hours. For the first time in many weeks, they had the opportunity to forget their responsibilities and concentrate on having fun. The respite made going to work this morning easier than normal.

Except for those who had been on overnight duty, the sounds of men awakening for their daily chores interrupted the camps' quiet at around 6:30 A.M. The hustle and bustle soon had a life of its own, with men washing up or bounding to the mess hall. Another lovely day, complete with the brilliant sunrise that bathed the atoll in its luscious beauty, had dawned.

In his quarters, Major Devereux applied shaving cream to his face. Commander Cunningham, a bit speedier than his Marine counterpart, had already plunged into his breakfast of bacon, eggs, and coffee. Dan Teters, hard-pressed by superiors to meet work deadlines, thought of the different projects that begged for attention. All three looked forward to another fruitful day's labor from their men—which meant that they would be one day closer to the time when Wake properly housed a fully manned and equipped defense battalion, ready to protect the atoll's shores from any aggressor. Cunningham also intended to check the results of VMF-211's gunnery practice. He knew the aviators badly needed the exercise to develop the skill and confidence required to perform at top levels, as well as to create an esprit among the unit.

A signal picked up at 6:40 by Army Sgt. Ernest Rogers in the communications center shattered the day's serenity. Sitting at his post inside the Army trailer, where he monitored radio traffic, Rogers was about to leave for breakfast when the receiver vibrated with a message he found hard to believe. sos . . . sos—the international distress signal alone grabbed his attention, but what followed transfixed the Army veteran. ISLAND OF OAHU ATTACKED BY JAPANESE DIVE BOMBERS, continued the message. As if the sender could read everyone's minds who picked up the broadcast, he added, THIS IS THE REAL THING.[1]

Rogers alerted his superior, Army Capt. Henry Wilson, who sprinted to Devereux's quarters to inform him of the development. Without bothering to remove the shaving cream on his face, Devereux rang Cunningham's office, but the naval commander had not yet left the mess hall. Devereux then ordered his bugler, FM1c. Alvin J. Waronker, to sound the call to arms. In the heat of the moment Waronker, a horrid bugler who rarely sounded any Marine call correctly, forgot the proper tune. Figuring any music was better than no music, he started playing tunes as they tumbled into his mind until he remembered general quarters.

Devereux might have laughed if the situation had not been so grim. When he spotted men casually strolling around and joking over Waronker's erratic concert, he yelled, "This is no drill! Pass the word!"[2]

The news shot to every part of Wake like a bolt of lightning. At 7:00, Cunningham learned of the attack when a messenger located him as he left the mess hall. Cunningham quickly issued orders for all Marines to man their posts and for Major Putnam to launch all aircraft to prevent their being destroyed on the ground.

Marines, trained for just such a moment, reacted quickly to the alarm. Lt. Woodrow Kessler had eaten four of his six pancakes when the news arrived. Instead of leaving the last two, he gulped down the final hotcakes as he sprinted outside. Officers rushed into the mess hall, where Cpl. Kenneth Marvin and some buddies were eating and ordered them to get to their positions. "Everybody's running around," said Marvin. "In each tent we had a case of ammunition and two cases of hand grenades, and we had to take those and put them on a truck. We then drove out to our position, Battery D on Peale Island."[3]

A warrant officer told Pfc. Martin A. Gatewood and his group to return to their tents, grab the ammunition that had been placed there, and report back to the mess hall, where trucks would transport them to their posts. Gatewood asked why, then reacted with the same incredulity exhibited by most men when told that the Japanese had just hit Pearl Harbor. "He said that we were at war and that Pearl Harbor had been bombed. Of course, nobody believed that. We were preached to all the time when we were in Hawaii that no one could bomb it because it was too well defended."[4]

It took longer for the civilian sector to realize that their peacetime days had ended. Workers noticed the increased activity near the Marine camp, but they dismissed it as a drill or some other military procedure. James Allen climbed into the flatbed truck taking him and others to their workstations when a jeep packed with Marines sped by. Young wondered why the men wore their combat helmets—the old World War I flat-brimmed style—and why they appeared so serious, but figured he would learn something during his midday break or after dinner.

A civilian crew had already applied a coat of paint to an unfinished barracks when they heard a yell. "Don't you know there's a war on?"[5] shouted Marvin's group of Marines as they headed out to Toki Point and Battery D.

A foreman broke the news to Hans Whitney, working on the top level of a four-story building. "The Japs are bombing Pearl Harbor, right now. They have sunk many of our ships and killed lots of service men. They may be here any minute."

Whitney thought about it for a few seconds, then reacted with derisive laughter. "Let them come," he boasted to his foreman. "The Marines will show them a thing or two."[6]

"Sir, Can You Use Me?"

No one knew what the Japanese might do next or when they might do it, but most military personnel assumed that one way or another, they would soon be in action. After all, the Japanese boldly struck the strongest American base in the Pacific, inflicting what early reports stated was heavy damage, and that base stood two thousand miles to the east of Wake. If the Japanese could mount a powerful attack against Pearl Harbor at such an extreme distance from their home waters, their arsenal could certainly handle tiny Wake.

One of the first items Cunningham and Devereux decided was the location for their command posts. As commander of the entire atoll, Cunningham had to be centrally located for speedier access, not just with Army, Navy, and Marine personnel, but with Teters and the civilians. Cunningham stopped by Devereux's office to inform him he would be situated north of the airstrip, along the road winding up Wake toward Peale Island. Devereux replied that as soon as a switchboard had been hooked up for him, he would operate out of a post in the brush on the lagoon side, near the Marine tents of Camp 1.

Cunningham then telephoned the manager of the Pan Am station, John B. Cooke, to urge him to recall the *Philippine Clipper* that had taken off less than an hour previously. Cooke sent out a prearranged coded signal to the airplane, informing the pilot that war had broken out and that he should immediately return to Wake.

Cunningham hurriedly conferred with Dan Teters and Lt. Comdr. Elmer B. Greey, the officer in charge of construction. The three agreed to allow the civilian work parties to proceed as scheduled, but that the civilian volunteers such as Joe Goicoechea should report to Devereux for further assignments.

Lt. Clarence A. Barninger and his tentmate, Lt. William W. Lewis, who had earlier seen Wilson speeding to Devereux's tent as they walked to breakfast and wondered what the problem was, attended a meeting Devereux hurriedly called for his officers. He informed them of the latest developments at Oahu and warned them that Wake could soon expect the same thing. He told his officers to man their positions and adopt war status.

All over the atoll, Marines arrived at their battle stations and prepared for battle. Gunnery sergeants, the iron men of the Marine defenses, checked that phone lines worked and ordered each man to inspect his ammunition supplies and rifle. Crews on the larger guns placed thirty rounds of ammunition in ready boxes for each of the 5-inch guns to be used against naval targets and fifty rounds for each 3-inch antiaircraft gun. By 7:35, less than one hour after the initial report of hostilities, every Marine position reported manned and ready to Major Devereux.

That included even the injured. Sgt. Walter Bowsher of Battery D had been in the dispensary with a swollen left leg due to a blood clot. The surgeon, Navy Lt. (jg) G. Mason Kahn, planned to operate on the leg in a few hours, but Bowsher refused to be separated from his men at such a crucial moment. Grabbing a pair of crutches, the injured Bowsher hobbled out to join his mates on Peale Island.

Devereux figured that if the Japanese were going to strike, they would first hit with an air attack. Since Wake's pounding surf would drown out the noise of incoming aircraft until they were almost directly overhead, he had to turn to some other expedient. Unfortunately, Wake's radar languished on Pearl Harbor's docks, so he had to improvise. He selected the highest point on Wake, the fifty-foot water tower in Camp 1 near his command post, and ordered two Marines to climb up and remain as lookouts. Wake's early-warning system thus consisted of two apprehensive Marines standing on the atoll's most visible installation, wondering if they made juicy targets for enemy aircraft.

Lieutenant Hanna ran through a mental list of items to consider in the war's opening moments. With only enough Marines to man half of the eighteen .50-caliber antiaircraft machine guns, and with no defensive position completely dug in and sandbagged, he fought with one arm tied behind his back. In addition, he supervised young men who had never seen battle, yet he could not show any traces of fear or indecision, even though he had never experienced combat either. Hanna reminded himself that the men looked to him for leadership; he had to show the men, many not yet out of their teens, that they could function despite any fears they had.

Once the Marines had spread throughout the atoll, Cunningham freed the handful of excess rifles, gas masks, and helmets for use by the Army and Navy personnel. He then scattered them around to help bolster the Marine defense or placed them in a reserve unit to be used wherever the fighting might be the hottest.

An anxious waiting game now started. Eyes scanned the skies for traces of approaching aircraft and scrutinized the sea for telltale signs of a naval armada. Some men dug deeper into the coral sand for more protection, while others stared straight ahead, alone with their thoughts.

At 10:00 A.M., after more than two hours of calm, Devereux placed the men on a partial alert. At every position, half the men were to continue watching for an invasion while the other half grabbed shovels to deepen bunkers, widen foxholes, and prepare for the inevitable assault.

At the airstrip, Major Putnam dealt with his own dilemma. Due to lack of space at the cramped airfield, his twelve new fighters stood closely together on the airstrip, which made them inviting targets to an opposing pilot. This may have been the most economical use of limited facilities, but it also created an invitation to disaster. One well-placed bomb by an enemy pilot could destroy multiple aircraft, and even machine gun bursts fired at random would be likely to hit something.

This is where Putnam faced his quandary. Military doctrine called for him to disperse the fighters to reduce the amount of destruction one hit could achieve, but he could not move the fighters without risk of damaging them on the rough coral surface that fringed the airstrip. On the other hand, construction crews would have protective revetments for his aircraft completed within a few hours. He could either disperse the unprotected fighters and hope that none were damaged, or leave them packed together on the airstrip and wait for the revetments to be finished.

He gambled that the construction workers could complete the revetments before a Japanese attack occurred, so he kept the fighters on the airstrip. At the same time, he ordered that four fighters should constantly be in the air, conducting searches. In that way, should the enemy hit sooner than expected, at least his entire air force would not be caught on the ground.

In this instance, the isolationist tendencies of the 1930s, combined with the economically depressed state of the nation, joined hands to deny the military the tools needed to conduct warfare. Putnam would not have agonized over such a decision had Wake's defenses been adequately prepared.

Cunningham faced another handicap by being limited to what the men in the tower could see and what his four aircraft might spot, and the chances of those few men locating or intercepting the enemy in the vast ocean or sky were slight. When Capt. J. H. Hamilton, captain of the *Philippine Clipper*, volunteered to fly a reconnaissance mission with his airplane, Cunningham at first agreed. He thought the *Clipper* could search to the south of Wake, a portion of the ocean that his fighters could not cover because of pressing duties, but after more thought he rejected the offer. It would be better to refuel the *Clipper* and get her out of Wake before any harm befell her.

Many of the civilians wished they could have boarded the aircraft and put Wake behind them, but they had to wait for another day. Most of the 1,145 civilian workers headed to the brush, some out of fear, some out of confusion, and some because no one told them otherwise. Before the war, Cunningham and Devereux avoided organizing all the civilians into military support parties. Another 1,000 men, even as ill-prepared for fighting as many of these might have been, could have considerably eased the crisis, but Cunningham and Devereux had to take care of military matters first. Developing Wake's defenses and shifting men and ammunition to the proper locations took precedence over training neophyte warriors.

Legalities also intervened. The civilians were not under military control, so issuing orders to them might have been nothing more than an exercise in futility. Cunningham and Devereux also feared that in combat conditions, any civilian who took up arms or aided the military might be considered by the Japanese to be a guerrilla fighter instead of a member of the regular military, an offense punishable by death.

Civilian supervisors, lacking any clear directive from Cunningham and Devereux, told the men to seek shelter in the brush covering Wake's interior and to wait for further instructions. Some men ignored the advice and immediately offered their help to the military. Most eagerly shuffled into the brush, as that would place them at least temporarily out of harm's way.

Already, some of the civilians had gathered near the Marine camp or come in to offer their assistance. A handful had previous military experience, like the man who walked up to Devereux and said, "Sir, Adams, former seaman United States Navy, reporting for duty. Sir, can you use me?"7 A group of about fifty civilians reported to Gunner Hamas, the Marine with whom they had received their training on Wake, and asked for weapons. On his own authority, Hamas forced open a storeroom and handed out rifles and ammunition.

Joe Goicoechea headed out to Battery D on Peale Island, ready to do whatever he could to help the Marines. The minimal training he had received under Corporal Gross gave him some knowledge, but the civilian knew that he, like the other civilian volunteers, was part of desperation moves by an undermanned defense contingent.

"Get Those Guns Firing"

Whether military or civilian, most men on Wake reacted similarly when they first spotted aircraft bearing toward them—they assumed they were American. Hans Whitney was working atop a four-story building on Peale Island not far from the Pan Am Hotel when he noticed twin-engine bombers approaching low over the airfield. "Look!" he shouted to his fellow workers. "Let the Japs come! We even have bombers now!"[8]

Standing near the airstrip, Cpl. Ralph Holewinski believed they were a new type of Army aircraft. Major Devereux was chatting on the telephone with Lieutenant Lewis at Peacock Point on Wake Island when Lewis said, "Major, there's a squadron of planes coming in from the south. Are they friendly?" Before Devereux could answer, a civilian ran in and yelled, "Look! Their wheels are falling off!"[9] Perched at his lookout spot at the water tower, Sgt. Donald R. Malleck wondered why these aircraft seemed to be headed straight toward him when they should be veering toward the airfield. At Peacock Point, Lieutenant Barninger saw the planes drop low and fast out of a rain squall around 11:50.

At the canteen, J. O. Young had just sat down with a milk shake, as he had so often done with Pearl Ann, when he heard planes shortly before noon. He thought they were U.S. aircraft and ran outside for a look. Suddenly, machine gun bullets kicked up dust around him. As bullets smacked into the ground and machine guns resounded with *rat-a-tat-tat*s, he and others dashed toward the lagoon and hid behind a coral outcropping.

Young's uncle, Forrest Read, sat in a truck taking him to lunch when the planes appeared. When one man said, "It certainly didn't take good old Uncle Sam long to get help to us," Read nodded his head in agreement. Then dirt spit up from the ground and explosions shook the truck. "Run for the beach and stay low in the rocks,"[10] someone shouted.

John Rogge heard the *clickety-click* of machine gun bullets on his barracks roof and tried to rush outside, but a wooden splinter hurled from a shattered plywood door pierced him in the back. Though fearing the projectile had mortally wounded him, Rogge scampered to a nearby drainpipe and waited out the attack.

To Johnson's north, Pfc. Martin Gatewood joined other Marines in filling sandbags in front of his 3-inch antiaircraft gun. "All of a sudden I heard bombs falling on the airfield, which was east of us. The next thing I saw was these planes coming over. All of us were dumbfounded. Godwin, the gun captain, was hollering, 'Get those guns firing!' " One of the Marines responsible for loading the shells into the gun was so engrossed with the sight of the bombers that he forgot to do his job. After the attack, Godwin elevated Gatewood to first loader, and "From then on we got our share of 'em."[11]

Civilian volunteer John M. Valov, who had been trained on a .30-caliber machine gun by Lieutenant Poindexter before the war started, also assumed the planes were American aircraft on maneuvers. Valov had so much confidence in the U.S. military that he had difficulty believing that any nation had the audacity to attack the powerful United States. When bullets scattered all around him, however, a surprised Valov dived for the nearest shelter.

What they had all witnessed was the opening moments of the first Japanese assault against Wake. Twenty-seven Mitsubishi Attack Bombers, nicknamed Nells, had come roaring in from their island base at Roi in the Marshalls, 620 miles due south. Shortly before reaching Wake, nine bombers veered off to bomb Wilkes Island, Camp 1, Camp 2, and Peale Island while the remaining eighteen focused on the airstrip. Two minutes before noon, war came to Wake.

Wilkes Island and Camp 1 escaped with minimal damage. The nine enemy aircraft strafed both positions, but they were appetizers for the more tempting airfield and military installations on Peale and Wake. Corp. John S. Johnson, on duty at his machine gun off Kuku Point on Wilkes, fired at the enemy bombers as they flew over Wilkes, then spun around to witness the attack on the airfield. Already he could feel the *whump* of the concussions from bombs smacking near the runway more than one mile away.

The nine Japanese bombers sped over the lagoon at such a low altitiude that Corporal Marvin and the other Marines at Battery D, along Peale's north shore, could not fire back. They began dropping their bombs while still over the lagoon, then ran them straight toward their intended targets at the Pan Am installations or the civilian barracks and buildings of Camp 2. Workers followed the progress of the bomb explosions, which sounded like an enormous flat hand swatting the water, until they came too near their own positions.

Benjamin Comstock Sr. and his son, Ben Jr., stood on a two-story building on the east shore of Peale when the bombs and bullets approached. Acting with the instinct that would mark the entire war—sons protecting their fathers and families—Ben Jr. tackled his father, shoved him behind a stairway, and then shielded him with his own body. Bombs tossed dirt and coral dust over the two men, but other than rattling their nerves, left both unharmed.

Not far away, Hans Whitney, whose friend had only moments before dared the Japanese to attack, watched the bombers head directly toward him on their way to strike the hotel. He and twenty men leapt for cover in the unfinished structure. "Bullets sounded like a terrific hailstorm, rattling on the steel," Whitney recalled. "We scampered down the framework and reached the ground where we were huddled together."[12]

Other civilians, caught in the open, ran for their lives. Earl Wilkerson jumped out of his seat at a card game in the barracks and rushed to hide in the brush. A group of aircraft swooped down on James Allen near the mess hall. He tried to reach the safety offered by a small bush, but a piece of shrapnel burned into his back before he got there. When those planes departed, he again rose—but hesitated as a second group of aircraft flew in. He suddenly recalled a 1940 conversation in California with a member of the Flying Tiger volunteers who helped the Chinese in their fight against the Japanese. The man told him he had been a tail gunner in China and laughed when he explained how the Japanese on the ground had turned into such easy targets by running and drawing attention to themselves. He added that the best thing to do in an air attack was to hug the ground and wait it out. Allen dropped to the surface, buried his face in the coral, and lay still, hoping that the man had been correct. In a few moments that seemed much longer, the planes sped overhead without noticing him.

Cunningham was working in his office along with his secretary, YN3c. Glenn E. Tripp, when the bombers approached. Tripp lay flat on the floor, while Cunningham dived under his plywood desk. Bullets splintered into the office from one end to the other, and when the attack ended, Tripp rested unharmed between two uniform lines of bullet holes.

Pfc. James O. King stood watch on a tower near Camp 1 when Sgt. Donald R. Malleck climbed up to routinely check on him. As they talked, aircraft suddenly dropped out of some clouds and adopted a course directly toward them. "Let's get the hell down from here!" shouted Sergeant Malleck to King, who replied, "You don't have to say that again!"[13] The pair safely reached the ground and ran for a nearby dugout.

Private Laporte, who at first had a hard time believing Pearl Harbor had truly been hit, now realized that what he had considered impossible had actually occurred. "Another guy and I left our gun [at Toki Point] to fill our mess kits and grab some coffee when we heard a roar," said Laporte. "I looked and about one and a half miles away the planes were dropping bombs on the airport. We threw the coffee and stew away—I'd regret that later—and got our butts in a hole and watched 'em come over. They hit the Pan Am Hotel. They flew right over us, but they weren't after our positions."[14]

They wanted Pan Am's facilities, and accurate bombing reduced much of the spot to smoke and flames. Twenty-three bullet holes riddled the *Philippine Clipper* at her mooring, and ten Chamorro employees lay dead. As gruesome a toll as this was on the commercial airline, it was dwarfed by the agony at the airstrip.

"The Destruction That Greeted Me Was More Than I Was Prepared For"

Less than two miles across the lagoon, Lieutenant Hanna chatted with Cpl. Franklin Gross at Gross's dugout south of the airstrip. As Hanna talked, Gross suddenly spotted a group of bombers drop out of a hole in the clouds. "What's this coming in?"[15] he asked Hanna. They guessed the aircraft must be more B-17s coming in for fuel, but bombs, bullets, and explosions awakened them to what was actually happening. Both men hastened to their posts as a fury of sound erupted all about them.

Major Putnam, the commander of VMF-211, saw the bombers at the same time and yelled, "Take cover—bombers."[16] He looked for a safe place on the airfield in which to hide, but when he found nothing, he sped toward a latrine one hundred yards away. Employing every ounce of athletic talent, the former high school track star dodged bullets and bombs and slid headfirst into the latrine moments before an explosion hurled deadly debris and shrapnel in all directions. There, stinking but safe, Putnam climbed out of the latrine to organize his defenses.

All around Hanna and Putnam, men strove first to stay alive, and then to fight back. S.Sgt. Robert O. Arthur had just squeezed into the belly of a Marine fighter to install a homing device when he heard shouting from outside. He peered through an opening, expecting to watch Army bombers land, but swore when he saw Japanese aircraft heading straight toward the airstrip. Knowing what a tempting target each fighter posed, Arthur edged out of the cramped quarters and hustled over to shelter.

Pfc. Jacob R. Sanders was standing on the back of a truck, laying telephone wire on the beach near the airfield, when the bombers struck. He had his back to the approaching aircraft, but turned around when the driver of the truck jumped out and hit the ground. Sanders dropped the telephone wire, retrieved his rifle, and scampered underneath the truck for cover.

He was one of the lucky ones, for during these opening moments on the airfield, to hesitate meant to die. A man either dived for any covering, no matter how slim, or stood exposed to enemy bullets and bombs on an open airstrip. Capt. Herbert C. Freuler used a narrow dip near the squadron's ammunition tent as shelter, while bullets ripped into ground personnel and airmen mere yards away and explosions eviscerated his mates.

In an attempt to eliminate Wake's major threat to their operations—the Marine fighters—the Japanese executed a meticulously crafted air strike. They seemed to know exactly what to hit and where to hit it, for in the first seconds of the strike, Japanese bombs destroyed two 25,000-gallon tanks of fuel and more than six hundred 55-gallon drums of aviation gasoline, stacked neatly together along the airstrip. Black clouds billowed skyward while flames, fueled by gasoline gushing out of damaged containers, threatened to engulf most portions of the airstrip.

Eight of VMF-211's twelve fighters stood unmanned and motionless in one section of the airstrip, causing surprised Japanese airmen to smile in anticipation of easy kills. The Japanese had expected to meet fighter resistance as they approached Wake, but they avoided the four Wildcats that had earlier taken off to search the skies. Now, instead of dodging American bullets, they raced straight toward silent targets to enact the massacre of VMF-211, Wake's tiny air force.

"We strafed the soldiers, as we determined to let not even one escape,"[17] mentioned Japanese correspondent Norio Tsuji, who accompanied the task force. Unlike Allen on Peale Island, who hugged the coral surface and remained motionless, Marine aviators and ground personnel raced about the airstrip, compelled by duty and courage to risk their lives.

As Lieutenant Hanna watched from not far away, the slaughter of VMF-211, a crucial portion of Wake's defenses, unfolded. Four Marine aviators rushed toward their Wildcats to take off before Japanese bullets destroyed their planes, but none made it. Machine-gun bullets tore into Lt. Frank J. Holden as he sprinted onto the runway. He slumped to the ground and died yards from his aircraft. Lt. Henry G. Webb raced toward his fighter, but bullets shredded his stomach, face, and legs and severely wounded the young airman.

Lieutenant Conderman and Lt. George Graves sat in the ready tent, preparing to escort the *Philippine Clipper*, when the alarm sounded. They rushed outside to the airstrip, where Graves actually reached his Wildcat. He climbed into the cockpit and prepared for takeoff, but a direct hit demolished the aircraft and instantly killed Graves. "I saw some of the men running to their aircraft and getting hit," said Hanna. "I saw Graves get in the plane just at the same time as the bomb got there."[18] Conderman, the boyish-looking aviator with a Tom Sawyer look, evaded bullets all the way to his plane. Just as he prepared to climb in, bomb fragments shredded his airplane and slammed him to the surface.

In other places, groups of ground personnel huddled beneath aircraft wings for protection, but perished when Japanese bombs demolished the planes. Men ran across the airstrip only to die before reaching their destinations. The impact of a bomb lifted Navy Machinist's Mate 3c. William O. Plate off the ground and slammed him into the brush near the taxiway. A stunned Plate lay in pain from shrapnel wounds and the rough handling, but he emerged in better shape than the men around him, who moaned in agony and bled profusely from gaping holes to their bodies.

The enemy arrived with such suddenness and departed so quickly that the Marines had little time to shoot back. Some Marines fired with the only weapons they had on hand—their rifles—which, against racing aircraft, is about as effective as trying to knock down a rocket with a pebble due to the excessive speed of the plane and the small size of the bullet. Other Marines along Wake's southern shore, including Holewinski, turned their .50-caliber and .30-caliber machine guns skyward and started shooting, but the Japanese were either too low, too fast, or too far away by then for them to do any good.

The airstrip resembled a scene from Dante's *Inferno*. Body parts lay scattered about the coral surface. Wounded and dying men moaned for help and begged to be dragged from the fires. The blackened hulks of the Wildcat fighters littered the airstrip, which became more dangerous by the seconds as a strong forty-mile-an-hour wind spread the fires toward fuel and ammunition supplies. Gasoline drums exploded, and machine gun bullets loaded onto the Wildcats screamed through the air after being ignited by the fires. Even spent Japanese bullets caused injury. When they struck the runway, the bullets flattened into hot metallic ovals that burned anyone who stepped on them.

Heroes sprinkle the pages of Wake, and the first appeared at the airfield. As flames approached a group of wounded Marines lying helplessly on the coral surface, Cpl. Robert E. Page jumped out of his shelter and began dragging each man to safety. For fifteen minutes, Page—who had to hug the ground as he ran to take in the meager supply of oxygen left by the fires—retrieved one man after another in the searing heat, including a sergeant whose nearly severed leg dangled on the few uncut tendons remaining.

The courageous youth battled fires and smoke to save fellow Marines. He stopped rescuing men only to beat out flames that ignited his clothes, but maintained a stream of reassurances to comfort the badly burned or the panicky. "I was scorched," Page later recalled, "my eyebrows burnt off, tips of my ears and my nose bloody, and I got all that dirt and had all that oil and gasoline and all that smoke had settled on me. And bloody as a hog all over, dragging those wounded men."[19]

Page rushed up to Lieutanant Conderman to help him, but the dying aviator pointed to other wounded men lying about the airstrip. "Let me go," he said. "Take care of them."[20] Page ignored Conderman's heroic words and dragged him to safety.

With the flames spreading, Page spotted one more Marine who needed help. He started out for him, but an officer, Maj. Walter L. J. Bayler, cautioned against it because some nearby gasoline tanks were about to explode. Without stopping, Page raced into the flames, saved the final man, sprinted away from the tanks, and slumped exhausted to the ground.

While Americans fought and died on the ground, four Marine aviators on air patrol continued their scouting. Capt. Henry T. Elrod, Lt. Carl R. Davidson, Lt. John F. Kinney, and T.Sgt. William J. Hamilton had taken off shortly after learning of the Pearl Harbor attack, but they had failed to detect anything approaching Wake. Unfortunately, the Japanese came in at a lower altitude and beneath a cloud cover. Oblivious of the horrors their VMF-211 mates faced on the atoll, the four flew at twelve thousand feet.

When they spotted columns of smoke gushing upward from the atoll as they neared Wake, the aviators knew something bad had happened. Looks of consternation and anger spread across their faces as the vague images took on the distinct look of burning buildings and smashed equipment. Kinney could not believe that so much damage could have been inflicted in their absence, and the four wondered which of their buddies would be alive when they landed.

"The destruction that greeted me when I landed was more than I was prepared for,"[21] wrote Kinney after the war, for the Japanese had virtually wiped out VMF-211 as an effective fighting force. Seven of the eight Wildcats left on Wake, sitting ducks for the Japanese aviators, had been reduced from sleek fighter aircraft to blackened shells, valuable now only for a few spare parts they might provide. The precious supply of spare parts already on hand, minimal from the start, had been destroyed. Much of the gasoline stock wafted in immense black clouds toward the sky. Even worse, of the fifty-five aviation personnel on the airstrip when the attack started, nineteen had been either killed or mortally wounded and thirteen injured, including over half of Putnam's aviators and every experienced mechanic.

Three of the four aircraft landed without mishap, but Elrod damaged a propeller as he taxied his fighter along the airstrip. Putnam, already staggering under the losses on the ground, saw his air strength pared to three serviceable aircraft and two others that, with repairs, might soon be ready. Kinney inspected the sole remaining fighter of the eight caught on the ground and thought it "might be able to fly again, although it had received hits in both wings, the tail fin, stabilizer, fuselage, elevators, hood, fuse box, radio cables, left flap, and auxiliary gas tank."[22]

Putnam turned to Kinney, who had previous experience as a mechanic for Pan Am, and told him he had to take Lieutenant Graves's place as engineer officer, the man in charge of keeping Wake's remaining fighters running. "If you can keep them flying," Putnam promised Kinney, "I'll see that you get a medal as big as a pie." Kinney answered, "Okay, sir, if it is delivered in San Francisco."[23] From then on, Kinney spent most of his waking moments scavenging through the seven ruined fighters in an effort to locate parts that could keep the other five in the air.

After removing every usable part that remained on the seven destroyed Wildcats, Putnam spread the hulks out over the airstrip to serve as decoys for the inevitable air attacks to come. He established a command post in the brush near the airstrip, ordered his men to dig foxholes, then split his squadron into two groups of defenders, and posted them at either end of the airfield, one end commanded by Captain Freuler and the other by Capt. Frank C. Tharin. Men grabbed gas masks, machine guns, and helmets, then hurried to their designated areas to dig foxholes. Putnam buried dynamite every 150 feet along the airstrip and issued orders to Captain Freuler to detonate the explosives should the Japanese attempt a landing through the air.

"Broken Bodies and Bits of What Had Once Been Men"

The battle ended as suddenly as it began. In fifteen nightmarish minutes, the planes had swooped down, smashed their targets, and departed. The Japanese laughed at Wake's feeble answer—a few rifles and antiaircraft guns retorted, but that was about all. As if to add insult to injury, as they flew away, the Japanese pilots dipped their wings to signify complete victory. "The pilots in every one of the planes was grinning wildly,"[24] added a Marine. They had reason to be jubilant—not one aircraft was lost, and only one Japanese had been killed, Seaman Second Class Iwai.

For the first time in fifteen minutes, silence returned to Wake. Calm replaced the sounds of exploding bombs and rattling bullets; only the crashing surf interrupted the tranquillity. Terns and frigate birds staggered about the atoll from the bombs' concussions, reminding Cunningham of "confused drunks trying to find their way home."[25] Dead fish floated in the lagoon's normally peaceful waters.

War had come stunningly, quickly, and lethally to Wake. Gruesome reminders lay all over Wake's airstrip and at the Pan Am facilities. Commander Cunningham raced over to the airstrip, where a dazed Putnam walked toward him "through broken bodies and bits of what had once been men." As he watched Putnam draw closer, bleeding from wounds and lugging an old Springfield rifle that had been shattered in the attack, Cunningham could not help thinking of "The futility of a situation where a man would try to protect himself from bombers with a rifle . . ."[26]

Able Marines rushed to help the wounded. M.T.Sgt. Andrew J. Paskiewicz, injured in the right leg by shrapnel, painfully hobbled around to the wounded and dying men at the airstrip to offer comfort. Pfc. Joseph E. Borne pulled up to the airstrip in a truck in which to place the dead, but was not ready for what greeted him. "At the airport, I have never before or since seen such devastation—dismembered bodies everywhere, planes on fire, the smell of burnt flesh; moaning, groaning and suffering everywhere. I immediately became sick . . . and thought I'd never stop throwing up."[27]

Borne set aside his revulsion and helped others drag bodies to the truck. Some were so shredded by Japanese bullets and bomb fragments that the men crumbled to pieces in their hands. Steam from the roasted bodies gagged Borne, and one enlisted man's body contained so many bullet holes that they could not even grab hold of him. They had to slide a mattress underneath the perforated remains and carry it to the truck in that manner. Civilian laborer Joseph Adamson had a more difficult task at the airfield—he sadly collected the remains of his son, Louis, who died in the bombing.

Since Devereux could not rule out the possibility that the enemy might soon attempt a landing, he ordered that the dead be taken to a large freezer in one of the civilian buildings. When time permitted, he would see that they were properly buried, but at this moment more important items called for his attention.

The wounded flowed into the civilian hospital at Camp 2 all day long. Civilian Theodore A. Abraham Jr., in charge of hospital records, saw some men arrive on foot, some on the backs of buddies carrying them in, and others disgorge from trucks. The wounded and dying streamed in far into the night, overtaxing facilities that were designed for peacetime injuries. Abraham dropped his clerical work and pitched in, but he found it hard to concentrate in a room with so much activity and pathos—the moans of the wounded blended with the scent of burned flesh and blood-soaked clothing to produce an image that haunted the young man. Some, like the civilian who witnessed the carnage at the airfield, lay on a cot in a total state of shock.

Two physicians supervised the hospital work. The Navy doctor, Lt. (jg) G. Mason Kahn, and the civilian physician, Dr. Lawton E. Shank, assisted by eight members of the civilian medical staff, labored through the night to patch up the wounded. Finally, nearing dawn of December 9, they treated the final man.

Murray Kidd had already been lying in the hospital from ptomaine poisoning when Marines carried in the first wounded. "They didn't have room for us, so they fixed up a barracks right next to it and we got in there. Some of the men were pretty well shot up."[28] Kidd, whose ailment seemed trivial compared with the hideous wounds he witnessed, was more than willing to yield his spot to the others.

Four men from VMF-211, too severely injured to help, died in the hospital that first night. Among the four was nineteen-year-old Sgt. Maurice R. Stockton and Lieutenant Conderman, the youth who tried to refuse help at the airstrip so others could benefit.

"We'll Take the Next Ship for Pearl"

While the military hastily prepared for a second Japanese strike, at the Pan American installations at Peale Island, Captain Hamilton inspected the *Clipper* to determine if the plane was able to fly. The bullet holes that punctured the fuselage worried him, but when he checked closer, he learned that, miraculously, nothing vital had been hit. He hurried over to Cunningham and asked permission to evacuate his crew, the passengers, and the station's twenty-seven white personnel. Taken aback, Cunningham asked why Hamilton had not included the company's Chamorro workers from Guam, but the captain replied the plane had no room for them. "I knew the plane had limited space, but it seemed to me an unfortunate time to draw the color line,"[29] wrote Cunningham.

Other individuals could have departed with the *Clipper* but chose to stay on Wake instead. A Pan Am employee offered to sneak aboard his friend, civilian John Wiggenhorn, but confident of rescue by the Navy, Wiggenhorn declined. J. O. Young and a handful of other workers walked over to the *Clipper*'s berth, where the pilot and crew prepared for their takeoff. The pilot turned to the group and said, "There is room for a few more, do any of you want to come with us?"

He had no takers. Most of the group believed they had little to fear and boasted that "Uncle Sam will be after us in a few days," or "We'll take the next ship for Pearl."[30] Young declined the offer because he did not want to leave his uncle.

The group hopped a truck piled high with ammunition and headed over to Wilkes Island, where they helped the Marines unload the material. After a quick search, Young located his uncle and learned that he had emerged from the bombings unscathed. The two dug a foxhole barely large enough for them to lie in, then covered it with wooden planks and sandbags. Young believed he would be quickly evacuated, but in case that did not happen, he wanted to have a shelter that would keep them safe during bombing attacks. From then until the battle's end, Young never left Wilkes.

Two other men intended to fly out, but were stranded on Wake when the airplane departed without them. Herman Hevenor, the government auditor, failed to receive word of the departure, and Pan Am carpenter August

Ramquist missed the plane because he was helping transport wounded men to the hospital.

Now loaded with five passengers, twenty-seven Caucasian employees, and eight crew members, the *Clipper* left at 1:30 P.M. Captain Hamilton twice failed to lift the heavily laden airplane from the lagoon, causing concern among the passengers that some might have to yield their seats to lighten the load. The forty individuals inside the *Clipper* silently waited as Hamilton gunned the engines for the third attempt. This time the aircraft slowly lifted from the surface, climbed to flying altitude, and veered northeast for Midway Island.

After refueling the airplane at Midway, Hamilton flew to Pearl Harbor, where authorities quizzed him and the other people about conditions at Wake. Hamilton then set course for San Francisco, where newspaper reporters and the public welcomed him as one of the war's early heroes.

"We Were Definitely on Their List for Elimination"

What had gone wrong in the attack? The United States government and the military shared the blame in leaving the defenders at Wake shorthanded and undermanned, but they operated in a restrictive time.

One item alone could have had an enormous impact on Wake's outcome. Radar had been developed sufficiently for use by the military. Wake, with its crashing surf drowning out noise, could have benefited from its installation, but the device never made it there. Devereux and Cunningham checked the manifests of each ship that arrived at Wake in hopes of finding the revolutionary invention among their items, but they always turned away disappointed.

"The radar could have made a big difference," stated Pfc. James O. King, one of Devereux's communications clerks. "Had it been installed, there is no way all eight fighters would have been caught on the ground like they were. With those additional planes, who knows what might have happened in the future course of the battle?"[31]

Ethnic stereotyping also played its part. Most men on Wake carried the same prejudices as those exhibited by the rest of the military throughout the Pacific—that the United States had little to fear from an Asian nation. The typical prewar racial stereotype lulled the men on Wake, and to some degree at Pearl Harbor, into a false sense of security. Americans learned a hard lesson that day—their opponents were far from the pushovers they imagined.

*   *   *

As December 8 closed on Wake, the military and civilians still looked ahead with optimism. The Japanese had struck and would probably soon hit again, but the next time they would be ready. Not realizing how badly damaged was Pearl Harbor, the Wake defenders expected that a relief force would soon dash out with more men and aircraft.

A more pessimistic Major Devereux concluded that the Japanese would stage repeated bombing attacks until they thought they had weakened the atoll, at which time their naval forces would move in for the kill. He hoped, however, that his men could repel any landing attempts until reinforcements arrived.

What neither Cunningham nor Devereux knew was that their superiors at Pearl Harbor had already begun the debate over sending help to Wake. Admiral Kimmel, still stunned from the devastating Pearl Harbor attack, received a new war plan from Washington stipulating that the Pacific Fleet's main task was to defend Hawaii and the West Coast. The island posts at Wake, Johnston, and Palmyra were to be reinforced if possible, but not at Hawaii's expense. Wake, lying the farthest distance from Pearl Harbor, dangled in front of the Japanese as a sacrificial lamb.

Every man played the same guessing game. They asked themselves and each other from where had the Japanese come, and when would they strike again. Most correctly figured the enemy had to take off from the Marshalls, 620 miles south, since that was the closest enemy base, but they had no idea when they would again attack. Putnam and Kinney, the most knowledgeable officers in aviation matters, calculated the average aircraft speed and the distance from Wake to the Marshalls, deduced that the Japanese would take off at dawn when it was light enough for operations, and concluded that the enemy would appear over Wake sometime about noon the next day.

Lieutenant Kessler figured that December 9 would unveil the likely course of events and, with it, their fates. He told the men in his gun crew on Peale Island, including nine civilian volunteers, that if the Japanese failed to bomb Wake Island again, that meant the enemy had administered a one-time punishment and had gone on to bigger fish. However, if they returned for a second raid, the men on Wake may as well start digging in, for it indicated that "we were definitely on their list for elimination."[32]

In the momentary lull, Marine Pfc. Verne L. Wallace finally had time to read a letter from his Pennsylvania girlfriend that had arrived just before the air strike. The words drew a rueful smile to his lips. "As long as you have to be away, darling," she wrote, "I'm so very, very happy you are in the Pacific, where you won't be in danger if war comes."[33]

CHAPTER 4

★

"I Used to Hear a Lot of Guys Pray"

"Don't Those Sons of Bitches Know That's Dangerous?"

Not only did the Japanese attack on December 9, but they also mounted a third straight raid on December 10. Almost on schedule, the Japanese returned shortly before noon on December 9. Americans stopped their work when they heard three shots relayed throughout the atoll, the signal that an air attack was under way, and rushed to their gun positions and bunkers. Twenty-seven bombers, glistening in the midday sun, roared in from the south, bombing and strafing as they stitched a lethal pattern on Wake's surface. Machine-gun bullets peppered the water tower, forcing the two men posted as lookouts to take refuge on the opposite side of the tank.

Pfc. John Katchak of Pennsylvania became the first Marine of the Wake Island Detachment to be killed when a bomb landed almost on top of him at Battery A at Peacock Point. The explosion eviscerated the young man, whose body was further torn to pieces when the bullets in his cartridge belt ignited from the heat. So little remained that fellow Marines gathered the pieces, tossed handfuls of dirt on top, and fashioned a rude mound as a hasty memorial.

"It was impossible to recover the body," Lieutenant Barninger wrote in a 1945 report, "and so surrounded by all the reverence and sympathy men have for a fallen messmate I spoke the burial service over him. It was crude, but if ever a body was committed to the earth and a soul to God with more depth of feeling or in closer kinship with the Almighty it was in a similar circumstance."[1] Throughout the battle, Katchak's burial spot served as an inspiration to the defenders.

After helping the Marines fire at the invaders, Young and Read rushed to their reinforced foxhole as bombs erupted within yards of their position.

Shaken, dazed, and numb, the men looked out as black, rancid smoke enveloped them. Another civilian, Charles Mellor, picked up a still-hot piece of shrapnel, looked at the departing Japanese, and shouted, "Don't those sons of bitches know that's dangerous?"[2]

Bullets and bombs inundated Hans Whitney's gun emplacement, causing the men to huddle closer to the coral for safety and comfort. When the planes left, six men lay dead, and Whitney writhed on the dirt with a shrapnel wound to the left hip.

Joe Goicoechea thought the entire Japanese air force had pinpointed him, as it seemed that every bomb and bullet dropped and fired at Wake headed directly toward him. With Marine Corporal Marvin and the others, Joe hid behind the gun shield, but the bullets still managed to find him. A piece of shrapnel wounded Marvin in the head, and a bullet punctured Goicoechea's ironworker's helmet, knocked it off, and hit the man next to him.

"I got hit in the face with shrapnel. There was nobody there to fix us, so we took care of it ourselves. It all hurt, but you just block out the pain. The guy next to me was hit real bad. His blood was on me. He had a big hole in his back—blood was just spurtin' out. We thought I was bleeding, but he was."[3]

Some civilians died when they panicked. Instead of jumping into one of the ditches that had been dug, they ran around trying to evade the bombs and died.

Mistakes like that irritated Sgt. Johnalson Wright, whether made by civilians or Marines. Determined to instill pride at his gun, as soon as the raid ended, Wright castigated the civilian crew manning one gun for not firing as many shots at the Japanese as the Marines. He bellowed that if they could not improve, they may as well not be near him. He stormed away, while the civilians huddled with Bowsher for additional training.

To most Wake Islanders, December 9 and the hospital are synonymous, for that was the day the Japanese hit the hospital. Death and injuries are a part of war, but amidst the bleeding and dying rests a sanctuary for those unable to fight. Combatants normally recognize the need for hospitals and consider them off-limits. Not so this day. Men who had already been wounded, or lay in the hospital from a work injury or an illness, now suffered even more. They lay helplessly in their cots, assuming the large red cross painted on the roof would shield them from enemy attack, even from such a ferocious foe as the Japanese, who had stunned world opinion with their atrocities in China and elsewhere. They paid for their incorrect assumptions.

The Japanese pilots so thoroughly devastated the hospital near Camp 2 that one man watching with Devereux quietly muttered, "Them poor bastards."4 Bullets ripped through the sheet metal roof to splinter cots and the floor, forcing Lieutenant Kahn to dive under a bed for protection. When he emerged untouched a few seconds later, Kahn noticed that a pair of shoes resting next to him had been torn apart by bullets.

Murray Kidd, who thought he had it better than Goicoechea or Rosendick out in the field, rested in a cot set up on the porch of the barracks next door. The staff originally told him and a few other patients to occupy the cots on the corner, but Kidd thought that spot would be too hot once the sun rose. "Let's move back a little bit where there's more shade," he mentioned to other patients. A few, including Kidd, shifted to cots a short distance away.

That small decision saved his life. A bomb hit the corner in which Kidd had been resting and killed the men in the first two cots. "I was in the next cot," Kidd explained. "The explosion flipped me over and tossed the cot on top of me. I never heard the bomb coming down. I don't remember anything except for this big *boom!* I couldn't hear for three hours afterwards."5 A rattled Kidd, slightly wounded by bomb fragments, quickly put on his clothes, veered toward the brush, and took refuge in a dugout being built by some friends.

He made another fortunate choice in running toward the brush. Other civilian patients ran outside and crawled under a Caterpillar tractor, thinking it had to be safer than the flimsy hospital walls. A direct bomb hit demolished the vehicle and killed every man.

As the flames spread, healthier men risked their lives to save those unable to move. Seventy-year-old construction worker Owen G. Thomas dashed into the fire to free two Marines trapped by the wreckage. Dr. Shank and Lieutenant Kahn repeatedly ran inside to move patients and to retrieve the precious supplies of medicine and medical equipment. Dr. Shank, who had endeared himself to civilians and military with his professionalism and affable nature, saved so many lives in those few moments that he was later recommended for a Medal of Honor.

The attack outraged both military and civilian camps. The men recalled all those stories of the Japanese raping and murdering thousands of Chinese, and now had no doubt about their veracity. An unprovoked attack on Pearl Harbor had been followed with a bombing on helpless men in a hospital. This war, only a few days ago so distant in their thoughts, had taken on a personal nature.

Now without a hospital, Cunningham selected one of the safest locations on Wake to house the wounded, in reinforced ammunition bunkers that lay in a neat row along the eastern end of the airfield. Each bunker, twenty by forty feet in size, held about twenty beds and contained a generator for power. Medical assistants equally divided the supplies between the two places, and Dr. Shank set up shop for the civilians in the bunker at the northern end while Lieutenant Kahn occupied the southern bunker for the military. In this manner, Cunningham hoped to prevent both hospitals from being destroyed by a single bomb. Two days later, Cunningham moved his command post into one of the middle bunkers with the Army radio unit led by Captain Wilson. Devereux switched his command post to a spot along the lagoon about four hundred yards east of the Marine camp.

Both physicians had plenty of men to tend, but each day the numbers dwindled. At least thirty civilians died in the attack on Camp 2, while seven Marines perished at various locations. The loss of life pointed out a serious predicament—the Japanese could afford to lose men and equipment, while the military on Wake could not. If a Japanese pilot died, another took his place, but each man and each gun lost at Wake irretrievably reduced the American garrison. More crucially, it reduced their ability to repulse the inevitable invasion attempt.

A Deadly Form of Chess

Across the lagoon, Major Putnam tried to mount some form of aviation response out of the shambles the Japanese handed him. Now with only four aircraft from VMF-211 left, he could not launch round-the-clock patrols, but he also could not hand the enemy a chance to strike while his Wildcats rested on the airstrip. Since he only had fifteen seconds' warning once the enemy was sighted, he had to play a guessing game as to when to send his men aloft and when to order them back to Wake for rest and refueling. He told his pilots that they would mount one scouting mission at dawn, one at dusk, and a combat patrol for noon, the most likely time for the Japanese to attack. He warned the aviators that once they spotted the enemy, they were to use their own discretion on attacking. In the meantime, he hoped that Lieutenant Kinney could work some miracles and rebuild an airplane or two out of what was left from the eight damaged Wildcats.

Lieutenant Kinney, aided by Sergeant Hamilton, worked nonstop to add another fighter to Putnam's arsenal. They stripped a cooling system here and an engine mount there, but without instruction manuals, the pair had to use all their ingenuity in creating a workable aircraft out of bits and pieces.

Fortunately, the fighters destroyed at the airstrip had been hit by the Japanese in uniform fashion—the bombs exploded in the middle of each aircraft. The impact flattened the middle into the ground while forcing the nose into the air. As a result, the subsequent fires failed to severely damage the engines. That left seven spare engines from which Kinney and his helpers could scavenge spare parts.

Elsewhere, Devereux engaged in a deadly form of military chess by trying to choose a safe spot to move his 3-inch guns. He started by ordering Lieutenant Lewis to shift Battery E from Peacock Point to a location just below the airstrip. He figured the Japanese pilots had accurately fixed Lewis's location and that the next wave of attacks would pinpoint the spot. All night long, a group of civilians and Marines, some wounded, others in a state of shock over recent events, all weary, labored to move the cumbersome 3-inch guns and their accompanying sandbags. After that arduous task, they had to install decoy guns made from steel pipes and cardboard in the old position to lure the Japanese pilots into thinking the former emplacement still existed.

This established one of the patterns that emerged at Wake—endure air attacks by day and move the guns at night in a constant game of outwitting the opposition. Devereux made educated guesses where the next day's attack would occur, then placed the guns somewhere else.

This was no simple task, for men had to be found to switch the guns to new positions, install the large weapons, and reinforce the locations with sandbags. Cunningham and Teters met each night to decide which batteries required help from civilians; then Teters took the responsibility of rounding up enough men. If Teters had a hard time meeting his quota, as he sometimes did, he shamed the men into working by calling them cowards or claiming they were abandoning fellow Americans.

For some reason, Cunningham excluded Devereux from these meetings. As island commander he had that authority, but it made sense for him to at least consult with his top defensive coordinator about what his men needed. Devereux did not appreciate what he considered a slight from Cunningham. Teters informed Cunningham later that Devereux "complained to me rather bitterly that you had not called him in to those meetings . . ."[6] This omission later led to hard feelings between the two commanders.

Across the atoll, details of men searched for wounded and retrieved the dead, which frequently meant picking up body parts. Dr. Shank and Lieutenant Kahn handled so many wounded and dying men that the supplies of morphine and anesthesia dipped dangerously low. At Camp 2, Theodore Abraham discovered the body of a construction worker who had apparently squatted down and clung to a vertical pipe for protection. A bomb explosion had remarkably ripped off every article of clothing from the man, except for the shoes, and killed him without leaving a visible mark.

As rigor mortis had already started, Abraham needed help prying the man from the pipe.

While Kahn and Shank tended to the wounded, the military on Wilkes, Wake, and Peale prepared for the inevitable Japanese landing attempt. No one enjoyed more than a few moments of rest. Too much work had to be completed before Japanese warships steamed over the horizon, and for all anyone knew, that could occur within a few hours. As was true at other Marine guns, Laporte and Gross filled sandbags, then stacked them around and inside the positions. At the airfield, military and civilian personnel worked through the night to construct blastproof revetments to shelter the four remaining fighters, and Lieutenant Kinney borrowed tools from Pan Am to replace the ones that had been destroyed in the attack. Devereux parked heavy construction equipment at various intervals on the airstrip to prevent an enemy landing. Marines also filled a Navy lighter with concrete blocks and dynamite and anchored it in the middle of Wilkes Channel to prevent small enemy craft from entering the lagoon.

Lieutenant Barninger's Marines completed their foxholes that afternoon, intending to later ring them with sandbags and chunks of coral. While he had time, however, near dusk Barninger sent some men to the Marine camp to retrieve extra toilet gear and clothing. The veteran knew that from now on, opportunities to walk over to camp would be few and far between.

Devereux faced a litany of problems, most revolving around lack of men, supplies, or ammunition. Without radar to alert Wake about incoming aircraft, every serviceman had to remain at his post in a constant state of readiness, half their attention focused on fortifying their positions while keeping watch on the skies, as well.

Devereux did his best to spread out his men, but Wake's twenty miles of shoreline were more than he could adequately cover with the limited resources available. All he could do was guess where the Japanese might land, and place men at those locations. The addition of eighteen naval personnel who reported for duty helped, but it was like placing another thumb in the proverbial dike. Devereux decided to post these men in a reserve force under the command of Lieutenant Poindexter—a group of about fifty cooks, clerks, and office personnel who in an attack would rush to the most severely threatened spots. Poindexter and other Marines administered a crash course in handling .30-caliber machine guns and in how to properly toss hand grenades to the men, then posted them to what was labeled the Mobile Reserve.

Lieutenant Hanna, who commanded the gun position that would later see the most ferocious fighting of the battle—the stretch of shore running just below the airstrip and northwest toward Wilkes—moved his command post from the airstrip to the beach area south of the airfield. Afterwards, he dug a foxhole into which he could jump during raids, then ordered the fifty men under him to fill and stack sandbags and to keep watch for any movement in the sky.

On Wilkes, Lieutenant McAlister rotated one-hour beach patrols among his Marines. Since he, like his fellow officers elsewhere on the atoll, lacked enough men, he filled in with civilian volunteers. He wisely paired a civilian with a Marine for each watch, so that every post always had at least one serviceman on guard.

On December 10, Corporal Johnson received orders to take six civilians and establish a gun position on Wilkes at the mouth of the lagoon. Johnson settled in with the crew and found that one man in particular, Leo Nonn, proved valuable. Every morning Nonn asked Johnson questions on military tactics and how to handle a weapon, and if Johnson needed a volunteer, he knew he did not have to look further than Nonn. If every civilian contributed as enthusiastically as Nonn and acted as bravely, Johnson concluded that possibly the Wake defenders might make the Japanese suffer when they arrived off the atoll. Maybe he and the other Marines, bolstered by the Army and Navy personnel and a handful of civilian volunteers, could hold them off after all.

"I Thought I Was the Only Person Left Alive on the Island"

The Japanese shifted the focus of the next attack to the Marine quarters at Camp 1 and to Wilkes Island. To seasoned military, the enemy's strategy seemed obvious—first eliminate Wake's air arm, then reduce the atoll's fortifications and guns in preparation for a landing attempt.

Since most Marines stood at their guns and positions, few casualties resulted from the strike on their camp, but most lost their personal possessions, including letters from parents and wives. Lieutenant Hanna lost the photographs of Vera and his daugher, Erlyne, and Corporal Richardson saw all the work he put into his 25,000-word manuscript literally go up in smoke.

Devereux's prediction that the Japanese would strike Battery E's former location proved correct, as the bombers destroyed two of the dummy guns and targeted the beaches directly above Peacock Point. When the Japanese also bombed Battery E's new location at the airfield, Devereux ordered a second shift, this time to a more camouflaged position on Wake's lagoon side above the airfield.

Wilkes Island bore the brunt of the day's bombing, which produced a tremendous explosion when bombs struck a shed packed with 125 tons of dynamite. The eruption defoliated much of Wilkes's interior and knocked men off their feet. Corporal Johnson crawled under a vertical limb of a tree about five inches in diamter for protection, but the explosion "bounced me around and shoved my face in the coral and I came out with a bloody face and a sore back. The shed was about two hundred yards from me. I could see it go way up in the air, even though I was horizontal on the ground. I thought I was the only person left alive on the island."[7] Ironically, Marines in foxholes closer to the center of impact felt little concussion because the waves went up and out toward Johnson and those near him.

Another Marine on Wilkes found two Guamanian workers buried to their waists in sand by the explosion. Rattled and in tears, the pair asked for help from their predicament. As the Marine freed them, one of the men exclaimed, "Boy, this don't happen on Guam."[8]

The Americans landed a few blows of their own during this raid. Captain Elrod plunged into the middle of the enemy formation, braved 3-inch shells fired from Wake by fellow Marines that could just as easily hit him as they could a Japanese, and splashed two bombers. American servicemen, heartened by the sight of enemy aircraft falling to the sea, christened the aviator "Hammering Hank" and muttered quiet thanks that Wake still had an air arm with which to greet the enemy. Elrod's two tallies should have made the Japanese approach the atoll with more caution, but the enemy disregarded the events. That casual attitude would soon cost them dearly.

The civilians at Wright's gun registered their own triumphs. After earning the Marine's wrath for a poor display on December 8, they performed much more smoothly in this raid. The crusty Marine admitted as much with a simple nod and an absence of cuss words.

"A Piece of Shrapnel Does Strange Things"

The citizen soldier army, so heralded by historians for contributing to victory in Europe and the Pacific, made its first appearance at Wake as volunteers dropped their shovels or stepped down from bulldozers to stand side by side with the four hundred Marines. They had traveled to Wake for money and adventure, not to fire weapons, but when the chips were down, they answered the call of duty like their military compatriots. Most were immediately sent to undermanned batteries and given speedy instruction on how to fire the weapons. Others filled sandbags and stood guard. All served the same purpose—to battle those who threatened the country's security.

Those construction workers who had received training from the Marines before the war started, like Joe Goicoechea, had already reported to their positions. Many of the rest gathered at the civilian mess hall to listen to Dan Teters explain what would occur and to answer questions. He told anyone who wanted to help the military to report to Major Devereux, who would then assign them a duty.

A steady flow of civilians headed over to the Marine side of Wake. James Allen had left the meeting and started walking to Devereux's command post when the Marines from Battery E at Peacock Point stopped him and asked him to work with them. He and eight other workers veered over to the battery, where Lieutenant Lewis welcomed them. They immediately started building the defenses and learning how to handle ammunition for the 3-inch guns.

Civilians showed up in groups as small as two and as large as ninety to offer help. John Rogge learned how to operate searchlights along Wake's eastern shore, then helped to carve out a dugout with five other men. A few needed minimal training because of previous military experience, such as Robert G. Hardy, a veteran of the World War I battles of Saint-Mihiel and the Argonne Forest, and Harold E. Lochridge, who fought on the Western Front in 1918. When fourteen civilians showed up at Toki Point, Sgt. Walter A. Bowsher placed them on his unmanned 3-inch antiaircraft gun and hurriedly instructed them on the fundamentals of using the weapon.

Putnam's depleted ranks received a boost when civilian John Sorenson led a group of fourteen volunteers, including Fred S. Gibbons and his son, George, to the airstrip and asked what they could do. Since the civilians were skilled repairmen, Putnam eagerly put them to work with Lieutenant Kinney.

Assuming the Japanese would reappear, Kessler started to train his nine civilians. He had no rifles to distribute, so he cracked open a case of hand grenades and handed three to each man. He showed George Harris, Arne E. Astad, and the others how to properly throw the grenade, then supervised the strengthening of their position.

At Battery D nearby, Sergeant Bowsher carefully explained the rudiments of gunnery to the civilians working with him. Seventy-two-year-old George Lawback, whose son also worked on Wake, listened intently, but he could not keep up with the physical demands of hoisting and moving the shells. When Bowsher asked if he wanted to leave, Lawback angrily declined. He wanted to remain with the crew, even if he could not contribute in the same fashion as his younger cohorts. Touched by this example of camaraderie, Bowsher let him stay and perform housekeeping chores.

The Morrison-Knudsen workers handled an array of tasks—they constructed dugouts and foxholes, filled sandbags, delivered ammunition to

Marines, and bulldozed coral sand into protective mounds. Some performed so well that Major Putnam later stated in his official report that he would have been proud to have claimed them as his own Marines.

Putnam's flattering words for these civilians, however, masked his and other Marines' disappointment that so many other workers chose not to help. The military appreciated the assistance they received, but they quietly asked why close to half the construction workers, all in good health, remained in the bush and away from the fighting.

This arose in part because of Devereux and Cunningham, who refused to enlist the civilians in the military on the grounds that they, as commanders, lacked the legal authority. Aside from the fear that they might be summarily executed as guerrilla fighters if captured, many men chose what they thought would be the safer and wiser course of hiding out in the bush and hoping for relief from Pearl Harbor or a victory by the Marines.

The civilians also lacked a clear directive about what to do. During his meeting, Teters told the men that if they decided not to volunteer, they were to head to the bush, dig a foxhole, and wait for instructions. Those instructions never made it to some fellows. One man, Pop Curtis of Idaho, explained to Goicoechea, "They told us to go into the brush and if they needed us they'd call us. Nobody ever called us."9

Joe Goicoechea wondered why Teters simply did not follow the same organization he had already formed. "Teters was a good man, but the only gripe I have was when the bombs fell, he should have kept every civilian in his own crew, with the crew boss, and that would have worked better. You can't blame the civilians who didn't come out of the brush."10 As a result, some of the men who would have helped, did not. At the same time, this confusion handed a convenient excuse to those who had no desire to contribute.

Finally, some men simply refused to fight, whether out of fear or principle. At Teters's evening meeting, workers angrily demanded an explanation for why Morrison-Knudsen failed to evacuate them before hostilities flared and stated that they had not come to Wake to fight. That, they contested, was why the Marines, Navy, and Army personnel were there.

Most Morrison-Knudsen workers avoided combat—barely one sixth of the 1,145 actually fought with the Marines during the subsequent invasion—but at least half contributed their labors in some fashion. However, the presence of a large group of healthy men hiding in the brush while others fought and died did not sit well with many Marines.

The men played another game, lonelier and more excruciating than the one unfolding on Wake, for this contest occurred inside, where emotions dwell. Each American, military and civilian, fought to control his fears.

They all had them—every person in the military will tell you only a fool or a liar will boast he has no fears in combat—but unlike the fighting for the atoll, where men stood side by side and shared the burdens, this one had to be resolved alone.

Those civilians who walked solitary nightly guard duty along one of Wake's beaches typified what every man experienced. Holding on to a rifle he probably had just learned how to operate, the civilian paced up and down the lonely stretch of beach, straining his eyes to detect unusual movement and listening intently for any sound out of the ordinary. Shapes that posed no threat by day—a large coral rock, for instance—at night suddenly took on the appearance of an enemy soldier sneaking onto the island. The thousands of tiny crabs that infested Wake's sand amused the men in daylight, but in the cover of darkness they sounded like humans approaching.

"I was frightened; you never get over it," admitted Goicoechea. "The first night was the worst night of my life. I was shaking and didn't know what the heck was happening. You could see that the older men were just as scared as you were. I used to hear a lot of guys pray. I was never backward in praying. These other guys would say they didn't know how to pray, but they'd sure beat me when times were tough."[11]

In the midst of the preparations, the wounded Goicoechea took advantage of a brief lull and ran across the bridge to the hospital to find out what happened to Murray Kidd. After a hasty search, he located his friend in his new dugout and shared experiences with him. They had barely begun talking when a medic asked Goicoechea if he could help retrieve bodies. Healthy workers were a precious commodity on Wake, and few could afford to relax for long. Goicoechea spent several hours laying bodies and body parts into the back of a truck.

"I had to help pull them out of the wagon, a leg here and an arm there. A piece of shrapnel does strange things. It just cuts you all up."[12] These sights, as gruesome as they were, did not bother Goicoechea as much as the Marine body he later came across in the coral sand, covered with crabs as they feasted on the carcass.

After checking on Kidd and learning he was safe, Joe Goicoechea returned to his spot at Battery D and tried to ignore the pain caused by his wounds. As Goicoechea talked with Corporal Marvin, also manning his post in spite of injuries, a naval officer strode up and ordered several of them, including the wounded Goicoechea and Marvin, to dash into a burning warehouse to remove whatever they could salvage. "You lead the way, and we will follow," Goicoechea instantly shot back. The officer refused, but still ordered the men into the warehouse. Knowing that Marvin and the other Marines had to obey orders, even though he sensed they agreed with him, Goicoechea angrily yelled, "You go to hell!"¹³ Much to their relief, the officer turned away.

As December 10 ended, the men of Wake could be proud of how the first three days unfolded. They had withstood repeated enemy attacks without collapsing, which is something that could not be said elsewhere in the Pacific. They also knew, though, that the Japanese had no intention of turning aside. Sooner or later the bombings would cease, and in their place would come trained soldiers armed with rifles and bayonets. Then the struggle would be up close, where they could see the faces of the men with whom they would engage in a life-and-death battle. Until then they waited and hoped that help would arrive from Pearl Harbor before the Japanese.

At least some men had the comfort of family. J. O. Young and his uncle, Forrest Read, waited with Marines on Wilkes Island, where they worked for Gunner McKinstry. The two Idaho men did not talk about home much, for that made matters worse, but they had each other, and that made things easier to bear. "Lonely, homesick and scared," wrote Read later, "I was very happy to share a dugout with my nephew, J. O. Young."¹⁴

"So Far the News Has All Been Bad"

While the Wake defenders waited for the Japanese, Franklin Roosevelt saw little in which to take hope. Reports of the devastation to men, ships, and material in Hawaii painted a gloomy picture, and people around the country reacted with dismay and despair. Conditions in his own White House had changed—blackout curtains adorned his windows; more guards, including Military Police, walked the halls; and plans had been drawn for a bomb shelter underneath the residence. Outside, soldiers carried rifles with bayonets attached, and sandbags appeared in front of government buildings, reminding him of the city of London during the infamous Nazi bombing attacks.

Roosevelt had to counter the flood of rumors that inundated the nation in the aftermath of Pearl Harbor, but he had little good news with which to answer. His wife, Eleanor, was heading to California for a scheduled trip when the pilot received a report, later proved erroneous, that San Francisco was under attack. Newspaper reporter Robert J. Casey noticed how worried the residents of Hawaii looked in those early days because they believed the Japanese would arrive at any moment. He wrote that "citizens who had believed the vast power of the United States unassailable and themselves secure" had become "men who now believed Heaven knew what, with faith behind them, hope crumbling and despair not far ahead."¹⁵

Citizens in both Hawaii and the mainland forty-eight states wanted to believe that their nation would quickly strike back, but hour after hour, nothing but bleak news and dreary bulletins poured in. One man in Washington, D.C., was so frustrated with the military's inability to answer the Japanese that he did the only thing he thought he could do to hit back at the enemy—he chopped down four of the beautiful Japanese cherry trees that lined the Tidal Basin.

Gloom hit at even the highest levels of government. Presidential aide Harry Hopkins angrily lashed out at those figures who contended the West Coast was lost and that our military lay impotent. Robert Sherwood, a noted author, wrote of the prevailing attitude at the time: "In going about Washington in those first days, it sometimes seemed that maybe the Nazi and Fascist propagandists were right, that maybe our democracy had become decadent and soft, that we could talk big but that there were too many of us who simply did not know how to stand up under punishment."[16]

The attitude typified how much of the nation felt after war's initial three days. Few doubted the nation would ultimately prevail, once it had time to assemble a potent military, but they wondered how it would hold on in the face of repeated calamities. Another acclaimed writer, Vincent Sheean, warned in a radio broadcast across the country, "Let us get ready for a series of shocks."[17]

Roosevelt, who countered the specter of millions unemployed and widespread hunger in the bleak days of the Depression by reminding his nation that they had nothing to fear but fear, now offered a mixture of hope and honesty. Talking to the press shortly before delivering a radio address to the nation, Roosevelt stated that every citizen had to do his or her part for the United States to triumph in a world at war. "We must share together the bad news and the good news. . . ." He then cautioned, "So far the news has all been bad . . ."[18]

What neither Sheean, Roosevelt, nor the nation counted on was the speed with which good news arrived. Unknown to them all, a small group of American military personnel, aided by a handful of civilian workers, waited in the wings on a tiny Pacific atoll. Wake was about to become the stage for the nation's first dramatic action of the war, and in the process offer hope to a nation mired in gloom.

CHAPTER 5

★

"The Island Was to Be a Cake Walk"

"The Enemy Would Soon Fold"

On December 8, as Japanese aircraft riddled Wake's defenders, Rear Adm. Sadamichi Kajioka stood on the bridge of his flagship, the light cruiser *Yubari*, in the vanguard of a unit of ships from the Marshall Islands. The fifty-two-year-old Navy veteran had gained a reputation as a dependable officer who gradually, if unspectacularly, rose through the ranks. Now a rear admiral, he faced the most important task of his career—seize Wake from the United States.

Japan needed the atoll to complete the first phase of its military operations. Control of Wake and other American possessions, such as Guam and the Philippines, following so quickly after the stunning annihilation of United States naval power at Pearl Harbor, assured Japanese naval dominance throughout the Pacific and endangered United States supply lines to Australia. Aircraft based at Wake could not only keep a constant watch for any American advance westward from Hawaii, but they would also pose a continuous threat to the Hawaiian Islands.

Kajioka's force of sixteen ships represented the final piece of Japan's far-flung offensive. Every other part of the Japanese plan either had been successfully completed or was well under way. Only tiny Wake, an insignificant dot in a Japanese-dominated ocean, remained to be swept aside.

The Japanese expected few problems, if any, from the assault. After all, they encountered a feeble response everywhere else. Allied forces mounted ineffective defenses throughout the Pacific, and the Japanese carrier aircraft darted in and out of the supposedly impregnable bastion at Pearl Harbor with surprising ease.

Sub-Lt. Shigeyoshi Ozeki, a young naval surgeon assigned to the Wake invasion force, typified the optimism with which the Japanese embarked upon the Wake expedition. "We were told that westerner[s] were weak and lacked the spiritual and mental fortitude that we possessed," he later wrote. "We were guaranteed victory in our 'Holy war' to rid the Barbarians from Asian soil and the respect and prominence that Japan should be alloted [sic] as a major power in Asia. . . . The island was to be a cake walk; with no enemy planes in the area our bombers would converge on the island and destroy its defenders before we had a chance to board the landing barges."[1]

Seishi Katsumi, who spent more than twenty years in the United States and attended Columbia University in New York before returning to Japan in 1941 to work as a civilian interpreter during the Wake operation, tried to warn a group of officers that their view of the United States contained dangerous misconceptions. He knew the Americans. He asserted that their fighting spirit equaled that found in the vaunted Japanese Army, and he urged that they approach Wake with caution. The officers, filled with enthusiasm over the coming victory at Wake, reacted with silent disdain.

They had a right to that cocky attitude, not only because of an unbroken string of victories elsewhere, but also because they steamed toward the atoll with a potent unit of ships. In addition to Rear Admiral Kajioka's flagship, the light cruisers *Tenryu* and *Tatsuta*, six destroyers, and three submarines escorted four troop transports. Though most of the ships were older, they packed a deadly concentration of firepower to deal with any opposition. Thirty-six bombers and twenty-four flying boats based out of the Marshalls provided the aerial offensive punch. Planners considered adding an aircraft carrier to Kajioka's arsenal, but they thought so little of Wake's defenses that they dismissed the notion.

The only part that bothered Kajioka was the number of soldiers allocated to seize Wake. Against what military intelligence estimated as 1,000 Marines and 600 civilians on Wake, he had 450 Special Naval Landing Forces, the Japanese equivalent to Marines. He decided that if needed, he would order some of his six destroyers run aground and use their crews as soldiers.

Kajioka considered that option a long shot, however. For three days, from December 8 until December 10, Japanese bombers had pinpointed every military target on Wake. They destroyed the airfield, and with it any American air defense, he assumed, on December 8. Over the next two days, aircraft wiped out antiaircraft batteries, seaplane facilities, and other installations. He believed that the enemy had been so weakened that he could take Wake within two days by landing 150 men on Wilkes and 300 on Wake. Everyone, including Kajioka, expected such a simple operation that his commander had not even given him a deadline for occupying Wake—he assumed it would happen as a matter of course. All his men had to do was file into the landing barges, wait for cruisers and destroyers to bombard the few remaining defenses, then move ashore, and take the atoll.

When Sub-Lieutenant Ozeki questioned Lt. Kinichi Uchida, commander of one of the companies assigned to hit Wake's beaches, about the December 11 attack, Uchida told him not to worry. "He assured me, much like a father would assure a frightened child, that the enemy lacked any aircraft and would soon fold under our ruthless assault."[2]

Ozeki relaxed as the flotilla droned toward Wake. His commanding officer was right—the United States could not hope to withstand the forces now coming toward them. Ozeki performed his chores content that "we could toss a few shells at the island and we'd be greeted by a white flag."[3]

"Well, There They Are"

Six hundred miles north, Lieutenant Hanna on Wake Island and Corporal Johnson on Wilkes waited in their improvised foxholes and bomb shelters. Over on Peale, Joe Goicoechea tried to sneak in a few moments of sleep in between strengthening his position and moving guns. No one knew when the Japanese would arrive, but the military veterans sensed it was only a matter of time.

Until the fighting erupted, the men—many of them hardly out of high school—grappled with different emotions and questions. The Marines, Army, and Navy personnel wanted to avenge the deaths of their friends and inflict punishment on the enemy. The civilians feared what would happen if they were caught in a battle for which they had no training. Devereux and Cunningham wondered whether the civilian volunteers could bear the incredible strain of bombardments, bullets, grenades. Would they stand their ground amid charging soldiers intent on killing them? J. O. Young worried that he would never have the chance to return to Boise to marry Pearl Ann, while others just hoped to see another Christmas.

Shortly before 3:00 A.M. on December 11, Marine lookouts on Wilkes Island thought they noticed movement far out to sea. Their eyes could have been playing tricks, for the early morning darkness and the casual sways of the ocean caused men to imagine all sorts of things, but they were pretty sure they had spotted something. To be on the safe side, they informed their commander, Captain Platt, who immediately relayed the information that ships had possibly been sighted to Major Devereux's command post.

The commander, who had been asleep, walked out of his dugout and down to Wake's beach to take a look for himself. He strained through binoculars to detect signs of motion, but at first nothing out of the ordinary caught his eye. As he swept the ocean from right to left, suddenly, in the distance, the vague outlines of ships appeared on the horizon. "Well, there they are,"[4] he muttered, and headed back inside. He knew the Japanese had arrived, for no American task force stood anywhere in the vicinity of Wake.

Devereux issued an order to all his officers to assemble their men and under no means open fire until he gave the word. He then contacted Commander Cunningham, who approved the plans and added orders of his own for the civilians to hide and for Putnam's aviators to take the four remaining aircraft of VMF-211 into the air as soon as possible.

At Peacock Point on Wake Island, Lieutenant Barninger snatched his binoculars and stood on top of his dugout directly behind his 5-inch guns to locate the enemy. While he scanned the horizon, Gunnery Sgt. Anthony Polousky prepared the battery for the coming battle. The Marines, including Cpl. Franklin Gross, did not worry him; they knew what to do. His concern centered on the group of civilian volunteers needed to fill in the gaps at their gun position. Sergeant Polousky grabbed John R. Burroughs and pointed out the powder magazine where shells and powder canisters were stored in separate stacks. "If we go into action," the Marine emphasized to the civilian, "pass up two shells—one for each gun. Then two powders—understand?"

Before Burroughs could answer, Polousky rushed to another spot, where he told Johnny Clelan and other civilians to take the shells and powder canisters passed out by Burroughs, and "Send a powder and a shell to gun No. 1, then a powder and a shell to gun No. 2—keep alternating."[5] Polousky had no time to answer any questions; he had to trust they understood his hasty instructions. The Japanese could start shelling any minute, and Polousky had his own responsibilities to handle.

Several miles out to sea, Admiral Kajioka gave the order for the assault force to climb into the landing craft. He had chosen the beaches along the atoll's southern shore as his landing zone because of rough surf on Wake's northern coast, but luck did not hold with him this night. Gusts of wind churned the water and shoved the landing craft against the troop transports, which made maneuvering into them more difficult for soldiers weighed down with equipment. Sub-Lieutenant Ozeki saw three men slip and disappear into the darkened waters, and several boats almost swamped in the heavy seas. "The face of heaven was against us from the beginning,"[6] wrote Ozeki, who thought the landing craft looked like kites being thrown about by a typhoon. Faced with disaster, Kajioka decided to wait until he could move closer to shore, where the seas might be calmer, before embarking the landing force. In the meantime, he intended to reduce the distance from Wake and bombard the atoll. He wanted as few of those Marine guns responding as possible when his men stormed ashore.

Kajioka hoped to achieve surprise at Wake, just as his compatriots did at Pearl Harbor, but he had no idea what would occur when he took his ships toward the atoll. Kajioka, aboard the *Yubari*, led the column of warships in, followed by his two cruisers and six destroyers. Off to the right steamed two troop transports loaded with 450 soldiers eager to kill Americans.

As the ships closed to within nine thousand yards, all appeared quiet on Wake. When Kajioka spotted no indications of American movement and received no fire, he thought that maybe the air attacks of the previous three days had accomplished more than anyone thought. December 11 just might be another resounding victory for the Japanese to post alongside their other triumphs—and another debacle for the United States to absorb.

Word rapidly spread throughout the atoll that ships had been sighted, and in the excitement some construction workers assumed the ships were American vessels from the United States Navy steaming to their rescue. "Look," a friend said to Hans Whitney as they stood on the beach. "Our Navy is at last coming after us."[7]

Whitney doubted his buddy, but others wanted to have nothing to do with any fighting and were more than ready to leave Wake. They had signed on to erect buildings, not hoist arms in combat, and in their opinion the government had a responsibility to extricate them from danger. Encouraged by the sightings, they filtered to the beach, suitcases in hand, waiting for the rescue ships to move in and rush them back to Hawaii. Nearby Marines shattered their illusion with frantic shouts to find shelter—fast.

"The Shells Were Shaking the Ground"

At his command post near Camp 1, Devereux concluded he had only one hope of survival. Since the more powerful Japanese guns could hurl shells much farther than Wake's 5-inch batteries, they could stand beyond the range of Wake's guns and fire at will, slowly eliminating every major point of resistance until the atoll was reduced to rubble. In that case, Marines, Army, Navy, and civilians could do nothing to respond. They could only wait for such a bombardment to end and hope they were still alive.

Devereux believed his only chance was to trick the opposing commander into thinking he had either achieved surprise or that the aircraft raids had smashed Wake's defensive capabilities. If he could pull that off, possibly the Japanese officer would carelessly bring his ships closer to shore, well within range of Wake's three 5-inch batteries.

The bold plan carried frightening risks, for it meant allowing the Japanese to fire at will while the ships inched inward. The plan required that his men endure a pounding naval bombardment in the interval, something most military men point to as one of the worst experiences of warfare. Each man, especially the inexperienced civilians and untested servicemen, would face a test of nerves the likes of which they had never before encountered. Devereux had to accept those risks, however, to retain any slim chance of repelling the stronger Japanese assault force.

At the airfield, Major Putnam prodded his men to ready the four fighters and get them into the air before the Japanese opened fire. Wake's defense heavily depended on the existence of these aircraft, not only for scouting and attacking, but also for the psychological advantage they gave to the men fighting on the atoll. As long as Wake sported an air arm, the Japanese had to approach the atoll with extreme caution; as long as Putnam, Elrod, Kinney, and the others climbed into the Wildcats, Wake's offensive bite extended hundreds of miles to sea. That provided a comfort zone for the men cringing in foxholes or huddling in dugouts and provided a security, however illusory it might be, that made life more bearable.

Shortly after 5:00 A.M., Putnam, Tharin, Elrod, and Freuler hopped into their fighters and started the engines. Three Wildcats surreptitiously lifted off at 5:15, with the final aircraft following forty-five minutes later because of a mechanical problem. The aviators flew to their assigned altitude and waited for daylight to give them the opportunity to strike.

Admiral Kajioka gained more confidence when he pulled to within eight thousand yards of Wake, point-blank range for naval guns, without receiving American fire. He ordered the *Yubari* and the other cruisers and destroyers to veer left and steam parallel to Wake's southern shore while the troop transports headed to the right and the invasion beaches.

At 5:30, *Yubari's* guns boomed an unwelcome notice that Wake, ignored for centuries by Pacific travelers, was about to become the stage for one of the war's most enduring epics. A series of bright flashes from offshore illuminated the darkness as Japanese guns fired. The first shells crashed into oil tanks in the southwest portion of Wake, close to where Devereux watched the drama unfold. That seemed to be the sign for every Japanese vessel to join in, and soon a furious volley of shells cascaded onto the atoll, destroying installations and hurling coral rocks in all directions.

The deafening noise stunned the Americans as the shells neared their targets. Shrieking, whistling projectiles rumbled above, sounding much

like railroad cars as they raced by to explode in an earth-shattering eruption. Dugouts rattled and shook from the blasts; coral dust fell on the men;
thick columns of black smoke rose from the atoll.

Japanese gunfire continued as the ships steamed to the western end of
Wilkes, where Kajioka reversed course to repeat the bombardment, this
time from only six thousand yards. Three destroyers broke off to swing
around the atoll's northern side and open fire from a second direction.
Japanese optimism about easily seizing Wake soared, for in spite of the
bombardment, they had still received no American response.

Not that the Americans did not want to react. From their outposts
spread throughout the atoll, Marine officers called Devereux's command
post, begging for permission to open fire, but each plea received the same
reply. Devereux, who calmly observed the Japanese from the roof of his
dugout, told his radioman, Corp. Robert Brown, to tell them they were to
remain out of sight, keep their heads down, and wait for his command. He
had to draw the enemy in closer.

In the brush near the civilian camp, Ben Comstock and his father
hastily dug a hole in the brush, then pulled a mattress on top as cover. It
was not much, but anything, even something as thin as a mattress, lent a
sense of security to the two men, isolated in their own little frightening
world—a minuscule hole on Wake that the Japanese wanted to destroy.
When a shell fragment sliced clean through their mattress, neither Comstock felt good about their chances of survival.

Each shell that rocked Wake seemed to produce more men who besieged Devereux to open fire. Battery A's Lieutenant Barninger at Peacock
Point on Wake and Battery L's Lieutenant McAlister at Kuku Point on
Wilkes—standing at the opposite ends of the Japanese bombardment
line—implored Devereux to let them respond. Lieutenants Kinney and
Hamilton of VMF-211 crowded together in a dugout near the airfield and
wondered why none of Wake's guns answered. Kinney, frightened by the
horrifying destructiveness and deafened by the sounds, felt that he would
rather be plunging straight through enemy antiaircraft fire than enduring
this bombardment. In the air, at least he could see Japanese tracers approaching his fighter. Down on the ground, hugging the dirt, all he could
do was wait and hope an unseen shell did not tear him to pieces.

Japanese guns continued to belch fire and smoke, but still Devereux
waited. The ships drew in even more, and Devereux kept silent. One officer, sporting a mixture of anger and fear, mentioned to the man next to him
that in practice at Pearl Harbor, his men had regularly hit targets at twelve
thousand yards, yet here the enemy was within six thousand yards and still
he could not fire. Another shouted to Corporal Brown, "What does that
little bastard want us to do? Let 'em run over us without even spitting

back?"[8] Devereux ignored the remarks and coolly waited, while Lieutenant McAlister called in the ranges.

Along Kajioka's intended landing zone on Wake's beaches south of the airfield, Corporal Holewinski listened to the terrifying whistle as the shells neared. He kept his head down, but that only made it worse, for a Japanese shell could strike at any moment. Men held their breaths as shells churned the ground and defoliated the brush. A frightened civilian on Wilkes asked Corporal Johnson if he were scared. "You're damn right I'm scared!" replied the veteran. "But that's healthy because you'll scamper to stay alive."[9]

In the bombardment, no one thought of home, they thought only of survival, and not survival until next week or the next day, but to the next second. They had become human bull's-eyes, targets for missiles that could obliterate all traces of their existence. Since it seemed that every inch of Wake rattled from explosions, it was not far-fetched to the men that sooner or later one of those shells would find their dugout or foxhole. They could do nothing but wait until the end came one way or another.

"The shells were shaking the ground and rattling," said Pfc. Martin Gatewood. "It feels like hell when you can't do anything or try to stop it. All you could do was stay low and hope they didn't hit you. It was a helpless feeling."[10]

Corporal Holewinski described the bombardment as demoralizing. He could hear the shells whistle and shriek, but could not see them or fight back. "A naval bombardment is some of the most fierce action you can be under," he explained. "It's frightening. It scares you."[11] For forty-five mind-numbing minutes, American Marines, Army, and Navy personnel, plus a handful of civilian volunteers, huddled near their positions while one thousand other civilians placed their faith in the makeshift holes in the brush.

Lieutenant Poindexter later compared Devereux's ploy to the celebrated action taken at Bunker Hill in the American Revolution when the American officer ordered his men to hold fire until they could see the whites of the enemy's eyes. At Wake, guns replaced eyes; shells substituted for bayonets. The Japanese drew so close that Lieutenant McAlister angrily raved about not being allowed to shoot back.

Around 6:10, when the *Yubari* reached the eastern end of Wake off Peacock Point, Admiral Kajioka pulled the ship to within a mere 4,500 yards and ordered a third run. Five minutes later, with the Japanese seemingly within spitting range, the Marines finally heard the command for which they had been waiting—open up with every 5-inch gun on Wake, Wilkes, and Peale. Devereux told switchboard operator Pfc. James O. King to relay the message, "Open fire. Fire at will."[12]

At Lieutenant Barninger's Battery A on Wake, the gun closest to the

Yubari, Sergeant Polousky rushed out of his hole to gather his civilian volunteers. "All right, you civilians, break out those shells," he barked. As he heard the sound of men running across the coral to their stations and the heavy cadence of labored breathing, John Burroughs scampered with the others toward the powder magazine, where Burroughs grabbed a shell and handed it to Johnny Clelan. Sergeant Polousky, irritated by their sluggishness, ran over and yelled, "Come on, you God-damned civilians, hurry up with those shells."¹³

Almost in unison, the six 5-inch guns at all three locations commenced firing in a round of shooting that Lieutenant Kinney claimed was music to his ears. Reminiscent of an old-fashioned Wild West duel between gunslingers, Wake's 5-inch batteries blasted away from short range against Kajioka's naval guns in a battle to see who remained standing when the smoke cleared.

Men around the atoll shook their temporary paralysis and started acting the way they were trained, as military personnel doing their duty under fire. Finally, their side had responded.

"You're In, Johnny Mac!"

Kajioka, unaware of the surprise that lay only moments away, continued his bombardment. The ferociousness of the Japanese shelling so awed Sub-Lieutenant Ozeki that he wondered not only how anyone could survive such brutality, but who would be left to surrender the atoll.

A frightening noise interrupted Ozeki's musings: "My thoughts were shattered by a sudden *whooom-clang* sound as American shore batteries hit our flagship. The vessel lurched amid ringing sirens and clanging bells. The thought of sinking in a ship, battened down trapped like rats, was an unpleasant one."¹⁴

A stunned Kajioka could hardly believe the Americans had fired at him, but he recovered in seconds to order the cruiser to turn about and speed away from the shore batteries. Devereux had outfoxed him, and if Kajioka failed to make the proper adjustments, he could end up in the water. As the *Yubari* executed a zigzag course, Kajioka ordered his guns to focus on the battery at Peacock Point that had opened fire.

The first two shots from Lieutenant Barninger's Battery A missed the *Yubari*, but from observing the shell splashes, Barninger corrected the fire until a salvo scored a direct hit. At a range of about 5,500 yards, two shells smacked into the *Yubari*'s midsection barely above the waterline. Smoke and steam gushed out of the stricken vessel, which limped slowly in the water. The ship strained to pull out of Wake's range, but when the *Yubari*

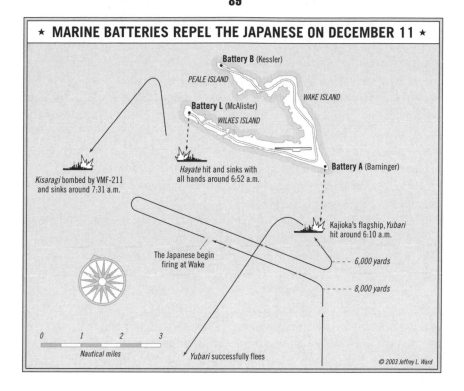

★ MARINE BATTERIES REPEL THE JAPANESE ON DECEMBER 11 ★

Battery B (Kessler)

PEALE ISLAND

WAKE ISLAND

Battery L (McAlister)

WILKES ISLAND

Hayate hit and sinks with
all hands around 6:52 a.m.

Battery A (Barninger)

Kisaragi bombed by VMF-211
and sinks around 7:31 a.m.

Kajioka's flagship, *Yubari*
hit around 6:10 a.m.

The Japanese begin
firing at Wake

6,000 yards

8,000 yards

0   1   2   3

Nautical miles

Yubari successfully flees

© 2003 Jeffrey L. Ward

was seven thousand yards away, Battery A poured two more shells into the damaged cruiser, close to where the first two hit. With one entire side of the ship engulfed in flames, Kajioka swerved the *Yubari* to starboard in an effort to put smoke between Wake and his ship. A destroyer rushed in between the flagship and the Americans to lay its own smoke screen, but another salvo from Battery A crashed into the destroyer, killing two and wounding fifteen Japanese sailors.

Battery A's lopsided gun duel with Kajioka took only minutes, but in that brief time, the Marine battery registered an impressive triumph. Their mates on Wilkes and Peale were about to deliver more punishment.

An abundance of targets steamed within easy range of Lieutenant McAlister's Battery L on Wilkes Island. McAlister selected the first of seven warships, the destroyer *Hayate*, but had to estimate the range because an earlier air raid had damaged his gun's range finder, the device that accurately measured distances.

Captain Platt called out the results as McAlister fired. The first salvo fluttered beyond the destroyer and the second splashed short, but the 150-pound officer found his mark with the third. "You're in, Johnny Mac!" cried Platt. "You're in, Johnny Ma— Oh, hell, he's gone, get another one!"[15] The shell punctured belowdecks and detonated the *Hayate*'s magazine, producing a ferocious explosion that lifted the destroyer fifty feet in the air. The doomed *Hayate* split in half and disappeared in less than two minutes, taking the entire crew of 168 sailors to their deaths. Those who were not killed outright by the blast either drowned or were devoured by the swarms of sharks that always ringed Wake. With this feat, McAlister and his men became the first Americans to sink a Japanese ship in the war.

"Whee! We got the son of a bitch!"[16] shouted McAlister to Pfc. King back in Devereux's command post. Devereux asked King what McAlister had said, and when informed of the accomplishment complimented McAlister for his excellent shooting.

"That ship stood on end and sank within a minute and a half," mentioned Lieutenant Hanna, who watched from his post along Wake's beach. "We really cheered. I don't think there was a man on the island who wasn't happy."[17]

Sgt. Henry A. Bedell might have been one, for work remained to be done. The veteran Bedell brought the celebrating men of Battery L back to reality with a few well-chosen words. "Knock it off, you bastards, and get back on the guns. What do you think this is, a ballgame?"[18]

The men halted their rejoicing and resumed their superb marksmanship. Before Kajioka pulled out of sight, Battery L landed other hits on a second destroyer, one transport, and one cruiser.

Across the lagoon on Peale Island, Lieutenant Kessler's men of Battery B delivered the final blow of the three-punch assault by the 5-inch guns. Heavy fire from the Japanese kept Kessler's crew partially pinned down, including one shell that screamed between two rows of ammunition handlers. Had the shell veered one way or the other, it would have killed half of Kessler's crew. Had it landed short, it would have knocked out the gun. His men kept up the firing, though, and landed hits on two of three Japanese destroyers that tried to race around Wilkes's northern coast. The destroyers altered course and, like the rest of Kajioka's task force, steamed away from Wake as quickly as possible.

Kessler, beaming like a proud father, could not have been more delighted with his mostly teenage gun crew. "There was no fear evident as the enemy shells fell about them," he wrote after the battle, "it was as though here at last they had been given an opportunity to fight back and they were determined to do so. There was no cheering but I sensed a feeling of great pride and satisfaction in the relaxed look in their faces. They had been tested and found themselves not wanting."[19]

By 7:10, approximately one hour after Devereux's command to open fire, quiet returned to the atoll. Instead of a landing on Wake and a quick victory over the Americans, Kajioka beat a hasty retreat to the Marshalls to lick his wounds and explain his defeat. As Kajioka limped away, Lieutenant Barninger gazed seaward toward the *Yubari*, from which steam and thick black smoke billowed, then watched the ship slowly gain speed and disappear over the horizon. His job, and the work of every man standing on Wake, was finished, but more lay in store for Kajioka. The smoke had hardly cleared from Wake's guns when the four aviators of VMF-211, Wake's tentacles reaching out to sea, plunged down to add the finishing touches to a remarkable morning.

"Hounded Out to Sea by Fanatical American Fighters"

While Kajioka and Devereux battled from point-blank range below, Major Putnam, joined by Captains Elrod, Tharin, and Freuler, scouted the skies at fifteen thousand feet to intercept Japanese carrier aircraft. Early reports mentioned the possibility of an enemy aircraft carrier in the area, but when none was sighted, the four decided to descend and help their mates fighting on land. Putnam radioed his companions, "Well, it looks as if there are no Nips in the air. Let's go down and join the party."[20]

Each aviator carried two 100-pound bombs under his wings in addition to the .50-caliber machine guns. As the pilots dipped toward the Japanese ships, antiaircraft bursts punctured the skies around them, but the Americans held fire until they dropped to within 1,500 feet. Putnam's errant pair of bombs missed one destroyer, but the officer made amends by peppering the bridge of a second destroyer with his machine guns. As he pulled out, Putnam saw pieces of metal and shards of glass—the enemy crew had apparently forgotten to remove the glass shield from the bridge—spray every Japanese officer and crew member nearby. Now out of ammunition, Putnam hurried back to Wake to land, reload, and return for another attack.

The four aviators, relieved at times by Lieutenant Kinney and Sgt. William J. Hamilton, flew ten different sorties that morning. For one hour, the Americans harassed the Japanese, much like hornets pursuing an intruder who had disturbed their nest. "We were hounded out to sea by fanatical American fighters who strafed us relentlessly and dropped bombs with impunity,"[21] wrote Sub-Lt. Ozeki. Machine gun bullets from one American fighter punctured the *Yubari*'s bridge and narrowly missed killing Admiral Kajioka. Other aviators damaged a transport and one other vessel.

Captain Elrod delivered the coup de grâce, however. In a run against the destroyer *Kisaragi*, Hammering Hank dropped a bomb that punched through the ship's deck and started a fire belowdecks. By the time Elrod disengaged to reload at Wake, the ship had slowed in the water, but still floated.

About 7:37 Putnam spotted the damaged *Kisaragi* thirty miles south of Wake and prepared to attack. Suddenly, an immense ball of flame consumed the destroyer, which disappeared in less than a minute, taking 150 men to their deaths. Putnam later attributed the sinking to Elrod's bomb, which started the fires that doomed the ship.

The six aviators dropped twenty bombs and expended twenty thousand rounds of .50-caliber ammunition at the enemy in sixty minutes, but they paid a price. Japanese antiaircraft fire punctured every Wildcat, especially Captain Elrod's, whose engine froze from a lack of lubrication. Elrod miraculously nursed the fighter back to Wake and alighted only yards from shore, but the hard landing, combined with the damage inflicted by the Japanese, knocked the Wildcat out of the fight. Elrod jumped out unhurt, but he seemed more concerned with the valuable fighter than about himself. He repeated over and over to Major Devereux, who had rushed to the beach to see if Elrod was all right, "I'm sorry as hell about the plane."[22]

Capt. Freuler's aircraft also suffered extensive damage, but Putnam concluded that by scavenging parts from destroyed fighters, the plane could be repaired. Until that time, however, he could put only two Wildcats into the sky to oppose the enemy.

Kajioka, already in shock over the fierce resistance fashioned by Wake's defenders, had had enough. He had lost not one, but two ships to a foe his compatriots dismissed as weak and lacking spirit. Somehow, he had to prepare an answer for his superiors in the Marshalls, who were sure to demand an explanation of why he could not seize an atoll they considered a pushover. Humiliated, still rattled by his near-death encounter with American machine-gun bullets, Kajioka headed for the Marshalls, where he intended to "make another attempt when conditions were more favorable."[23]

Later that day, Lt. David D. Kliewer put the finishing touches to December 11. As he patrolled twenty-five miles southwest of Wake around 4:00 P.M., he spotted a submarine, most likely the *RO-66* commanded by Lt. Comdr. Hideyuki Kurokawa. Kliewer dipped low to ensure better results before dropping his two 100-pound bombs, but he plunged so far that bomb fragments from the explosion pierced his aircraft. He gained altitude and then turned back for a second sweep with his machine guns. Kliewer strafed the submarine until he ran out of ammunition, and as he changed course to head back to Wake, he thought he saw the submarine disappear. When he landed and reported the outcome, Major Putnam hopped into an aircraft and flew out to check the location. He spotted an oil spill where Kliewer encountered the submarine, so he assumed the boat had been destroyed.

Doubt remains whether Kliewer destroyed the submarine on December 11, or whether he damaged its communications equipment so severely that it later sank in a December 17 collision with a second Japanese submarine of which *RO-66* was unaware. In either event, Kliewer deserves the credit, for his actions led to the boat's demise.

"It's Been Quite a Day, Major"

Wake's defenders recorded an impressive tally on December 11. The atoll's three 5-inch batteries, the aviators of VMF-211, and Lieutenant Kliewer sank two surface ships and one submarine, damaged at least seven others, and downed two aircraft. At a cost of two Wildcat fighters and five wounded Marines, Wake inflicted a punishing human toll on their enemy—340 Japanese sailors died.

The military registered three "firsts" on Wake that day. For the first and only time in the war, shore batteries repulsed a Japanese invasion. Wake sank the first Japanese warship of the Pacific conflict. Most important, for the first time since the war started, an American force had prevented the Japanese from seizing an objective.

Morale on Wake skyrocketed. For three days the men had suffered through bombing raids and seen companions die, lost personal possessions and friends, yet they had little opportunity to fight back. When given the chance on December 11, they proved their mettle against a force that should have handily swept them away. Kajioka commanded such a powerful conglomerate that all he had to do was stay outside Wake's range, reduce the defenses with his larger guns, and then send in his landing force to sweep up the few surviving Americans. Instead, he fell to Devereux's strategy and lost.

In an interview after the war, Devereux maintained they should never have defeated Kajioka, whose force "should've wiped us out with ease."[24] The Japanese admiral certainly helped by steaming in close to Wake, but from then on, the courage and determination of Devereux's men took over. Each Marine, each sailor, and each soldier drew on that performance to help sustain them in the days to come.

On Peale Island, Private Laporte shouted and cheered with others over what he called a big morale booster, and elsewhere around the atoll military and civilians celebrated. "The tension, & concern over our ability to match the Japs['] superior guns, numbers etc. was gone," wrote Sergeant Donald R. Malleck. "We suddenly were invincible. I am very certain every man on that Island grew a good two inches—at least."[25]

Private First Class King sensed a surge of confidence swell in the men around him. They were certain that the United States would soon dispatch a naval relief force to their aid, and with that assistance the Japanese could never take the atoll. "The attitude of the men after the December 11 attack was that we could handle pretty much anything," said King. "There was no doubt that help was coming at this stage. We were all optimistic and never dreamed the Japanese would take the island."[26]

After joining delighted aviators and mechanics at the airfield, Cunningham walked to Devereux's command post to congratulate the officer and his Marines for the marvelous defense. He then dashed over to the Marine Officers' Club for a hasty celebration. "It was like a fraternity picnic," Cunningham wrote. "War whoops of joy split the air; warm beer was sprayed on late arrivals without regard to rank; already the memories that would last a lifetime—a tragically short lifetime for some—were being recalled, relived, and even embroidered."[27]

Beer in hand, big John Hamas joined Cunningham for a drink, then left to collect a group of civilians and deliver ammunition to Wilkes. Cunningham departed shortly after Hamas to complete what he called one of the proudest tasks of his career—inform Pearl Harbor of the victory. Admiral Kimmel, busy trying to regroup the shattered forces at the Hawaiian base, still found time to praise Cunningham and every man on Wake for performing their duties "in accordance with the highest traditions of the Naval Service."[28] Cunningham read the notice to Devereux and Putnam at his first opportunity.

"We felt good, almost cocky," Cunningham wrote. "Surely help would come from Pearl Harbor any day now, and meanwhile we could wait it out."[29]

Back at Devereux's command post, Corporal Brown turned to the major and said, in understated terms, "It's been quite a day, Major, hasn't it?"[30]

Devereux could not spare much time for celebrating, for he and every other man on Wake knew that the Japanese, though embarrassed and licking their wounds, would inevitably return in greater numbers. Devereux had to prepare his men for what would be a more violent, bloody clash.

Fortunately, he could count on Dan Teters for aid. Close to 450 civilians joined Marine batteries to handle ammunition and stand night watches, deliever food and build shelters. The civilians, highly technical tradesmen and skilled workers, had little training in handling weapons or dealing with the type of fear they faced during the bombardment, yet they came through when the military most needed them and collaborated with the military to inflict a shocking defeat on Japan. In a report, Lieutenant Barninger of Battery A wrote that he could never have enjoyed the success he achieved on December 11 without the help of the civilian volunteers at his battery, who not only handled ammunition, but also helped construct shelters for the men. The citizen soldiers had rolled up their sleeves, braved enemy fire, and stood side by side with their military counterparts.

Other Marines, however, cursed the fact that so many civilian construction workers declined to help the undermanned Marines. Lieutenant McAlister of Battery L had to halt the firing of his 5-inch guns when he could not coax any civilians to help bring up ammunition. Instead, his Marines had to leave the guns to carry ammunition up from the magazine. Eventually a few civilians emerged from hiding and assisted McAlister, but the thorny issue of civilian assistance would plague Cunningham and Devereux all through the battle.

"One of the Most Humiliating Defeats"

Out at sea, Admiral Kajioka led the dejected task force back to Kwajalein in the Marshalls. Along the way, the Japanese buried the dead in traditional style by wrapping the bodies in white cloth and dropping them overboard. The somber ceremony did nothing to improve the men's mood.

To cover their embarrassment to the people back home, the Japanese Navy explained that Kajioka returned because of poor weather. One Japanese newspaper reported, in words that now seem comical, that "The Imperial Navy shelled Wake Island on December 11, and dealt heavy losses to the remaining military establishments of the enemy. Our side suffered some damage, too."[31]

The Japanese military knew the truth. *Yubari*'s action report admitted that Wake's batteries and aircraft proved more effective than they assumed, and in the process disrupted the Japanese timetable for the Pacific. Instead of holding Wake as planned and freeing ships and men for other operations, Japan now had to commit more forces in a second assault they never thought would be necessary.

One officer accurately concluded that "Considering the power accumulated for the invasion of Wake Island, and the meager forces of the defenders, it was one of the most humiliating defeats our navy had ever suffered."[32]

They would be back, however. Sub-Lieutenant Ozeki noticed that every man aboard *Yubari* spoke of nothing but revenge. December 11 had been an abberation, an accident no one could have foreseen. They would make amends the next time they saw Wake.

"Old Glory Still Waves over the Island"

Nowhere did the heroics at Wake have more impact and create a more emotional reaction than back home. American citizens, reeling from continuous bad news from the Pacific, almost hesitated to read the next day's headlines. The Japanese moved in the Pacific with impunity, and American military forces had given little reason to hope they would soon reverse the trend. The nation's most popular news magazine, *Time*, included in its first wartime issue that early information from the Pacific indicated that Japanese bombers " 'smashed' Wake in no-time flat."[33]

An unsettled country even feared invasion of the continental United States. School authorities in New York City sent the district's children home when air raid sirens blasted a warning, and frightened children ran crying through East Providence, Rhode Island, streets. Press reports from Topeka, Kansas, referred to growing pessimism in the area, and Boston officials placed guards around power plants and reservoirs when enemy aircraft were reported flying only two hundred miles away. Patrolmen in the state of Washington stamped out brush fires they claimed created an arrow pointing toward the huge Bremerton Navy Yard.

What turned out to be imaginary raids by Japanese aircraft caused panic in both San Francisco on December 9 and Southern California on December 10. Japanese ships supposedly prowled the coast of California near Catalina Island. The U.S. Army convinced organizers to move the famed Rose Bowl football game on New Year's Day from Pasadena, California, to Duke Stadium in Durham, North Carolina.

Then news arrived on December 10 that Japanese aircraft had sunk Great Britain's two powerful ships, the battle cruiser *Repulse* and the majestic battleship *Prince of Wales*, off the coast of Malaya. Considered the pride of the British Navy, the ships disappeared after a brief encounter, leaving not only Great Britain, but also the United States without a battleship in the Pacific. A distraught British Prime Minister Winston Churchill, the revered leader whose stirring optimism pulled his country through the darkest hours of the war against Hitler, claimed that "In all the war I never received a more direct shock. . . . As I turned over and twisted in bed the full horror of the news sank in upon me. . . . Over all this vast expanse of waters Japan was supreme, and we everywhere [were] weak and naked."[34]

*   *   *

Then, like a beacon suddenly illuminating the path home, the men at Wake breathed hope and optimism into a depressed nation with their December 11 rejection of the Japanese. Maj. Gen. Thomas Holcomb, the Marine commandant, informed Secretary Knox that same day that "A cheery note comes from Wake and the news is particularly pleasing at a time like this." In Nampa, Pearl Ann read headlines in the the *Idaho Daily Statesman* that Wake was STILL UNDER AMERICAN FLAG,[35] meaning her fiancé, J. O. Young, might be all right.

President Roosevelt, fresh from meeting the dynamic Churchill, brightened even more at learning what his military had done at Wake. When asked by a reporter at a press conference on December 12 to express his thoughts of Wake, a heartened president replied, "So far as we know, Wake Island is holding out—has done a perfectly magnificent job. We are all very proud of that very small group of Marines who are holding the Island."[36]

Headlines and articles in the nation's newspapers and magazines trumpeted the news as if the nation had found a savior. MARINES KEEP WAKE proclaimed the *New York Times*. The *Washington Post* called Wake an "epic in American history, one of those gallant stands" that stir the soul. *Time* concluded that "At Wake a tiny band of Marines made more of the Corps's imperishable history that had its beginnings in the fighting tops of John Paul Jones's *Ranger* and *Bonhomme Richard*. They had been there since the first day of war, beating off attack after attack by the Jap, shooting down his planes, sinking his surface ships, probably knocking the spots out of his landing parties."[37]

The *Honolulu Advertiser*'s headline read, TINY GARRISON HOLDS OUT AGAINST ATTACKS. The *Detroit Evening Times* boasted MARINES HOLD OFF WAKE ASSAULT, credited the defense of Wake with raising the American fighting spirit, and bragged that the Wake defenders "are standing firm in the midst of flying steel. . . ." The article added with pride, "Old Glory still waves over the island possession."[38]

"Out there a couple of thousand of miles west of us," wrote reporter Robert J. Casey from Hawaii, "the Marines were still holding Wake. . . . And as Americans we got a bit of thrill and plenty of consolation out of that. In a few outposts the United States of Valley Forge and The Wilderness and the Argonne was surviving and our ancient swaggering faith in ourselves and our Destiny didn't seem quite so ludicrous."[39]

Newsweek stated that "out in the middle of the Pacific, on tiny Wake Island, a Marine Corps garrison gave the Japs the surprise of their lives" by repelling the December attack. The magazine added that "all America was watching to see what the next move of the heroic leathernecks would be."[40] Instead of opening the newspaper with trepidation over what tragedy the

Japanese had next inflicted, as the country had done since Pearl Harbor, people now eagerly looked forward to more news.

The nation swiftly reacted. A new war slogan, "Wake Up!" swept across the country, and thousands of young men swamped military recruiting centers. In Hartford, Connecticut, a woman walked into the Connecticut Employment Service and asked for work making ammunition. When asked why she wanted such a job, she replied, "My husband's in the Marine Corps. He's at Wake Island."⁴¹ She got the job.

Americans could once again hold their heads high. People compared Wake to Davy Crockett and the Texans fighting Santa Anna at the Alamo, the Spartans holding off the Persians at Thermopylae, and other names associated with extraordinary military feats. Like an irritating pebble stuck in Japan's shoe, Wake tenaciously held on when other places had succumbed or absorbed catastrophic losses. The Japanese steamroller had been halted just as it appeared to gain momentum, stopped not by an immense naval task force or a fleet of bombers or an entire army, but by a handful of military personnel and their civilian volunteers. The event harked to those days in 1776, when farmers dropped their plows, picked up their muskets, and headed to do battle with the British. The men of Wake resurrected optimism when the nation most needed it.

"We Had Done It Today"

Festivities on Wake quieted later that night when a group of men gathered near the civilian camp to bury the bodies of eighty military and civilian personnel killed since December 8. With so many events unfolding at rapid speed in the war's opening days, there had been no time to bury the bodies, which had instead been placed in a refrigeration unit. Commander Cunningham now arranged a ceremony to honor the slain men. With Devereux and Teters at his side and an honor guard of four Marines, Cunningham enlisted the help of a civilian preacher, a carpenter from Wyoming named John H. O'Neal.

Other Morrison-Knudsen workers used construction equipment to dig a long trench about one hundred yards from the east end of the airfield, then carefully placed each of the eighty bodies into the common grave. After the Marine honor guard fired three volleys, O'Neal recited prayers for the fallen Americans, including Conderman and Graves from the airfield. Since most men had to remain at their posts, only a small crowd could gather. Among them was a construction worker whose son had accompanied him to Wake because of the excellent wages. Instead of compiling a financial nest egg for his future, the boy, killed in Wake's early action, now shared a resting spot with other fallen men.

That night, hoping to confuse the Japanese bombers, Devereux ordered Capt. Bryght D. Godbold to move the four 3-inch guns from Battery D on Peale's western edge across to the island's eastern corner. Teters arranged for a large group of construction workers to help, and by the next morning the men had the guns emplaced in their new location.

Elsewhere on Wake, men tried to catch a few moments of sleep in between assignments or watches, for no one knew when they would again enjoy a full night's sleep. At least they could doze off or stand duty with a fresh optimism born of the day's events. December 11 had been a good day.

"Well, we had done it today," wrote Commander Cunningham. "Surface ships, bombers, and now a submarine. If they'd just give us enough time, we'd lick the whole Japanese Navy by ourselves.

"I went back to my cottage thinking the hell with the dangers of a night raid, threw open the window to the soft breezes and the soothing sound of the surf, and slept like a baby."[42]

It would be Cunningham's last deep slumber in almost four years, but he had a right to be elated. His men notified the Japanese that the Pacific Ocean was not their private domain. They may have scored impressive victories at Pearl Harbor, Guam, and other places in the war's opening days, but Wake reminded the Japanese that the United States had not disappeared. The nation only needed time to regroup. When ready, it would strike back with the ferocity exhibited by Lieutenant Hanna, Captain Elrod, Joe Goicoechea, and the other military and civilian personnel on Wake.

The men of Wake answered the Japanese, not only for themselves, but for their nation, as well. In those heady December 11 moments, they gained a small measure of revenge for Pearl Harbor and vengeance for slain comrades, and in the process gave hope to the people back home.

They could not celebrate too much, however. With limited resources, a battalion at half-strength, and an air force of only a few usable fighters, they had to hold on against an angry enemy until help came.

★

CHAPTER 6

"Our Flag Is Still There"

Foxholes, Dugouts, and Trenches

The men on Wake could not celebrate for long, for a Japanese air raid could be expected at any time. By inflicting the first humiliation of the war on the Japanese, the Wake Islanders only gave the enemy more reason to seek redress. Sooner or later, a second Japanese assault force, equipped with additional men and guns and fueled by vengeance, would come knocking on their door. This one would not be so easily deterred.

Servicemen performed their duties with an extra jaunt in their step and with the attitude that they could withstand anything the enemy hurled at them. After all, they had just pounded a superior force into submission. Imagine what they might do once they strengthened their defenses. Besides, by the time the enemy reappeared off Wake, reinforcements from Pearl Harbor would certainly have taken their place beside the veterans of December 11. Tokyo might send more troops, but more would be on hand to greet them.

December 11 injected such renewed optimism into the Wake defenders that Marines joked with each other over their accomplishment, and Lieutenant Barninger thought his men looked forward to another encounter with the Japanese. Corporal Marvin heard Marines from Texas boasting, "This is the Alamo of the Pacific."[1] Marvin joined in their fun, but he saw something ironic, almost ominous, about being compared to the famed 1836 battle. At the Alamo, every Texan died after staging an heroic defense.

The military, helped by civilians, took immediate steps to improve the atoll. They placed additional sandbags inside and around the edges of foxholes and gun positions, inserted pieces of lumber to fortify bunker roofs, cut down branches from the brush to camouflage their positions, and moved 3-inch guns to different locations almost nightly.

On Wake, Lieutenant Poindexter organized a group to dig foxholes and construct dugouts near Camp 1. To fashion the dugouts, bulldozers scraped out trenches, across which were placed twelve-inch-by-twelve-inch pieces of wood. Men then shoveled coral rocks and sand on top of the wood to a depth of four or five feet to absorb the shock of bombs. These shelters, though hastily improvised, could withstand anything but a direct bomb hit.

On Wilkes, Corporal Johnson directed his men in fashioning a rude shelter near their machine guns. The finished product, complete with wooden slabs covered with a layer of sand, may not have matched the Marine manual for correctness, but under the circumstances it served the purpose. Johnson would later recall with a grin that one civilian complained they made the entrance to the shelter too small, but in the very next air raid he handily dashed inside before anyone else.

Lieutenant Kinney faced enormous problems in piecing together remnants of broken aircraft to fashion usable ones, but a group of civilians helped by creating a partially underground aircraft hangar out of an old shelter. They dug a ramp leading below the airfield's surface, then placed steel beams across the ramp, and covered them with wood and cloth. With this hangar, Kinney and his assistants could work in relative safety, and the enclosed hangar also allowed them to repair aircraft around the clock without worrying about enemy bombers spotting their lights.

"What the Hell Am I Doing Here?"

Having endured a December 8 attack and then repelling a landing attempt three days later, Americans on Wake now entered a twelve-day span in which hopes of rescue alternated with fear of death or capture, joy alternated with hunger, comradeship alternated with weariness. The Siege of Wake had begun.

In the early days of the siege, the men faced the situation with a buoyant optimism that eased the strain. Everyone, military and civilian alike, blissfully unaware that the fleet in Hawaii, and with it their hopes, suffered a near-catastrophic blow, expected reinforcements to arrive from Pearl Harbor to strengthen the military and evacuate the civilians. The workers around Murray Kidd, for instance, claimed the U.S. Navy would arrive within a few days to remove them from danger. "That raised our spirits, but then every day we waited and waited."[2]

Even though the Japanese scheduled most of their bombing raids around noon, the men could not relax the rest of the day. Sometimes enemy aircraft materialized later in the day, during the night or, on a few occasions, not at all. The men, shorthanded already, had to maintain a constant vigilance. Jittery guards posted on the water tower sometimes added to the confusion by sounding "Air raid!" when all they actually spotted was a flock of birds or shadows in the clouds. Even though the alarms proved false, the men still had to rush to their dugouts, which could in some cases be a distance away. Over a period of time these supposed sightings irritated the weary defenders, who had better things to do than scamper into hiding from phantom attackers.

In the early phases of the siege, heady with their December 11 triumph and certain of quick help, the burden appeared small, but as the days wore on, the men grew weaker and more fatigued. "We could never be certain if they were going to come at other times, as well, so we were in a constant state of alert," wrote Pfc. Jacob R. Sanders of Battery E. "It was nerve-racking. We worked long hours and then stood long hours of watch. As this was before radar, they would have us just staring at the horizon and sky looking for enemy planes. I got so used to just staring at the sky I was even able to see stars during full daylight."[3] Other men told of gazing so many hours into the tropical sun that they suffered momentary periods of blindness.

Daily bombing raids rivaled the December 11 naval bombardment for sheer terror. During the attacks, the men—like Private First Class Gatewood—fired at the aircraft until they spotted the bombs falling, raced for their dugout or foxholes, then jumped back on the gun again as soon as the bombs exploded. Corporal Marvin had to navigate fifty yards to reach the dugout from his gun, but he handled the distance with ease. "I was never fast on my feet, but I fell down twice and I was still the first one there!"[4]

Bombs screeched downward; roofs of dugouts rattled from near-hits; gritty coral sand sifted through the cracks; dust particles flew around and lodged in men's eyes, noses, and ears; flames leapt from demolished structures, and men gasped for air in the thick acrid smoke. Concussion waves knocked men off their feet and smacked them so hard to the ground that they felt as if they had become part of the surface. "We mashed into the sandbags in that hole like we was part of 'em,"[5] said Private Laporte of his efforts to avoid the bombing on Peale Island. Some men compared the ordeal of a bombing raid to being inside a huge steel kettle while someone pounded on the outside.

A handful of men panicked under the strain. Pfc. James O. King waited out one attack with a group of servicemen and civilians. In the midst of the bombing, a civilian started shouting, "They're gonna kill us! They're gonna kill us!" Already frightened by the thought that an enemy projectile could viciously end their lives, the Americans did not need any further burdens. Sgt. James W. Hall walked over to the terrified construction worker, looked straight at him, and yelled in a booming voice, "Shut the fuck up!"[6] The tactic worked, as the civilian remained silent, although scared, for the remainder of the raid.

To divert his attention from the bombs during one raid, John Rogge flattened himself at the bottom of his dugout and stared at another creature struggling to remain alive. "We were close to the lagoon and when the high tide came in, some water'd get in our dugout. I watched this fly come into our dugout, and then he got into the water and was flopping like a fly does, trying to get free. I watched him for a little bit and then thought, 'You poor little bastard! If you want to live half as bad as I do, I'll help you out.' So I took my finger and lifted him out and threw him out the hole. Any other time he'd be dead."[7]

Corporal Johnson claimed the worst part of the bombing on Wilkes Island was the inability to fight back. He could do nothing, since his machine guns could not reach high enough to affect the enemy bombers. Across the channel separating Wilkes from Wake, Lieutenant Hanna waited out the attacks in similar fashion:

"You're trying to make yourself as small as possible. You know there's not anything you can do because you have nothing that can reach that high. I've never felt more helpless in my life. It's the luck of the draw. You couldn't be on an island like that, with those circumstances, and not have been scared, but you don't dwell on it. Those people who say they were never scared in battle—they're damn liars!"[8]

Most admitted they could not allow themselves to think of home. Corporal Marvin claimed he was too busy surviving to worry about his family, and Lieutenant Hanna only sporadically wondered how Vera and Erlyne were doing in between the attacks. The men had to keep their minds on the battle, and thoughts of loved ones made that harder.

On Wake, prayer was a popular occupation. Some of the men explained they were too frightened or occupied to pray, but most stated the bombings provided extra incentive to turn to a higher power. Forrest Read needed little prodding; he looked to what had always been a source of strength and inspiration—God. His nephew, J. O. Young, drew comfort from a patriarchal blessing he and Pearl Ann received from their minister before he left for Wake. "He said I would safely return. That helped me during the bombardments. I knew I was coming back. It calmed me down. Pearl knew I would be home, so it helped her, too."[9]

George Rosendick repeatedly beseeched God to let him survive the next bombing raid, while others thanked the Lord that at least their families were safe back home. At Devereux's command post in one bombardment, someone heard radioman Corporal Brown mumbling. "What the hell are you doing, Brown?" asked the Marine. Brown retorted, "I'm praying, you God-damn fool!"[10]

With their world disrupted due to the battle, animals wandered about, dazed, or ran into dugouts. Rats, rattled by the bombing, scampered into foxholes and crowded into dugouts. One terrified rat crawled across Commander Cunningham's face, and another scurried into a foxhole, bit a Marine's nose, and held on while the repulsed Marine beat it to death. Birds meandered about the beaches, and crabs interrupted the men's sporadic attempts to sleep. Thousands of animal carcasses littered the atoll, forcing weary Marines to waste precious time burying them to prevent diseases from spreading.

Once a bombing raid ended, men shook off the dust, looked around to see who else survived, and then realized that they had made it through another attack. Major Devereux wrote that men gazed about them, "as though they could not quite comprehend, and then it was like a great weight lifting from your chest. You wouldn't die today. Not this morning, anyhow."[11]

Major Devereux was the image of fearlessness. He usually stood on top of his dugout, watching the raid—as if his presence in the open could reassure his men that all was well. Marines close to Devereux claimed he showed no fear whatsoever, though the officer had to tremble inside. Private First Class King, stationed at Devereux's command post, had numerous opportunities to observe the major. "One day they were bombing and strafing up the beach and I could hear them coming. Devereux stepped out of the dugout, watching the bombs come, and I knew the next one was going to hit us. A bomb hit so close that I had to grab him to prevent him from falling onto me. As soon as that bomb hit, he was back outside watching. He was one calm Marine."[12]

In between raids he visited as many men as time warranted, believing they appreciated their commander emerging from his command post to check on their well-being. At one spot he chatted with a Marine who had safely endured a particularly heavy bombing attack. The pair stared at the many bomb craters that dotted the area and remarked on the good fortune that no one was killed. Then, after a few moments, the Marine mentioned to Devereux, "We're sure gonna run out of luck quick if we keep using it up at this rate."[13]

The bombings intensified to the extent that Devereux eventually had to move his command post to a safer location. On December 14, he abandoned the dugout near Camp 1 and shifted into the concrete magazine next to Cunningham's at the eastern edge of the airstrip. All four concrete structures now housed men—Dr. Shank's civilian hospital occupied the northernmost one, followed by Cunningham's and Devereux's command posts, then Kahn's military hospital at the southernmost bunker.

After each bombing, Lieutenant Hanna communicated by phone with each position under his command to check on casualties. After relaying the information to Devereux, he visited his fifty men, believing they received a boost from his physical presence. Hanna made a point of talking to each individual for a few moments to relax him, then moved on to the next foxhole along Wake's southern beach.

Captain Platt did the same on Wilkes Island, emerging from his dugout almost before the final bomb hit to see how his men fared. Nineteen-year-old Pfc. William F. Buehler later recalled a conversation with Platt following a raid. "He came by my foxhole and asked if anyone wanted a cigarette," mentioned Buehler. "He was very calm and said, 'If you get into the foxhole, you're pretty safe. There isn't much else we can do, so take cover and stay in there until the all-clear. Unless you get a direct hit.' He sort of looked off in the distance, and he said, 'I guess if you're that unlucky, perhaps goddammit, you're supposed to die.' "[14]

The daily bombings offered a mixed menu of terror, courage, and humor. The civilians manning the gun at Battery D, who had earlier incurred Johnalson Wright's wrath for ineptness, now made it a point of honor to remain at their gun until every Marine had departed. One time Sgt. Raymon Gragg, who wore earphones as captain of a 3-inch gun, raced to the dugout as bombs exploded, but was jerked to the ground only five feet from the entrance. In the excitement he had forgotten to remove his set of earphones, and a balky cord slammed him down.

Joe Goicoechea, who spent his time on both Wake and Peale Islands, crept over to where his friend, George Rosendick, huddled, intending to visit his buddy. "I snuck over there, and a goddamn raid came over. One guy went crazy. I just dove under a little bush, and I told George I'd never come back because of that crazy civilian. I saw another guy do the same — go nuts. One Marine lost it, too. Most men held their own pretty good, though."[15]

Some went to extreme measures to provide for their safety. John Rogge was walking near a warehouse one day when he thought he saw a head sticking out of the sand. When he veered over to investigate, he recognized the civilian dentist. The man had dug a hole in the dirt so deep that only his head showed.

During raids, Pfc. Verne L. Wallace often thought of a 1940 day in Philadelphia, Pennsylvania, when he and a friend discussed joining the Marines. His friend claimed Wallace was too small to be a part of such a heralded outfit but Wallace, fortified with a few beers, bet the bulkier man he could do it. The pair walked over to a recruiting station, where the Marine officer accepted Wallace into the Corps while rejecting Wallace's friend. Now, in the middle of bursting bombs and shrapnel, Wallace wondered if he had, indeed, won the bet. He remarked to a Marine next to him,

"Every time I'm under fire I keep thinking, 'What the hell am I doing here? I ought to be in Philadelphia!' "[16]

One constant sight reassured those in the immediate vicinity of Battery D—during every raid, in spite of every bomb, Sgt. Johnalson Wright stood outside the dugout near his gun, squeezing the lucky dollar from Nicaragua. The hefty Marine claimed that the dugout cramped his style and was too crowded, but his men knew the real reasons—he did not want to take up so much space in an already-congested dugout, and he had trouble squeezing through the opening. If anyone tried to entice the sergeant inside, Wright told him to mind his own business. His lucky dollar would pull him through.

Magicians at the Airfield

Little except miracles and earnest wishes appeared to help at the airstrip, where Lieutenant Kinney and a handful of mechanics, including civilians Fred S. Gibbons and his son George, labored to keep the remaining two aircraft flying. Kinney understood what the fighters meant to the men on Wake—as long as the aircraft rose to meet the enemy, the Japanese first had to barge through them before attacking the atoll. He and the others worked ceaselessly to repair damaged aircraft or to fashion workable planes out of spare parts.

As was true of most men on Wake, Kinney had to improvise to keep an air force going. He borrowed an air compressor from the former Pan Am facility to help dislodge sand buildups in engines. He scrounged for parts in wrecked Wildcats that he could use in operating planes. He so often patched together aircraft that some wondered how the makeshift planes could even fly.

One day the supply of oxygen for the aviators ran out, meaning the pilots could no longer fly at the higher altitudes demanded to meet Japanese bombers. Lieutenant Freuler solved the dilemma by arranging a manner of switching welding oxygen from their storage cylinders to the smaller containers used by VMF-211. The aircraft may not have won any contests for their appearances, but as far as the military and civilians were concerned, those two Wildcats were true beauties.

Putnam and other officers heaped praise on Kinney and his crew. Major Walter L. Bayler, who worked in communications, called them "magicians" whose efficient work must have made the Japanese think "we were turning out planes from some assembly line concealed in the woods." Major Putnam bestowed even higher accolades, calling their work the "outstanding event of the whole campaign." In a report after the war, Putnam stated, "With almost no tools and a complete lack of normal equipment, they performed all types of repair and replacement work. They changed engines and propellers from one airplane to another, and even completely built up new engines and propellers from scrap parts salvaged from wrecks. They replaced minor parts and assemblies, and repaired damage to fuselages and wings and landing gear; all this in spite of the fact that they were working with new types [of aircraft] with which they had no previous experience and were without instruction manuals of any kind."[17]

Despite their labors, Lieutenant Kinney and the others could not compete against repeated enemy attacks, a lack of spare parts, and increasing damage. On December 17, an accumulation of coral sand ruined the engine of one Wildcat, temporarily reducing Wake's air arm to one fighter. The day they could no longer field an air force had almost arrived.

"Some Deserve Credit and Some Don't"

Unique to Wake is how the civilian and military worlds merged in time of need to help one another battle a common foe. Marines, Navy, and Army units stationed at the atoll entered the service knowing that one day they might have to fight for their country. The workers who signed on with Morrison-Knudsen had no such understanding.

From the conflict's initial moments on December 8 until the final battle on Wake, civilians contributed in numerous ways, including fighting. John O'Neal continued to perform the religious functions that he started with the December 11 burial service. He frequently shuffled from foxhole to foxhole, inquiring how each man was and if he needed anything. He could not provide anything material, but the moral boost and spiritual contributions benefited many of the men.

To free the military for defense purposes, Cunningham asked Dan Teters to handle the food for all 1,600 men. Teters not only opened his supplies of rations, candy, and clothing to the military, but "Dan Teters's Catering Service" picked up food cooked in the civilian mess and trucked meals out to the soldiers and civilian volunteers manning the guns. Twice each day, before the sun rose and after it set so a Japanese scout plane could not follow a truck and detect one of the hidden gun positions, civilians brought welcome provisions to the men. They dropped off the food at determined locations, then one man from each gun headed out to retrieve it.

The system worked fairly well, although deficiencies existed. Some of the food was barely edible, especially the chocolate bars, which became worm-infested in the humid conditions. Military and civilian volunteers manning the guns believed they deserved the food more than the men who willingly chose to hide in the brush. On Wilkes, for instance, Captain Platt ordered that if any civilian wanted to eat, he had to work at one of the guns. When he needed more workers on Peale Island to construct defenses, Captain Godbold collected all the food and threatened to give it only to those who volunteered. Seventy-five men soon arrived and helped build a dugout.

Men supplemented their diets in different ways. Out on Peacock Point, where the men were a bit farther removed from the road, Corporal Gross's crew often went hungry when the men sent to retrieve the food arrived at the drop-off point and found most of it gone. Fortunately, a civilian named Sonny Kaiser headed out each day, in complete disregard for his safety, scrounged around the buildings, and returned with beans, fish, candy, or other items.

"He was a godsend to us," explained Gross. "We were at the end of the chow line, and they all but forgot about us, so he'd go out and come back with canned goods, cigarettes, and candy while we were on position those days."[18]

Joe Goicoechea, never one to remain still when something can be done, took an abandoned truck out one day to load up on food. While two men stood on each side of the cab, ready to bang on the doors if a Japanese bomber appeared, Goicoechea dodged bomb craters along a tortuous route to a warehouse, where the men piled boxes of canned juice, milk, and cigarettes into the vehicle.

More civilians contributed to the defense of Wake than is often assumed. Murray Kidd claimed that everyone he knew worked at something, whether it was actually manning a gun or helping fortify a position. Each evening the civilians gathered at some location, such as the airfield, where they received their jobs for the night. Usually it entailed strengthening defenses or moving guns. "Someone would come get us to do the work," said Kidd. "Every night we sandbagged, moved guns, or whatever the military needed. I never got on any gun. Very few men did get on the guns. We just did what they told us to do. All the guys I knew helped out. A lot of the others didn't."[19]

Just under 200 civilians manned various military posts around the atoll. Another 250 helped dig shelters, sandbag gun positions, or complete other construction work that aided the military. Altogether, 450 out of 1,100 civilians, or just over 40 percent, participated in some fashion.

Most, however, did not. Some Marines claimed they could already point to examples of where the civilians abandoned them. Marines stationed closer to the points of the heaviest bombings, such as those near the airfield or at Barninger's Battery A at Peacock Point, received fewer food deliveries than those in relatively calm sectors. Major Putnam badly needed work done at the airstrip, but saw the numbers of civilian helpers dwindle as the bombings intensified, particularly following night raids. Each time the Japanese executed such an attack, the civilians headed for the brush and refused to come back out until dawn, costing Putnam a full night's labor. He even asked permission from Commander Cunningham to let him organize armed groups of Marines who could head into the brush and force the civilians to come out and help. "Dammit, they've got to hold up their end!"[20] he shouted.

Cunningham knew that many of the civilians appeared only at food time, but he wisely denied the request. He sympathized with their feelings that they had been cheated by not being evacuated in time and that their futures had been affected by a war they had not expected, and he wondered what Putnam's Marines would do if they met with resistance from the civilians. Eventually, Dan Teters promised to deliver more men by personally appealing to their sense of duty, a promise he fulfilled.

On Wilkes, Corporal Johnson supervised four civilians manning machine guns. Three men cooperated and followed Johnson's orders, especially Leo Nonn, who always seemed to ask questions and volunteer to do things, but the fourth, Johnson said, "irritated the hell out of me. Every morning he would get out his contract [with Morrison-Knudsen] and show me where it stated that in case of hostilities, the civilians would be removed. I finally stopped it one morning by telling him two of the things you need that first disappear in battle are soap and toilet tissue. I told him, 'Hold on to that contract and all you got to worry about is soap.' After that he didn't show it to me too often."[21]

The feelings toward the civilians ranged from the outright harsh to the sympathetic. Most Marines recognized that the civilians had not bargained for a battle, but also wished they had received more help. Pfc. Jesse Nowlin castigated the civilians as a "thieving, stealing, disruptive, unruly, disorganized mob that came out like a pack of rats at night and ripped and raided and caused an inordinate amount of trouble that we at that time were not in a position to deal with."[22] The situation created a dilemma for the military. When the real fighting occurred—the expected second landing attempt—who could the military count on, and how many would be there? The lack of participation by so many civilians is a point that irritates some Marines to this day, who wonder whether the civilians who headed to the brush had "chickened" out when the military most needed them.

On the other hand, Lieutenant Hanna typified how the majority seemed to feel at the time. Hanna stated three of the four men who served near him were superb fighters, but he sure could have used more help. "I could understand some of them, with the fact they weren't trained and knew nothing about what was going on. The bombing they received wasn't conducive to good morale. I wished more had fought, but I understand why they didn't. Some of the men deserve credit and some don't. The ones that stayed in the brush don't deserve more credit, but some helped quite a bit."[23]

Private First Class Gatewood agreed that most civilians remained in the brush instead of helping. "We were kind of mad about it, but hey, they wasn't in the service to protect, so it was up to them if they wanted to do something."[24]

Marines lavished praise on those who volunteered, however. An officer walked over to a machine gun manned by civilian John M. Valov and a few other Morrison-Knudsen workers, slapped them on the back, and called them true Americans. Lieutenant Kessler complimented the bravery of the civilians who showed up at his guns. They asked for rifles, but when none were available, they were given three boxes of hand grenades and taught how to use them. However, Kessler had choice words for the others. "After the bombs started to fall, many of the summer soldiers disappeared into the brush, not to be seen again during the fight."[25]

Even Major Devereux stated similar thoughts. He sorely needed additional men, but he understood why many chose to avoid the battle. Instead of criticizing, he diplomatically claimed that the arduous days on Wake only made the contributions of those civilians who helped all the more admirable. In light of the heavy fighting and the possibility of worse to come, it is not surprising that many men remained hidden.

"Send Us More Japs"

For the twelve days of the siege, contact with families back home came to a standstill. With near-daily bombings and a second invasion attempt expected at any time, no mail could be flown in or out. As a result, families had no way of knowing about their loved ones on Wake, and the defenders could only guess how their families fared. Lieutenant Hanna yearned to let Vera know he was fine, but he had to settle for hoping she coped with the situation and assumed her husband lived. People like Vera and Pearl Ann existed on the morsels of information about the atoll they read in newspapers, which was not much, and clung to the belief that Lieutenant Hanna and J. O. Young would return to them.

For information back home, the men on Wake listened to radio broadcasts, a very unreliable source. The Army communications unit filtered some news to the men, while a handful of Marines listened to programs over their own receivers. They did not always appreciate what they heard. One radio commentator drew derisive laughter when he likened the Wake defenders to the biblical David challenging Goliath. Lieutenant Kinney listened in astonishment as a reporter stated that while no one knew how many Americans fought at Wake, the number had to be small. The United States military had never released details of the size of the military contingent on Wake, but now Kinney listened as a fellow American openly divulged material that could help the enemy and adversely affect his future.

In one of the first days of the siege, Private First Class Gatewood learned that excited Americans had given the Wake Islanders a nickname, an appellation acknowledging their heroic defense and the inspiration they breathed into United States society. "The first word we got was when that crew from the radio trailer told us we were known as the Alamo of the Pacific."[26] Gatewood enjoyed the comparison but hoped he experienced a happier outcome than the fighters in 1836.

Radio also brought good news, however, and let the defenders know they had not been forgotten. Hans Whitney heard a news announcer say, "That faraway little garrison of Wake Island is still holding out, with her handful of Marines, even after raid upon raid of Jap bombers."[27] Members of the Army and Navy units stationed on Wake, as well as the many civilians who helped, chafed at the lack of mention of their presence while the Marines received the accolades, but at least they realized the home front cared for the events taking place.

On December 13, the famous band leader, Kay Kyser, dedicated a song to the men at Wake. Pfc. Max J. Dana, on duty at his machine gun on Wilkes Island, surreptitiously listened over the open communications line as Major Devereux and Captain Platt discussed the issue. "Hey, Captain, we had a song dedicated to us on the radio," said Major Devereux. "Kay Kyser on his program dedicated a song to the Wake Island Marines."

Captain Platt, who impressed everyone with his dry wit, replied in his slow Southern drawl, "What did they play, taps?"[28] His reference to the traditional military tune played at burial ceremonies cast a realistic bent on the event, while at least producing smiles on Devereux's and Dana's faces.

Each day the men of Wake held on, they more firmly embedded themselves in the nation's consciousness, especially after one of the greatest propaganda stunts, however unintentional, of World War II. Shortly after the December 11 attack, Cunningham transmitted a message to Pearl Harbor. As was common in those days, the men operating the radio transmitter, in this case Ens. George H. Henshaw and Ens. Bernard J. Lauff, added what was called padding, or nonsense words, to the front and back of the message, to confuse the Japanese and to make it more difficult to successfully translate the information. On one of their messages, the pair added the words SEND US to the front and the words MORE JAPS to the end. Someone at Pearl Harbor lifted the four words, combined them into one phrase, and instantly created a new national rallying cry. Americans did not learn until after the war that Devereux had never uttered the phrase, but by that time the slogan's impact had long had its effect.

The American media transformed the slogan into one of the war's most famous retorts. According to most major radio programs, newspapers, and magazines, when Pearl Harbor asked Major Devereux if he needed anything, he replied, "Send us more Japs." The slogan raced across the United States, with citizens reveling in the defiant nature of the response. Newspapers splashed the phrase across their front pages and magazines devoted articles to its supposed origin. Tiny Wake, already renowned for producing the war's first victory, now had given the nation a slogan. Outnumbered and outsupplied, the gritty little Major Devereux and his battlers had an answer for the arrogant Japanese, who had enjoyed nothing but victory until now: Send us more, and we will destroy them. Americans adopted it as a national retort to the enemy. It typified the manner in which the nation wanted to believe its soldiers would fight—determined, aggressive, insolent—not the way the war had begun at Pearl Harbor. "Send us more Japs" quickly took its place alongside "I have not yet begun to fight," "I only regret that I have but one life to lose for my country," and other heralded slogans from American military history.

"From the little band of professionals on Wake Island came an impudently defiant message phrased for history," boasted *Time* magazine. "Wake's Marines were asked by radio what they needed. The answer made old Marines' chests grow under their campaign bars: 'Send us more Japs.' "[29]

While Americans celebrated the phrase, the men on Wake reacted incredulously to the news that their nation had rallied behind what they considered an absurd phrase. Tired, hungry, dirty, and facing a second round with a brutal foe, the last thing any servicemen or construction workers wanted was more Japanese. Major Devereux claimed they already had enough, and Commander Cunningham stated that only a person with a death wish would send such a message.

The men understood the importance of propaganda, but this involved their own skins. Would the rallying cry prod the enemy to greater effort? "When we heard that slogan we said, 'Who in the crap said that! He's out of his gourd!' " explained Corporal Marvin. "We figured it was the newspapers that did that. They were trying to get the United States all worked up, get more people involved."[30]

"An Epic in American Military History"

The slogan, while dominating the news of Wake for a time, was not the only item of information the home front received about Wake. For the duration of the fighting, Vera, Pearl Ann, and the entire nation bled with the men on Wake. They could not comprehend what their loved ones endured, for one has to be in combat to understand that, but as Lieutenant Hanna, Corporal Holewinski, Joe Goicoechea, and the other defenders shook off the dust from the daily Japanese bombings, citizens in the United States avidly followed developments.

Since the U.S. government and its military could not divulge many details, both for security reasons and because they lacked specific information, family members of Wake defenders relied on radio, newspapers, and magazines for information. Daily newspapers yielded the bulk of the information, and as Vera or Pearl Ann read each day's developments, their emotions fluctuated from despair to hope, fear to joy.

Headlines on December 9, for instance, hardly reassured family members when they proclaimed, WAKE AND GUAM REPORTED TAKEN.[31] At that time it appeared Wake had succumbed to the Japanese, as had other places, but worse, the articles provided no details on what had happened to specific individuals. Their loved ones fought on an island in an ocean that bordered the U.S. West Coast, but as far as family were concerned, the men might as well have been on Jupiter. They could do nothing but wait each day, latch on to anything that appeared positive, and hope that additional good news would arrive.

The first specific information arrived on December 11, when Capt. John H. Hamilton landed the Pan American *Clipper* on San Francisco Bay after his harrowing flight out of Wake. Newspapers, including Pearl Ann's *Idaho Daily Statesman* in Boise, ran lengthy stories in which Hamilton described the December 8 attack and showed reporters the sixteen Japanese bullet holes that ornamented his aircraft. Pearl Ann could not have taken comfort in his remark that the Japanese opened by machine-gunning the civilian camp, but at least Hamilton added that morale was high on Wake.

Newspaper reporting over the coming days offered a mixture of hope and doom. On December 12, the *Detroit Free Press* stated that Washington officials, including President Roosevelt, assumed the Wake defenders would die, but that their efforts would not be in vain, for "here in one of the Nation's most remote possessions men have repelled the attack of the Nipponese." Although the newspaper claimed "They must die," the *Free Press* stated that "every American may well be proud of the Alamo of the Pacific—Wake Island."[32]

A headline in the *New York Times* read, MARINES KEEP WAKE, and mentioned in an article that "the American flag up to noon yesterday was still flying over Wake Island." The reporter ended less optimistically by stating, "Wake may be captured; its capture, indeed, had long been anticipated, but if its 'leathernecks' add another glorious chapter to their history and inflict further losses on the enemy, they will not have died in vain." The *Washington Post* labeled Wake "the stage for an epic in American military history, one of those gallant stands such as led Texans 105 years ago to cry, 'Remember the Alamo!' " The paper added that when news of the December 11 victory arrived in the State Department press room in Washington, D.C., reporters turned their thumbs upward and created a new victory slogan, "Wake up!"[33]

Headlines over the next few days claimed that WAKE AND MIDWAY HOLD OUT, JAPS AGAIN RAIN BOMBS ON ISLAND, and U.S. MARINES STILL FIGHTING TO SAVE WAKE. The *Detroit Free Press* praised what it called "The valiant back-to-the-wall Marine Devil Dogs on Wake Island" for their spirited defense.[34]

Morale and pride soared every time that Americans opened their newspapers or listened to the radio as reporters described another setback for the Japanese attempt to take Wake. Each additional day the stand lasted, each hour the men on Wake held on, nudged the home front further from the shock of Pearl Harbor and closer to optimism.

For instance, in a December 16 article under the banner, MARINES ARE STILL THERE, the *New York Times* remarked that the stand at Wake "cheered the capital and perplexed military strategists" who had earlier abandoned hope for the atoll. "It had been contended that the outposts could not be successfully defended, but the Marines are still there. What price they are paying has not been revealed."[35]

From the home front vantage, the outlook improved over the next few days. On December 17 came news of Devereux's reported answer, "Send us some more Japs." Two days later the Marine newspaper at the Quantico Marine Base in Virginia, the *Quantico Sentry*, boasted that IN THE PACIFIC "OUR FLAG IS STILL THERE."[36]

"What the Hell Did You Expect the Marines to Do?"

Citizens in the United States, energized by the boost in morale, exploded in extraordinary displays of patriotism and national fervor. Wake became a symbol of defiance for all. The slogan "Remember Wake!" influenced young men to enlist, and posters bearing the image of a Marine and that slogan blanketed the United States.

"America remembers Wake Island and is proud. The enemy remembers Wake Island and is uneasy," wrote Marine Comdt. Maj. Gen. Thomas Holcomb.[37] People wrote letters to the editors of newspapers urging everyone to "Wake! America!" and begging for increased production of tanks, airplanes, guns, and ammunition. They pointed to Wake as an example of how Americans fight when under pressure.

Political cartoonists included Wake in their drawings. One pictured three sinking ships off the coast of a small island bearing a sign, WAKE ISLAND—U.S. MARINES ONLY! Others showed a Marine standing amidst smoking ruins on the island and raising a defiant fist toward the heavens, or a hand writing the name "Wake Island" to a lengthy list of previous Marine glories. Another pictured a Marine writing a letter to Santa Claus in which he asked for more Japs.

(National Archives)

A Chicago police officer helped resolve a labor dispute at a defense plant when he remarked to picketing machinists that if the men on Wake Island could fight so courageously, the least they could do was settle their differences with management. Dr. Walter Snyder of the University of Richmond in Virginia compared the heroism at Wake to that shown by the Spartans at Thermopylae, when three hundred Greeks gave their lives to save their country.

Amateur poets used Wake to inspire the nation. Harry H. Scarritt penned the poem "David Crockett's Spirit," in which the spirit of the famed battler of the Alamo looked down from heaven as the Japanese assaulted Wake on December 11. In the poem, Davey Crockett admired the Americans' fighting spirit and accurate shooting, then promised to shake the hand of each defender who perished on the island. Other poets compared Wake to soul-stirring battles in American history, such as Lexington, Saratoga, and San Juan Hill.

Recruiting centers enjoyed a bonanza, in part because of Wake. In Los Angeles, former world heavyweight boxing champion Gene Tunney swore 385 men, supposedly equal to the number of Marines and Navy on Wake, into the Navy. The men first formed a huge W for Wake, then repeated the oath in unison. *Time* reported that in Waterloo, Iowa, five Sullivan brothers enlisted in the Naval Reserve together. (Sadly, on November 13, 1942, all five died when a Japanese torpedo sank their ship, the cruiser USS *Juneau*, off Guadalcanal in the South Pacific.)

Hollywood chipped in by starting work on the first of what would become the major wartime movies. On December 17, the same day that the American public learned of the "Send us more Japs" quotation, Paramount Pictures announced plans for a motion picture about Wake. To be based on a screenplay by W. R. Burnett and Frank Butler and tentatively starring Brian Donlevy, Robert Preston, and William Bendix, Paramount hoped to have the film in theaters by the summer of 1942.

In the publicity that surrounded Wake, the Marines received the lion's share of accolades, while the nation's media ignored Navy, Army, and civilian personnel in their reporting of the Wake story. Why? That occurred, in part, because the defense of the atoll, the portion of the story containing the most gripping drama and thus the feature that received the heaviest publicity, had been assigned to the Marines. The Navy, on the other hand, staffed the seaplane base, and the six Army personnel maintained the radio communications for the Army Air Forces bombers. The Marines served in combat roles, the "glamorous" assignments as far as reporters were concerned, and were mentioned more frequently.

Second, the public associated the Navy with the disaster at Pearl Harbor, where the military had been caught off guard and where the nation had absorbed a hard blow. A few days later they learned that Wake, manned largely by Marines, had scored a triumph. While the Navy bore the stigma of disaster at Pearl Harbor, the Marines hoisted the banner of victory.

An astute Marine public relations department quickly jumped on the national enthusiasm for the leathernecks. The department issued daily bulletins apprising the country of Wake's progress and worked with the news media to publicize the feats of Captain Elrod, Lieutenant Kliewer, and the rest. Bombastic statements by top Marine officers cast the Devil Dogs in heroic terms. "What the hell did you expect the Marines to do? Take it lying down?"[38] said Marine Comdt. Maj. Gen. Thomas Holcomb in *Time*.

A proud heritage also contributed to the Marines' overshadowing their compatriots on Wake. The Corps enjoyed a reputation as being the nation's elite combat force, established by triumphs on battlefields far and wide. The atmosphere in the nation that the Marines represented what was best in the military made it easier for people to accept that Wake, too, was a Marine domain.

"Surely, Help Would Come from Pearl Harbor"

Stirring battle cries and exultation back home did little to aid the men on Wake, though. Ammunition, weapons, and aircraft meant more. Some were available, but how could a Navy weakened by December 7 ship the needed reinforcements and supplies to Wake while protecting Hawaii and the West Coast from Japanese aggression? Much of the fleet lay on Pearl Harbor's bottom, and the main weapons remaining—three aircraft carriers—could not be carelessly expended. Navy officials knew, however, that the American public demanded a victory to avenge Pearl Harbor, and they could hardly stand by and do nothing while America's first heroes succumbed.

Wake's military expected the Navy to come to their aid. After all, that is what fellow servicemen do. They had battled the Japanese on behalf of their nation, so it was only logical to assume their nation would do everything possible to save them. As long as the defenders believed help would come, they were never totally cut off from the outside world, and they could more easily accept the severe conditions. Each day that unfolded without help arriving, the sense of isolation gripped Wake more tightly.

In fact, at Pearl Harbor, Pacific Fleet Comdr. Husband E. Kimmel had already prepared a daring plan to relieve Wake centering on the aircraft carrier *Saratoga*. Even before the war, Kimmel had foreseen that Wake could present an opportunity to engage the Japanese fleet, and he now seized his chance. He issued orders forming Task Force 14, commanded by Rear Adm. Frank Jack Fletcher. Besides the *Saratoga*, three heavy cruisers, nine destroyers, one seaplane tender, and one oiler would rush additional supplies to Wake. Kimmel understood the risks involved should a stronger enemy naval force appear, but he felt the impact on morale for both the military and the public back home outweighed the negatives. Help was coming to Wake.

On December 12, two hundred Marines of the Fourth Defense Battalion began boarding the seaplane tender *Tangier* for shipment to the atoll. In addition to the Marines, Navy crews loaded onto the ship nine thousand rounds of 5-inch shells, twelve thousand rounds of 3-inch shells, over three million rounds of belted machine gun ammunition, boxes of hand grenades, barbed wire, mines, and pistols, and replacement parts for Wake's damaged guns. Excited Navy personnel on shore yelled "Good-bye and give 'em hell!"[39] as the ships pulled away on December 15, bursting with men and war matériel.

Back on Wake, Marines impatiently watched and waited. "Why the hell doesn't somebody come out and help us fight?"[40] Captain Elrod asked Major Devereux. His answer seemed to be steaming its way west.

CHAPTER 7

★

"They Don't Guarantee You're Coming Back"

"Foggy Blur of Days and Nights"

If the Japanese were the main enemy for the men on Wake, fatigue came in a close second. Rested men fight better and think more clearly, but as the siege wound into its second week, the demands made on the men left no time for sleep. A succession of mentally and physically exhausting days sapped their energy—they stood guard, ate cold food, hoped to avoid Japanese bombs, stood guard some more, stole a few moments of sleep, then awoke to repeat the process all over again.

Men already weakened from poor diet and battling to contain their fears still had work to do. They had to constantly search the sky for signs of approaching aircraft. The strain caused men to imagine things—flocks of birds became a squadron of Japanese bombers, for instance. False alarms frequently interrupted the defenders' routine and cut into badly needed rest.

The bombing raids became more difficult to endure. Since Japanese aircraft could suddenly appear at any time, the men could never relax. In a diary he kept on Wake, Private First Class John R. Himelrick mentioned bombing raids on ten of the eleven days from December 12 to December 22. "At 0515 this morning a jap [sic] 'P' Boat came over very high and dropped a few bombs," he wrote on December 12. Two days later, he added that aircraft attacked the beach near his position by the airfield and that "Some came too Darn Close for comfort." On December 17, he admitted "They are sure getting regular" and that when the Marines expected a raid "everythings quiet as hell just before a raid & the Boys stay pretty close to their dugouts."[1]

The men stared from gun positions, foxholes, and dugouts with blank expressions. Their bodies and muscles yearned for rest, but that was an unaffordable luxury. Sleep would come at a later date, when the outcome had been settled.

Major Devereux called this time the "foggy blur of days and nights when time stood still," a period when men pined for sleep, yet willingly went without. "The days blurred together in a dreary sameness of bombing and endless work and always that aching need for sleep," wrote Major Devereux. "I have seen men standing with their eyes open, staring at nothing, and they did not hear me when I spoke to them. They were out on their feet. They became so punch-drunk from weariness that frequently a man would forget an order almost as soon as he turned away. He would have to come back later and ask what you wanted him to do, and sometimes it was hard for you to remember."[2]

The longest period of uninterrupted sleep Devereux enjoyed during the siege was two hours, and the men and officers under his command had little more. Devereux once issued an order to his executive officer, Maj. George H. Potter, and then left for Commander Cunningham's command post in the concrete bunker adjoining his. By the time he arrived, Potter was on the telephone, asking the major to repeat what he had just told him. Lack of sleep impaired Potter's power of concentration.

Lieutenant Hanna managed an hour here and there in between his duties overseeing the atoll's machine guns. As was true with every man, he rarely left his post, meaning he could never allow his concentration to slip. "You didn't dare relax at any time. I actually slept on my feet sometimes. I might be standing there talking to somebody, and the next thing you knew you drifted off, then you snapped your eyes open and left off where you were."[3]

Corporal Johnson always took the 8:00 P.M. to midnight and the 4:00 A.M. to 8:00 A.M. watches instead of giving them to the civilian volunteers because he feared they might fall asleep. He considered those times the most likely periods for a landing attempt, and he wanted to be sure someone dependable stood guard and was ready to respond. To make sure he did not nod off, Johnson periodically pressed his bayonet against his thigh or leg hard enough to produce a sensation of pain but without drawing blood.

Drowsiness overcame nearly every man at one time or another. During one nighttime outing to locate food, Joe Goicoechea, exhausted from his duties, slumped to the harsh coral surface and dozed off for an hour on the uncomfortable terrain. Pfc. Jacob R. Sanders dived under a truck after being caught in the open by a bombing raid, then quickly fell into a deep slumber, oblivious of the exploding bombs.

The effects of fear and a sense of isolation compounded the problems caused by exhaustion. The defenders faced an array of unspoken fears—

fear of death, fear of capture, fear of failing their fellow Americans when the fighting began, fear of losing what they now had. On top of that, each day the men's world seemed to shrink more and more until it became the few feet around their foxhole or gun; each day home and help seemed more distant. Trapped in the middle of an ever-increasingly Japanese ocean, it was as if a noose slowly tightened around their necks, and only help from Hawaii could save them. But would relief puncture through the enemy and arrive in time?

Under the stressful conditions, men could not control their emotions as they would in normal circumstances. Tempers flared and men argued. In Dan Teters's presence, Major Putnam and Commander Cunningham engaged in a heated exchange.

But it was fear with which they most grappled. Experienced soldiers like Johnalson Wright and Major Putnam, who had fought in Nicaragua and seen men die, could more easily handle fear, but many Americans on Wake, like Joe Goicoechea and Corporal Holewinski, had come straight out of high school. Before December 8, the worst crisis they confronted concerned girls or alcohol. Now they faced an enemy who wanted to kill them.

"It was fear for everybody, including myself," claimed Corporal Johnson. "You were especially afraid after dark. You had to control yourself because you kept seeing things in the bushes. You had to tell yourself the Japanese couldn't get on here."[4] One time Johnson and another Marine heard scratching noises along the shoreline. When they carefully inched away from their machine guns to investigate, they discovered the noise had been caused by a bunch of hermit crabs.

Standing guard at night proved particularly hard for the men, both civilian and military. Civilian Earl Row called his time walking the beach on Peale Island on night patrol one of the worst experiences of his life, because imagination transformed every shadow into a Japanese soldier.

Corporal Marvin was nearing the end of his watch one night when he heard something move in the darkness. As the noise grew louder, Marvin tightened his hold on his rifle, then ordered the man to halt and repeat the password. "He threw up that Springfield rifle and he said, 'You tell me first.' I said, 'Christ, put that thing down.'" Both men were so frightened they had forgotten the password and had no idea how to respond. "This was after we had the December 11 battle with the ships, and we figured maybe some of the Japs had washed ashore."[5]

To make sure his men did not become paralyzed by fear, Lieutenant Hanna kept them busy filling sandbags and doing other tasks. Corporal Holewinski maintained a constant chatter about any topic that came to mind, such as how long the war might last or when the Navy would arrive, and Corporal Johnson diverted attention by casually chatting with his men about items he knew would take their minds off their predicament: "I tried to keep their minds on activities, on what we were gonna do when we arrived home, other diversionary talks. Some were going to a baseball game. I said I was going to the Ozarks to hunt squirrels. I felt it was my duty to do this to calm them down and take their minds off the situation as much as possible. I guess every person in war thinks every bullet and bomb is coming right at him, but you have to realize how minute you as an individual are compared to all the space around you. We tried to get that."[6]

One night after finishing work at a 5-inch gun at Peacock Point, a sergeant told Joe Goicoechea that some food had been stored near the airfield and he could head over there if he liked. Goicoechea lost no time and, in the darkness, cautiously crept through some brush near the road separating the gun position from the airfield. Suddenly a pair of Marines, rifles in hand, rose and asked Goicoechea where he was going. When he explained his reason for being out at night, they eased their guard and Goicoechea proceeded to the airfield. "God, were they scared. So was I," said Goicoechea later. "They called me every damn name you can think of. You talk about nervous? They were nervous, too. Everybody was scared, and anyone who says he wasn't hasn't been to the confessional for a while."[7]

Physical maladies compounded the mental torments. Almost every man on the atoll, civilian and military alike, suffered from diarrhea brought on by improper sanitation practices. The military knew to dig trenches for field sanitation, but many of the civilians in the brush urinated and defecated in the open. That attracted flies, which quickly spread disease to every point.

The inability to thoroughly wash themselves increased both the discomfort and the chances for illness. In most cases wearing the same clothes they donned on December 8 and showing the stubble from eight or ten days' growth on their chins, the disheveled men adapted, but not much helped. Private First Class Gatewood used a five-gallon can of water and his helmet to clean up whenever he could. Goicoechea claimed that the men were so busy being scared that washing was not a priority, which in turn created an offensive odor in the cramped spaces of shelters. He and the others with him solved the problem by spreading oakum, a pleasant-smelling compound used by plumbers, all around their dugout.

"An Ever-Increasing Apprehension"

As Christmas approached, one topic dominated every discussion on Wake—when would the United States Navy bring reinforcements? The men had an easier time early in the siege, believing that relief would arrive, but as they grew wearier, their mood turned more pessimistic. Construction engineer John R. Burroughs wrote that "as time wore on, one question loomed in the minds of civilians and servicemen alike: 'Where, in Christ's name, was the U.S. Navy?' When would our people send reinforcements?"[8]

On December 12 the men thought they had to hold on for only a few days before help arrived. Six days later they faced the possibility they could be left on their own. Burroughs referred to an "ever-increasing apprehension. The feeling of exhilaration arising from our success in the battle of December 11 had worn off." More and more, Major Devereux acted according to a Marine adage, "Maybe you oughta get more, maybe you will get more, but all you can depend on getting is what you already got."[9]

Superiors in Pearl Harbor could not provide a definite answer about when relief would come. After sailors loaded ammunition and other supplies aboard the seaplane tender and Marines filed onto the *Tangier*, the relief force remained at anchor pending the arrival of another aircraft carrier, due in any day from California. In the meantime, Wake waited.

Instead of the welcome news about the Navy rushing to Wake's aid, Commander Cunningham received routine messages from his superiors asking about conditions on the atoll. The most frustrating one came from an admiral who inquired about the completion date for the dredging operations begun before the war. Cunningham stewed over this transmission before sending a restrained reply that since December 8, he had been quite busy conducting Wake's defenses. He could not predict any completion date, but mentioned that prospects for its finish would dramatically improve if the Japanese stopped their daily bombing attacks.

In subsequent communications, Cunningham informed Pearl Harbor that almost every structure on the atoll had been either destroyed or damaged, including the main warehouse, barracks, aviation facilities, and machine shop. Japanese bombs demolished half his heavy equipment and trucks, 80 percent of his diesel oil, and much of his dynamite.

Cunningham alerted Pearl Harbor that if Wake was to remain in U.S. hands, the civilians had to be speedily evacuated. Most did little but hide in the brush, yet they still had to be fed. Cunningham believed he and Devereux could better focus on defending Wake if they did not have to worry about the civilians.

Cunningham's superior, Rear Adm. Claude C. Bloch, responded on December 17 that Cunningham should begin organizing for a possible civilian evacuation, but to retain about 250 skilled laborers who would be needed to complete the construction projects. Bloch hoped that enough civilians would volunteer to remain so the military would not have to force men to stay.

*   *   *

Time ran short for Wake. An ominous development brewed in the Pacific Ocean on December 16, when two Japanese aircraft carriers, on their way back as part of the assault on Pearl Harbor, detached from the victorious unit and veered southwest toward Wake. When they steamed within air range, 118 fighters and dive-bombers would be able to blast Wake, supplement the daily bombing raids already in progress, and support a landing assault. The Japanese circle surrounding Wake suddenly drew tighter.

Three days later, Japanese bombers added another alarming factor when they dropped potent thousand-pound bombs in their raids. The 132-pound bombs previously used, terrifying enough in their own right, now had a more destructive weapon as an ally. The monster bombs smacked with such an intimidating violence that they created holes seven feet deep and thirty feet wide. Marines and civilians, already numbed by the week-long aerial barrage, abandoned their dugouts and flopped into foxholes out of fear that the dugouts would collapse under the more powerful explosions. Just when the defenders thought conditions could get no worse, the Japanese fine-tuned their bombings to a new intensity that made wooden crossbeamed, dirt-covered shelters appear a hazardous place in which to reside. The Americans preferred to place their luck with the foxholes that, while resting in the open, proved smaller targets to hit.

John R. Burroughs recalled the impact made by the more powerful bombs. "It was only a matter of seconds until we realized that this was no ordinary raid: the nerve-shattering roaring of the engines close overhead was exceeded only by the repetitive swish and scream and crashing crescendo of the falling bombs. Each earsplitting detonation shook the timbers in our dugout. There was no surcease, no breathing spell between explosions."[10] In reaction to the disturbing events, Captain Elrod and Lieutenant Kliewer urgently destroyed the squadron's papers to keep them out of enemy hands.

Had they known what else transpired in the ocean, the two officers might have been more concerned, for twenty-five miles out to sea, three Japanese submarines arrived off Wake to begin patrolling the waters around the island in preparation for the second landing attempt. Their presence indicated that the assault was only days away.

The news was not all rosy for the Japanese. Unaware that another Japanese submarine plied the same waters—most likely the *RO-66*, the boat damaged by Lieutenant Kliewer on December 11—one of the newly arrived submarines accidentally rammed and destroyed the *RO-66*, killing all her crew. When a Japanese admiral learned of the tragedy, he wrote in his diary that Wake was "somewhat of a jinx."[11] The prophetic words contained more truth than the admiral wished to believe.

"Where's the Wake Island Hotel?"

Despite the rash of unfortunate activities, Wake held on. The American public continued its admiration for their defense, even as it grew apprehensive about the garrison's ultimate fate. Hints appeared that while the men might have been mounting a gallant defense, they faced a better-equipped foe that could send unlimited resources against the atoll while their own dwindled.

On December 20, the *New York Times* reported that Wake had been under almost constant enemy attack since December 8, and when a reporter asked President Roosevelt if any relief forces headed to Wake, he declined to answer, leading many to speculate that military leaders had given up the atoll as lost. A handful of papers even added that, without reinforcements, the atoll could probably not hold out much longer. The *Washington Post* called it a miracle that the defenders had kept the stronger enemy at bay for so long, and cited military experts who claimed they expected to learn of Wake's demise at any moment.

On the atoll, men took heart in the exploits of VMF-211, and watched with admiration as aviators, at times down to one Wildcat, plunged directly into antiaircraft fire to pursue Japanese aircraft. Private First Class Himelrick wrote in his diary for December 21 that "30 Jap Dive Bombers cam[e] over. Murph & Me were in the 'C.P.' on watch. . . . I saw one Jap plane come spinning down out of a cloud & explode. Boy that sure looked good."[12]

It took two naïve, brash pilots from Hawaii, Ens. J. J. Murphy and Ens. Howard Ady, to bring in the best news, however. The aviators landed a PBY flying boat on Wake's lagoon on December 20, hopped out, and asked the first group of Marines they saw, "Where's the Wake Island Hotel?"[13] The haggard Marines did not know whether to laugh or throw the young officers into the lagoon, but instead pointed to a pile of rubbish and explained that was what remained of the hotel.

Murphy and Ady, symbolic of how little both superiors in Hawaii and the American public knew about the crisis at Wake, stared incredulously at the destruction on all sides. As they walked to Cunningham's command post, they stumbled through debris and skirted defenses manned by shabby-looking servicemen. Murphy and Ady realized that Wake had been under strain, but neither officer expected this.

Once with Cunningham, the pair delivered the news they had been ordered to fly into Wake, information so sensitive that Pearl Harbor hesitated to transmit it by airwaves lest the Japanese intercept it. Murphy and Ady explained to Cunningham that a relief force, anchored by an aircraft carrier, at long last steamed toward the atoll with Marines, aircraft, and vital supplies and, barring any unforeseen circumstances, should arrive on Christmas Eve. They told Cunningham he was to immediately begin preparations to evacuate all but 350 essential civilians, who would remain to further fortify Wake's defenses.

The news raced about the atoll and revitalized the tired defenders. "That message was like a shot in the arm for us,"[14] mentioned Major Devereux, who now guardedly believed that his superiors had decided to contest Wake. Men near Private First Class Gatewood wondered if they might even be back in Pearl Harbor for Christmas.

After what seemed like endless days and hours of fighting and waiting, someone finally rushed to their aid. Bolstered by an additional two hundred Marines and another fighter squadron, to say nothing of a carrier task force, the Marines on Wake argued they could repel any Japanese attempt. Men boasted that the enemy had best approach cautiously and talked eagerly of getting another crack at their foe.

Commander Cunningham assumed that the Japanese needed time to regroup after December 11 and would not arrive for at least a few more weeks, which meant he could organize the expected reinforcements and rebuild positions. Delighted that his men's faith in their nation had been justified by the news, Cunningham also looked forward to embarking one thousand civilians for a journey out.

Major Devereux's enthusiasm dampened after he visited with the ensigns and learned how badly the naval base in Hawaii had been mauled. Suddenly, he doubted the Navy possessed the capability to spare ships and men for Wake, and he certainly questioned the Navy's willingness to sacrifice their few remaining vessels.

Dan Teters compiled the list of civilians who would have to stay. Some volunteered, such as Joe Goicoechea and the entire sixteen-man civilian crew helping out Sgt. Johnalson Wright at Battery D on Peale Island. Teters deemed others so vital that he gave them no choice. Dr. Shank and five nurses assisting him at the hospital made his task easier by refusing to leave their posts.

In the meantime, officers compiled reports for Murphy and Ady to carry to Pearl Harbor on their return flight the next day. Taken together, the reports would give officials at Pearl Harbor their first accurate glimpse of the conditions at Wake. For instance, in his report, Commander Cunningham mentioned two factors as preventing more serious damage to Wake— effective Marine antiaircraft fire and Putnam's aviators, who attacked air and surface targets with disregard for personal safety. Major Putnam described the daily operations of his aviators, then stated that Kinney and Hamilton, assisted by Aviation Machinist's Mate First Class Hesson and a group of civilian volunteers, kept VMF-211 flying with their tireless work and hasty improvisations. Major Putnam included a glimpse of the human cost involved by sending a list of the horrendous losses suffered by VMF-211—four of twelve officers and thirty of forty-nine enlisted had already perished in the fighting.

"Keep the Old Chin Up, Girl"

Those reports paled in impact to the letters written home by a handful of Marines the night of December 20. One officer who had been on Wake since the battle's opening, Maj. Walter L. J. Bayler, had been ordered to accompany Murphy and Ady out of Wake so he could construct a radio network on Midway Island. The Marine officer, surely the envy of every other serviceman on the atoll, agreed to forward any letter given to him.

The Marines, who had not allowed themselves to think of home and loved ones during the fighting and siege, took a brief respite from their labors, picked up paper and pencil, and scribbled a few sentences to wife or family. As far as they knew, this could be their last contact with home in a long time—or ever.

Lieutenant Hanna did not write a lengthy letter, for as commander of the machine guns he had much to do, but in his brief note he attempted to maintain a positive outlook for Vera and Erlyne. "I didn't want to upset her," he said. "You got to make the best of it, and you tried to keep from upsetting them too much, but at the same time you try to put on paper how you feel. That's never easy."[15] As Lieutenant Hanna finished his letter, he noticed that some of the men near him wrote notes while others, mainly the single Marines, declined. Later that evening the truck delivering food picked up Hanna's letter and started it on its way home to Vera and Erlyne.

On Wilkes, Corporal Johnson also kept his note short and simple—he hoped that everyone was well and that he would soon see them. Major Devereux struggled to write words that conveyed his thoughts, including advice for his young son Paddy, but tore up the paper after nothing appropriate came to mind. At his position, Private Laporte chose not to send a letter. "I don't think anybody wrote a letter. I think a lot of us didn't know what to say."[16]

On the other hand, Lieutenant Kinney and others tried to infuse optimism at home by mentioning some of their recent feats. Kinney claimed he was "getting some good gunnery practice although the targets shot back," then added information that may have been more than his family wanted to read. "Had my goggles shot off last week when I went in on eight bombers—seven got away." Navy Lt. Comdr. E. B. Greey wrote to his wife that "Heroes have been made hourly and many will go unsung but the Stars and Stripes are still at the top of the mast. Too much praise cannot be given to the Marines, and those damned Japs know what our steel feels like."[17]

Dan Teters sent thoughts of his wife, Florence, along in a letter he wrote to his construction boss, George Ferris. He added that many of his civilians had offered valuable assistance to the military to that point, but many others suffered from the effects of the battle. "I strongly recommend getting them off here before I have more mental and shell shock cases on my hands than I have now."[18]

Other Marines poured out their hearts to their families in emotional letters that openly proclaimed their love. Major Putnam's note to his wife, Virginia, as cited by historian Robert Cressman, illustrated what many of the men felt but were unable to so movingly convey.

> Sweetheart: War sure is hell—I've grown a beard! But don't worry, I will shave it off before you get a chance to complain about it in person. Everything not OK, of course, but getting along as well as might be expected. Got a small knick [sic] in the back, but just a knick and it is doing fine—didn't miss a day of work. Not much squadron left, but what there is, is still in there swinging at 'em. Like the Limeys, we may be dumb and slow, but we sure can come up grinning and asking for more. Keep the old chin up, girl. Don't know just when I can get home to see you all, but I surely will get there. Give all my little gals a great big piece of my love, but keep a piece as big [as] all of them for yourself. Take great big pieces—there's plenty of it. Your Paul.[19]

Commander Cunningham was less romantic to his wife, Louise, but offered the insight that even though fighting and dying were constants, many men still thought of more gentle items.

> We are having a jolly time here and everything is in good shape. I am well and propose to stay that way. Hope you are both in the pink and having a good holiday season. Trust you haven't worried about me, for you know I always land on my feet. . . .

Cunningham purposely painted an optimistic picture in an effort to ease his wife's concern for her husband.

> The situation is good and getting better. Before long you won't hear of a Japanese east of Tokyo. The climate is good, the food isn't

bad, and I only have to wash my face once a day. Baths even scarcer, though we work in a swim now and then.

You know I am waiting only for the time of our joining. Circumstances may delay it a little longer, but it will surely come.[20]

Finally Captain Elrod, who had already gained distinction with his accomplishments in the air, crafted two letters to his wife, Elizabeth. In a hasty note he scribbled before heading to the airfield, Elrod mentioned,

We are still clinging grimly on to what little that we can still call our own. Everything is very secret to everyone except the Japs who seem to know it all before the rest of us.

Later, when he had the chance to add a second note, Elrod slowed down, realizing that he had rushed with his first letter. This time, emotion and love shone from every word.

I am missing you terribly and am undergoing a few *new* experiences but also is everyone else.

He added that

I am writing this in something of a hurry and under somewhat difficult circumstances. I'll think of a million things that I should have said after I have gone to bed tonight. But now I am going to say that I love you and you alone always and always and repeat it a million times or so. Give my love to Mary also. Between the two of you, you have it all—There isn't any for anyone else. I know that you are praying for me and I have nothing more to ask then [sic] that your prayers be answered.

Capt. Elrod signed the letter, "Your devoted and loving—Talmage."[21]

Unfortunately, not every serviceman had the opportunity to send a letter. Many never learned of Bayler's offer, especially those on duty some distance from the airfield. Corporal Marvin did not know of the incident until after Bayler departed, and Private First Class Gatewood heard of it shortly before Bayler left. Gatewood admitted he would have loved to send a letter home "because I wanted them to know I was still living."[22]

That night Bayler visited the wounded in the two hospitals to collect any letters from them. The men appreciated Bayler's efforts in their behalf, but they were also somewhat jealous that he would soon leave the beleaguered atoll. What no one, including Bayler, added was that he first had to safely wind his way through the skies, still largely dominated by Japanese aircraft.

Close to 7:00 the next morning, Ensigns Murphy and Ady climbed into their PBY to prepare for takeoff. Major Bayler, complete with a stack of letters, stepped aboard, but Herman Hevenor, once more scheduled to leave Wake, was absent. The budget inspector who had barely missed flying out on the *Clipper* on December 8, once again fell victim to a cruel fate. Murphy and Ady appeared to be his second chance for a ride home, but Navy regulations stipulated that anyone traveling on a PBY had to have both a parachute and a life jacket or he could not fly. Since the PBY's only spare set went to Bayler, whose mission held priority over Hevenor's safety, the civilian auditor watched forlornly as another aircraft, and with it his best opportunity for survival, disappeared over the horizon.

"Boy, They've Got Us"

News that a relief force headed toward them brightened everyone's mood, but the men on Wake could not rest until they sighted the first American ship over the horizon and knew help had arrived before the Japanese. Until then they faced more unsettling days in the deadly race in which they unwillingly participated—would rescue and relief from home arrive first, or would the Japanese and death beat them? Would the noose that tightened ever so slightly each day finally close around their necks, or would the task force from Pearl Harbor burst through and save them?

Reactions varied. Cunningham and Devereux maintained optimistic outlooks, primarily for the benefit of the men. They wanted to keep morale up among the military, and they did not want to alarm the civilians, who were obviously not as well disciplined. The commanders wisely understood that men with hopes of survival fight better than those who have none.

Lieutenant Hanna, on the other hand, tried to be realistic. Rather than saying anything and falsely raising everyone's expectations, he kept the men busy at their posts and reminded them that their first jobs as Marines was to fight.

Corporal Johnson claimed that he, like most veteran Marines, discarded the chances of help from Pearl Harbor as early as the sixth or seventh day of the siege. He did not think the Navy wanted to risk losing any more ships, and if Pearl Harbor had been serious about sending help, it should have arrived by December 14 or December 15. "We all knew it was a wash out after the sixth or seventh day. There were 1,700 people on the atoll, and a battleship cost so much, so what are they going to risk? The consequences of trying to rescue us might be more severe than not rescuing

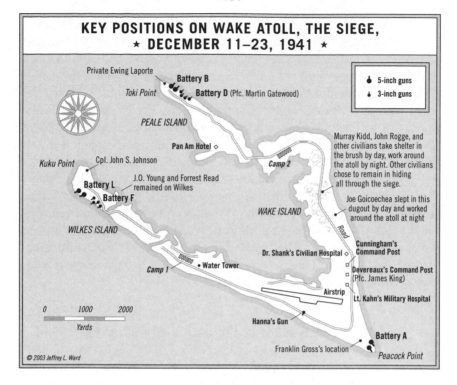

KEY POSITIONS ON WAKE ATOLL, THE SIEGE,
★ DECEMBER 11–23, 1941 ★

Private Ewing Laporte

Battery B

Toki Point

Battery D (Pfc. Martin Gatewood)

🔥 **5-inch guns**

🔥 **3-inch guns**

PEALE ISLAND

Pan Am Hotel ◇

Murray Kidd, John Rogge, and other civilians take shelter in the brush by day, work around the atoll by night. Other civilians chose to remain in hiding all through the siege.

Kuku Point Cpl. John S. Johnson

Camp 2

J.O. Young and Forrest Read remained on Wilkes

Battery L

Battery F

WAKE ISLAND

Joe Goicoechea slept in this dugout by day and worked around the atoll at night

WILKES ISLAND

Cunningham's Command Post

Dr. Shank's Civilian Hospital ◇

Devereaux's Command Post (Pfc. James King)

Camp 1 • Water Tower

Airstrip

Lt. Kahn's Military Hospital

0   1000   2000

Yards

Hanna's Gun

Battery A

Franklin Gross's location

Peacock Point

© 2003 Jeffrey L. Ward

us."[23] By December 15, Johnson had assumed that help would not be forthcoming, but he was careful not to say anything around the civilians.

Sunday, December 21, intensified the deadly race. Only one day after receiving news of a relief force and writing letters home, the men endured another air raid, but this was ominously different from all the previous attacks. Instead of high-flying bombers, forty-nine low-level fighters, dive bombers, and torpedo bombers lambasted the atoll. Rather than staging one or two bombing runs, as had been the practice, these aircraft pounded Wake for over an hour.

The civilians did not realize the significance of what had just occurred, but every serviceman on Wake knew their predicament had worsened. The previous raids originated from long-range bombers based out of the Marshall Islands to the south. Carrier aircraft, however, with their shorter range, meant that the Japanese prowled much closer to Wake than feared and that at least one aircraft carrier, probably supported by a mixture of cruisers and destroyers, could not be far away. That, in turn, indicated that a second landing force, this time buttressed by a more powerful naval presence, must already be at sea and headed toward the atoll. If help from Pearl Harbor was to arrive, it had better reach Wake fast, before the Japanese cut off every available water route to the besieged atoll.

The December 21 attack by carrier aircraft extinguished any slim hopes for many Marines. "Then it was, hey, they got to be only about one hundred fifty or two hundred miles off," said Corporal Marvin. "That's when we said, 'Boy, they've got us.' "[24] Lieutenant Kessler shook his head in dismay. Less than twenty-four hours before, he and the rest of the atoll had cele-brated the great news of relief, but now the Japanese Navy seemed to be moving in for the kill. Commander Cunningham, aware of the slim wire upon which he and the other Wake Islanders trod, sent an urgent dispatch informing Pearl Harbor of the new development. Aid had to arrive soon.

Once more, the military grabbed their rifles and manned their guns. Few complained, though, for that was their job. If they did, and if they stood anywhere near Sgt. Johnalson Wright, they knew he would curtly re-mind them, "You ain't paid to think, Mac. All you're paid to do is fight where they tell you to." Most servicemen carried the realistic attitude ex-pressed by Corporal Marvin, who explained, "When you joined the service, they don't guarantee you're coming back."[25]

"Where, Oh Where, Is the United States Navy?"

The news that Japanese carrier aircraft had entered the picture profoundly affected events in Pearl Harbor. In the aftermath of the Pearl Harbor attack, Adm. Chester W. Nimitz was named to replace Admiral Kimmel as com-mander of the Pacific Fleet. Until Nimitz arrived from Washington, Vice Adm. William S. Pye, a man as cautious as Kimmel was daring, held the reins. Pye dreaded losing more of the battered Pacific Fleet before Nimitz assumed command and thus acted with reticence toward anything that might endanger the ships.

As the relief force inched across the Pacific, a cautious Pye kept a wary eye out for the Japanese Navy, especially their aircraft carriers. He allowed Fletcher to head west, but was ready to recall the unit should any signifi-cant opposition suddenly appear. As the ships slowly churned toward a Wake garrison begging for help, December 21 wound to a conclusion with the relief force still six hundred miles distant.

News from Washington increased Pye's apprehensions when Adm. Harold R. Stark, the Chief of Naval Operations, informed Pye that the Navy Department now considered Wake a liability and that the decision to relieve the garrison rested solely in his hands. Pye understood what this message meant—he could continue the operation to save the atoll's heroic defenders, but superiors would hold him responsible should the Pacific Fleet absorb heavy losses.

On December 22, Fletcher further impeded the task force's progress by ordering all ships to refuel. This lengthy operation required that every vessel slow its speed by six knots and to steam into the wind, which took the ships farther from Wake. By the end of the day, Task Force 14 stood no closer to helping the Wake Islanders than it did one day earlier.

The progress of the task force turned out to be irrelevant. Just as the Wake Islanders and the Japanese engaged in their climactic December 23 battle, Admiral Pye, worried that he might lose the few remaining ships of the Pacific Fleet to prowling Japanese carriers and operating with the knowledge that Washington now deemed Wake as good as lost, ordered the relief expedition back to Pearl Harbor. The recall produced angry outbursts among Marine and Navy personnel aboard the ships at sea, who urged superiors to ignore the order and steam to the rescue of their fellow fighters. Henry Frietas, who served aboard the *Tangier*, said, "Here we were, loaded for bear with a carrier and cruisers, and we didn't go in! Everyone was distressed." Frietas claimed that every man on the ship would have voted to head into Wake, even though it meant placing themselves in danger. "It was wartime. We would have gone in."[26]

The language grew so inflammatory on the bridge of the *Saratoga* that Rear Adm. Aubrey Fitch stormed off so he would not hear possibly mutinous talk and be forced to take action. One Navy officer aboard the *Enterprise* dejectedly wrote, "It's the war between two yellow races." Even in Japan, propagandist Tokyo Rose ridiculed the Navy by sarcastically asking in a broadcast, "Where, oh where, is the United States Navy?"[27] The order stood, however, and the task force reluctantly turned away from Wake.

Should Pye have allowed the ships to continue? He properly concluded that the carriers could not be foolishly risked, but his caution blinded him to an opportunity to inflict damage to the enemy. Task Force 14 would not have arrived until after Kajioka reached the atoll, but the ships could still have disrupted the landings and possibly altered the outcome. To a nation starved for good news and seeking revenge for Pearl Harbor, this would have been a welcome development.

Military authorities averted an outcry back home by keeping news of the recall from the public. The nation hardly needed to learn of another failure, and the Navy Department certainly preferred to gloss over the affair. By the time most Americans learned of the details after the war, domestic matters had risen to the forefront and had cast war-related affairs to the back burner.

The episode created a controversy within the military, however, as some top officers castigated Pye's vacillation. Adm. William F. Halsey supposedly swore for half an hour when he learned of the recall and had to be talked out of impulsively leading his own charge into Wake. The failure to support fellow servicemen grated at the crusty warrior's sense of duty.

Admiral Nimitz commented that while no one could deny Pye's intelligence, he sorely lacked the gumption that top commanders required.

The incident produced no scandal or charges of cover-up similar to those fomented by the Pearl Harbor debacle, but the outcome held severe repercussions for Admiral Pye. He lingered on for ten additional months in the Pacific before spending the rest of the war in stateside positions, while Nimitz and Halsey occupied key posts in the nation's successful wartime march across the ocean to Tokyo.

The men on Wake did not learn about the recall until after the fight for the atoll ended. Though disappointed, they accepted their fate with few traces of bitterness. "The military did not resent the Navy, at least I didn't hear anything," said Corporal Johnson. "We just happened to draw a bad hand at poker, if you want to look at it that way."[28] Joe Goicoechea said that he later discussed the issue with some buddies, and they concluded that the mathematics of the situation pointed to the outcome—what would be easier for the United States to lose, a group of critically needed ships, or the men on Wake?

"We lived on 90 percent rumors and a little bit of realism tucked in between," mentioned Pfc. James King. "Relief was on the way. It will be here tomorrow was a rumor almost every day. Tomorrow never came for that."[29]

Though the Wake defenders did not realize it at the time, they now stood alone. After two weeks of bombardments, fear, hunger, and weariness, the beleaguered men dug in and prepared for what they knew would be the determining clash for the atoll. Not far away, Kajioka moved in for the final act.

"Like Losing All the Best Friends"

Three December 21 events emphasized that Wake, for all its noble labors, was running out of luck. Battery D on Peale Island provided the first indication. The man who symbolized good fortune by placing his faith in a lucky coin from Nicaragua, Sgt. Johnalson Wright, died in an early afternoon raid. Wright sat, as always, outside the dugout entrance, clutching his coin as Japanese bombs approached. Private First Class Gatewood heard him reassure the men that he would be all right, then describe the raid as if he were a play-by-play announcer broadcasting a game. Suddenly, Wright said, "The bombs are coming pretty close."[30]

Up to this point in the siege, he had miraculously avoided harm, thus building credence in his coin, but this day the talisman held no luck. A bomb explosion hurled a tree limb through Wright's body and propelled pieces of metal that tore open his side and severed an arm. The bomb's ferocity ripped helmets off men near the veteran Marine, but Wright was the only fatality at the gun position on that day.

"The damn fool wouldn't get inside the sandbags, and that's the reason he got it," explained Corporal Marvin. "He said the lucky dollar would save him, and he was the only one killed in that raid on our gun position. Wright thought he was invincible."[31]

As an officer spread the word that "They got Big Wright on that run,"[32] other Marines buried him near the battery. The following morning another bomb explosion tossed Wright's body out of the makeshift grave, forcing his buddies to inter him again. This time Wright's remains stayed where they were, resting in a spit of land on Peale Island, symbolic of what had become of Wake's luck.

VMF-211, the mainstay of Wake's hopes through so much, also ceased to exist that same day. The final two aircraft, piloted by Captain Freuler and Lieutenant Davidson, rose to meet the bombers attacking Wright and the others at Battery D. Lieutenant Davidson chased an enemy plane out to sea, but never returned.

Wake's air force now consisted of Captain Freuler and his fighter. In a furious dogfight, the outnumbered Freuler shot down one enemy plane, barely missed colliding with a second as it exploded from his bullets, then fell victim to a Japanese fighter piloted by PO3c. Isao Tahara. Tahara, who supposedly also shot down Davidson, leapt on Freuler's tail and pumped bullets into his fuselage. After three attempts at landing his damaged craft, a bleeding Freuler finally alighted on the fourth, then slumped unconscious in a pool of blood. Freuler survived the episode, but his Wildcat could no longer fly.

VMF-211, Wake's gallant little air force that had withstood a massacre on December 8 and repeated aerial combat afterwards, was no more. Freuler would have taken solace had he known that in one of the two Japanese aircraft that fell to his bullets perished Noboru Kanai, the bombardier who accurately dropped the bomb that destroyed the USS *Arizona* in Pearl Harbor.

The loss meant far more to the men on Wake than a single aircraft. Even though only two Wildcats could be put into the sky, they provided a semblance of an air shield for Wake. Nothing now stood between the enemy and them; the Japanese could boldly charge in at will. They had lost their tentacles, their ability to hit from a distance, which meant the Japanese enjoyed a huge tactical advantage.

"When that last Wildcat was gone, it was like losing all the best friends one has," said T.Sgt. Charles Holmes. "It began to give me a feeling that we were doomed. . . . I had this terrible feeling that I would be killed the next day. Depression became worse as the hours passed by. . . . I prayed and ask[ed] God to take care of the folks back home."[33]

Without an air arm with which to conduct a defense, Major Putnam collected the remaining aviators and mechanics, walked over to Devereux's command post, and reported for combat duty. Devereux asked Putnam to join Lieutenant Poindexter as an infantry reserve.

As VMF-211 fought its last gallant battle over Wake, on the morning of December 21 Admiral Kajioka, still licking his wounds over the December 11 thrashing, guided another fleet out of the Marshalls and steamed toward Wake. In addition to the force he commanded ten days earlier, Kajioka sported two new destroyers to replace the two he lost on December 11, four heavy cruisers, and extra Special Naval Landing Forces. He could now land three companies of Japanese soldiers instead of two—one each commanded by Lt. Kinichi Uchida, Special Duty Lt. (jg) Yakichi Itaya, and Special Duty Ens. Toyoji Takano. Kajioka, stung once by Wake's guns, was not about to allow another fiasco to occur.

"This May Be Your Last Night on Earth"

Any doubt that a Japanese landing force would soon strike disappeared on December 22, when Japanese carrier aircraft pounded Wake for a second straight day. The air strike meant that the carriers had not just hit Wake on December 21 as they sped by on their way to another destination. They obviously had remained in the area with the intent to destroy as many defensive installations as possible in preparation for a landing attempt.

Lieutenant Kessler saw the writing on the wall and ordered the men at his gun to work even harder at completing their defensive positions. Civilian John Burroughs labored right with them and noticed the Marines were "grim and silent. This sort of thing could not go on indefinitely. Everyone sensed the coming of a crisis."[34] Some, remembering the graphic scenes and reportage of Japanese atrocities in China, doubted now that they would ever leave Wake alive.

The night of December 22 contrasted greatly with that of December 20, when energized men, buoyed by news of the relief force, wrote notes to families. Somberness replaced hope. Men resigned themselves to another fight, this time probably involving land combat.

At their position at Battery E, bordering the lagoon just north of the airfield, Sgt. Gilson A. Tallentire ordered James Allen to break out two boxes of hand grenades and to prepare himself for close-in fighting. Not far away, Captain Elrod told a group of men, "I want you all to clean up. This may be your last night on this earth."[35]

*   *   *

People in the United States sensed the end, as well. An editorial in the *Washington Post* sent best wishes to the Wake defenders for Christmas. The newspaper wanted to express how much the men meant to the nation even though the editors knew the Americans fighting on Wake would probably never read the article. The editors stated that while it appeared the Marines and civilians would not enjoy their happiest Christmas ever, they helped make the holidays for millions of Americans back home better than expected.

> From what we hear by the grapevine, Santa Claus is going to give you boys on Wake Island the go-by this year. . . . It may be you will be too busy even to remember that it is Christmas Eve. . . . But some of you will remember. And some of you will think of other Christmases at home. . . . You may get a little tight in the stomach for a minute or two, thinking of this.
>
> But we want you to know that you are the best Christmas present this old U.S. ever had.
>
> Because of you, we all stand straighter, eyes ahead.
>
> Because of you, there is new hope in the faces of liberty loving people.
>
> Because of you, the American flag seems to give a special, prideful flirt as it snaps in the breeze these days.
>
> Because of you, American boys are storming recruiting offices, young soldiers in camp are on the double quick, sailors live for their ships, factories are working day and night, and the President, and Joe Doakes in the street, are busting their buttons.
>
> For all we know, because of you, that a Christmas will come when there will be Peace on Earth, Good Will to Men!
>
> Merry Christmas, Marines . . . and give them Hell![36]

★

CHAPTER 8

"I Was Surprised at Some of the Younger Ones"

"A Sort of Stubborn Pride"

Unexpectedly stung one time by the numerically inferior Americans at Wake, a cautious Admiral Kajioka drew up plans to prevent a second occurrence. While his fellow naval and Army commanders scored stirring triumphs at Pearl Harbor, Guam, Hong Kong, and elsewhere, he alone had been humbled by the foe. Kajioka could not afford another defeat; to lose again to the Americans would mean the end of his career as a naval commander.

He headed toward Wake with a more powerful force this time, in both ships and men. In addition to the nine vessels he brought up from the Marshalls, the aircraft carriers *Soryu* and *Hiryu*, both veterans of the Pearl Harbor campaign, steamed north of Wake and launched the carrier raids that had so alarmed the defenders. To the east, six cruisers and six destroyers took up station to intercept any American naval flotilla that might sally forth from Hawaii. Kajioka literally ringed Wake with Japanese vessels. Instead of the 450-man landing force he transported on December 11, he now boasted 2,000 soldiers.

Kajioka learned from his earlier mistakes. Rather than steam into view of Wake during daylight, he intended to sneak in under cover of darkness to avoid Wake's deadly batteries, and he eliminated the opening barrage that hallmarked the December 11 attack to increase the possibility of surprise.

He planned to throw his two thousand troops against Wake in three groups. The first, consisting of seven hundred Special Naval Landing Forces commanded by Lt. Kinichi Uchida in Patrol Boat 32 and Special Duty Lt. (jg) Yakichi Itaya in Patrol Boat 33, both converted destroyers, would crash onto Wake's southern beaches below the airfield, almost exactly at the point where Lieutenant Hanna and Corporal Holewinski waited. After brushing aside the beach opposition, the men were to sweep across the island and eliminate pockets of resistance. In the meantime, two hundred men led by Special Duty Ens. Toyoji Takano would rush ashore aboard smaller landing craft in two locations—near Camp 1 at the far western tip of Wake, and in the middle of Wilkes Island. Once these units established a beachhead, a third force of eleven hundred troops would land after sunrise to finish sweeping the atoll.

That should have been more than sufficient to seize Wake, but Kajioka took no chances this time. To draw attention from the southern shores of Wake and Wilkes, he ordered two cruisers to bombard Peale as his men approached the other islands, hopefully pulling some of Devereux's men away from Wake and Wilkes and toward Peale. Should his two thousand men fail to gain a toehold, he intended to issue rifles to the crews of his six destroyers, run them aground on Wake, and add their numbers to those already fighting the Americans. Kajioka risked his reputation on this invasion, so the loss of a few destroyers meant little if it guaranteed a victory.

On the other side of the beaches, Major Devereux faced the dilemma of trying to meet a landing assault with limited resources. Since he had to keep half his men at the 5-inch guns to answer any naval fire and at the 3-inch guns to counter air attacks, he had only around two hundred servicemen and civilian volunteers to contest whatever force Kajioka mustered.

Hamstrung by small numbers, Devereux could not adequately guard every yard of the atoll's shores, so he had to guess Kajioka's most probable landing spot. Since the coral reef surrounding Wake jutted closest to shore along the southern beaches of Wake, he figured his opponent would choose that spot. That is where he would come ashore if he were the Japanese admiral, for it would place the Japanese near Wake's most important military feature—the airfield. Accurately predicting that Kajioka would likely split his invasion force into separate groups, Devereux stretched his line south along the airfield and toward Camp 1. Thinking that Kajioka might also send men against Wilkes, Devereux ordered his commander on Wilkes, Captain Platt, to post his defenders along the same shore.

Captain Platt faced the same quandary as Devereux—where to station his few men. He placed most of his approximately seventy men in the northern half of the island, near the 5-inch and 3-inch batteries. Four .50-caliber machine guns guarded the beaches above the new channel that split Wilkes almost in half, while two additional guns below that channel kept watch on Wilkes's southern half. In case the Japanese decided to sweep around Wilkes's northern tip and try to enter the lagoon, Platt placed two machine guns, under Corporal Johnson, near the northern lagoon shore.

Platt told Marine Gunner McKinstry, commander of the 3-inch guns of

Battery F that guarded the northern half, that in a landing attempt he was to fire at the enemy as long as he safely could, then fall back as infantry and establish a line near the new channel. Since the beach sloped so sharply in front of McKinstry's 3-inch guns, he would not be able to use the guns once the Japanese landed, so his contributions to the battle would come more as an infantry commander than as a battery officer.

Major Devereux walked around the island on the eve of December 23, visiting gun positions and talking to his Marines. Instead of weary men with pessimistic attitudes, he found a determination that bolstered his hopes about the inevitable battle. "It was an unspoken thing, an intangible, but it was as real as the sand or the guns or the graves," he wrote after the war. "My men were average Marines, and they had bitched and griped among themselves like any soldiers. Now their nerves and bodies had been sapped by two almost sleepless weeks. Now the chips were down for the last roll of the dice, and they knew it, and they knew the odds were all against us, but now they were not grumbling. There seemed to grow a sort of stubborn pride that was more than just the word 'morale'."[1]

"Island Is Sighted"

Corporal Johnson felt he had an omen. Many times during the siege he wondered if he would live to see his birthday, and here he was, at midnight on December 23, celebrating his twentieth birthday, his exit from the teenage years. This was hardly the manner in which he hoped to enjoy it, for he had just completed four hours of watch, and in another four hours he had to again man his post for a second stint. He planned to use the brief interlude as his quiet little party.

When civilian volunteer Leo Nonn replaced Johnson at midnight, the corporal noticed that something seemed to bother him. Johnson asked the construction worker, whose contributions during the siege had been impressive, what was wrong. After a few moments Nonn wondered how Johnson felt about the carrier aircraft blasting the atoll.

Johnson knew what was on Nonn's mind—the presence of carrier aircraft indicated an imminent invasion—but he did not want the civilian to stand four hours on watch with that specter haunting him. Instead, Johnson told Nonn the planes probably came from a Japanese squadron on its way somewhere else, and the planes simply used Wake as target practice. "I wanted to get his mind off it. I also told him I had lived to see my birthday and we were going to have a hell of a party tomorrow. I said I was gonna call Dan Teters [and invite him], which I knew I couldn't do."[2]

The ploy worked. Nonn headed to his post, and Johnson returned to his dugout to catch a little sleep. He had no idea what he would tell Nonn later in the day when he could not pull off the party.

Corporal Johnson would speak to Nonn much sooner than expected, for during the civilian's watch Kajioka moved in. About 2:00 A.M. on December 23, tired lookouts posted along the atoll's northern portions reported seeing flashes far off in the distance, as if a naval battle had ensued. One of Lieutenant Kessler's men saw what he thought were lights in the water north of Peale. Worrying that they could be landing craft swaying in the waves, Kessler forwarded the information to Devereux's command post. Cpl. Robert Brown immediately awoke the major.

"The enemy are reported on Toki Point, sir," he told the sleepy officer.

"Any confirmation?" asked Devereux.

"No, sir."

Devereux then rang Lieutenant Kessler on Peale. "Any boats beached?" he inquired of his battery commander.

"Negative."[3]

Devereux believed that what his men spotted was, at most, an enemy feint to the north to draw his attention from the likely beaches to the south. Devereux called for general quarters and prepared for battle. On Wilkes, Captain Platt ordered the men of Battery L under Lieutenant McAlister to deploy as infantry along the lagoon beaches.

Private First Class Gatewood thought the sighting was the Japanese fleet positioning itself to bombard the atoll. Others hoped that the United States Navy had suddenly arrived and engaged a Japanese unit, since the flashes reminded them of nighttime training exercises at sea, or that a relief force was battling its way through to the atoll. Lieutenant Hanna and Corporal Holewinski could not see anything from their places south of the airfield, nor could Major Devereux, but all knew that these numerous sightings meant that something was about to happen.

The light show lasted one hour. What the men detected was Kajioka's cruisers trying to move above Peale Island and bombard it as a feint to the main thrusts against Wake and Wilkes. In the darkness, however, the ships lost their bearings and fired on a stretch of ocean far to the north, accomplishing little more than disrupting the sharks. The inauspicious start was not what Kajioka hoped for.

With Devereux's call to be on the alert, Leo Nonn woke Corporal Johnson, who shook his head to clear his mind and asked if it were already time for his next watch. Nonn replied that it was only 2:30 A.M., and that Johnson had to come to the machine gun because of possible landings at Toki Point. Johnson hurried up to the gun and strained his eyes and ears to pick up signs of activity, but he noticed nothing out of the ordinary. Just as he prepared to relax, the sound of machine guns clattering in the distance arrested his attention. He knew from the direction that the .50-calibers along the southern beaches had opened up. That could mean only one thing—the enemy had landed on Wilkes.

Out at sea, Sub-Lieutenant Ozeki donned his battle gear in complete darkness. Admiral Kajioka did not want to take a chance of alerting the Americans and their dangerous guns, so he forbade the use of light. Ozeki claimed that no one wanted "to be on the receiving end of more 'love letters' from Wake's trigger-happy defenders."

Fumbling about in the darkness and with the ship swaying from heavy winds and churning seas, Ozeki had trouble locating his shoes. He asked other soldiers near him to help, but they just whispered for him to be quiet. Figuring that someone had stolen his shoes, Ozeki grabbed the only item available, a pair of rubber thongs, and slipped those on his feet.

As Ozeki walked to the assembly point, the flip-flop noises made by the thongs seemed comical, as if he were a clown attempting to maneuver with oversize fake feet. No one around him said anything until he stepped on deck, where the officer assigned to check each man glanced at the thongs and then mumbled, "The honorable lieutenant surgeon is an idiot!"[4] Ozeki tried to hide his embarrassment and told himself that he would not have to wait long to retrieve another good pair of shoes. Once he hit the beach, he could take his pick of shoes from the feet of dead Japanese soldiers. If he died before replacing the thongs, then he had no worries anyway.

On a second Japanese vessel, a young journalist, Kayoshi Ibushi, waited with the soldiers for the order to begin the run into Wake. A sudden storm jostled the nervous young Japanese and caused others to become physically ill. "The angry waves tossed the ships around as if they were toys," Ibushi later wrote. "Suddenly a blinking light was seen on a destroyer up ahead. It was the signal 'Island is sighted.' Our course was changed, and our speed gradually reduced. The island appeared faintly in the darkness. The admiral ordered, 'Break off and land the naval party.' "[5]

Officers and men, wearing white sashes as a sign of courage, leapt into the landing barges, followed by correspondent Ibushi. The Japanese youth then waited silently as the craft churned toward shore. The larger ships, including Kajioka's flagship, remained outside of Wake's range.

"If I Couldn't Be Seen, I Quite Likely Couldn't Be Hit"

After fifteen days of waiting, the fight for control of the atoll started around 3:20 A.M. Gunner McKinstry contacted Captain Platt at his command post in the island's midsection when he thought he heard the sound of motors approaching from the sea.

"Can you see anything?" asked Platt.

"Not a damned thing, but I'm sure it's there."

"Then fire,"[6] said Platt. The commander also ordered the .50-caliber machine guns along that section of beach to commence firing at the sounds. As it was still pitch dark, Platt could not see anything ahead of him, but he hoped the light created by the .50-caliber tracer shells would let him know precisely where the enemy was.

When that did not help, Platt ordered a nearby searchlight crew to illuminate the beach directly in front of the 3-inch guns. The bright light captured Takano's one hundred soldiers just as they poured ashore from a landing craft. In less than a minute, a Japanese bullet knocked out the searchlight, but Platt glimpsed enough to let him know the Japanese headed straight toward McKinstry's 3-inch guns.

The Japanese, after firing a red rocket as a sign to Kajioka that they had landed, charged forward with fixed bayonets. McKinstry tried to fire the powerful 3-inch guns at the enemy, but he could not lower the weapons enough to have any effect—the Japanese had already moved in too close for those guns to be helpful. Instead, McKinstry relied on the .50-caliber machine guns to ward off the enemy. A furious volley of machine-gun bullets temporarily halted the attack, as bullets splattered into the coral sand, pinged against the landing barges, and smacked into Japanese. In the darkness, both sides fired at opposing gun flashes as they could not yet see their foe.

The Japanese quickly seized the upper hand, and in some places along the outer fringes opponents engaged in bitter hand-to-hand fighting. When the Japanese started to move around McKinstry's flank and lob hand grenades at the Americans, the veteran Marine, about to become trapped and worried about the unarmed civilians in his command, decided to pull away from the gun position and head toward the new channel, as Platt earlier ordered him to do. He realized that the enemy, now alerted to the location of the 3-inch guns by the gun flashes, would quickly direct their efforts toward the spot. After shouting to his civilians to scatter into the brush and wait for daylight, and after telling his Marines to remove the firing locks from the guns to make them useless for the enemy, McKinstry supervised an orderly withdrawal eastward through the brush to join T. Sgt. Edwin Hassig and a group of searchlight operators. Once there, McKinstry established a skirmish line near the new channel and prepared for more fighting.

Platt attempted to contact Lieutenant McAlister, who had formed a defense line near the new channel, but his communications had been severed by the fighting. He ordered the .50-caliber machine-gun crews along the beach to maintain a steady volume of fire for as long as possible, while he

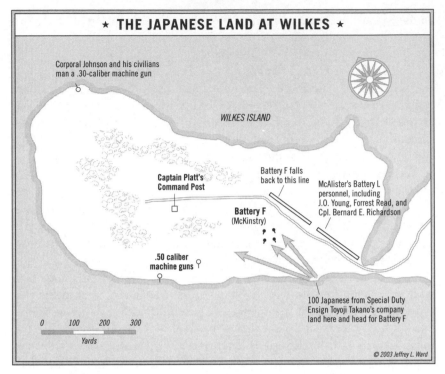

★ THE JAPANESE LAND AT WILKES ★

Corporal Johnson and his civilians
man a .30-caliber machine gun

WILKES ISLAND

Captain Platt's
Command Post

Battery F falls
back to this line

McAlister's Battery L
personnel, including
J.O. Young, Forrest Read, and
Cpl. Bernard E. Richardson

Battery F
(McKinstry)

.50 caliber
machine guns

100 Japanese from Special Duty
Ensign Toyoji Takano's company
land here and head for Battery F

0   100   200   300
Yards

© 2003 Jeffrey L. Ward

tried to ascertain the situation confronting him. Already, he could pick up the sounds of fighting where McAlister should be.

J. O. Young heard the sounds even better. He stood right in the middle of the action. He and five other civilians, including his uncle, Forrest Read, passed 3-inch shells to McKinstry's gun crews while the landing barges neared shore, but once the Japanese stepped on land and began sprinting forward, McKinstry shouted for everyone to fall back. Without a rifle to defend himself, Young rushed toward the new channel in search of a safe place.

Forrest Read felt secure near the 3-inch guns and wondered why McKinstry had ordered them back, but trusting the Marine veteran's expertise, Read rushed away, clutching three hand grenades. As Read stumbled through the brush, he hoped the darkness would help protect him, figuring that "if I couldn't be seen, I quite likely couldn't be hit."[7] He began to doubt his logic when tracer bullets zipped by and momentarily lit the area.

Read, separated from his nephew, headed toward McKinstry's skirmish line beside the new channel, located a crop of coral rocks that provided a decent hiding place, and squeezed into a hole as far as he could go until only his feet protruded from the makeshift dugout. McKinstry had already placed his Marines to the immediate right of Lieutenant McAlister's nine men and commenced a barrage of fire and hand grenades to check the enemy's advance. Japanese bullets kicked up clouds of coral sand all around the two Marine lines, but few did any damage in the dark.

Adrenaline and terror energized J. O. Young in equal measure as he hunted for his relative. He hated to be separated from Uncle Forrest just as the fighting took on a heightened brutality, but the darkness impeded his chances of locating the man. Finally, he spotted something familiar—a pair of boots sticking out of the rocks that he immediately recognized as belonging to his uncle. He shouted to the man in the hole, using his uncle's nickname, Comanche, then grinned when his relative, dirt smudged and grimy, appeared. The two asked if the other was all right, then, relieved to once again be in the company of family, located a more accommodating and safer hiding place.

After advancing 150 yards to the 3-inch gun position, Takano's troops halted, dug in, and placed flags around their position so that when daylight arrived, Japanese aircraft would not bomb the sector. Takano's men maintained a steady volume of fire throughout the night, but stubborn resistance on the left from a .50-caliber machine gun along the beach manned by Pfc. Sanford K. Ray and one other Marine, as well as the opposition mounted by the McKinstry-McAlister line to Takano's right, prevented Takano from making additional progress.

The Marines' stout defense on Wilkes blunted the enemy's assault, but most battlers realized they faced an awkward, almost impossible predicament. They could fight with every ounce of fiber and determination, but they had no reinforcements to bolster their lines, while the Japanese could pour in many more to replace the soldiers killed. All they could do was fight valiantly and take solace from the fact that they performed their duties.

"We knew we would never see the sun set on that day," explained Pfc. Max J. Dana, who manned a machine gun near Private First Class Ray, "because Marines don't surrender and Japanese don't take prisoners. I assumed I was going to be dead that day, and we intended to do the best we could."[8]

"Loaded With Lurking Japs"

One of McAlister's troops, Cpl. Bernard E. Richardson, had been at his post since first being awakened from a deep slumber by Sgt. Henry A. Bedell's gruff, "Wake up, Rich! Wake up! Japs! They've landed!" As Richardson related in an extraordinary memoir he wrote after the war, he slowly shook the cobwebs from his head, lay for a few moments longer in the foxhole he and Pfc. Robert L. "Red" Stevens had so meticulously shaped, then crawled out and smacked into Sergeant Bedell, who had returned to make sure Richardson was awake. As the pair hurried over to the grenade dump, crouching as they ran to make smaller targets, Richardson was "startled completely awake by the whine of rifle fire and the terrifying streaks of tracer bullets."9 He checked his Browning automatic rifle and the heavy magazine belt pulling at his waist to make sure he could instantly return fire if necessary.

At the dump, Bedell passed out grenades to nine men, including Richardson and Stevens. He reminded the group that as they headed to the channel, they were to keep low and zigzag. Then, as Japanese tracers brightened the area, Bedell raced off.

Richardson and the other eight made their way back to the channel, where they found Sergeant Bedell already waiting for them. He placed each man in a separate foxhole with the curt warning to stay there until he returned.

In the darkness, Richardson took a few moments to get his bearings. The half-dredged channel rested to his left, the invasion beaches stood to his front, and open territory lay to the rear. Happily, the presence of another Marine in a foxhole only a few yards away reassured Richardson.

The darkness played tricks with Richardson's weary mind as he waited in his foxhole. Alone with his thoughts, the Marine tried to control the fears that assaulted him as he imagined all sorts of horrors approaching in the pitch blackness. "My mind, already a little fuzzy from the grueling routine of the past two weeks, painted vivid pictures of the underbrush loaded with lurking Japs. Time and again, I imagined Japs surrounded me, though, actually, I could neither see nor hear any. Artillery fire became heavier. The misty rain eased almost to a stop."10

He saw the searchlight beam sweep the beach before being shot out, then waited anxiously for something to happen. By the sounds, staccato bursts from one side met by steady pumpings and grenade explosions by the other, he knew that a battle raged along the beaches of both Wilkes and Wake, but so far his line received little gunfire. Amidst the din of distant battle and the roaring surf, Richardson strained his eyes and ears to pick up the telltale indications of movement. Anything out of the ordinary, such as leather boots scraping against rock, twigs cracking, or safety bolts closing, in his words, "might mean the end of me"11 if he failed to notice them.

While Richardson and the other eight Marines dug in and waited for their sergeant to return, Sergeant Bedell rushed back to the beach area, where he learned that landing barges had been spotted close to shore.

Lieutenant McAlister ordered Bedell to send two men down to throw hand grenades into the barges, a near-suicidal mission since they would have to move within close range before pitching the grenades. Bedell selected nineteen-year-old Pfc. William F. Buehler to accompany him, ordered him to grab some hand grenades, and stuffed others into his own pockets.

The pair cautiously advanced toward the beach, surprisingly without drawing fire in the darkness. When they moved to within thirty-five yards, they rose and started tossing their grenades toward the landing craft. Within a few minutes Bedell slumped to the beach from enemy fire, gasped for air, and died.

By the time of Bedell's death, Buehler had already thrown his supply of grenades at the Japanese, so he turned back to rejoin the other Marines. One hundred yards of open terrain lay between Buehler and safety with his unit, but the youth dropped close to the ground, tried to ignore the bullets that kicked up sand near him, and started crawling for his life. "I don't re-call being under fire so much when we went down to the beach, but when I was moving back I was," explained Buehler after the war. "I was crawl-ing, face down low, when I felt a tug at my foot. Later I saw that a machine gun bullet had cut through the leather of my shoe and grazed the top of my foot. If that bullet had arrived a split second sooner, it would have hit my head."[12]

For ten minutes, McAlister and the others waited to learn how the two courageous Marines fared. Finally, Buehler returned to report that Japa-nese gunfire pushed him back before he could determine if they damaged the landing craft. He added that Sergeant Bedell, nicknamed Bullhorn be-cause of his booming voice, had been killed.

"Get the Hell Over Here! They're Killing Us!"

Two men on the island, both lacking details about the battle's course, now took matters into their own hands and, by their combined efforts, helped turn events on Wilkes in the Americans' favor. For much of the fighting, a frustrated Captain Platt operated from his command post in Wilkes's mid-section completely in the dark, since the Japanese severed his communica-tions line. Around 4:40, he decided to leave his command post and take a look for himself, a move that surprised few Marines since the popular offi-cer had a reputation for ignoring danger.

He walked from his command post a short distance to machine gun Number 11 on the beach north of where Takano landed, checked on the men there, and then swerved to the sounds of firing to his east. Shortly af-ter 5:00, with the sun's first rays lighting the sky, Platt crept close enough to the 3-inch position to observe the enemy. He noticed that instead of advancing to the right toward the Marines near the new channel, the Japanese had gathered around the American antiaircraft guns. In their concern for resistance from the east, where Platt knew McKinstry's and McAlister's men should be, the Japanese had completely ignored the rear, precisely where Platt now stood. He instructed Sgt. Raymond L. Coulson to retrieve a .30-caliber machine gun from the lagoon side of Wilkes and to meet him as quickly as possible for an assault on the Japanese rear.

As Platt headed back to prepare for the charge, he met another group that had been doing its own reconnoitering. Two Marines and six civilians, led by the just-turned twenty-year-old Corporal Johnson, had completed their own remarkable odyssey from the lagoon side of Wilkes across to the scene of fighting.

In the battle's opening hours, Johnson guarded Wilkes's northern coast with two .30-caliber machine guns and his seven men. He heard the firing in the brush behind him, the heavier roar of the American rifles clearly distinguishable from the faster crack of the smaller-caliber Japanese weapons, and debated whether to leave his post and join the fray or to remain in case the Japanese tried to slip by into the lagoon. Since the Japanese had cut his communications with Platt, Johnson faced the decision on his own.

"I had a great amount of fear because after the enemy got on the island they were in the bush behind us. Two times I was *extremely* afraid on Wake, and this was one. I could tell where they were fighting at," Johnson explained later, "but the lines were always cut. Should I go in there firing? I wanted to, but I wondered if I would hit my own men. I decided that the other Marines knew where we were, so the best thing was to stay at the lagoon. It would have been easy to turn the machine gun around from the sea and spray the whole area, but I kept facing the sea."[13]

When daylight arrived without the Japanese endangering his position, Johnson tried to contact Platt for instructions. Once again he could not get through, but he managed to communicate with another machine gunner, Sergeant Coulson. Johnson explained that, other than sporadically firing a few tracers over the lagoon to see if any enemy rafts came in, they had engaged in no fighting. When Johnson asked Coulson if he thought Platt wanted him to change his position, Coulson shouted, "Platt may be dead. Get the hell over here. They're killing us!"[14]

Johnson asked Coulson to alert other machine gunners along Wilkes's southern beaches that he intended to advance along the coast before swinging inland and joining the Marines battling the Japanese. Johnson assigned two men to carry each of the machine guns, another two men to handle the ammunition belts, and the remaining two civilians to bring the

Aerial reconnaissance photo of Wake Island, May 1941. Wilkes Island is at the top center, Peale Island is to the top right, and Wake forms the "V." Notice the surf pounding off the coral reef. (National Archives)

Maj. James P. S. Devereaux, commander of Wake's Marines. (United States Marine Corps)

Lt. Winfield S. Cunningham, commander of the Wake garrison, in a 1928 photo. (National Archives)

Pan Am Hotel, Peale Island, 1940. (National Archives)

Pfc. Max Dana (left) during prewar training in San Diego. (From the personal collection of Max J. Dana)

Close friends Pfc. Max Dana and Pfc. Clifton Sanders pose in the typical World War I–style uniforms the Marines wore on Wake. (From the personal collection of Max J. Dana)

Cpl. Kenneth Marvin in California shortly before shipping out to Wake. (From the personal collection of Kenneth L. Marvin)

Cpl. John Johnson. On December 23, 1941, his twentieth birthday, Johnson almost single-handedly wiped out a contingent of Japanese huddling under a truck on Wilkes Island. (From the personal collection of John S. Johnson)

J. O. Young and Pearl Ann on their wedding day in 1945. (From the personal collection of J. O. Young)

A 3-inch gun, similar to the one manned by Hanna and Holewinski on December 23. The protruding legs and gun platform offered little protection for the Marines and their civilian volunteers. (From the personal collection of Ralph J. Holewinski)

The Japanese light cruiser *Yubari*, which participated in both the December 11 and December 23 attacks. (National Archives)

This December 1941 newspaper cartoon made good propaganda but it was anything but what the Wake Island Marines wanted—for Santa to "Send more Japs." (National Archives)

Marines board *Tangier* in Pearl Harbor on December 15, 1941, hoping to come to the relief of their comrades slugging it out with the Japanese on Wake. (National Archives)

Robert Preston (standing) and William Bendix hunker down in a camouflaged machine gun nest for the Paramount picture *Wake Island*, released in 1942 and garnering four Oscar nominations. (Photofest)

Capt. Henry Elrod was awarded the Medal of Honor posthumously for his exploits, first in the air with VMF-211, then on the ground near Hanna's gun. (United States Marine Corps)

The airstrip on Wake resembles a junkyard, the wrecked Grumman F4F-3 fighters now only good for spare parts. (National Archives)

Following their capture of the atoll, Japanese military personnel examine one of the protected revetments used to house Wake's dwindling air force. (National Archives)

Japanese soldiers raise their flag following the December 23 battle. (National Archives)

A December 1941 newspaper cartoon showing holes in Japan's Rising Sun flag blatantly indicates that the Imperial Japanese juggernaut hit at least two major snags on its way to domination in the Pacific. (National Archives)

収容所へ急ぐ大鳥島の捕虜

Captured Morrison-Knudsen workers being led away following the climactic December 23 battle. (National Archives)

A painting by Japanese artist Matsuzaka Yasu shows the defeated Wake Americans being rounded up and put in trucks by their captors. (National Archives)

The *Nitta Maru*, the ocean liner that took most of the Wake military and civilian personnel from Wake to POW camps in China and Japan. (National Archives)

Rear Admiral Sakaibara was the Japanese commander on Wake. He was hanged in June 1947 for the execution of ninety-eight American civilians. (National Archives)

Commander Cunningham (seated right), Dan Teters (seated left), and a collection of captured Americans pose for a 1942 propaganda photo aboard the *Nitta Maru* when the ship arrives in Yokohama. (*Freedom* magazine, from the personal collection of James A. Allen)

Morrison-Knudsen worker Allan A. O'Guinn on the deck of a ship taking him back to the U.S. His emaciated state is typical of the Wake POWs, who spent three and a half years in prison camps, upon liberation. (From the Victor Lane/ James A. Allen Collection)

A 1943 sketch on POW camp tissue paper by Pfc. Max Dana gives a rough idea of the typical living quarters in the prison camps. (From the personal collection of Max J. Dana)

A group of American POWs, including Major Devereaux (seated at far right), Lieutenant Hanna (standing, second from right), and Navy surgeon Lieutenant Kahn (standing, far left), gather around a radio provided by the Japanese. (*Freedom* magazine, from the personal collection of James A. Allen)

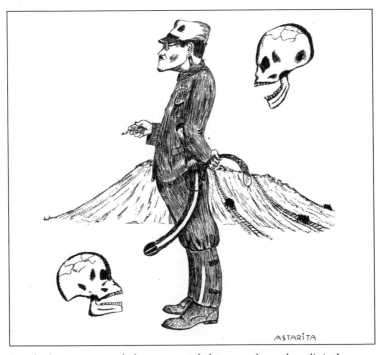

Joseph Astarita captured the essence of the most detested, sadistic Japanese guard—Isamu Ishihara—during Astarita's captivity in China. Known as the "Beast of the East," Ishihara frequently beat American POWs with his riding crop. "Mount Fuji" stands in the background. (Reprinted by permission of Joseph J. Astarita, from *Sketches of POW Life*, 1947)

American bomber crews frequently bombed Wake after it fell into Japanese hands. This photo, from June 24, 1945, shows plumes of smoke from exploding bombs. (National Archives)

American POWs celebrate the end of the war in the Omori Prison Camp near Tokyo. (From the personal collection of Joseph Goicoechea)

Col. Walter Bayler, the last man to leave Wake before its fall in 1941, is the first to return to Wake in 1945 as part of the party sent in to accept the Japanese surrender. Directly below him, wearing glasses, is Sgt. Ernie Harwell, covering the surrender for *Leatherneck* magazine. Harwell later became the longtime radio voice of the Detroit Tigers and is a member of baseball's Hall of Fame. (From the personal collection of Ernie Harwell)

Admiral Sakaibara (left) signs over Wake Island to the Americans. Colonel Bayler, holding a pipe, looks on. (National Archives)

Japanese and American soldiers salute the Stars and Stripes as it is raised on Wake Island, September 4, 1945. (National Archives)

Major Devereaux with his son, Paddy, being greeted back home after his return from prison camp in 1945. (National Archives)

Commander Cunningham sits with his wife, Louise, during a meeting with reporters after returning home. (National Archives)

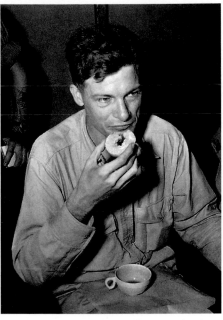

Lt. Robert Hanna enjoying coffee and a doughnut after liberation from prison camp, 1945. (From the personal collection of Col. Robert M. Hanna)

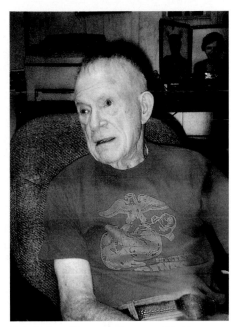

Col. Robert Hanna at home in Florida, 2002. (From the author's collection)

Cpl. Ralph Holewinski, before he left for Wake. He played a key role in the battle at Hanna's gun. (From the personal collection of Ralph J. Holewinski)

Ralph Holewinski in Gaylord, Michigan, 2002. (From the author's collection)

The three Idaho friends and Morrison-Knudsen workers pose for a photo in Hawaii, 1941, before leaving for Wake. From left to right—Murray Kidd, George Rosendick, and Joe Goicoechea. (From the personal collection of George Rosendick)

Joe Goicoechea (left) and George Rosendick, still best friends after all these years, in Boise, Idaho, 2002. (From the author's collection)

Murray Kidd and his wife, Lena, in Boise, Idaho, 2002, shortly before he passed away. (From the author's collection)

Marines' rifles and ammunition. Then, "looking like Mexican bandits,"[15] the group set out on their trek along Wilkes.

They carefully advanced around the northern coast and down to machine gun Number 9, Private First Class Ray's gun, encountering nothing but a few dead Japanese who obviously had met stiff resistance somewhere, for the entire lower half of one Japanese soldier's face—nose, jaw, and mouth—was missing. When they moved closer to the combat area, Johnson saw someone at the gun, waving toward the brush. Johnson took that as a sign that the enemy had infiltrated the brush, collected his band of eight men, and issued orders to attack.

Johnson, acting more like a twenty-year Marine veteran than a twenty-year-old, told Pfc. Marvin P. McCalla, the only other Marine with him, that the Japanese must be trying to outflank gun Number 9 by heading through the brush. Johnson picked up one machine gun, put McCalla on the other, and advanced toward the enemy. First Johnson and his civilian helpers rushed forward while McCalla covered them with fire; then McCalla and his civilians sprinted up while Johnson kept the Japanese pinned down. Johnson drew no fire, but when McCalla moved out, Japanese rifle shots lit up the brush. Since the Japanese uniforms blended perfectly with the foliage and camouflaged his targets, Johnson randomly sprayed the area with .30-caliber bullets until he heard screams and noticed a lessening of opposition. He then waited for McCalla to join him.

Together again, the eight Americans plunged into the brush. Johnson and McCalla answered Japanese fire with their own guns as they surged forward, stopping momentarily when they stumbled across four dead enemy soldiers. Johnson, who most likely killed them with his earlier burst, thought it odd that the Japanese wore split-toed canvas shoes.

The group continued forward, encountering more dead. Finally, after safely leading his gritty group across Wilkes, Johnson joined Captain Platt and his Marines.

Platt and Johnson joined forces around 5:35 A.M. Bolstered by Johnson and his seven men, Platt could now stage a stronger counterattack than he originally thought possible. He placed fourteen men in a 130-foot line, positioned Johnson with one machine gun at one end, McCalla and the other gun at the other, and kept three Marines behind to act as a reserve in case his line bent in front of enemy resistance. He ordered Johnson and McCalla to continue their alternating advance once the enemy discovered their presence, and reminded the men to shoot only at clearly identifiable targets, since McKinstry's and McAlister's Marines had to be somewhere in the area. He added that they should shoot short, well-aimed bursts, and to keep moving toward the Japanese.

Platt stood behind Johnson, a .45 in each hand, and ordered the line to advance without firing—if they were fortunate, the enemy would not spot them until too late. Surprisingly the line moved to within fifty yards before the Japanese, busy repelling an attack from the other side, realized another American force had closed in from the rear.

Platt was astonished by the ease with which he moved toward the enemy. He later credited the Japanese preoccupation with the other American unit, their tendency to bunch together in one spot, and their lack of aggressively pursuing the Americans with giving him such a golden opportunity to counterattack. The Japanese company lacked initiative and audacity, qualities that Platt possessed in abundance.

Once the Japanese turned their fire on Platt's men, Johnson and McCalla implemented their alternating advances, each man peppering the front immediately ahead of the other. Marines and civilians, their heartbeats racing madly and their faces so black from the grime of battle and the gunpowder that Johnson could barely recognize them, moved amidst popping rifles and the staccato rhythm of machine guns. Every once in a while Johnson heard a high-pitched scream, and guessed that his bullets had found their mark.

Johnson had to cease firing a few times because his gun jammed. When it did, he opened the top plate, extracted the guilty shell, shut the plate, and resumed firing. He hoped the gun would not jam while a bayonet-wielding Japanese charged toward him.

Platt's counterattack steadily closed on the enemy, who collapsed on the 3-inch guns and a searchlight truck nearby. Johnson, his machine gun barrel glowing with heat from constant use, noticed a group of about twenty Japanese crowding together under the cramped confines of the truck, a vehicle about twenty-two feet long and six feet wide. "They reminded me of a bunch of suckling pigs on a farm," Johnson recalled.

Believing the Japanese might want to surrender, Johnson tried to think of a word he could use to convey that notion to the trapped enemy, but a Marine distracted Johnson's attention. "The guy [Pfc. Severe R. Houde] next to me said, 'They can't hit anything.' I told him to get down." The words had barely issued from the Marine's mouth when a bullet struck and killed the young soldier. In the same burst, a bullet grazed Johnson's right arm and others kicked particles of coral into his face.

"The bullet had to come from under the truck, and I—I guess it was an emotion, a controlled emotion," said Johnson. "It was either kill or be killed and I was there to kill 'em." He later added, "It was a machine gunner's dream."

Johnson fired his machine gun at the collected Japanese under the truck until one 250-round belt emptied; then he loaded another and continued to

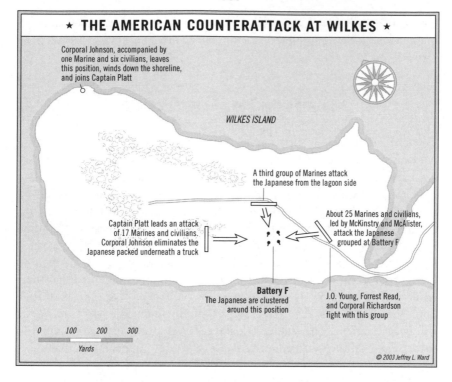

★ THE AMERICAN COUNTERATTACK AT WILKES ★

Corporal Johnson, accompanied by one Marine and six civilians, leaves this position, winds down the shoreline, and joins Captain Platt

WILKES ISLAND

A third group of Marines attack the Japanese from the lagoon side

Captain Platt leads an attack of 17 Marines and civilians. Corporal Johnson eliminates the Japanese packed underneath a truck

About 25 Marines and civilians, led by McKinstry and McAlister, attack the Japanese grouped at Battery F

Battery F
The Japanese are clustered around this position

J.O. Young, Forrest Read, and Corporal Richardson fight with this group

0   100   200   300

Yards

© 2003 Jeffrey L. Ward

shoot. He started at one end of the truck and methodically pumped rounds underneath until he reached the other end, at which time he repeated the process. All the anger, the rage that had accumulated since December 8 gushed out of the youngster, who exacted a heavy price from the enemy. "I sat behind the machine gun and loosened bursts, and every fourth round was a tracer and I could see where my bullets were going. You could see the bodies contort and their arms flail up in the air. I must have fired 375 to 400 rounds into the bodies under the truck."[16]

The attack virtually ceased with Johnson's one-man offensive. In the sudden calm, a corpsman moved up to tend to Johnson's injuries. When the corpsman tore off Johnson's shirt, blood gushed down his arm, but the wound was not too severe. The corpsman then used a pair of tweezers to pluck the coral from Johnson's face.

While the corpsman treated him, Johnson looked back to see two Japanese soldiers with their hands raised in surrender, the only survivors of the twenty who took shelter underneath the truck. Johnson asked his most dependable civilian, Leo Nonn, to take the pair of Japanese under guard to Captain Platt for interrogation.

As he gazed about him at the destruction and death, Johnson concluded that his seven men had behaved splendidly under difficult conditions. The corporal, less than one day removed from being considered a teenager, remarked later, "I was surprised at some of the younger ones. They all performed well."[17]

"Be Sure the Dead Ones Are Dead"

While Platt and Johnson counterattacked the enemy from the west, McKinstry and McAlister organized their own offensive punch from the east. Takano's men, trapped in the middle, had no chance.

Corporal Richardson, who had been ordered by Sergeant Bedell to remain in his foxhole near the new channel, started the action from the McKinstry-McAlister side. He had listened to the sounds of fighting for too long now, so he crawled over to Pfc. Gordon L. "Gunny" Marshall to ask for his advice. The pair lit cigarettes and discussed the matter. Even though the sun had not yet risen, enough light filtered in that they could see the shadows of numerous ships off Wake, "big ones and little ones, waiting only for dawn to move in and finish us off," wrote Richardson in his memoir. That settled the issue. "We knew this and admitted it to ourselves and to each other. Isolation was now unbearable, inactivity impossible."[18]

Richardson and Marshall collected six other men as they slowly advanced around a bend toward the beach. Resting on the sand, half still in the water, loomed an empty landing barge. Not far inland to their right were the 3-inch guns, now manned by Japanese soldiers. As the eight attempted to move into a better position, the group encountered McKinstry and additional men, including Forrest Read and J. O. Young, who also had crept forward to charge the Japanese. Around 6:00 A.M. the third American unit in the vicinity of the guns, the men led by Lieutenant McAlister, arrived.

McAlister and McKinstry now commanded about twenty-five men, strong enough to mount a frontal assault on the 3-inch position. They split into two forces, a smaller unit led by McAlister that veered out in a flanking attack, while McKinstry took the larger group and attacked head-on. The Americans had barely begun moving forward when an enemy patrol appeared. Seeing the larger force, the three Japanese soldiers hid behind a huge coral boulder. The large, red-bearded McKinstry closed on the boulder but was halted by McAlister's admonition to send one of his men instead.

"I've got 'em, Gunner," offered Cpl. William C. Halstead. The corporal rushed the boulder, leapt on top, and pumped rounds into the three stunned Japanese before they had a chance to open fire.

With that opposition removed, the attack proceeded. J. O. Young grabbed a rifle from the body of a dead Marine, while Forrest Read stayed close to McKinstry to pass along hand grenades for the gunner to throw at the Japanese. The unit of Marines and civilians formed a rough line at a right angle to the beach and cautiously approached the enemy until they were spotted. Then all hell broke loose. As Richardson recalled, "Jap voices lifted in shrill, strange battle cries. Gunny [Marshall] answered with an angry tortured rebel yell. It was a release from the tensions of the silent night. We picked up Gunny's cue and drowned the enemy voices. Then, as unexpectedly as the screams had sprung from us, they died away and ceased. We inched along, firing and feeling our way."[19]

The Americans, after venting their anger, advanced slowly. Richardson cursed when his loaded ammunition belt dropped down over his hips and sagged to his ankles, further impeding his movement. As he awkwardly stumbled toward the enemy, he wondered what idiot back in the States had designed a belt to carry ammunition instead of a shoulder bag.

The Americans engaged in a furious melee that included hand-to-hand fighting. Pfc. Artie Stocks saved Pfc. Henry H. Chapman's life when he shot a Japanese as the enemy soldier prepared to run Chapman through with his bayonet. Private First Class Halstead, who only moments before had killed the three Japanese, slumped dead at McKinstry's feet when an enemy bullet struck him down. Corporal Richardson eased into the firing position he learned during training and slowly aimed at another enemy soldier. "The patch of cloth raised and enlarged. I held my breath, squeezed the trigger and killed the first game I had ever stalked—a human being."[20]

The red-bearded McKinstry seemed to be everywhere, cheering and coaxing his men forward and complaining in his booming voice that he had only a .45 with which to shoot the enemy. As McKinstry shuffled about the battlefield, he tossed grenades toward the Japanese as fast as Forrest Read (whom McKinstry later praised in a report as being outstanding) and the other civilians could hand them to him. Men marveled that such a huge individual could rush around in the midst of such heavy fighting, yet avoid being hit. If anyone lagged behind, whether civilian or Marine, McKinstry administered a verbal reprimand and threatened to shoot him in the ass unless he kept going.

Richardson heard Gunny Marshall yell that a man near Richardson, Pfc. Wiley W. Sloman, had just been hit in the head. When Richardson looked over, blood covered Sloman's face and streamed down to his chest. Marshall, thinking that Sloman was dead, shouted to McKinstry that he could have Sloman's rifle. In the heat of the fighting, Richardson had no time to feel shock or revulsion over the injury sustained by Sloman, but moved on with the line of Marines. A corpsman later tended Sloman's wounds, and the man miraculously survived after being left for dead.

This group of Marines and civilians was one of the first in the war to experience a battlefield technique later employed elsewhere by the Japanese. In the heat of the fighting, McKinstry turned back to observe supposedly dead Japanese rise from the ground and bayonet Americans from behind. At one time, while McKinstry paused to put a new clip into his .45, he saw a Japanese soldier stand up and lunge toward an American. McKinstry yelled to the Marine and tried to fire his .45, but the gun jammed. The American swung around and thrust at the Japanese soldier with his bayonet just as the Japanese thrust at him. They both dropped lifeless to the ground, their bodies locked by the bayonets.

From that moment on McKinstry walked around the battlefield and pumped rounds into what he had assumed were already-dead Japanese. He urged his men to be cautious, shouting, "Be sure the dead ones are dead."[21]

McKinstry and McAlister slowly reduced the area controlled by the Japanese. While McAlister closed in from the right and McKinstry moved in against the Japanese front, another American unit suddenly arrived from the lagoon side and attacked from the north. Almost completely surrounded, the Japanese had no chance to escape the trap.

Fed by Read, McKinstry tossed hand grenades into the final enemy position until the sound of gunfire ceased. After waiting a few moments in the silence, McKinstry spotted someone slowly stand up on the other side of the battery.

"Mac," the man called out, "that ugly voice of yours sounded like an angel's when you came through."[22] A grinning Captain Platt walked across dead Japanese toward McKinstry. The counterattack, mounted independently by three different groups, unknowingly turned into a coordinated assault that eliminated all Japanese opposition on Wilkes. By 7:40, the fighting on the island terminated.

Other than the two Japanese prisoners who survived Johnson's onslaught, Takano's force no longer existed. Nearly one hundred officers and men lay slain on the island, defeated by a smaller force of more determined, aggressive Marines and civilians. If the men on nearby Wake enjoyed similar success, the Wake defenders would register a second, more resounding defeat on Kajioka.

"On Our Way to Make a Last-Ditch Stand"

After the fighting ended, Platt ordered his men to sweep throughout the northern half of Wilkes, from the new channel to Kuku Point, to remove any pockets of Japanese soldiers that may have survived. The men found nothing but dead Americans and Japanese.

As Corporal Johnson moved around Wilkes, he saw a Japanese body lying near a foxhole occupied by a Marine. When Johnson walked over to make sure the Japanese soldier was dead, the Marine explained that he had killed him. Johnson remarked that he could see no wounds on the enemy body, but the other Marine replied that he had choked the Japanese. When Johnson wondered why he had not used his rifle, the American answered, "I wanted to feel him. They had been bombing us all this time and I wanted to get my hands on him and feel him."[23]

The Americans still had to be careful, for Japanese pilots assailed them with repeated fighter and dive-bomber attacks. Men jumped into and out of foxholes and ditches as they moved through the brush, then rose after the planes departed and continued mopping up the island.

Corporal Richardson reunited with his buddy, Red Stevens. Stevens mentioned that if he had the opportunity, he planned to return to the foxhole the two had constructed earlier. "I've got some cigarettes there I could use," he told Richardson. As the two neared their old foxhole, Japanese aircraft charged down for another strafing run. Red Stevens dived into the familiar foxhole while Richardson jumped into another that was closer.

He soon wished he had not. "To be in a hole alone is terrible," he wrote. Richardson cringed as bombs shook the ground and heaved dirt on top of him. "They came and kept coming until I could shake no more. I just lay there in the coral sand and waited. And for the first time I began to relate this day, this action to me. It came to me that I was about to die. And I didn't want to die, that day or ever. There was [sic] so many things I wanted to do. So many places to see. So many girls to love. So many books to read. Millions of books, and me not reading them."[24]

Images flashed through Richardson's mind as he waited for a bomb or bullet to take his life. He saw the many pages of his novel being destroyed; he thought of family and friends; he imagined the funeral service held in his honor in the Methodist church back home in Arkansaw, Wisconsin; he thought he could smell the family barn; he was pleased that he had not agreed to the tattoo that his buddies urged him to get.

Suddenly, calm returned. Richardson rose, looked around, and rushed over to Red, but where the shelter and Red should have been, Richardson found only a fifteen-foot crater. A direct bomb hit had obliterated his buddy and left no trace that a human being had occupied the foxhole only moments before.

After two hours, the Marines completed their sweep through the brush and reported Wilkes secured to Captain Platt. They counted ninety-eight dead enemy against the loss of seven Marines killed. Platt attempted to interrogate the two prisoners with sign language, but could obtain little information from them. Since the officer had no way of communicating with Major Devereux or anyone else over on Wake, he had no idea what had been taking place over there. All he could do was keep his men ready and hope that sooner or later he heard from Devereux.

Around noon, Platt sighted small boats drawing toward the island across the old channel that separated Wilkes from Wake. He looked farther offshore and found several cruisers and transports about four thousand yards out. Platt ordered Lieutenant McAlister to fire at the ships with the 5-inch guns, but when McAlister arrived at the battery, he found both out of commission. With his 5-inch and 3-inch guns useless, Platt told McAlister to lead the men to the old channel, take up positions as infantry, and fire on the small boats.

The men hurried eastward. Dead bodies, both Japanese and American, littered the way. J. O. Young, still armed with the rifle he removed from a dead Marine, assumed this was the final action. "It was supposed that the Japanese did not take prisoners, so we were on our way to make a last-ditch stand."[25]

Richardson passed by the bodies of three friends killed in the morning's fighting. Pfc. Clovis R. Marlow, a man everyone called Skinny, had apparently put up a valiant struggle before succumbing, since several dead Japanese lay beside him. Richardson said, "Skinny's head was thrown back and his mouth was open as if he were snoring as he had done almost every afternoon after lunch in our tent before the war. His wasted blood had fired in the hot sun to a polished ebony. Flies crawled in his mouth and out his nose. For the first time, I realized how hot the day had become."[26]

The men passed the new channel around 3:30 P.M. and had made it almost halfway to the old channel when a Marine shouted, "Someone's coming down the road."[27] Everyone tried to ascertain who the individual might be. Their hearts lifted when they saw a white flag attached to a pole. Could it possibly be that Devereux and his men had checked the Japanese at Wake as they had just done on Wilkes? Could this be the second victory for the American defenders? Captain Platt moved forward to find out.

CHAPTER 9

★

"We'll Make Our Stand Here"

"Shells Came Shrieking Like a Thousand Demons"

While Takano's men swarmed ashore on Wilkes, the other Japanese contingents, among whom was Sub-Lieutenant Ozeki, silently approached Wake. Still unable to locate his shoes in the dark, Ozeki awkwardly tried to keep pace with his fellow soldiers of the Uchida Company as they filed to their embarkation points, but the rubber thongs made walking difficult. Nature proved to be an unreliable ally. A stiff wind created seas so rough that one Japanese officer said the waves were "raging like huge mountains."[1]

The two converted destroyers headed toward their landing points, still apparently unobserved by the Americans in the moonless night. Soon the ships would crash onto the beach, giving the soldiers the opportunity to finally close with the enemy and at long last make amends for the December 11 debacle. Five hundred Japanese Special Navy Landing forces waited patiently for the battle to begin.

If the operation unfolded according to plan, the fighting would be over in a short time. Kajioka's main force was to thrust straight inland to seize the airfield, in the process charging directly across Lieutenant Hanna and his small group of defenders. A second unit would land to the east to swing behind any opposition at the beach and to cut off any help from Peacock Point, while a third company crashed ashore near Camp 1 to eliminate opposition in that sector.

Nerves nearly immobilized each Japanese soldier and stomachs churned as the vessels closed in. The signs so far seemed good—the Americans on Wake had not yet opened fire. Maybe Kajioka had his surprise this time.

Around 2:30 each man's thoughts suddenly halted when an officer shouted, "Shore ahead!"[2] Men fell to the deck to brace themselves against the coming crash, and a shrill crunching sound emitted from below as the ships' hulls scraped against Wake's reef in an abrupt halt. Sailors tossed ropes over the side for the infantry to descend into the water, and men grabbed hold and prayed they could reach land before the enemy commenced firing.

The soldiers quickly learned they would have no such luck when an American shell crashed into the ship's bridge, killing several men and sending tardy soldiers hastening to the ropes. "Out of the darkness in front of us, shells came shrieking like a thousand demons let loose," remembered one Japanese officer. "Quick! Quick!"[3] prodded another in a hasty attempt to move men over the side.

Phosphorescent tracer bullets, used to indicate the direction of fire, so thoroughly filled the air about the ship that they reminded Ozeki and the others on the rope of swarming bees. Bullets slapped men off ropes, then followed others into the water as the Japanese waded toward shore. Ozeki moved through such intense fire that he felt he was walking straight "into the jaws of a hungry beast that made its lair on Wake Island." At the same time he could not help noticing the beautiful tapestry formed by the enemy's tracer bullets, which lit up the sky as they crisscrossed in murderous majesty, as if a giant spider had spun an illuminated web. "Nothing is as enchanting as an approaching tracer round. It approaches you in slow-motion growing larger until at the last possible second it speeds up and flys [sic] by at incredible speed leaving a 'vviipp' sound buzzing in your ears."[4]

Ozeki plunged into the water beside his ship and turned toward shore. Within moments, Patrol Boat 32 disembarked the 290 men of Uchida Company on the beach below the airfield, Patrol Boat 33 disgorged 140 men to the west, and a landing barge brought in WO Kiroku Horie's 70 men just to the west of Peacock Point.

Ozeki had not expected such fierce opposition. In water less than three feet deep, Lieutenant Uchida led his men toward shore. The soldiers held their rifles over their heads while bullets whizzed by at chest and head height, some thumping into Japanese soldiers while others clanged off the destroyer's metallic side. Ozeki splashed to dry land, thinking he "must have looked like a complete fool hitting the invasion beach in my thongs screaming 'Banzai!' (flipitty-floppitty) 'Charge!' (flipitty-floppitty)."[5]

Once the survivors reached the beach, they fell flat onto the sand, while artillery shells and bullets raced above. Few dared raise their heads even a little, for to do so meant giving the enemy a better target. Even as close to the ground as they were, soldiers still felt bullets tear into the gear they carried on their backs until it was shredded to tiny cloth strips.

Sub-Lieutenant Ozeki lay on the beach, hoping that this nightmare would end. He and other Japanese had assumed they could brush aside minor opposition on the beaches and quickly head inland, but that did not seem to be the case: They had not counted on Marines like Lieutenant Hanna and Corporal Holewinski, or civilians like Paul Gay and Bob Bryan.

"Every Damn One of 'Em Was Ready to Do His Duty"

As he had done throughout the siege, Lieutenant Hanna frequently left his command post located in the middle of his two-and-one-half-mile defense line stretching east-west from Peacock Point to Camp 1 along the beaches south of the airfield. He liked to check on his men, especially since Devereux believed the main Japanese thrust would hit his line. The Marines seemed ready, but he wished he had more than the four .30-caliber machine guns with which to greet the enemy.

So did Corporal Holewinski, who sat with his machine gun one hundred yards from where Patrol Boat 32 would soon appear. Seven other Marines waited in their positions along the same section of beach, trying to spot any unusual movement. The fatigued warriors gazed from bloodshot eyes set deep in grimy faces, and stubble covered their chins, but they seemed ready. Private Laporte noticed the calm attitude of the men near him. "It wasn't a desperation look, but a look you got when you know you had to do something. Of course there was some fear involved, but every damn one of 'em was ready to do his duty."[6]

The haggard Marines bolted alert when the sounds of fighting erupted on Wilkes. Commander Cunningham dashed a message to Admiral Pye in Pearl Harbor that ENEMY APPARENTLY LANDING,[7] and when Lieutenant Hanna noticed the shadow of a vessel approaching his lines, he rushed over to an unmanned 3-inch gun that had been moved to a small elevation south of the airfield. Corporal Holewinski, whose rifle had been stolen during the siege when he left it unattended for a few minutes, grabbed an older Springfield rifle and joined Hanna as the lieutenant raced by, as did civilians Paul Gay and Bob Bryan.

They reached the gun only moments before Patrol Boat 32, containing Lieutenant Uchida and Sub-Lieutenant Ozeki, rammed ashore. Hanna peered into the darkness, trying to obtain an accurate fix on the vessel, when a Japanese soldier unknowingly aided him. From out of the void, a light suddenly flared. "Some damn fool on the ship was hanging lanterns on there,"[8] said Lieutenant Hanna later. What he saw were lanterns placed along the ship's side to aid Ozeki and the other men dropping into the water, but instead of helping the Japanese, the lanterns handed Hanna a perfect target at which to aim.

With a loud, sharp crack, Hanna's gun rocketed the opening shot toward Patrol Boat 32. The first shell dropped short of the ship, but Hanna's second missile crashed directly into the bridge, casting flames about the deck that illuminated the craft and signaled every other Marine gun in that portion of the beach to open fire. As Hanna pointed the 3-inch gun at the lanterns, Gay and Bryan handed shells to Corporal Holewinski, who then fired the 3-inch gun as quickly as the two civilians brought up the next shell. In an amazing display of accuracy, Lieutenant Hanna hit Patrol Boat 32 with eighteen of twenty-one shots.

Instead of an easy landing, the Japanese stepped into a slaughter, as soldiers dropped into the water or spun around from bullet hits. When one of Hanna's shells hit the ship's magazine and ignited the ammunition, a tremendous explosion illuminated the beach and the enemy soldiers wading ashore. Marines took advantage of the light and added their guns to the carnage. The captain of the Japanese ship, mortally wounded by the latest hit, ordered every man to abandon the blazing vessel, which he refused to leave. Sailors stepped toward him to help him off, but the captain waved them away and disappeared in the inferno.

Lieutenant Hanna swung his gun from the burning vessel toward the enemy soldiers, now crawling up the beaches. The Japanese knew they had to eliminate Hanna's gun, or many more of their comrades would die, but fire from other Marine positions, including Kessler's guns on Peale, forced the Japanese to hug the ground.

"It appeared as if all the island's defenders had me in their sights," wrote Ozeki. "Their bullets headed straight for my nose, then at the last second they'd change their metallic minds and veer off coarse [sic] missing me by centimeters."[9] Bullets splattered in the sand all around him, and tracers continued to light the night in eerie patterns. Ozeki heard what he at first thought was a bunch of bees buzzing around his head, then realized that rather than insects, bullets zipped by.

Explosions, shouts, and confusion reigned as Uchida's men laboriously inched toward Hanna, while machine guns, 3-inch guns, rifles, pistols, and grenades joined in a symphony of destruction. The quick staccato of the .30-caliber and .50-caliber machine guns blended with the slower *putt-putt-putt* of the Japanese machine guns, while the more powerful Marine rifle overshadowed the snappier crack of the Japanese. Soldiers stumbled on the beaches, moaning in pain, and officers exhorted their men to greater effort. So many explosions lit the sky that men compared the event to a Fourth of July fireworks display.

"Do You Think You're Really Big Enough to Make Us Stay Behind?"

While Lieutenant Hanna and his group battled in the center of the mael-strom, Devereux took quick steps to shift reinforcements to the embattled Marines and civilians around the 3-inch gun. Already hamstrung from a lack of personnel, the major risked weakening other positions on the atoll, but he felt he had to rush aid to Hanna, holding a crucial sector of beach, or quickly lose the fight. He ordered Major Putnam to take the remnants of VMF-211, now serving as infantry, and fight his way through to Hanna from the airfield. He told Captain Godbold to send nine men down from Peale, and requested that Lieutenant Lewis fire the 3-inch guns of Battery E as close over the invading Japanese as possible.

The tactics had an immediate effect on the enemy. While Hanna's group mounted a heavy volume of rifle and pistol fire, shrapnel from Lewis's exploding shells rained metal fragments on the invaders from as close as fifty feet above. Corporal Marvin, now with Battery E after being switched from Peale, could not see what they fired at because of the darkness, so they aimed where they thought the ships and Japanese would be and set the fuses to explode above them.

Hit from two sides, many Japanese fell wounded or dead before they left the beach. Kiyoshi Ibushi, the Japanese war correspondent who accompanied the troops, wrote that "Shells burst directly over our heads, and there was a continuous and intense horizontal fire from the high-angle guns. . . . We hugged so close to the ground that our helmets dug into the earth."[10]

Major Devereux altered earlier orders given to Lieutenant Poindexter to take the Mobile Reserve and head up to Peale Island. Instead, around 2:45 Devereux told Poindexter to set up his guns and men between the airfield and Camp 1, about a half mile to Hanna's west. Within ten minutes, Poindexter positioned his men in a line to the west of Hanna, where he engaged Japanese troops in a heavy firefight through the night.

Poindexter's men, helped by the illumination from Japanese Very lights, inflicted severe casualties on the Japanese. At first, the enemy advanced cautiously, but as the night went on, they became bolder. Civilian laundry worker John M. Valov spotted a group of shadowy images less than fifty yards away and fired into it. The Japanese moved toward him, but machine-gun fire from other Americans halted their advance and forced them back toward the beach.

When he heard the sounds of fighting to his rear at Camp 1, Poindexter left G.Sgt. T. Q. Wade in command at the line while he rushed back in his

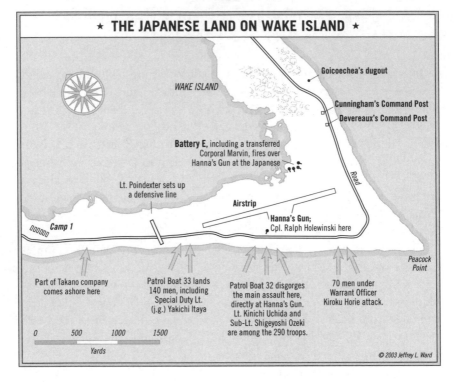

★ **THE JAPANESE LAND ON WAKE ISLAND** ★

WAKE ISLAND

Goicoechea's dugout

Cunningham's Command Post

Devereaux's Command Post

Battery E, including a transferred
Corporal Marvin, fires over
Hanna's Gun at the Japanese

Lt. Poindexter sets up
a defensive line

Airstrip

Hanna's Gun;
Cpl. Ralph Holewinski here

Camp 1

Road

Peacock
Point

Part of Takano company
comes ashore here

Patrol Boat 33 lands
140 men, including
Special Duty Lt.
(j.g.) Yakichi Itaya

Patrol Boat 32 disgorges
the main assault here,
directly at Hanna's Gun.
Lt. Kinichi Uchida and
Sub-Lt. Shigeyoshi Ozeki
are among the 290 troops.

70 men under
Warrant Officer
Kiroku Horie attack.

0   500   1000   1500

Yards

© 2003 Jeffrey L. Ward

truck to investigate. When he arrived, a Marine pointed seaward, where Poindexter spotted a landing barge that had drifted off course from the Wilkes fighting, as well as Patrol Boat 33 churning toward shore. He directed the Marines near Camp 1 to concentrate their fire on the craft, which forced the barge to back off and try to land several more times, but the metal sides deflected most of the ammunition.

According to one Marine, Poindexter was either "crazy as a bedbug or the bravest guy alive." A native of Madison, Wisconsin, the twenty-four-year-old 2d Lt. Arthur A. Poindexter joined the Marines in November 1939, following his graduation from the University of Kansas. Popular with both officers and enlisted men, Poindexter earned a reputation for fairness and for keeping his word. "He was a straightforward guy who gave you no bullshit," said his close friend, Lieutenant Hanna.[11]

Poindexter proved his worth during this action. He organized two teams of volunteers to wade into the water and toss hand grenades into the barges. Poindexter ordered the other Marines to hold their fire so he and his group could creep within hand grenade range, even though he knew the command meant that the Americans would have to advance in the open without covering fire. One team consisted of Sgt. Gerald Carr and civilian

R. R. "Cap" Rutledge, while Poindexter and Navy Mic. James Edward Barnes formed the second.

The four, each carrying six hand grenades, crept out of the brush toward the two enemy vessels and slid among coral outcroppings until they reached the shoreline. As waves lapped at their feet, the men lobbed their grenades at the two targets, but they all fell short. Poindexter rushed back to the brush to retrieve more grenades, then made a second attempt from closer range. Poindexter and Barnes waded ten yards out, stopped, and hurled their grenades into the barge, killing or maiming every occupant.

Back at the airfield, Putnam posted Lieutenant Kliewer and five enlisted men at each end of the strip with orders to detonate a series of mines planted to destroy the airfield should the enemy appear to be taking Wake. Putnam then took twelve other Marines, including Captain Elrod, to help his fellow Marine, Lieutenant Hanna.

Before Putnam traveled far, civilian John P. Sorenson, a hard-nosed construction worker twenty years older than Putnam, arrived with twenty-two civilian volunteers ready to fight. The offer moved Putnam, but he told Sorenson to head for the safety of the brush instead. "If you're captured in combat, your chances are mighty poor. You can't go with us."

The warning meant nothing to the bulky individual. "Major, do you think you're really big enough to make us stay behind?"

Putnam tried once more to rebuff what he called in his report the "humorous defiance to the squadron commander's advice and request that they leave the combat area and seek security." Putnam had once bitterly complained about the lack of civilian assistance, but he now had trouble finding the right words to express his appreciation to Sorenson. "I'm proud of you. I'd be glad to have you as Marines. But take off. Join the other civilians."[12] Putnam led his Marines away, but close behind followed the stubborn Sorenson and his band of civilian soldiers.

Putnam arrived alongside Lieutenant Hanna just as the Japanese closed in. Putnam immediately placed his men along a line extending from Hanna's gun to the airfield.

The Japanese, still enjoying the advantage of numbers, tried every maneuver to overwhelm the Americans. They attempted to swerve behind Putnam and outflank Hanna—but each time, accurate American fire pinned them down. Bayonet charges dented Putnam's line, but failed to puncture it. Americans and Japanese engaged in one of war's most fearsome acts—hand-to-hand fighting. They grappled with one another, shot each other from inches away, plunged bayonets into stomachs, gouged skin and twisted arms, bit hands and strangled necks.

Due to the courage and directions of their leaders, plus the fighting spirit of the Marines and civilian volunteers, the Hanna-Putnam line held, but each sortie by the Japanese further depleted their ammunition and, more important, their numbers. Hanna did not know how much longer he could hold out or, for that matter, survive.

"I Reckon We Can Make Out a Little Longer"

Besides the main action around Hanna's gun and the subsidiary fighting along Poindexter's line, military personnel and civilians battled the Japanese at three other locations on Wake. In the first contested area, Cpl. Winford J. McAnally and about ten men contested the eastern end of the airfield against Horie's seventy soldiers. During their skirmish, a strange apparition materialized at the end of the airfield that some Americans compared to men from Mars. Two Japanese soldiers, wearing large goggles to shield their eyes and carrying tanks on their backs, started to advance. "What the hell's that?"[13] asked one Marine. McAnally had never seen anything like it, but he was not going to waste time analyzing the sight. A quick burst of fire caused one of the Japanese to explode in a ball of flames, but the other hid behind a coral rock. McAnally directed a steady stream of bullets at the rock until they chipped through and killed the second soldier. He and his unit had just encountered the first flamethrowers of the Pacific War.

The combatants struggled at the airfield for ninety minutes. Horie's men inched close to McAnally's line to throw hand grenades, but the Americans cut down the soldiers before they inflicted any harm. As happened elsewhere, Japanese superiority in numbers gave them the advantage. With the enemy moving in, McAnally pleaded for assistance from Devereux. When the major replied that he had no one left to send, McAnally said, "Well, sir, I reckon we can make out a little longer."[14]

Shortly after this exchange, Devereux lost communications with McAnally. He sent a two-man patrol from his command post to reconnoiter the airfield, but when that patrol failed to return, Devereux concluded they had been killed and that the airfield was most likely lost. For the first time, he considered the likelihood that the Japanese had overrun many spots on Wake and that he might soon have to establish a last-ditch line along the road near his bunker.

To the airfield's east at Peacock Point, Lieutenant Barninger's forty men remained at the 5-inch guns, as ordered, in case enemy ships attempted to move in closer. Every explosion and every machine gun burst made them want to rush to the aid of their fellow Marines, but orders were orders, and they sat with their guns.

They drew fire from the airfield a quarter mile away, but surprisingly the bullets came from McAnally's squad shooting eastward toward the Japanese. "We were scared," said Cpl. Franklin Gross. "McAnally was firing from the airport right into us. I could lie on my back and watch the tracers go right over us. If we stood up, he'd a killed us."[15]

Lieutenant Barninger later wondered if he made the correct choice in keeping his men around the guns, but he felt that with the information available at the time, he could take no other course. As a result, the men at Battery A played little part in the December 23 struggle for the atoll.

The final scene of fighting occurred at the airfield's western end, where Lieutenant Kliewer and the Marines posted to detonate the mines battled the Japanese. Throughout the night the men, armed with two submachine guns, three .45s, and two boxes of hand grenades, rejected repeated enemy bayonet charges.

Around 9:00 A.M., Kliewer noticed the presence of Japanese flags along the beach and throughout the island. He decided to set off the mines before the enemy overran his position, but the motor designed to detonate the charges failed to work because of damage caused by a recent rainstorm. Kliewer's group fought for another hour before falling back toward other American forces.

"We Might as Well Die on the Attack"

To the west, Lieutenant Poindexter's line faced serious threats from enemy units. The officer returned from his grenade attack about one hour before daylight and directed the defense while Japanese soldiers infiltrated the brush to his left. He could tell from the large amount of shouting among Japanese and from the frequent use of flares that the Japanese were massing for a final assault on his line.

At dawn, the Japanese added grenade launchers to their arsenal and quickly knocked out one of Poindexter's machine guns, inflicting several casualties on his men. One civilian, John Valov, heard someone shout to look out, but before he could react, a hard object smacked into the back of his head. A grenade had exploded nearby and propelled shrapnel in his direction. Valov felt a trickle on the back of his neck, which he at first thought was sweat running down, until another man yelled that his head and back were drenched in blood. Valov still felt fine, so he shrugged off the wound and continued.

When G.Sgt. Q. T. Wade muttered to Poindexter that, "They're all over, on all sides,"[16] the officer had no choice but to extricate his men from an increasingly hopeless situation. He ordered a withdrawal to Camp 1 in two groups. While half the men pulled back, the other half laid down cover fire. In this fashion, the Marines leapfrogged back to Camp 1, where by 7:00 Poindexter established another line across the island with ten machine guns and interlocking fields of fire.

Poindexter expected a strong attack at any moment, but he waited with his men for two hours, receiving nothing more than occasional fire. At that point, the aggressive Poindexter decided that if the Japanese were not going to attack him, he may as well attack them. After all, he commanded one of the most powerful units of Americans on the island, with ten machine guns and Marine riflemen. Though he had lost contact with Major Devereux, that was even more reason to assume the initiative. Years later he explained his decision to charge the Japanese. "To hell with that old saw about 'a gallant last stand' like George Armstrong Custer at the Little Big Horn. The Marine Corps had taught me that the only way to accomplish anything is to take the offensive. If we were to fight 'to the very last man,' we might as well die on the attack."[17]

Poindexter sent a messenger back to Camp 1 to round up additional Marines for a counterattack. The man located a group of Marine clerks and truck drivers dug in near a supply dump and told the assembled Marines that the lieutenant wanted everyone with a rifle to move up to the line on the other side of the water tower, but his pleas at first had no effect.

The youngest man present, eighteen-year-old clerk Cpl. Cyrus D. Fish, led the way. Rising from the floor, Fish, whom Poindexter later praised for his "inspiring initiative and courage," picked up his gear and shouted, "What are we sitting on our asses here for?"[18] With that display of courage by the teenager, the other men grabbed their rifles and started toward Poindexter's line.

A few Navy personnel joined them as they moved forward, including two who had been trapped on a water tower since the battle's opening moments, F1c. William O. Plate and S2c. James M. Mullen Jr. The men had been standing watch atop the tower near Camp 1 since shortly before midnight. When they climbed the sixty-foot ladder to relieve the men who had been on duty, Plate ignored the fact that he manned his post with neither rifle nor handgun. Weapons remained a precious commodity on Wake, and as naval personnel, he had no access to any, but he relaxed in the knowledge that all the previous nights had passed without incident.

Kajioka's sudden arrival jarred Plate back to reality, for here he was, in the midst of an enemy invasion, without a means of fighting back. Since he had orders to remain on the tower, he intended to watch the Japanese through his night glasses and relay the information to Mullen, who would then communicate enemy movements through his telephone to Lieutenant Poindexter's machine gun positions below.

Plate's discomfort magnified geometrically through the course of the battle, as firing from both the Americans and the Japanese streamed toward and near them. Marine 3-inch shells swooshed by the tower on their path toward the landing craft, while enemy bullets sped up from more than one direction. Puncture holes in the tower caused by the shooting produced rivulets of water that made standing on the platform perilous.

"We felt like a sore thumb sticking up there," recalled Plate years later. "Anyone on the island could take a shot at us. If we moved from one side of the tower to another, we would get fired on from that side, too. There were a lot of Japs out there. We felt pretty naked up there without a rifle. It was not a good feeling."

Instinct saved Plate's life at one opportune moment. As he observed the beach through his night glasses, Plate suddenly had a funny feeling. "I swung my glasses down to a bulldozer not far below and there was a Jap who had his rifle aimed directly at me. I could see his finger tightening on the trigger through the night glasses. I dropped right where I was on the platform, and he hit the tower right where I had been standing. If I hadn't glanced down, I would have been drilled dead center."

Plate and Mullen remained on the tower for almost five hours while the battle swirled around them. Finally, around 7:00, they contacted Lieutenant Poindexter, who gave them permission to leave their post and join other Marines fighting on the ground. Quitting the tower would be much more difficult than imagined.

"We wondered how we were going to do this," explained Plate. "It was quite a ways to the ground, and then we had to go all the way across open land to reach Poindexter's line, all in plain view of the Japanese." Plate started down first, achieving what he considered record speed for descending the twenty yards to the surface. He and Mullen made a mad dash across the open area while bullets kicked up dirt on all sides.

"It looked like a plowed field when rainstorms start and those big drops of rain hit the ground. The bullets kicked up that much dirt and dust. I've always wondered how I made it across,"[19] said Plate.

Corporal Fish and the reinforcements moved away from Camp 1 toward Poindexter and the sounds of battle, but Poindexter, eager to begin his offensive, thought the men moved too slowly. He shouted for them to quicken their pace, and when one man still lagged behind, Poindexter sprinted out and kicked the man in the rear.

Reinforced with the additional twenty Marines from Camp 1, Poindexter divided his fifty-five men into three squads of about ten men each, two attacking on either side of the road paralleling the beach and a third following to protect the left flank. The other men stayed behind with the machine guns, ready to lunge forward in support at Poindexter's command. Poindexter assumed that all the Marines, including Lieutenant Hanna and Corporal Holewinski, had been killed at the airfield or driven back, so he did not count on receiving any help from that sector. He hoped, however, that the Marines on Peacock Point would rush westward along the beach. If they did, the two forces might trap the Japanese in between.

Poindexter kicked off his assault at 9:00, but quickly experienced difficulty when the men on the left moved more slowly because of the thick undergrowth. Whenever he encountered any Japanese, Poindexter halted his advance and ordered some of the Marines to lay down covering fire, while others rushed closer to the Japanese and dispatched them with a shower of grenades.

Poindexter moved eastward in this fashion until reaching a fork in the road near the airfield's western end, where enemy resistance stiffened considerably. Rather than expend his men, around 11:15 Poindexter halted his counterattack and sent word back for the machine-gun crews to rush forward with their guns.

At that moment, a rifleman shouted that a large cluster of Japanese approached down the road with a white flag. Poindexter scanned the group for signs of any American soldier among them, but he failed to perceive any. Could his counterattack have succeeded? Could the Japanese be surrendering to him? Telling his men to shoot only if the Japanese opened fire on him, Poindexter stepped onto the road, tightly clutching his weapon, and walked forward to meet the opposition.

"In My War We Were Losing"

While Poindexter enjoyed success at the eastern edge of the airfield, one mile to the west, Lieutenant Hanna and his small band of defenders held off endless attacks by hundreds of enemy soldiers, most roused to vengeance by Hanna's accurate shooting. His 3-inch gun had severely damaged Patrol Boat 32, killing many men, and even now he cut down more with his smaller weapons as they attempted to close in. Determined to destroy this pesky group of Americans, Japanese soldiers crawled forward until they lay twenty yards in front of Hanna, jumped up, shouted "Charge!" and ran straight at the lieutenant. American hand grenades, rifle fire, and 3-inch shells from Battery E halted the Japanese before they advanced half the distance.

One of those soldiers facing Hanna, Sub-Lieutenant Ozeki, hugged the ground near Captain Uchida when a hand grenade bounced by. He shoved his face deeper into the coral sand, every limb and muscle trembling, and waited for the explosion and for what he thought must be his death, but the American grenade failed to detonate. He raised his head to witness a gruesome sight—instead of Japanese soldiers charging to a glorious victory, the bodies of comrades cloaked the ground leading to Hanna. Men near Ozeki cursed when they dropped bullets as they tried to chamber the rounds in the darkness. The Japanese may have outnumbered the Americans at this gun, but as far as Sub-Lieutenant Ozeki was concerned, the battle had not gone as expected. "They say that in war each man knows only what he sees in front of him. In my war we were losing."[20]

Finally, a group of soldiers stood and yelled, *"Totsugeki!"* the Japanese word for "charge." Ozeki, now wearing the boots of a dead comrade, tried to rise, but at first his legs would not move. He made a few more attempts before he lifted from the sand and stepped forward, but he trembled so badly that he stumbled with every move he took. Ozeki squeezed off two shots with his pistol, but his hands shook so hard that the bullets smacked into the sand only a few yards ahead of him. Around him, the fallen bodies of other men who had tried to charge Hanna's gun reminded him of rag dolls tossed in a heap.

Despite the deadly return fire, enough Japanese pressed ahead that they threatened to surround Hanna's gun. When Devereux ordered Lewis's 3-inch guns to cease firing at the enemy in front of Hanna, the Japanese closed in even more. The commander, unable to obtain a clear picture of the fight from his command post because so many communications had been cut, later admitted that this move might have been premature, for it left Hanna's and Putnam's line on its own and gave the Japanese an opportunity to close in.

As enemy bullets clanked off the 3-inch gun and its platform, Lieutenant Hanna decided he could no longer fire the weapon. The Japanese had drawn so near that the weapon could not be lowered enough to have an impact, and since the gun offered little protection behind which to fight, he and the others would be dead within moments anyway. He ordered everyone to jump off the gun's circular platform, scoot as far underneath as possible, and lie behind the four eight-foot-long gun legs. The one-and-one-half-foot-thick metallic protrusions provided sparse cover, but it was better than being in the open on the platform. "We'll make our stand here. This is as far as we go," Hanna told Holewinski, Gay, Bryan, and Eric Lehtola, a third civilian. The officer admitted later that his order "was almost like telling the men this is where we are going to die, but I didn't quite put it that way."[21]

As Japanese bullets ricocheted off the platform and enemy soldiers shouted encouragement to one another, Hanna, Holewinski, and their civilian volunteers scampered underneath the 3-inch gun and lay down beside its legs. The sharp crack of Japanese rifles and the bullets pinging against the platform drowned out most noise around Hanna, who had so much adrenaline coursing through his body that he failed to notice the sparks caused by enemy bullets striking metal directly above him. The officer continued to fire his .45, but he realized the end could not be far off.

Twenty yards toward the beach, Sub-Lieutenant Ozeki saw Captain Uchida raise his sword, shout a command, and rush forward. He drew his own sword and ran after him, screaming at the top of his lungs as American tracers laced the nighttime sky. He drew inspiration from his leader, Uchida, and comfort knowing that hundreds of his fellow soldiers followed closely behind him, but when the pair fell to the sand after a short sprint, they realized they had been the only two to advance. Ozeki tried to shout something to Uchida about the predicament they faced, but the officer's head suddenly slumped forward. When Ozeki turned Uchida's head toward him, a huge hole existed where the captain's forehead used to be. A bullet had hit the commander directly below the brim of his helmet and sliced away an entire section of his face.

Alone on the beach, Ozeki pressed into the sand and waited for the other soldiers to join him. To his surprise, at such a perilous moment Ozeki remembered a friendly conversation he had with other soldiers who joked that in combat a man's testicles shrank because of fear. There on the beach, with bullets nipping the ground and men yelling and dying, Ozeki slipped his hand inside his trousers to see if the theory was true. To his delight, he found that fear had not seemed to affect him in any manner.

"I Assumed I Wasn't Going to Make It"

Back near the 3-inch gun, Corporal Holewinski fired as fast as his old Springfield rifle allowed, but because the weapon did not function properly, he could shoot only one round at a time. As he lay in the prone position and pushed off his chest, Holewinski inserted a bullet into the rifle, took aim, fired, and then repeated the process. Holewinski had clear shots at numerous targets, for explosions lit the battlefield and fires in the brush nearby outlined the advancing enemy, but the sight proved to be a mixed blessing. The illumination only reinforced how hopeless was their situation. For a split second Holewinski wished he had signed on for additional life insurance for his family; then he maintained a steady fire while bullets smacked into the platform above and hand grenades bounced close by and exploded.

The enemy, bayonets gleaming in the night, repeatedly rushed Hanna's and Putnam's line, then fell back in the face of heavy fire from the Americans. On a few occasions the Japanese raced completely through the American lines, for at times Lieutenant Hanna shot to his front and then to his rear as the Japanese ran right past. Hand-to-hand fighting again broke out in some spots.

With his band of men from the airfield, Putnam set up a skirmish line immediately to Lieutenant Hanna's right, determined to prevent Uchida's men from rushing by and controlling the land directly south of the airfield. In the midst of the fighting, a Japanese sniper wounded Putnam in the left jaw, causing so much blood loss that blood drenched the photographs of the officer's daughter he always carried in his breast pocket.

With Putnam slipping in and out of consciousness, Elrod, Sorenson, and the rest fought like cornered beasts. Sorenson, the bulky civilian, stood his ground and lobbed grenades at the onrushing Japanese until his supply ran out. With no other weapons at hand, Sorenson picked up large rocks and threw them at the enemy until a volley of bullets cut him down. Captain Elrod jumped up, shouted, "Kill the sons of bitches!"[22] and fired his submachine gun as the other Americans rallied around him. When a Marine nearby ran out of ammunition, Elrod handed him his weapon, grabbed a similar gun from a dead Japanese soldier, and continued to fight. Elrod's courage, combined with the actions of Sorenson and the other men along Putnam's line, momentarily halted the Japanese momentum.

Captain Elrod's heroics formed the stuff from which legends are made. He rarely sought cover, even as the battle raged about him. A Japanese officer, most likely referring to Elrod, mentioned that, "One large figure appeared before us to blaze away with a machine gun from his hip as they do in American gangster films."[23] When Elrod ran out of ammunition, he grabbed a handful of grenades to continue the fight, but the odds of his surviving so many bold actions finally caught up when a burst of Japanese fire killed him. For his actions, both on this day and earlier in the battle for Wake, Captain Elrod was later awarded the Medal of Honor.

As the fight stretched into the second and third hours, Hanna and Putnam faced a critical situation. Every officer was wounded or killed except Captain Tharin, and three enlisted men had fallen. Ten Morrison-Knudsen men, including Sorenson, died and another three suffered wounds in the fierce fighting. Only three civilians emerged unharmed, one of whom was Fred Gibbons, who battled side by side with his son until the younger Gibbons slumped dead.

Nearly surrounded and down to just a few men, Putnam, still weak

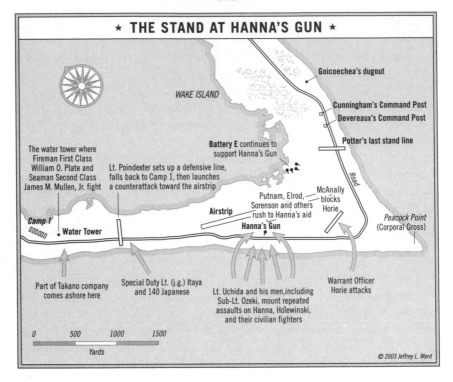

★ **THE STAND AT HANNA'S GUN** ★

WAKE ISLAND

Goicoechea's dugout

Cunningham's Command Post

Devereaux's Command Post

Potter's last stand line

The water tower where Fireman First Class William O. Plate and Seaman Second Class James M. Mullen, Jr. fight

Battery E continues to support Hanna's Gun

Lt. Poindexter sets up a defensive line, falls back to Camp 1, then launches a counterattack toward the airstrip

Putnam, Elrod, Sorenson and others rush to Hanna's aid

McAnally blocks Horie

Road

Airstrip

Hanna's Gun

Peacock Point (Corporal Gross)

Camp 1

Water Tower

Part of Takano company comes ashore here

Special Duty Lt. (j.g.) Itaya and 140 Japanese

Lt. Uchida and his men, including Sub-Lt. Ozeki, mount repeated assaults on Hanna, Holewinski, and their civilian fighters

Warrant Officer Horie attacks

0   500   1000   1500

Yards

© 2003 Jeffrey L. Ward

from blood loss and fending off enemy soldiers with his .45, fought his way over to Hanna's gun, where the lieutenant and his men had already taken shelter under the platform. Hanna glanced over from his position in time to spot three Japanese, neatly silhouetted against the nighttime sky, stalking Putnam from less than ten feet away. Hanna took aim with his .45 and shot each man in the forehead from such a close range that he saw the bullets enter their heads and exit through the back, creating holes large enough for him to sink a fist into.

The fighting now collapsed on Hanna's 3-inch gun, a temporary haven for the cluster of Marines and civilians who huddled underneath. The Japanese took such large casualties in attacking that they at first retreated to the brush, from where they kept Hanna and Putnam pinned down with rifle fire and lobbed hand grenades toward the Americans. Holewinski learned to ignore the grenades that smoked, since those weapons always failed to explode. When a grenade tumbled in that did not smoke, he squeezed as close to the metal leg as he could and hoped for the best.

Sub-Lieutenant Ozeki had another reason besides the heavy losses for not being so aggressive in grappling with the Americans. He had been taught in training never to let the Americans move within an arm's reach, since every American soldier was a trained boxer who could snap their necks with one punch. He did not know if it was true, but Ozeki was not about to give one of his opponents a chance to prove it one way or the other.

The battle dissolved into a series of repetitive actions. When the Japanese thought they had the advantage, they scrambled out from the brush and raced toward the gun, shouting words of exhortation to each other. Hanna, Putnam, and the few men underneath or near the gun answered with their rifles and .45s, while Bryan hurled hand grenades. The Americans repelled attack after attack, always preventing the Japanese from closing the circle around them and bringing fire from all sides.

For more than two and one-half hours the beleaguered men at Hanna's gun kept the enemy at bay. Hanna and Putnam fought side by side, lying on the ground underneath the platform while they fired their .45s. No one expected to survive—too many Japanese soldiers and too few Americans occupied a small radius of action.

"That was a foregone conclusion," Lieutenant Hanna said after the war. "I assumed I wasn't going to make it. We weren't going anywhere. You're feeling that you don't have any choice, so you might as well make as much of it as you can."[24]

Corporal Holewinski harbored similar thoughts, but he pushed them out of his mind as quickly as he could. If he was a dead man, at least he intended to behave honorably during his final moments and take as many Japanese with him as he could. Holewinski watched one Japanese soldier lift his head to look around; then he fired his rifle. "We were close enough that when my shot hit him he spun around and the blood spurted out, just like in the movies. When he went down, his buddy jumped up, and I got him before he got his rifle out. I shot him, he spun around and went down."[25]

At least thirty dead Japanese littered the ground around Hanna's gun. Bryan became so absorbed in throwing his grenades at the enemy that he refused to share any with Holewinski, who instead kept using his rifle. At the same time, Holewinski heard Bryan yell to Gay that he should save two bullets in the gun he was using. In case the Japanese were about to overrun their position, Bryan wanted a bullet left for each civilian rather than allow them remain alive and face possible torture.

Putnam continued to briefly lose consciousness from the wounds to his neck and chin. He grabbed Hanna's first-aid kit, hastily bandaged his neck, and then returned to the fighting, but he could not shake his drowsiness. That became the least of his worries when two Japanese soldiers suddenly appeared above him. He fired two quick rounds at the Japanese, who slumped dead to the ground beside Putnam.

Dozens of hand grenades bounded near the platform, but fortunately either they failed to detonate or the platform's legs absorbed most of the impact. One grenade tore a chunk of flesh the size of a baseball out of Holewinski's back, but in the heat of the action he did not realize he had been hit until after the battle, when he finally felt the blood trickling down his back and legs.

"Where's the Cavalry Now?"

Daylight, normally an ally in that it enabled one to see better, worsened the situation for Hanna, as carrier aircraft started bombing and strafing the position around 7:00 A.M. Aircraft swooped down on the gun and peppered the entire area with bullets, killing Gay and Bryan, the two civilians who had battled so valiantly through the night. Holewinski, who was hit in the left leg by the same aircraft, saw Bryan's body lift up off the ground from the bullets' impacts, then slump back onto the sand. The enemy planes returned for more runs as the few survivors shrank closer to the steel legs for protection.

"The second attack the Japanese got me in the right leg," explained Holewinski. "Those bullets were like hot knives going through you. I was lying on my back, looking straight up at the airplane, and I could see the rear gunner's glasses, the plane came so low. He started making a third run, and I'm scooting under the gun some more."[26]

Holewinski, with wounds to his back, both legs, and to his buttocks, lay still, hoping the pilot would think he was dead. His gamble worked, as the enemy bullets splattered into the sand beyond his body.

Hanna praises Gay, Bryan, and Lehtola for sacrificing their lives to assist the Marines, but he blames himself for their deaths because he could not train them properly. Marines are taught to stay low to the ground at all times, but the three construction workers died when they raised their heads to take a look at the battle area. "They didn't hug the ground like they should," said Hanna. "They'd stick their head up at the wrong time, but they had no training. You have to know that somebody is looking for you at the same time you are looking for them. That bothers me. I didn't take the time to explain that to them. It was my fault. I didn't have much time to show them much of anything."[27]

The trio perished, not because of Hanna's fault, but because they did what they thought they should do, fight alongside their military brethren, and no amount of training by Hanna or any other officer in the limited time available before the landing assault would have likely altered the outcome.

The civilian and military worlds united at Hanna's gun to produce a roster of heroes who willingly risked death to do their duty.

For five and one-half hours, from 2:30 until 8:00, Hanna and Putnam orchestrated the defense around Hanna's gun, holding off repeated attacks until they began to run out of ammunition. They could never take a breather, for they never stopped fighting during that time, and Hanna does not even recall taking a drink of water. In a report after the war, Major Devereux tried to describe the intense situation facing Hanna, and to make it easier for the reader he simply compared it to that of Custer's Last Stand, the renowned frontier battle in which American soldiers fought to the death battling larger numbers of Sioux warriors.

They had held out for most of the night, but the aerial attacks at daylight and Japanese numerical superiority proved more than the group could handle. The Japanese gradually drew closer, and as they did, one by one the Americans ran out of ammunition. Finally, weak from blood loss and the constant fighting, both Hanna and Holewinski came down to their final three bullets. The seemingly hopeless situation caused Holewinski to think of those Hollywood films in which surrounded soldiers heroically battle hostile Indians, then are rescued at the final moment by the cavalry. As the Japanese neared the gun, Holewinski thought, "Where's the cavalry now?"[28]

"I Guess We'd Better Give It to Them"

As the long night wound on, Cunningham and Devereux tried to obtain a clear picture of events from inside their command posts, but because communications had been severed, they had to rely on the word of runners sent from battery commanders. Cunningham realized he faced a critical situation when he attempted to order a submarine he thought to be in the waters off Wake to join the fighting, but received instead a transmission from Pearl Harbor explaining that no friendly vessels, surface or otherwise, stood near Wake and none were to be expected. After reading the message, Cunningham concluded his chances of survival were slim. "We were on our own,"[29] he later wrote.

Around 5:00, Cunningham sent another dispatch informing Pearl Harbor of the battle's progress. Without clear communications to Wilkes, Peale, or to Hanna, Cunningham could not accurately assess matters, but he knew the enemy had landed in many places with overwhelming numbers. He transmitted a phrase from a book he had read, Anatole France's *Revolt of the Angels*, which stated, ENEMY ON ISLAND. ISSUE IN DOUBT.[30]

With the situation deteriorating, Devereux shifted Marines from other locations around the atoll to his command post, where he organized a final defense. He placed his executive officer, Major Potter, in charge, then ordered Captain Godbold to rush troops down from Peale and Corporal McAnally to fall back from the airfield. By 7:00, about eighty men supported by four machine guns, the largest American force on Wake, manned Potter's line. Interspersed with the Marines were the civilians from Sergeant Bowsher's crew on Peale, armed with hunting rifles and shotguns they removed on the way down from the demolished Pan American Hotel.

Gunner Hamas left Devereux's command post to join the line, which extended from the edge of the airfield across to the beaches. Already, Japanese fire burst into the Marines, who wanted to prevent the Japanese from breaking through and heading north toward Peale.

The group of Americans could do little to change the dramatic situation. At 7:30 Devereux contacted Cunningham to inform him that, as far as he could determine, the battle fared poorly at every point. He mentioned that "the Japs had secured Wilkes Island, Camp One, the channel, the airstrip and probably Barninger's position [Peacock Point] as well, and that now the enemy was eating his way into the island with Potter's line as the next bite."[31] Devereux had no contact with the Hanna-Putnam line, and he assumed Poindexter fared poorly, as well. He added that he did not think Potter could long hold out against overwhelming numbers.

Devereux made these judgments with the best available knowledge. Some information came from unusual sources, such as the civilian who screamed hysterically that the Japanese along the airfield were bayoneting every American who had been with Poindexter. "They're killing 'em all!" he shrieked as he raced into Devereux's command post. Corporal Brown called Devereux over to listen to an unidentified American who kept repeating in hushed tones over the communication lines, "There are Japanese in the bushes. . . . There are definitely Japanese in the bushes. . . ."[32] Devereux attempted to coax the man into letting him know who and where he was, but before the individual could respond, Devereux heard a burst of fire, followed by silence. These events seemed to indicate the Japanese held the upper hand everywhere.

Then daylight arrived and handed Devereux a glimpse of what surrounded the atoll—more than twenty sleek Japanese ships steaming not far off the coast. He and the Americans could continue to fight, even kill every Japanese then on the atoll, but those ships ringing Wake would either simply bombard Wake into submission or disgorge more forces to clean up the mess.

Devereux could no longer bring his batteries into the battle, for they had all run out of ammunition. Enemy pilots, emboldened by the lack of opposition from the once-potent weapons, humiliated Americans on the silent guns by waving to them as they made runs against the batteries, as if indicating they knew the Americans could not return fire.

All this followed the grim news that the relief expedition had been recalled to Pearl Harbor, information that made it difficult for Devereux and Cunningham to continue the battle. Major Potter recalled later that "I don't believe the situation looked hopeless, or was so considered by anyone, until word was received, prior to the decision to surrender, that the relief force approaching Wake had turned back."[33]

Devereux and Cunningham continued their conversation, each trying to avoid being the first to actually use the word *surrender*. As overall commander, the decision to yield the atoll rested with Cunningham, but he asked Devereux if he felt it was necessary. The Marine skirted the issue by reminding Cunningham the decision was his, then wondered if there was not something he and the military could do to affect the battle. After quick reflection, Devereux concluded that Cunningham also bore the responsibility for over one thousand unarmed civilian lives and that any action he as a Marine officer took would only delay the inevitable while costing the lives of more people.

"Well, I guess we'd better give it to them," said Cunningham to a dejected Devereux. The word *surrender* is anathema to Marines who, according to Corps tradition, never yield to an enemy, so the major attempted once more to think of a different solution. "I tried to think of something— anything—we might do to keep going, but there wasn't anything. . . . It was a numbing realization, bitter to take, but Commander Cunningham's decision to surrender was inevitable, beyond argument. We could keep spending lives, but we could not buy anything with them.

"So I said, 'I'll pass the word.' "[34]

Just then Gunner Hamas returned to Devereux's command post and asked for instructions concerning the fighting along Potter's line. Devereux looked at him and, obviously moved, said with a touch of self-interest, "John, it's too late; Commander Cunningham ordered me to surrender. Prepare a white flag of truce, go outside, and give the order to 'cease firing.' "[35] Hamas and Devereux stared at each other in silence for a few moments, each Marine doing the best he could to contain his emotions at such an awkward moment. Hamas, the warrior who fought in two wars for two different nations, then walked out the door to carry out his superior's wishes.

CHAPTER 10

★

"Remember Wake Island"

"Oh Brother, We've Had It Now"

Now that the decision to surrender had been made, Cunningham and Devereux had to spread word throughout the atoll. In some places, the fighting continued, especially Platt's successful counterattack at Wilkes and around Hanna's gun, so Devereux had to proceed cautiously as he moved from section to section. The men who fought closest to Devereux's command post received the word first, and thus surrendered earlier than did Americans fighting farther away. As a result, combat raged on Wilkes while Americans had already laid down their weapons at certain parts of Wake.

Gunner Hamas left Devereux's command post first, to begin what he later called "Our saddest chapter." From inside, Devereux heard Hamas shout to those Marines nearby, "Major's orders! We're surrendering. . . . Major's orders . . ." Devereux, with tears running down his face and sensitive to the issue of Marines surrendering, hurried to the entrance and yelled at Hamas, "It's not my order, God damn it!"[1]

Seeing the anguish that his commander felt, P.Sgt. Bernard Ketner walked over to him and offered his hand for a handshake. "Don't worry, Major. You fought a good fight and did all you could."[2]

Cunningham grappled with his own misery. He glanced at the men in his command post, futilely trying to think of something he could say to ease their fears, but could find no words to express any comforting thoughts. He then walked out, dumped his .45 into a latrine, and drove away to his cottage, where he shaved, cleaned up, put on a clean blue uniform, and drove back to his command post to officially surrender the atoll to the Japanese.

As men learned of the surrender, they took precautions to prevent the enemy from using anything of value. They removed the bolts from their rifles, shattered the stocks against rocks, hurled pistols into the lagoon, and shoved sand or blankets down gun muzzles. Army Capt. Henry S. Wilson burned the codebooks, dismantled the cipher machines, and tossed the parts into the ocean to preserve the secret American codes.

At the hospital, civilian laborer Theodore Abraham noticed that a Japanese flag had replaced one of the American banners on Wake. The distasteful image seemed an omen of hard times ahead, a fact emphasized by his first encounter with Japanese soldiers. Working as a secretary in the hospital, Abraham tied a white sheet on a long stick and placed it outside the bunker's entrance so the Japanese would not expect any opposition. Despite this precaution, a group of Japanese soldiers stuck their rifles inside and fired randomly, killing one American. Abraham then realized that he was in for a tough time. "This was the final feeling of defeat and the beginning of an uncertain future,"[3] he later wrote.

Meanwhile Devereux, accompanied by volunteer Sgt. Donald Malleck, began his long walk to the various Marine emplacements. Finding nothing more suitable for a sign of surrender, Sergeant Malleck tied a white cloth to the end of a mop handle; then the pair headed over to order Potter's men to cease firing.

"When Devereux came around with a white flag, I said, 'Oh brother, we've had it now,'" explained Private First Class Gatewood, a member of Potter's skirmish line. "Devereux came and said, 'Men, it's over with. We haven't got anything else to work with. Strip your rifles and throw them into the bushes. Stand by and wait for the Japanese to come around.' I think we were too scared to cry. I figured it wouldn't be too long before we were killed, because the rumors were that the Japanese did not take prisoners."[4]

Private Laporte tossed his rifle bolt away and waited. Soon, a group of Japanese slowly approached from the road, forced the Americans to remove their clothes, took rings or other valuables, then tied their hands behind their backs, and ran a cord around their necks. "The Japanese soldiers were small," said Laporte, "but it don't matter what size you are as long as you got a rifle. We hated this. Can you imagine! Our creed was supposed to be you don't surrender. It was hard to take."[5]

Devereux and Malleck started for the hospital a short distance away, but before they took many steps, a Japanese soldier motioned for them to empty their pockets and drop their helmets and pistol belts. The soldier led the officers toward Japanese lines, where another Japanese emerged from hiding. From somewhere, a rifle shot rent the air, and the second man dropped dead. Devereux immediately whirled toward the nearest group of Americans and shouted, "The order has been given to cease firing, and damn it, you'll obey that order!"[6] Devereux hoped to prevent a mass slaughter right there on the road with his quick action.

The first Japanese soldier rolled the body of his dead comrade over, then escorted Devereux and Malleck toward the hospital as if nothing had happened. At the hospital, a Japanese officer handed Devereux a cigarette and explained that he had visited San Francisco in 1939. As they chatted, Commander Cunningham drove up in his truck, stepped out, and walked over. The Japanese officer, a bit confused at seeing two top American officers, asked, "Who Number One?"[7] Devereux pointed to Cunningham.

The Japanese searched Cunningham for jewelry or weapons, then placed him in the back of the truck and asked him to point out the location of land mines. Other than the mines set at the airfield, however, none existed, but the Japanese drove Cunningham away anyway.

A pair of odd circumstances occurred on Cunningham's forced tour. He watched while some Japanese soldiers tried to coax a drunken, shoeless civilian into surrendering. When the man refused to yield until he found his shoes, Cunningham expected the enemy to lose patience and bayonet the man. He was surprised that the soldiers allowed the reeling man to find his boots.

When Cunningham drove past the ruined Pan American buildings, mail and other items from the *Phillipine Clipper* lay scattered about the spot from bomb explosions. Among the refuse fluttered hundreds of pieces of American paper money, enough for any man on the atoll to retire, but Cunningham could do nothing but watch the fortune drift in the wind.

The Japanese used the hospital bunkers to store the first group of American prisoners, which included Gunner Hamas. After being tied with wire and packed into the crowded hospital bunker with many other Marines, some of whom were badly wounded, Gunner Hamas tried to obtain help for the injured men. With the few words of Japanese he learned while stationed in the Far East, Hamas asked an elderly officer if at least Lt. Kahn's hands could be untied so he could tend to the wounded. The Japanese officer looked around to see if any other officer noticed, loosened the wires around Kahn's and Hamas's hands, and gave Hamas some cigarettes. The same officer later permitted Hamas to walk outside and pick up clothing for the men.

Farther from the command post, Lieutenant Lewis's Battery E, nestled along the lagoon less than ten minutes' walking distance from Devereux, had already begun destroying their guns. After sabotaging the guns, Lewis rounded up his men, including Joe Goicoechea and other civilians, and marched them toward Devereux's command post. The emotional moment almost immobilized some of the Marines, who felt sick that they had to be part of a surrender. "Some of the old-timers were damn near bawling and crying that the Marine Corps doesn't surrender,"[8] said Corporal Marvin about the trying march.

Joe Goicoechea feared he and the others would be bayoneted, especially when some Japanese soldiers shoved two of the Guamanian workers around and acted as if they were going to slit their throats. Goicoechea told himself that if the Japanese started slaughtering people, he was going to try to take one of the enemy with him. Fortunately, no violence erupted.

"Hell, This Can't Be Happening"

Devereux next stopped at Hanna's 3-inch gun, where the numerous signs of brutality attested to the viciousness of the fighting there. Both American and Japanese bodies littered the sand, and those who survived, including Hanna and Holewinski, hobbled around or lay on the ground with injuries. At the moment of surrender, the Japanese had drawn to within ten feet of Lieutenant Hanna, who faced them with only three bullets left in his .45. Before the Japanese closed in farther, Hanna threw his handgun in one direction and the clip another way. "Hell, this can't be happening," Hanna thought. "Marines don't surrender. Then after I got thinking about it, of course Marines did surrender." None of his men had much ammunition left, which meant that had they continued, they would have resorted to fighting with bayonets, knives, fists, and teeth.

Lieutenant Hanna and Corporal Holewinski, the two who had been at the scene ever since the initial shot had been fired, slowly extricated themselves from underneath the platform, happy about being alive, yet miserable over having to surrender to guarantee it. Holewinski welcomed the end to the fighting, for he could feel the blood pouring down his leg and needed it treated. An unbelievable thirst also gripped him.

"This was the lowest I felt during the battle," said Lieutenant Hanna. "Up to the surrender, I had no hope of getting away alive from the island. I had already consigned my soul to hell and planned to do what I could until I died."[9]

Hanna tried to stand, but his right leg caved in, and he collapsed to the surface. He at first thought his leg had fallen asleep from being confined underneath the gun platform, but then he realized that he had been hit in the right leg. He had no idea that he had been wounded there; he had concentrated on the battle so intensely during all those hours of fighting that he felt no pain from his right leg until the combat ended. When Holewinski arose, he, too, discovered that a bullet had struck him in the knee, the fourth wound sustained by the young Marine.

Hanna and Holewinski, bloody and bruised, stood on wobbly legs for a moment, two fatigued combatants surveying the gruesome scene around them, surprised that they had survived such a savage contest. Among the fallen rested the bodies of Captain Elrod, the game battler of the air and land, as well as the civilian duo that had so ably helped Hanna and Holewinski on the gun—Robert L. Bryan, an engineering clerk; and Paul J. Gay Jr., the man who served milk shakes at the canteen. The construction workers fought like seasoned veterans instead of the newcomers they were to combat, and in the process helped fashion the legend that became the battle for Wake.

Devereux walked over to the equally grimy Putnam, whose jaw had been partly shot away, thinking that his bloodied aviation officer looked like hell. Instead of complaining about his wounds, Putnam said, "Jimmy, I'm sorry, poor Hank [Elrod] is dead."[10]

Devereux next headed for the western edge of the airfield, where Major Putnam had stationed Lieutenant Kliewer with orders to blow up the airfield. Around 10:15, Kliewer saw men carrying a white flag down the beach. Major Devereux and a group of Japanese officers halted about fifty feet away, from where Devereux gave the order to surrender. Kliewer's men begged him to ignore the command, which they claimed Devereux gave under duress. "Don't surrender, Lieutenant. The marines [sic] never surrender. It's a hoax."[11] Kliewer briefly assessed the situation, then put down his weapon and raised his hands.

The final two locations Devereux contacted—Lieutenant Poindexter's line and Wilkes Island—proved to be the most difficult of his walk, for at those places servicemen and civilians had not only held off the Japanese, but staged successful counterattacks, as well. They assumed the battle had gone in their favor, so when Devereux issued the order to surrender, the men at first did not know how to react.

Lieutenant Poindexter emerged from hiding to greet Devereux, at first expecting to learn the Japanese had been defeated. Within seconds he had to readjust his thinking and prepare his men for the capitulation.

A unit of Japanese soldiers, enraged with Poindexter's successful counterthrust, charged out of the brush with fixed bayonets, intent on killing the Americans. At the last moment, a Japanese officer stepped between the Japanese and the Americans, thereby preventing a slaughter. Poindexter and his men, still reeling from the unlikely course of events, headed along the road with Devereux to Camp 1.

Along the way, Poindexter, accompanied by a Japanese lieutenant, searched the brush for wounded Americans. In their hunt the pair came across a dead Japanese officer who had been shot in the face. The Japanese lieutenant gently placed a small flag over the man's chest and tucked the ends under the belt and shoulder straps, then, with Poindexter's help, carried the body to the road and placed it on a truck. Poindexter, who had seen a can of pears along the path, went back to retrieve the food. As he opened the can, the Japanese lieutenant sat next to him and offered Poindexter a handful of cigarettes. Poindexter accepted, and in return motioned for the Japanese to share some of the pears. There, along a road which wound through death and devastation, with the sounds of battle barely silenced, opposing officers quietly shared food and cigarettes.

As Devereux neared Camp 1, a Japanese soldier scaled the tower to yank down the Stars and Stripes. The image of their flag being so shabbily treated was more than combat-weary men could handle. A few started toward the tower, hatred burning in their eyes, but Devereux shouted, "Hold it! Keep your heads, all of you!"[12] The Marines instantly obeyed and watched tight-lipped as a soldier from a foreign land grabbed the American flag, stuffed it into a camouflage net, and climbed back down with the prize.

A miscalculation almost produced a massacre. G.Sgt. John Cemeris, who had yet to learn of the surrender and still manned his .30-caliber machine gun, shot down an enemy dive-bomber while Devereux and Poindexter led their men through Camp 1. The officers rushed over to where the Marine squatted and ordered him to raise his hands above his head. The tactic worked, for the Japanese herded the Marines together for a march to the airfield without reprisal, while Devereux walked to the old channel for a quick boat ride across to Wilkes. He received the surprise of his life there.

"Who the Hell Gave That Order?"

All things considered, Captain Platt could label the day's events on Wilkes a success. His men had eliminated enemy resistance on the island, and now they advanced toward the channel, fresh with optimism and eager to see what the white flag ahead meant.

The closer he moved toward the oncoming group, however, the more concerned Corporal Johnson became. He discerned Marines among the throng, but he also noticed a larger number of enemy soldiers. When the distance narrowed even more, the wide smiles that dominated the Japanese faces and the looks of dismay that enveloped the Marines indicated ill news.

"It's me: Major Devereux," shouted the commanding officer. "Lay down your arms! Lay down your arms! The island has been surrendered. Lay down your arms! The island has been surrendered!"

Bewildered by the unexpected words, the Wilkes Marines looked at each other as if uncertain of what they heard. Captain Platt bellowed, "Who the hell gave that order?"[13] Major Devereux identified himself, then walked closer to Platt.

"Trudy [a nickname for Platt], tell your men to lay their weapons down. It's an honorable surrender."

In his southern drawl and holding back tears, Platt replied, "Major, do you know what you're asking us to do?"

"Yes, Trudy," replied Devereux. "Tell your men to lay their weapons down."[14]

Platt angrily slammed his .45 to the ground, then shouted to his men to do the same with their weapons. Japanese soldiers rushed to Corporal Johnson and smacked his hands with their bayonets to move him away from his machine gun. Johnson, who so was so thirsty he tried to lick his lips but couldn't, remembered the two hand grenades he carried in his pockets, but when he pulled them out, the enemy soldiers ran back. Using arm gestures, Johnson indicated to a Japanese officer that he only wanted to throw them into the channel. The officer nodded his approval, then stepped over and took Johnson's watch and ring.

"You talk about being startled, that [the surrender order] was the last thing in the world I had expected to see,"[15] mentioned Corporal Johnson about the strange course of events his birthday had taken. He worried that when his captors came across the dead Japanese piled around the truck back at the battery, largely his doing, they would storm around searching for the perpetrators. If so, Johnson doubted he would live more than a few hours, but surprisingly the Japanese did nothing. Johnson concluded that the enemy spared their lives because the Marines gave first aid to the two Japanese prisoners they had seized during the fighting.

Now that the fighting had ended, Private First Class Buehler noticed how pretty the day had been. Blue skies and gentle white clouds framed a brilliant sun. Buehler studied nature for a few moments and tried to recall when he experienced a more lovely day. He could not. "My most vivid memory of December 23 is that it was such a beautiful day, and I thought, 'This is a hell of a day to have to die; what a shame to die on such a beautiful day.' "[16]

As the group with the white flag neared J. O. Young, he discarded the Marine shirt with corporal's stripes and the rifle he used in the battle. If the Japanese thought he was a civilian, maybe they would spare him, but if they found him with military paraphernalia and weapons, he feared they would execute him on the spot for being a guerrilla soldier.

Young was not the only man altering his appearance for safety purposes. Gunner McKinstry brandished his pocketknife and hurriedly cut off his thick red mustache. The Marine learned that the two Japanese they took prisoner had been alerting their unit about a huge American with a red mustache who had gone around the battlefield shooting Japanese on the ground. McKinstry figured if he wanted to live, he had better remove his telltale growth.

Corporal Richardson, the aspiring novelist, realized the irony of what had transpired. While Cunningham and Devereux had been arranging the surrender across the channel on Wake, he and the other men under Captain Platt fought and killed on Wilkes. Five of his buddies died after the battle had already ended near Devereux's command post.

As Richardson dropped his rifle in a pile, another Marine asked him what was wrong. For the first time, Richardson noticed that he had been crying. "What a hell of a way for it to end!" he replied. "What the hell does it matter, we're still alive." Richardson, who like most men assumed during the battle that he would not survive, hoped that whatever the future held for him, he would face it "with a conscious courage I did not have as I faced death."[17]

Civilian and military alike reacted in similar fashion to the surrender. An initial period of disbelief preceded gratitude over being spared. Forrest Read doubted he would ever see family and friends in Boise until Devereux with his white flag, which Read called "the most beautiful sight I ever beheld," stepped on Wilkes to arrange the surrender. "All I can remember," said Corporal Johnson, "is when Devereux told us to lay down our weapons, it was like a thousand pounds was lifted off my head. I knew I was going to die, but I didn't want it to be a senseless death. I was hoping hand-to-hand combat or something like that. I thought well, he's the major and he's in charge. I was no longer responsible for the men around me or their lives."[18]

Young and his uncle had not been the only relatives fighting on Wilkes. When Devereux and the surrendering party arrived at Platt's command post, the Japanese freed the two prisoners taken in the fighting around the 3-inch guns. As soon as one of the soldiers was released, he rushed to a dead Japanese on the ground a short distance away and cried, "My brother . . . my brother . . ."[19]

At other pockets around the atoll, Marines prepared for the Japanese to arrive. Lieutenant Kessler at Battery B on Peale Island told his men to consume as much food as they could, since it might be a long time before they ate again. They broke out emergency rations and some candy bars, but under the circumstances, most did not feel like devouring much. Kessler coaxed them into eating until the supply disappeared. After their hasty "meal," Kessler ordered the men to clean the area so the Japanese would not think they were living in a pigpen.

Due south of Kessler, Lieutenant Barninger destroyed all the weapons of Battery A, then waited at Peacock Point all afternoon for the enemy to arrive and take them prisoner. When no one appeared near dusk, Barninger marched the men to the airfield, where other prisoners from Wake had already been deposited. He thought the chances of yielding without mishap were far greater in the daylight than to remain at Peacock Point and risk surrendering to a nervous enemy after dark.

To civilian Rodney Kephart, the end came as a relief. He had no idea what lay ahead, but he could worry about that later. He had survived the battle, and that was all that counted to him. He wrote that "when the word came in to us that the island had been surrendered, and I wormed my way through the brush to the highway, I felt so relieved and free that I could almost whistle. I felt as though I had walked out from under a load of bricks. It certainly was a relief to be free from the suspense of it all, and to be through dodging hell in small places."[20]

"I'm Going to See You Spit Your Fire"

Throughout the afternoon and evening of December 23, Japanese soldiers escorted every American on Wake to the airfield. The first groups came from near Devereux's command post and from the hospital, followed by the men of Hanna's gun, Poindexter's ragtag army, and Platt's unit from Wilkes. Some men walked to the airfield on their own strength, some hobbled on bare feet scratched by the coral, others leaned against friends or grasped a proffered hand. One group of prisoners, dirty, weary, and demoralized, walked with T.Sgt. Edwin F. Hassig, a muscular ox of a man, when Hassig spotted Major Devereux along the road. Not wanting his commanding officer to see his men in such sorry shape as they trundled by, and hoping to cheer an obviously depressed Devereux, Hassig barked at the exhausted men, "Snap outta this stuff! God damn it, you're Marines!"[21] Almost in unison the men's heads rose and their backs stiffened as they marched by their commander. Devereux, touched by this display of pride, felt more like an officer than he had in a few hours.

As the Americans streamed toward the airfield from all corners of Wake, they passed by signs indicating their stay at the hands of the Japanese might not be pleasant. A civilian, his throat slashed from ear to ear and his body sliced by repeated bayonet thrusts, lay dead on the side of the road, while the headless corpses of two other civilians served warning that the Japanese expected ready compliance.

At the airfield some of the men, already suffering from the wires looped around their hands and necks, had to kneel for several hours on the coral surface. Lieutenant Hanna, Major Putnam, and Gunner Hamas scratched shallow trenches into the harsh terrain in an attempt to avoid the biting wind they knew would sweep across Wake after dark. Diarrhea and dysentery caused a revolting stench, and Joe Goicoechea stood in the middle of a large group of men, naked, and afraid, listening to the moans of wounded men. Sunburned backs, heads, and shoulders afflicted more men as the long day wore down.

J. O. Young worried when some Japanese soldiers took out their swords and polished them with a cloth while glaring toward Young's cluster. He later learned the Japanese were simply wiping salt water off their swords to prevent rust, but the episode caused a few moments of anxiety among the prisoners. Corporal Gross watched a different Japanese soldier, bleeding from a horrible hand wound, hack a stack of wood with his sword. He and other Americans feared that the man would next vent his rage on them. A Japanese guard even boasted to Private First Class Dana that he and the other Marines had less than one hour to live.

With well over one thousand Americans to care for, Japanese treatment depended on when and where the Americans were seized. Some men still wore shoes and undershorts; others lacked both items. Some could move around more than others; some were wire bound while some other men had no restraints.

In the section of the airfield where Major Putnam stood, a Japanese soldier lost control and attacked two of the wounded prisoners with his bayonet. He killed one man, but the second deflected several bayonet thrusts with his unwounded arm and fended off the soldier until a Japanese officer ran over and beat the Japanese with the flat of his sword.

Corporal Holewinski, who because of his wounds could not easily move on his own until the following May, was carried to the airfield, where Lt. Kahn, the naval surgeon, issued a stern warning to one of the men responsible for so many Japanese deaths. "The doctor told me, 'Remember, you *weren't* by the 3-inch guns.' He repeated it a couple of times. We heard later that a Japanese interpreter had told him they had lost so many men at that gun that they were looking for the Americans who were on it."[22]

For a while every American, military and civilian, thought he was about to die. Around 4:00 P.M. the Japanese placed machine guns along the perimeter and turned the weapons toward the captives. Believing they were about to be massacred, the Wake Islanders prepared to meet their deaths. "I was staring at the gun barrel," said Corporal Gross, determined to go out a brave man, "and I knew as well as I was going to take another breath that they were going to kill us. I looked right at that barrel and thought, 'Well, I'm going to see you spit your fire.' I was beyond praying. Nobody seemed scared. We knew we were dead, and our defense mechanisms kicked in. When all is lost you have no fear anymore."[23]

Pfc. John Edward "Ed" Pearsall forced himself to look at the sun one more time because he thought he would never get another chance. Pfc. James King decided with a small band of other Marines that at the sound of the first shot, they would all rush one machine gun and at least try to take out that position before dying. J. O. Young talked with the man next to him about what they could do if the Japanese opened fire, then stopped when they realized they could do little but accept the inevitable. "We figured this was the end—sick, wounded, civilians, Marines, Navy, Army—we were all together,"[24] said Joe Goicoechea. The men from diverse worlds—civilian and military—who forged sturdy bonds during the fifteen-day battle for Wake, now stood in open defiance of the Japanese, doomed men mounting one final retort, this time with their attitudes rather than their weapons. Some men actually moved closer to the front lines to ensure they were killed in the initial rounds of fire rather than wait on the airfield, wounded yet not dead, for a Japanese officer to walk up and put a bullet in their heads.

At the last moment, Admiral Kajioka—dressed in a pressed white uniform and on the atoll to formally accept the surrender—rushed to the airfield and ordered the Japanese to halt. He engaged in a heated debate with the Army officer in charge, with each man wildly gesticulating and screaming back and forth. After fifteen tumultuous minutes, Kajioka finally won the argument, and the Army officer reluctantly ordered his men to secure their guns and leave the airfield.

Having survived one intense confrontation, the defenders tried to improve conditions for their wounded and naked comrades. By midafternoon Major Putnam obtained permission to separate the men into civilian and military and to place the wounded and sick in one location to make it easier for Lieutenant Kahn and Dr. Shank to provide care.

Before the Japanese moved the captives away from the airfield, an interpreter read a proclamation to the prisoners about their fates. The men would not be harmed as long as they obeyed orders, but anyone who caused problems would be harshly treated. The interpreter ended by announcing that the emperor of Japan had kindly agreed to spare their lives. From somewhere in the middle of the conglomeration, a Marine shouted,

"Well, thank the son of a bitch."[25] The comment crystallized what most men felt, but they at last knew they would not be shot that day.

Later that day Admiral Kajioka proclaimed the atoll a possession of Japan and renamed it Bird Island.

The men spent the remainder of December 23 at the airfield, alternately huddling against the cold and moving about to keep warm as the sun set. By nightfall, most at least had some article of clothing. "Still naked, we were assembled on the airfield," wrote Cpl. Robert M. Brown. "After several hours the order was given to recover our clothing. Because it was piled helter-skelter at several sites, and because those prisoners who happened to be closest to a pile got to grab first, I wound up with one short-sleeve khaki shirt, one pair of khaki trousers and a pair of shower clogs. But it was better than being naked."[26]

That night the Japanese moved most of the men into the airfield hangar, more than one thousand men crammed into a structure with a capacity for less than half that number. The conditions quickly became intolerable, as men fainted in the stifling heat and became sick in the fetid atmosphere. Lieutenant Barninger kept his men together as much as possible and told them to move as closely to the hangar door as they could, where they might catch some fresh air.

Finally, to relieve the situation, guards allowed some of the men to return to the open air. Even though the night would be cold and wet, at least outside they had room to move about. There were times that night, though, when the men wished they had remained in the hangar, for a rain squall drenched everyone and cold winds swept across the open field.

"Tomorrow Is Christmas Day"

A little more organization appeared over the next day and a half for the badly sunburned men, who had to sit under Wake's scorching sun for much of that period. Other than a little jam and bread and some foul-tasting water that had been trucked to the airfield in huge gasoline drums, the defenders enjoyed no food, and their weary, battered bodies had little opportunity to rest and recover.

On Christmas Eve, the Japanese formed a work detail of thirty men under Captain Tharin and Gunner Hamas to bury the American dead. They retrieved the bodies that had been stored in the refrigerator since the siege's early days, now badly decomposed because bombings had destroyed the unit. Hamas picked up a jar of maraschino cherries in the same storage room and shared them with the other men. Later, when he returned to the

United States after the war, Hamas discovered that he could not eat cherries without becoming ill.

Workers gently moved the bodies of four Marines and twelve civilians to a four-foot-deep grave dug seventy-five yards inland, close to the area of Hanna's gun. Decomposition and battlefield wounds hideously disfigured the bodies near the gun. When Cpl. Robert Brown and another Marine lifted Captain Elrod's body, completely riddled and torn with machine-gun wounds, the shattered body broke in two pieces.

The work detail laid out the bodies so they faced the sea, covered them with ponchos weighed down with gravel, and then filled in the trench so a mound two feet in height appeared. This had to suffice as the grave marker, since no other materials were available with which to fashion a cross.

A handful of Japanese admired the valiant effort the Wake Island military and civilians had displayed over the past two weeks and wished them well. WO Nemeto Kumesaka wrote on December 24, "Tomorrow is Christmas Day for foreigners, the hearts of the defenders of Wake and their families who have been defeated just before the day must be full of deep emotion. I feel sympathetic despite the fact that they are our enemy. . . . I hope the best thought will be given to the defeated officers and allow them to spend their last Christmas night in comfort. Pity your enemy, but hate his deeds."[27]

On Christmas Day, Lieutenant Hanna's third wedding anniversary, the Japanese moved the Wake Islanders into more permanent housing, the enlisted men occupying the barracks at Camp 2 and the officers and a few high-ranking civilians the cottages nearby. Barbed wire surrounded each building, but otherwise the men were left largely to their own in the shelters. Commander Cunningham resided in one cottage with civilian John Rogge, Captain Platt, Captain Wilson, and the hapless auditor, Herman Hevenor, while Devereux, Teters, and a few others moved into a second cottage.

The Japanese posted as many as 150 servicemen and civilians to each barracks, which had been designed for far fewer. An additional barracks served as a sick bay into which all the seriously wounded or ill were placed so Lieutenant Kahn and Dr. Shank could provide the most efficient care. However, since the Japanese appropriated most of the American medical supplies to treat their own men, Kahn and Shank had to make do with little.

Living conditions improved in the newer quarters, although men still did not receive enough to eat and the wounded failed to enjoy proper medical treatment. A bit of stew augmented canned food, and men generally relaxed inside the confines of their quarters.

A Japanese guard whose parents lived in Hawaii befriended the Americans in Cunningham's cottage. He kept asking Cunningham if he thought his parents would be safe in Hawaii, and often told the captives, "Pretty soon war over—everybody shake hands."[28]

"A Debt of Deep Gratitude"

The human cost of the struggle for Wake reflected the high price the American defenders exacted for yielding their atoll. When you add the loss of lives on December 11, when Wake's batteries and aircraft sent two ships and their crews to the ocean's bottom, to the tally for December 23, which most probably cost the Japanese another five hundred men killed, as many as one thousand enemy soldiers perished trying to wrest tiny Wake from the outnumbered garrison.

Against this enormous loss of life, 124 Americans died at Wake, including 49 military and 75 nonmilitary personnel. The men of VMF 211, the Guamanian workers, and Morrison-Knudsen's construction crews suffered the highest casualty rates—more than half of Putnam's aviation squadron died, while 10 Guamanian and 65 civilians fell during the battle.

When one measures contributions to the fighting at Wake according to casualties suffered, the final tally indicates that the workers from Morrison-Knudsen played a significant role, despite the fact that so many chose to remain in the brush. It is hard to absolve every man who fled into hiding, but most can be forgiven for avoiding something about which they had little prior knowledge and for which they were ill suited.

Through the years the Marine who contributed as much as anyone to Wake's defense, Lieutenant Hanna, softened his attitude toward those civilians who did nothing. "I didn't have a thought about it until after the action was all over, and then I thought, 'God damn it, you could have done something!' Where were they when we needed them? I don't feel that way now," he said in 2002. "What training did they have? They had no rifles, no pistols. If we had had too many civilians, they may even have gotten in the way."[29]

The official Japanese reaction disregarded the losses and focused on the result, which on the surface showed a victory for Japan. A report concluded that "the enemy forces are, after all, easily beaten. Although they had forces equal to the invasion force and were in a fortified position, they were defeated in a half day's fighting." However, more balanced Japanese observers concluded differently. Sub-Lieutenant Ozeki said that when he realized the Americans had surrendered, he felt he had been granted a reprieve from death. Correspondent Ibushi visited various points around the atoll and described seeing "mountains of dead and rivers of blood," and a naval officer asserted the battle to seize Wake was "one which would have made the gods weep."[30]

Weeping was not in the picture for the Americans. They may have been overwhelmed in the end, but by then the impact of their struggle had already left its mark. In addition to the tremendous boost given to morale at home, the Japanese timetable for expansion in the Pacific had been stalled for two weeks, which gave the United States sorely needed time to recover from Pearl Harbor and assemble men and matériel for a counteroffensive. Since the Japanese had to delay their advance toward Midway, the U.S. had an opportunity to reinforce the island, rebuild damaged ships, and rush other vessels from the West Coast to the front lines in time to hand the Japanese a resounding defeat in June 1942 off Midway.

"Wake may have fallen at last," stated the *Washington Post* on December 24, "but the extraordinary fight made by the Marine defenders has served a two-fold purpose. It has kept a considerable portion of Japanese forces diverted and thus aided the defense of our other possessions in the Pacific. And it has been a thrilling inspiration to all other defenders of freedom, with corollary repercussions at busy recruiting stations. The Nation, indeed the entire Allied world, owes a debt of deep gratitude to the heroes of Wake Island."[31]

"Semper Fidelis"

When news of Wake's fall first arrived in Washington, D.C., top naval officials realized how crushed the president would be at receiving the information. Already beset by problems throughout the Pacific, President Roosevelt at least had Wake to brighten his day. He knew that hopes for their survival were slim, but each day he awakened with the thought that at one spot, a group of isolated individuals showed the world how the American military fought.

The Chief of Naval Operations, Adm. Harold R. Stark, refused to be the one to break the news to the president, so Secretary of the Navy Knox headed to the White House. After listening to Knox's report, a devastated Roosevelt called the news "worse than Pearl Harbor."[32] Roosevelt castigated the Navy for its failure to save the Marines and other men serving on Wake and demanded that the military soon find a way to strike back at the Japanese.

British Prime Minister Winston Churchill happened to be in Washington when Wake fell. Secretary Knox later asked him what he would do to some of the Navy's top officers for recalling the relief force. Churchill, sensing the emotions of the moment and also not wanting to become involved in an American affair, answered that "it is dangerous to meddle with Admirals when they say they can't do things. They have always got the weather or fuel or something to argue about."[33]

Other public figures lambasted Admiral Pye and the Navy for bungling the relief force. Adm. William F. Halsey, soon to become a national hero, said that the relief expedition could have caused severe damage to the Japanese had it continued toward Wake. Respected journalist Clark Lee wrote that the Navy, feeling the effects of its Pearl Harbor debacle, seemed more intent on not losing ships than with saving Marines.

By the time of his State of the Union address on January 6, 1942, Roosevelt had replaced anger with determination. The day before, he signed a Presidential Unit Citation, an award that recognized the achievements of the First Defense Battalion, VMF-211, and their commanders, Major Devereux and Major Putnam, for inspiring the nation and the democratic world.

The next day, in typically powerful fashion, Roosevelt moved the American people with stirring words, including comments about the heroic stand at Wake Island. After declaring the bitterness he felt at not being able to save Wake, Roosevelt stated that the atoll's loss would · only make the United States more determined to once again have the possession under its wings. He continued that "There were only some four hundred United States Marines who in the heroic and historic defense of Wake Island inflicted such great losses on the enemy. Some of these men were killed in action and others are now prisoners of war. When the survivors of that great fight are liberated and restored to their homes, they will learn that a hundred and thirty million of their fellow citizens have been inspired to render their own full share of service and sacrifice."[34]

Ironically, rather than demoralize the nation, the fall of Wake magnified the impact the atoll's defense had already made on the home front. In its December 24 issue, the *Washington Post* admitted that the Japanese had landed on Wake, and since then "there has been only silence from the island's defenders." The nation reacted tensely to the ominous quiet, but considered the siege as an indication that the men had provided evidence of how Americans fight when their backs are to the wall. Six days later, the *New York Times* asserted that "An island or two may be lost, in spite of all that brave men can do. But the issue of this war will never be in doubt if freedom's side is truly represented by Major Devereux, and his Marines, and his civilian mechanics."[35]

Newspapers, again focusing on only the Marine role to the detriment of the other contributors, splashed Devereux's image across their front pages. In its Christmas issue, the *New York Times* spread the Marine motto, *semper fidelis*, across a photograph of Devereux, while other publications ran a picture of a concerned Mrs. Devereux in New York, their son Paddy on her lap, waiting for word of her husband. Other newspapers continued the comparisons to the Alamo, Thermopylae, and the 1879 struggle at Rorke's Drift in Africa, where a small band of British soldiers nobly repelled a numerically superior force of Zulu warriors. They elevated Wake to the model of how the nation should react—resolute, tough in body and spirit, motivated by sacrifice. *Time* wrote of a grateful nation praising the men at Wake, who added another glorious chapter to match the feats performed at Trenton, Belleau Wood, and other Marine victories. Other publications pointed out that if one rotated an image of the atoll 45 degrees to the left, the *V* for Victory sign appeared.

In San Antonio, Texas, the home of the Alamo, a recruiting office began forming an all-Texan one-thousand-man "Avengers of Wake Island" group and announced plans to swear them in as a unit at the historic Alamo. *Family Circle* urged its readers to forget Pearl Harbor and instead remember Wake. Poets flooded newspapers and magazines with their verses, most forgettable, but a few memorable.

A radio broadcast on January 12, 1942, shortly after Wake's fall, trying to bolster enlistments with the Marines, claimed that because of Wake Island, the nation had "a new rallying cry, a new war motto that rings from one end of America to the other and across our far-flung possessions—that cry is 'REMEMBER WAKE ISLAND.' " Later in the year *Look* magazine made heroes out of Devereux, Putnam, Kinney, and a handful of other Marines in a stirring article, and Ray Krank spread the story to youth with a popular comic book version of the battle, complete with colorful images of Marines battling as "the little brown hordes swarmed ashore," air and naval clashes, and Devereux sending his mythical "Send us more Japs" message. The saga even entered the music field when Patrick Andrew Crorkin wrote the song, "Wake Island," in 1942.[36]

While the rest of the nation celebrated Wake's feats, the relatives of the men on the atoll worried about the fates of their sons, husbands, and brothers. They had no way of knowing if their loved ones were alive, dead, or harmed, and they were not likely to receive information soon. All they could do was wait and hope.

The first contact from the government arrived in early January. The Navy Department sent letters notifying families that their husband, son, brother, or father had been on Wake at the time of its capitulation and was most likely a prisoner of war, but that they knew little more. Additional information arrived in May 1942. Some families received word that their relative's name had been found on a list of prisoners, "which definitely confirms the fact that he has been captured by the enemy and is still alive."[37] The two-paragraph notes mentioned that the American Red Cross would furnish them with the best manner of sending packages to their relative. The mother of Private First Class Pearsall had even less information— her December 4 letter to her son returned unopened, with capital letters stamped on the envelope stating the reason as MISSING IN ACTION.

The families of civilians heard less than military families. Morrison-Knudsen attempted to find out all it could about the men, but for a time had nothing to pass on to families. Like the Pearsall family, some parents or spouses received letters they had mailed before Christmas, unopened and marked RETURN TO WRITER, since the mail could not be delivered. For many, this disturbing news was all they had for many months.

*　　　*　　　*

In the meantime, the Wake Island legend machine churned out fresh material almost weekly. Authors transformed Major Devereux into a titanic figure who ranked with George Washington, Ulysses S. Grant, and other prominent figures of American history. One author claimed that the Japanese expected light resistance at Wake, but "They did not know Major James P. S. Devereux. They had never even imagined him. . . . This small, supple man proved under stress to be a fighter and a phrase-maker to equal John Paul Jones."[38]

The single most influential medium in promoting the Wake saga proved to be Hollywood. On December 22, 1941, before the battle had ended, screenwriters finished the initial script for the Paramount Pictures planned release about the atoll, called *Wake Island*. Producers shot the movie, the first World War II combat film to be produced in the United States, off California with Marine Corps cooperation. The movie opened in the fall of 1942 to critical acclaim. Audiences responded to its warm portrayal of the Marines, epitomized in the playfulness of Robert Preston and William Bendix—the comic relief—and they reacted tearfully at movie's end, which depicted the Japanese closing in on a pair of Marines—supposedly the final two on the island—in imitation of the Alamo.

Starring Brian Donlevy, Preston, Bendix, and others, the movie glorified the Marines. Critics, however, loved what *Newsweek* called its "intelligent, honest, and completely successful attempt to dramatize the deeds of an American force on a fighting front." Theaters advertised the movie, which eventually garnered four Oscar nominations, with huge posters bearing the slogan, TODAY! WITH GUNS AND GRIT AND GLORY! WAKE ISLAND, while a movie ad in *The Saturday Evening Post* carried a color picture about the movie showing bandaged, nearly surrounded Marines behind sandbags, shooting Japanese soldiers mere feet from their position. Calling the battle "those fourteen days that will live forever," the ad urged patrons to "Avenge Wake Island" by purchasing war bonds. The Earle Theater in Washington, D.C., announced that it was shifting the screening of another film to free the theater for *Wake Island*. Few customers complained that the establishment bumped the movie *Are Husbands Necessary?* to a later date.[39]

"When Old Glory Did Not Fly, There Is No Freedom"

While the United States elevated Wake to legendary status, back on the atoll the Japanese targeted the top commanders, aviators, and civilian foremen for interrogation. The Japanese seemed concerned that the Americans had so severely punished Kajioka's ships with nothing stronger than the 5-inch guns and even organized search parties to scour the atoll in hopes of finding larger weapons that fired monstrous projectiles. They argued that more powerful batteries had to exist and demanded that American officers explain what happened to them. They questioned Major Putnam for three straight days about aviation matters, but he evaded their queries by answering that they now possessed whatever remained of his aircraft and could learn whatever they needed by examining the planes.

When Devereux sat down with an interrogator, the Japanese officer inquired about radar equipment and other electrical apparatus. Devereux attempted to explain that he knew only generalities about these topics, since that was not his field of specialty. At that comment the officer checked a list of American names and duties and nodded in the affirmative. To Devereux's astonishment, the Japanese possessed the background on him and many of the other officers.

One Japanese interrogator asked Commander Cunningham whether he had actually sent the famous "Send us more Japs" message. When Cunningham explained that no one had been foolish enough to request additional enemy soldiers, the officer replied, "Anyhow, it was damned good propaganda."[40]

Until the first group of prisoners left Wake on January 12, the Japanese had some of the enlisted and civilians clean rifles, locate food and ammunition supplies, string barbed wire around positions, and rebuild some of the defenses in case the United States mounted a counterstrike. Most of the men, looking more like a group of hoboes since they had not shaved in over two weeks, worked haphazardly, or surreptitiously ruined weapons by pouring sand down barrels and removing key parts that had not already been tossed away. Others smuggled canned food and cigarettes into the barracks from the caches they uncovered and shared it with the other prisoners.

Joe Goicoechea stumbled across a small fortune in American money when the Japanese assigned him to sort through the undelivered mail from the *Clipper*. He and a few other Americans slit holes in their pants, stuffed the money inside, and then shared it with the men in their barracks. They had no idea of what lay ahead, but they figured that money might one day help them. Goicoechea and the group handed out about fifty dollars to each man in their barracks.

On his way to a work detail one day, J. O. Young glanced over at a building being used by the Japanese as an office and noticed a crumpled American flag that had been stuffed into a fish net and wedged into the door's bottom as a stopper. Young and the other men bristled at the offensive sight, but they could do nothing as they marched by but stifle their tears and corral their emotions. Accustomed to freedom all their lives, the men suddenly faced a world in which their every move would be dictated and their fates determined by someone else. "One can not imagine what a horrible and helpless feeling that was to see our flag so desecrated," Young wrote after the war. "One thing we found out at once was that when Old Glory did not fly, there is no freedom."[41]

Dr. Shank, whose optimistic outlook raised morale among the patients, did his best along with Lieutenant Kahn to ease the conditions for the wounded men in the makeshift hospital, but they could do little since they worked without sufficient medical supplies. Corporal Holewinski, hobbled by the multiple wounds suffered around Hanna's gun, required extensive treatment, but the Japanese only permitted his bandages to be changed each day. Holewinski had to lie in bed with maggot-infested wounds and rely on inner strength to carry him through the ordeal.

Despite having to yield the atoll, most Americans on Wake still believed the United States would rush to their rescue. They expected to awaken any day to see the U.S. Navy ringing the atoll. At worst, some of the men guessed the war would end within six months and they could return to the United States. Corporal Johnson, unimpressed by the dismal Japanese performance in the December 23 battle, bet one man fifty dollars that the war would be over by July 4, 1942. Some men taunted their captors by claiming an American landing force would sweep in and destroy them.

Commander Cunningham, depressed over the loss of Wake, figured that if an American squadron appeared, it could handily destroy the Japanese cargo ships moored to buoys. "At any moment, I kept telling myself during those first days, American submarines or aircraft would come in for the attack. All of us in the cottage were sure it would happen, and soon."[42]

John Rogge, the civilian construction worker from Idaho, served as Cunningham's orderly after the surrender and lived in the cottage with him. Cunningham and the other officers spent hours discussing the recent operation and what they should or should not have done. Rogge heard Captain Platt blame himself for not somehow sending word to Devereux of his success on Wilkes. Platt believed that if he could have done so, he could have shifted his men to Wake, where the combined forces might have eliminated the rest of the opposition. According to Rogge, Cunningham hated yielding the atoll but did not place all the blame on himself. Cunningham and Platt agreed that the relief force "turned chicken."[43]

The interlude between the battle on December 23 and the departure of most of the atoll's defenders on January 12 passed peacefully. Some officers tried to lift spirits on January 1 by shouting, "Jappy New Year."[44] Lieutenant Kinney found a broken portable radio in one of the barracks and repaired it so that the men obtained some news from the outside, including

Roosevelt's promise to build fifty thousand aircraft in 1942, a vow that cheered everyone.

When he was not tinkering with the radio, Lieutenant Kinney tried to determine a way he could escape. He believed that as an officer, he had a duty to flee at the first opportunity, and along with Captain Tharin, Kinney laid plans to steal a Japanese seaplane floating in the lagoon and set course for Midway. Kinney realized the escape was a long shot, but the preparation kept him busy and helped to pass the time.

In another barracks, each day after Corporal Johnson ate his morning ration, he walked outside barefoot, covered his scarred and blistered feet in the sand, and hoped the sun and sand would help heal them. Since he had not been able to remove his shoes or socks during the fifteen-day battle, his feet had given him many problems.

As he sat with his feet in the sand one day, one of the two Japanese soldiers he helped capture on Wilkes entered the barracks area and began inspecting each man's face. Johnson recognized him and hoped the soldier would not walk over to him, for, says Johnson, "I thought he was going to cut my head off."

When he located Johnson, the soldier slowly walked over, took a good look into Johnson's face, then pulled up his own shirt to show the dressing on his back that covered his wounds. He motioned for Johnson to follow, but instead of taking the Marine to his execution, the Japanese led him to a building packed with personal belongings, such as clothing and suitcases, and beckoned for Johnson to help himself. "I guess he was trying to tell me it was cold where we were going, and he gave me this suit and a shirt. I guess he thought I had saved him from being bayoneted at the gun on Wilkes, when I was only telling some men to take him to Captain Platt for questioning."[45]

On January 11, the most prominent question on every American's mind was answered when the Japanese notified them that most of the men would board a transport the following day for shipment across the Pacific. An interpreter read the names of three hundred men who were to remain on Wake as laborers to finish the construction projects already under way, but promised they would receive good food and good treatment. As soon as the work was completed, including repairing and repaving the airfield, the interpreter claimed the Japanese government would release the three hundred and allow them to return to their homes in America.

Herman Hevenor, the government auditor, encouraged John Rogge to claim he was Hevenor's secretary. As a civilian government employee, Hevenor would most likely be repatriated in the coming months, while the military and civilian workers faced lengthy incarcerations. Had Rogge gone along with the ruse, he stood a decent chance of returning to Idaho long before his coworkers. Rogge, however, hesitated to leave his friends and declined the offer, an act he later regretted when the Japanese in fact included Hevenor in a group of repatriated diplomats a few months later. "I didn't have the brains to say all right. I probably could have gone home to the United States when he did in 1942, but I was twenty-one years old and scared shitless. That was one of the greatest mistakes of my life, and every time I thought about it in prison camp, I wanted to beat myself over the head. But you never know what might have happened. I could have gone home, been drafted, and ended up being killed somewhere else."[46]

Most Wake Islanders considered the order to pack for an unknown destination a bad omen. The move negated any chance of rescue by the U.S. Navy, and since they would be steaming west toward Japan, they would be even farther from their loved ones and everything they knew. A stark sense of isolation gripped the men, who had to somehow pull together their remaining strength to face the ordeals that lay ahead. It would prove to be almost as difficult a task as fighting their recent battle.

★

CHAPTER 11

"I Was Torn from Everything I Knew"

"When the Brutality Started"

The period of uncertainty about whether the men would remain on Wake ended January 12, 1942, when the first of three groups embarked on the *Nitta Maru* for a voyage to parts unknown. Two groups remained behind—one all-civilian unit to complete construction of military positions, and the other consisting of those military and civilian personnel still too severely wounded to move.

For men who endured the fifteen days of combat on Wake and then had to deal with what many saw as the humiliation of surrender, the journey represented another step wrenching them from what was familiar. Every mile away from Wake meant one mile farther from home.

Some even had to contend with being separated from the men they had known since childhood. Joe Goicoechea and George Rosendick headed to the *Nitta Maru* with the 1,187 men on January 12, but their friend, Murray Kidd, had to stay behind since he was one of the few who could operate the tug going from Wake to Wilkes. Saying good-bye to lifelong chums, men with whom he'd shared so many laughs and escapades, proved one of the most difficult moments of his life.

"I saw Joe on the lighter and waved to him," said Kidd. "I wanted to go with them so bad. Seeing them steam away made me feel like I was torn from everything I knew."[1]

A few men, like Major Devereux, were allowed to pack a handful of items into small bags. He chose a pair of shoes, a toothbrush, some underwear, and a pack of cards. The rest of the men assigned to the *Nitta Maru*, including Goicoechea, Hanna, and Rosendick, headed to the lighter with nothing but the clothes on their backs. After Kidd transported his mates through heavy seas to the ship, the prisoners boarded in one of three ways—through a hatch on the port side, by climbing a heavy rope net onto the deck, or hauled aboard by means of a cargo net.

A different world waited for them once they stepped on the transport's deck—they had to run a forty-foot gauntlet of angry, armed Japanese as their rude initiation into what would be a life of hell. "We were put on a lighter and taken out by these tugs operated by civilians," said Corporal Johnson. "That's when the brutality started. It was planned brutality. I sheltered my head as best I could. The worst part was when you had to go down into the hold, because then you had to use both your hands and your feet, and you were totally exposed. No blood was on me, but I sure had some sore shoulders and I had a big knot on the right side of my head. They used bamboo sticks." Explaining this part of his incarceration sixty years after the event, Johnson added, "It's going to take me a long time to forget what happened on the *Nitta Maru*."[2]

"As soon as we stepped on the boat, these Japs are in a line," recalled Private Laporte, "and one of 'em knocked the hell out of me. We had to run the line, and they hit us from behind, on the head, with rifles and clubs."[3] Lieutenant Hanna, wearing only a pair of lightweight trousers, shirt, and shoes designed for duty on a tropical isle, was smacked about the body and head with covered bayonets. If he or anyone else slumped to the deck, the Japanese beat him until he rose and continued forward.

The civilians fared no better. Ill from indigestion or nerves, Joe Goicoechea spent most of the trip out to the transport vomiting, his condition aggravated by the rough seas and churning craft. Weakened and demoralized, both by this and by being separated from Murray Kidd, Goicoechea tried to climb up the net but slipped. For a second he feared either being crushed between the barge and the *Nitta Maru* or falling into the shark-infested water, but a man behind him gave Goicoechea a helpful push onto the deck.

Japanese soldiers searched Hans Whitney's group for valuables when it stepped aboard. The Japanese burst out in laughter when they found a set of false teeth in one man's pocket. They casually tossed them to the deck, and when the American tried to retrieve the teeth, they kicked him in the face. Marine Cpl. Robert M. Brown was punched in the stomach and ribs, then handed over to a line of Japanese armed with broom handles, pieces of pipe, belts, and clubs.

The *Nitta Maru* had been a luxury liner before the war, but only misery and a foretaste of hell greeted these unfortunate men. The Japanese shoved Cunningham, Devereux, and twenty-eight other officers into the ship's tiny mail room directly over the engine room, spacious quarters compared with what lay ahead for the rest of the military and civilian prisoners in the ship's sweaty confines of the cargo spaces in the forward portion of the vessel.

Every man received a typed list of rules governing their conduct during the trip. The first sentence made clear that "The prisoners disobeying the following orders will be punished with immediate death." Hanna, Goicoechea, and the others scanned a list of twelve such punishable offenses, including trying to obtain more food than given, attempting to leave the room, "showing a motion of antagonism," and "disordering the regulations by individualism, egoism, thinking only about yourself, rushing for your own goods." In classic understatement, the notice warned, "Since the boat is not well equiped [sic] and inside being narrow, food being scarce and poor you'll feel uncomfortable during the time on the boat." The sheet ended with the ominous statement that the Empire of Japan "will not try to punish you all with death."4 Each American wondered what the rules meant and how strictly the Japanese would enforce them, especially the one about egoism. They lived not only with the specter of being taken farther from loved ones, but also with the uncertainty of knowing which action, whether intentional or not, might bring about their deaths.

"We Must Never Give In"

Conditions for the officers differed slightly from those faced by the enlisted and civilian personnel. For Lieutenant Hanna and each of the other officers, what turned out to be "home" for the next ten days was approximately six square feet of living space in the mail room, which the Japanese kept illuminated around the clock. A single five-gallon bucket, emptied once a day, served as the bathroom facility, and each man had to stand or sit in complete silence all day.

Each evening the officers assembled for an inspection by the guard commander, Capt. Toshio Saito. They had to line up in neat rows, then respond instantly to orders given by Saito or any other Japanese to avoid a beating. Many of the men, including Hanna, endured slaps to the face for not understanding orders given in a foreign language. During one of these inspections, the Japanese took Commander Cunningham's Naval Academy class ring that he had managed to hide from previous searches.

Twice a day, a cabin boy brought food into the room. The fare usually consisted of water and a meager handout of rice or barley, sometimes supplemented with bits of fish, an olive, radish, or pickled seaweed. The men learned to eat everything to maintain their strength, no matter how foul-tasting or -smelling.

One day the Japanese cabin boy brought in something other than their meal. With a boastful attitude, he handed around photographs of the devastation at Pearl Harbor taken by Japanese aircraft. The images stunned the gathering and caused morale to plummet. Lieutenant Kinney recalled later that "We had heard that the damage at Pearl Harbor had been considerable, but the destruction revealed in the pictures was numbing. The capsized and burning battleships alongside Ford Island seemed to dash any hopes we might have had for a short war."5 Left alone with his thoughts and time on his hands, each officer faced the numbing realization that before help could arrive, their nation had to rebound from what appeared to be a resounding defeat. That meant that their involuntary stay in Japan or wherever the ship headed could be measured in years instead of months. As the *Nitta Maru* chugged westward, a sense of hopelessness cut through the men.

Captain Platt, who relaxed his men on Wake with an ever-present cheerfulness, restored a semblance of morale by his demeanor during a beating. The Japanese had grown lax in enforcing the no-talking regulation, but one day they burst in and grabbed the affable Platt, who had been one of the most audible violators. They hanged him from ceiling pipes and severely beat him with clubs, expecting to make an example out of the vocal American. When Platt refused to cry out, the Japanese struck him harder. Platt gritted his teeth and remained silent. After the Japanese departed, Platt told his fellow officers, "Twarn't nothing."6

Platt's example heartened the Americans. They had seen that even though they could no longer battle with guns and hand grenades, they could fight the Japanese with attitude. Lieutenant Kinney remembered this incident well after the war and wrote, "The manner in which Captain Platt withstood this punishment set an excellent example of resistance for the rest of us to follow during our period of captivity. We must never give in. We must always show our enemies that we were stronger—at least in spirit—than they were."7

As bad as it was in the mail room, it did not compare to the miserable conditions for the men in the *Nitta Maru*'s hold, where sweltering air, mixed in with the odors of diarrhea and vomit, hung over everyone. The Japanese packed the men in so tightly that they all could not lie down to go to sleep. In the cramped conditions, they had to take turns stretching out on the metal deck while the others knelt. Standing would have improved the situation, but the Japanese forbade anyone from taking a position higher than kneeling.

Five-gallon buckets in each corner served as the lavatory facilities. When one was full, a prisoner had to take the container to the middle of the hold, where the Japanese hoisted it up and dumped the contents overboard before returning it to the men waiting below. Their "meal" consisted of a cup of gruel and a cup of water once or twice a day.

"There were no Japanese guards down there," stated Corporal Marvin. "You could see them standing above in the passageway, looking down. Every once in a while they would come down and tell us they were winning the war. They sank the *Enterprise* three times! They sank all our battleships over and over."[8] Even though the war news sounded too fantastic to believe, men like Marvin and Goicoechea could not casually dismiss it. After all, the Japanese had overrun Wake and smashed Pearl Harbor, feats once unimaginable.

Like the officers in the mail room, the civilians and enlisted had orders to remain silent. Like their officers, they often ignored it. Most of the time the Japanese stayed away, for few had any desire to enter such a stinking, depressing place as the hold, but sometimes their captors hurried down, selected a man, and beat him senseless. A friend of Hans Whitney came back after a beating and exclaimed, "Those damned bastards don't pull any punches!"[9] Goicoechea noticed that the Japanese most often vented their anger on tall, light-haired, light-complexioned men.

The men never knew when the Japanese might select someone for punishment. As retribution for talking, the Japanese took Pfc. Jacob R. Sanders and Pfc. Robert E. Shores over to some pipes. "Shores was told to reach up and grab onto an overhead pipe," Sanders wrote after the war. "They then proceeded to flog him with a club about the size of a baseball bat. I watched this and thought I had a good idea. I decided that when it came to be my turn, with my hands up on the overhead pipe, I would be able to bend away from each blow, thereby lessening the severity of the beating. Boy was I wrong! Our captors weren't stupid and quickly caught on to what I was doing. Another Japanese sailor then stood in front of me with the tip of his saber right at my navel. I then had to lean into each blow so that I wouldn't get gutted by that sword!"[10]

Some of the men suffered nightmares about the *Nitta Maru*'s hold for years. They could not move without the cooperation of those next to them, and traveling to and from the buckets in the corner to relieve themselves was an experience in itself. Men had to step over and squeeze around other men on their way to the buckets, where an overpowering stench assailed their senses. Diarrhea and vomit turned the deck into a slippery obstacle course.

In the early days of the voyage, the men prayed that Japan was not their final destination. They believed that a camp in China or any other Japanese-controlled area would be preferable to being confined deep inside Japanese home territory. As the *Nitta Maru* churned its way toward her destination, though, hopes dissipated when the hull turned progressively colder. That seemed to indicate a northerly destination—the same direction as Japan.

The weary days blurred into an indistinct stretch of time, framed by defeat on Wake at one end and incarceration in an unknown location at the other. Few men panicked and screamed, but every individual faced those moments when he wondered what the outcome would be. Ironically, some worried that they might even die at the hands of fellow Americans, for some of the men swore they heard submarine torpedoes zing by the hull.

Corporal Johnson kept track of time by counting the cups of water—every two cups meant one day at sea. To keep a strong mental edge, he consciously thought of his school days. "I transplanted my mind to football games at Chaminade College or the tea dance at Sacred Heart Academy, an all-girls' school in Saint Louis. I tried to think of things that were pleasant to get my mind off things."[11]

"We Wondered What in Hell Was Going to Happen to Us"

After six days of hell aboard the *Nitta Maru*, the men felt the ship slow, then halt. Their concerns intensified when a group of Japanese sailors removed a small number of Americans while keeping the rest in their confined quarters. Other sailors placed a large box at the entrance and ordered everyone to deposit any remaining possessions into it. Watches, rings, and money disappeared into the container, after which the men were thoroughly searched. If anything other than a toothbrush was found, the item would be confiscated and the man punished.

As the prisoners would soon learn, the ship had pulled into Yokohama, a port city immediately south of Tokyo. The vessel remained in port two days, long enough for the Japanese to transfer a handful of prisoners and to use others as propaganda tools. The Japanese permitted Commander Cunningham, Dan Teters, Commander Keene, and Lieutenant Kahn to wash their faces and comb their hair, then led them above decks, where a waiting line of Japanese reporters and photographers snapped their pictures and scribbled notes of the incident. Since the Japanese wanted the world to think that they treated the Americans decently, the photographers waited until a prisoner smiled to snap his picture. This initial Japanese propaganda attempt only confirmed fears back home for the men's welfare, however, when a close examination of one photograph showed all four Americans looking relatively healthy, but weary.

The Japanese next allowed these four and a few other Americans to record radio messages for broadcast to the United States. Everyone knew the propaganda purposes, but the men happily accepted an offer that permitted them to make contact with home and loved ones. Lieutenant Kinney sent a message to his family and to his girlfriend. Civilian Harold Sutherland tried to slip a subtle message through to his family by saying, "So far we have been treated fine, I think."[12]

Cunningham, fresh from witnessing Platt's beating, painted a positive picture so that his wife and child back home would not worry. "To my wife in Annapolis, I wish to send my best greetings and hopes for her welfare and that of our child, and I also wish to assure her that I am in perfect health and expect to stay that way for a long time."[13] Cunningham then added greetings to President Roosevelt and praised his men for the stout defense they mounted, but Japanese propagandists cut this portion from the broadcast.

Ham radio operators in the United States picked up the transmissions and relayed them to the government and families. This news from the Pacific did not contain much information, but at least some of the families knew their loved ones survived. For the parents and wives of the other prisoners, however, the suspense continued.

In a separate action, the Japanese removed eight officers and twelve enlisted men at Yokohama for interrogation, hoping to pry out information about American codes and communications before sending them to prison camps located in Japan. All had been involved in aviation, such as Major Putnam and Lieutenant Kliewer, or in communications, such as Major Potter, Ensign Henshaw, and RM3c. Marvin C. Balhorn.

The men staying aboard the *Nitta Maru*, which constituted most of the Wake Island defenders, breathed a sigh of relief that they had not been selected for removal, for Japan was the last place in which they wanted to be confined. If their final destination was China instead of the Home Islands, they would at least be closer to friendly Chinese forces and freedom.

On January 20, the *Nitta Maru* departed Yokohama and headed toward the Japanese-controlled Chinese port at Shanghai. During the voyage, the Japanese committed an atrocity that no Wake Islander learned about until later.

Glenn Tripp, Cunningham's yeoman, watched the Japanese drag away two men near him, S2c. John W. Lambert and S2c. Roy H. Gonzales. Two hours later the men returned, obviously frightened by what had occurred, and told Tripp that the Japanese had accused them of lying and that they were to be punished. The shaken men had no idea why they had been charged, and the terrified looks on their faces emphasized the worry they had about their treatment. After a few moments a guard came and took the two topside.

Neither Tripp nor anyone else ever saw them again. In fact, they did not learn what happened to Lambert and Gonzales until after the war. The Japanese led the pair, plus S2c. Theodore Franklin, M.T.Sgt. Earl R. Hannum, and T.Sgt. Vincent W. Bailey, to the quarterdeck, blindfolded the five, and tied their hands behind their backs. As 150 Japanese sailors crowded around to watch the proceedings, Lt. Toshio Saito stood on a box, drew his sword, then read a proclamation stating the five Americans would be executed as revenge for the many Japanese killed at Wake.

A Japanese sailor who gave an account after the war claimed that the prisoners did not know the fate that awaited them until guards shoved them to their knees. The most muscular members of Saito's prisoner guard, wearing the traditional *Hachimaki* headband indicating a desire to do their best, stepped behind the Americans and readied their swords. A guard bent over and brushed aside the long hair that blocked the first victim's neck, raised his sword, and decapitated the individual. The sailor told a war crimes investigating commission that "After the first victim had been executed, it is my personal belief that all the other remaining four victims knew what was going on. The sword as brought down on the neck of the first victim made a swishing noise as it cut the air. As the blade hit and pierced the flesh it gave a resounding noise like a wet towel being flipped or shaken out. The body of the first victim lay quietly, half across a mat and half onto the wooden deck. Plenty of blood was around the body."[14]

Other Japanese guards then executed the four remaining Americans. Crew members mutilated and bayoneted the five bodies, then unceremoniously dumped them overboard. All this occurred while Goicoechea, Hanna, and the rest huddled below, oblivious of the crime.

On January 24, the ship pulled into Shanghai, where a small group of interested Chinese civilians and a few reporters noted the ship's arrival. The *Nitta Maru* headed down the Whangpoo River to the port at Woosung, a Chinese village ten miles from Shanghai. On a cold, blustery day, 1,162 Americans filed onto the docks, where members of the Japanese Army waited to take them to the Woosung Shanghai War Prisoners Camp, their first prison camp.

As a Japanese officer harangued the men in Japanese, the vociferous Joe Goicoechea impetuously muttered something within earshot of a soldier. When the guard turned and smacked Goicoechea hard on the head with his rifle butt, the civilian realized he had best exercise more discretion in the future.

The five-mile march to camp tested the endurance of men already weary from the exhausting weeks on Wake and the arduous ocean journey. The hungry, tired men huddled close together to ward off the snow and biting winds, a difficult task since they all were ill dressed for winter. They had boarded the *Nitta Maru* in the tropics, wearing lightweight shirts and pants, or shorts, and now they had to rely on the paper-thin accoutrements to shield them from winter's sting.

"It was cold, by God!" stated Corporal Marvin of the trek to Woosung Camp. "There was a drizzly rain, and everyone was just in khaki, and we wondered what in hell was going to happen to us."[15] Groups of Chinese peasants quietly watched as the stream of American prisoners wound by, some Marines wearing shower togs as shoes. When the Japanese ordered the men to quicken their pace, even though their leg muscles were cramped from being confined so long, the men drew upon inner sources of strength to comply.

"Our Misery Started"

Wake Island defenders languished in many prison camps in China, Korea, and Japan. While they all shared common features, each location also displayed unique tendencies. To simplify matters, I have divided the prison camps into two sections—those outside Japan and those inside Japan. The main difference between the two was the severity of treatment.

Since most of the men captured at Wake Island were first confined at Woosung, then the nearby camp at Kiangwan, eight miles outside of Shanghai, those camps provide an accurate glimpse into prison existence outside the Home Islands. Consisting of seven wooden, unheated barracks surrounded by two rings of electrically charged fences, Woosung was a former Chinese cavalry camp taken over by the Japanese to house prisoners. In freezing weather, the 1,162 men walked through the gates around 4:00 P.M., then stood at attention while the commandant, Colonel Yuse, stepped onto a chair to address the throng. For more than one hour, the officer shouted at the Americans, but since he spoke in Japanese, none of the men understood his words. From Yuse's demeanor, however, they grasped that he issued warnings about their behavior.

A camp interpreter followed Yuse and spoke to the men in broken English. Civilians, like Forrest Read and his nephew J. O. Young, who had been accustomed to taking orders only from their foremen or from Dan Teters, and military personnel like Private Laporte, trained to obey their officers, now had to listen as an enemy officer, handling himself with the arrogance that sometimes comes with victory, recited a list of rules. "You will obey orders or be shot," ominously commenced the lengthy list. The interpreter also cautioned, "Do not touch the fence because it is full of juice and will make you died [sic]," "When you hear the voice of the 'clarinet,' get out of bed," and "Do not drink water unless it is made hot or you will be died." The proud Japanese interpreter then ended with the admonition, "You will remain here until Japan has beaten America."[16]

Shivering against the cold and depressed with the interpreter's "suggestion" at the length of their stay, the men collected the pair of thin, musty-smelling blankets, a cup, bowl, and spoon handed out by Japanese soldiers and headed toward their barracks. The wooden structures, one hundred feet long and twenty-five feet wide, each housed around 288 men. Each of the five barracks—the other two comprised officers' quarters and a hospital—was divided into eight sections with thirty-six men forming a section. Instead of beds, the buildings sported six-foot-wide sleeping platforms that extended from the sides about two feet above the floor. Large enough for eight men to a platform, the wooden planks provided little comfort and no privacy. Each man slept on a one-inch-thick cotton mattress stuffed with straw and a pillow of the same composition, and ate their meals while sitting on the platform's edge.

As the seemingly endless day neared an end, the men gulped down the "soup" dispensed by the Japanese—little more than tepid water containing a piece of gristle. With that first meal, the men stretched out on the platforms, huddled against each other for warmth, and settled in for what they hoped would be a decent night's sleep. In his barracks, Lieutenant Hanna and seven other men slept spoon fashion for warmth and to maximize the space. In another building, Joe Goicoechea and the civilian next to him placed one of their blankets on the platform, slid close to one another, then shivered under the other three threadbare blankets. Finally alone with their thoughts at night, the one time when the men could evade the Japanese tormentors, most slept fitfully as thoughts of home and family flooded in.

Day one at Woosung, their initial taste of what their life would be like for more than three and a half years, finally ended. "Our misery started,"[17] Goicoechea later wrote.

Any American who awakened in the middle of the night to visit the latrines received a hint of the treatment that lay ahead. Ten stalls, hardly more than wooden planks with holes cut into them and heavily populated with rats, stood at the end of the barracks. Large earthenware pots underneath collected the refuse, which Chinese farmers retrieved every few days to use as fertilizer for their fields. According to Lieutenant Kinney, the Japanese handed out only ten sheets of toilet paper for the entire year, so everyone had to improvise. Most men kept a rag and a small can of water with which to clean themselves afterward. Whoever went to the latrine then had to return to his platform and crawl between the other men, which meant that few Wake Islanders ever enjoyed a solid night's sleep.

A shrill blast from a Japanese bugler began the first full day at Woosung. The men had only a few moments to clean the barracks, fold their blankets, mop the floors, and stand in front of their platform for the daily inspection. When the Japanese officer arrived, the men had to bow, then count off in Japanese with their *horyo*, a number given each man the first day. James Allen's number, 4428, indicated he lived in Barracks 4, Section 4, and was man 28.

After the inspection, Lieutenant Kinney walked outside the barracks for a quick glimpse of his surroundings. Across from a dirt road that circled the camp stood a storage facility, the prison galley, and a few other buildings. Electrical fences separated the camp from the Japanese living quarters. Open fields later used for sports and gardening flanked the barracks to the east and south.

Kinney met other men who had been in Woosung before the Wake Island men arrived. British embassy personnel from Shanghai awaiting repatriation chatted with him, as did members of the crews of two captured or sunken gunboats, the British vessel *Peterel*, and ironically, the American gunboat *Wake*.

J. O. Young received the first beating administered at Woosung when he saw a group of Americans dragging their straw mattresses outside for more straw. He joined the men, not realizing that a guard nicknamed Rocky had specifically marked which mattresses were to be moved. Since Young's was not among those marked, Rocky forced Young to stand at attention, then smacked him on both sides of his head as hard as he could. Trying not to mutter a sound, Young absorbed the blows with dry eyes.

His reaction exemplified the struggle that started with the first moment of incarceration and lasted until the day of liberation—the battle to endure, to absorb whatever the captors handed out, to show by doing so, that, while they may be prisoners of war, they had not been defeated. "Hidden behind the routine, under the surface of life in prison camp, was fought a war of wills for moral supremacy—an endless struggle, as bitter as it was unspoken, between the captors and the captives," Major Devereux wrote after the war. "The stake seemed to me simply this: the main objective of the whole Japanese prison program was to break our spirit, and on our side was a stubborn determination to keep our self-respect whatever else they took from us. It seems to me that struggle was almost as much a part of the war as the battle we fought on Wake Island."[18]

Nature provided one of the battlegrounds. Men endured the summer's heat without much complaint, even though it meant dealing with the presence of what seemed millions of mosquitoes and flies, because that was far more tolerable than the frigid winter temperatures that frequently dropped below zero. Lieutenant Kessler wrote, "The days and nights became one long misery of wet and cold. The shivering became so prolonged that muscles ached and grew tired."[19]

The men battled the cold in different ways. They heated bricks in makeshift fireplaces and stoves during the day, then wrapped the bricks in blankets and placed them on the platform beside them at night. So many men surreptitiously hooked up improvised hot plates to the camp's electrical power lines that they caused a blackout. When engineers from a Shanghai power company investigated, they discovered the reason and put an end to the practice.

Other men paced back and forth all night in futile attempts to ward off the cold. "The winter at Woosung was rough," said Goicoechea, whose feet hurt so bad from the cold that he shouted in pain as he walked. "I seen grown men with tears in their eyes because it was so cold. I still think about that. Remember, we only had light clothing."[20]

Besides the weather, rats constantly plagued the men, sometimes running across their faces at night. The worst pests, however, proved to be smaller—bedbugs and lice. Bedbugs, about the size of a pencil eraser, so harassed Private First Class Gatewood and his friends that they dampened their top blankets because they heard bedbugs would not move around on a wet surface. It worked to a degree.

"The bedbugs just started climbing up to the ceiling and dropping down on us," mentioned Gatewood. "They felt like rain falling down on us. They'd get on you someplace and suck blood out of you until they were full, then they'd roll off. Then we'd roll over on them in the night and squash them, and there'd be a big bloody spot. There were thousands in your blankets, in cracks in the walls. You could easily have a hundred of 'em on your body at any time when you were sleeping."[21]

The men eventually learned to live with the critters. They could control the lice—the size of a pencil point and anywhere from one-quarter to one-half inch long—a bit easier by boiling their clothes, but nothing they tried solved the bedbug problem. If they squashed too many bedbugs, an atrocious smell inundated the barracks. Eventually, Gatewood and the others fell into a nightly routine—like robots, they periodically waved their arms about their bodies to swipe off the bothersome pests.

The lack of cleanliness vexed many of the men. Accustomed to showering and brushing their teeth every day, the men now had to readjust to grime and sweat. The prisoners grew dirtier by the week, although they had the dubious advantage of everyone being equally filthy. Cpl. Robert M. Brown later wrote that no one knew how bad anyone smelled because they all smelled the same.

A shipment of safety razors and hair clippers somewhat alleviated the conditions and made the men feel a bit more human. Each man received one razor blade, but he had to make it last for the rest of his confinement. For more than two years Kinney maintained his single blade by repeatedly sharpening it on the inside of a drinking glass.

"The Japanese Weren't Ever Going to Take away Our Pride"

Most days, the enlisted men and civilians had to work in factories, mines, or on outdoor projects, while officers tended gardens or labored on other smaller endeavors. At first the enlisted men and the civilians polished shell casings to be used in large guns. Since the rules of the Geneva Convention governing conditions in prison camps prohibited men from working in anything war-related, the men objected, but the Japanese countered that they had not signed the articles of the Geneva Convention and ignored the complaint. The men turned to their second alternative and purposely did such a poor job on the shells that the Japanese eventually abandoned the idea and switched the men to other work.

No matter which task they received, the Wake Island men looked for ways to either sabotage the work or to insure the finished product did not perform properly. Men assigned to repair trucks, for instance, acted as if they corrected the problems, but instead altered the trucks to guarantee frequent breakdowns. A group of men storing oil barrels at the Shanghai Race Course loosened one end of the 55-gallon drums, then stacked them upside down so the liquid leaked out. These small victories boosted morale and gave the men a sense that they contributed to the war effort.

A project called Mount Fuji, however, provided a harsh challenge to their spirits. Early in 1943, guards marched the men to a spot outside of Shanghai and told them to begin building a hill. The Japanese commander explained it was to be used as a recreation area, but the Americans soon realized the project was a mound to stop bullets in a rifle range. Every day for almost a year one thousand men shoveled dirt into woven baskets attached to two poles, carried these on their shoulders to carts, pushed the carts along narrow-track railway lines to the hill, and dumped the contents onto the slowly expanding rise. Mount Fuji eventually grew to be five hundred feet long and more than thirty feet high.

A few lighthearted moments occurred during the building of Mount Fuji. One time a Japanese guard needed to ride down the hill in one of the carts. He ordered a civilian worker to take him down slowly, but as Joe Goicoechea watched, the man handling the brake jumped out, the car derailed, and the Japanese guard flew through the air.

Pfc. Jacob Sanders and other Marines loved to leap back in the cars after dumping the contents, then ride back down as quickly as possible, laughing like schoolchildren on a playground. Even if the carts tipped off the tracks and injured someone, the men thought it was worth it for a few laughs.

The Japanese guards' reaction to the levity amazed Sanders more than anything else. "They assumed that since we had surrendered on Wake, we were totally shamed and without any self-respect," wrote Sanders. "Instead, we never forgot that we were United States Marines and tried to show our captors that we had a lot of pride in who we were and what we had accomplished. The Japanese weren't ever going to take away our pride in being Americans."22

As the hill rose higher, the men had to work harder to push the carts to the top. They also had to be more careful because they worked under the scrutiny of the most feared Japanese official in camp, Isamu Ishihara. The Wake Islanders encountered all sorts of Japanese guards and camp officials, some decent men who offered help to the Americans and others who loved to torment the men. The worst was Ishihara.

The man, who served as an interpreter, fit the stereotypical image of Japanese that then existed in the United States—short, thin, and wearing horn-rimmed spectacles. He walked around the camp, clutching his ever-present riding crop, hoping to catch an American doing something wrong. When he did, he descended on the transgressor with such a vicious flurry of blows that the victim often stumbled away in a senseless daze. The Americans universally detested Ishihara, to whom they gave the appellation "Beast of the East."

"The cruelest one we had in camp was the interpreter," Lieutenant Hanna recalled later. "He would deliberately misinterpret what you said and then use that as an excuse to beat us."23

Ishihara hated the Americans with equal venom. Apparently he had fallen prey to a group of bigoted Americans in Hawaii before the war, who beat Ishihara. Ever since, he sought vengeance on others. He shouted to the captives that when Japan won the war, he would shit on the American flag, and the level of animosity he displayed even disturbed some of his fellow Japanese. A group of officers once took away Ishihara's sword when he started to use it to beat the prisoners. Nevertheless, Ishihara remained in power for the duration of the war.

Hans Whitney was one of the few who got the better of Ishihara. One day he and two other men hid behind a shed to avoid work. All of a sudden, Ishihara appeared and demanded to know why they were not helping with Mount Fuji. Whitney knew that Ishihara had a paralyzing fear of dying from disease, so Whitney quickly replied, "We have spring fever."[24] Ishihara hurriedly walked away as Whitney and his two friends burst out in muffled laughter, but the interpreter later whipped them with his riding crop when he learned what the phrase meant.

The Americans tagged the guards with a humorous array of nicknames. Woosung and Kiangwan had "Rocky," "the Pig," "Bucktooth," "Whiskers," and "Dog Face." A guard named Morisako gained the appellation "Mortimer Snerd" because he reminded the men of the humorous-looking country bumpkin dummy used by famed ventriloquist Edgar Bergen. When Morisako asked who Snerd was, the prisoners told him he was a popular movie star in Hollywood. The guard loved the nickname until he learned the actual identity. The next man who called him Snerd received a horrible beating.

Some guards, like Ishihara, gained notoriety for their cruelty. Hans Whitney claimed "They were all bad, vicious, overbearing, cruel, sadistic, the only difference being some were worse than others."[25] Corporal Marvin, George Rosendick, and many others received beatings for minor offenses, such as dropping a cigarette on the ground. Joe Goicoechea was so severely beaten about the head that blood freely gushed from his ears, nose, and mouth. The guard named Whiskers, who loved to use his belt buckle to inflict pain, beat Whitney and forced him to stand at attention in the hot sun for four hours after the civilian accidentally broke a shovel handle in the garden. A guard named Clubfist, so christened because of the artificial left hand with which he smacked Americans, earned his harsh reputation from the repeated beatings he administered.

The smart prisoners learned to avoid these guards whenever possible. Private Laporte kept a low profile and rarely brought attention to himself. Corporal Gross avoided confrontations. "You had some guys who lived kinda reckless, but I never confronted a Jap unless I had to. If I could go around him rather than have to face him and salute, I did. Some guys didn't think, and that's why they beat the hell out of you. In one barracks we had a guard right outside the door. Every time you left the barracks you had to stop and bow to him. Sometimes guys wouldn't do it right away and get beat. Hell, I'd go out the back door. I played it smart every way I could. Staying out of sight was the best thing."[26]

At the same time, other guards developed a reputation for fairness and decency. Camp commandant Col. Satoshi Otera, nicknamed Handlebar Hank because of his mustache, allowed more Red Cross supplies into Kiangwan camp than was the case elsewhere. A guard called Popeye secretly passed out cigarettes and money to the men, and Dr. Yoshihiro Shindo, Kiangwan's medical officer, tried to guarantee the men received the best medical attention available under the circumstances.

"Shindo would go out of his way to help you," stated Goicoechea. "He couldn't care less if you didn't salute him. The rest of 'em would've come back and worked you over. He even got in trouble for helping us. Some Japs we knew we could get away with stuff, and others we knew we had to work because they took their jobs seriously."[27]

"I Was Just Too Ornery to Die"

It is amazing that the military personnel and the civilian construction workers endured so many physical and mental hardships as well as they did. Everyone longed to be with their families, and the Marines, especially, constantly battled with the specter that they, as professional soldiers, could not take an active part in the huge conflagration unfolding all around the world.

To a man, the Marines pointed to Major Devereux as one of the main factors in their survival. Devereux constantly reminded the men they belonged to the First Marine Defense Battalion, and he insisted on maintaining the same discipline and system that every Marine camp followed, whether inside or outside the United States. Thus he demanded that every enlisted man promptly salute officers of any branch of service. He believed this put order into the men's life, instilled pride in being Americans, and gave them a feeling of importance. Devereux also expected his officers to conduct themselves with the proper demeanor, a rule he so closely followed that even Japanese guards saluted Devereux when he walked by.

"His discipline helped pull us through," claimed Corporal Johnson. "A corporal and a sergeant got into a fight one time, and Major Devereux had the corporal locked up in the Japanese brig for striking a superior noncom. He had us all between the barracks, and he, a very devout Catholic, said, 'Goddammit! We're trying to get you out of here alive, and you're trying to kill yourselves! I won't put up with it.' "[28]

In the early months of confinement, the hungry men so heatedly argued over food that some Marines suffered broken noses and busted teeth. Finally, Devereux lined up all the men and told them he would severely punish anyone if the arguing continued. "I will sacrifice a few to get the rest of you back,"[29] he added.

The major later faced another predicament over food when camp cardsharps conned unwitting servicemen out of their daily ration allotments. Devereux turned to that old gambler himself, Gunner McKinstry, who collected the neophyte gamblers to show them the tricks being employed by the more experienced card players.

In like manner, Teters established a routine for the civilians. He saw how efficient Devereux could be, and realizing the military knew more about survival than he, Teters copied their example.

The men employed all sorts of tricks to make life more bearable. Some took solace in the fact that, unlike other Allied forces, before surrendering they had put up such a stout defense. Whenever a Japanese guard shouted at Sergeant Bowsher, he muttered under his breath, "We've already whipped you. Now you can do your damnedest—you can't hurt us. . . . We've had our victory. Now what are you going to do about it?"[30]

The men also relied on the buddy system. A person can tolerate much more if he has someone with whom to share thoughts and emotions and someone else to look out for. Goicoechea and Rosendick benefited in camp from their longtime friendship, which brought a feeling of normalcy into their otherwise abnormal existences, while Murray Kidd felt the pang of separation from his friends. Private Laporte claimed that even guys who rarely spent time together before the war now forged close bonds. "There was people there who wouldn't talk to a guy before, but in camp they became best friends. You could support each other and get your morale up quite a bit."[31]

A few others brought a built-in system of support because a member of their family was incarcerated with them. The civilians had a handful of father-son combinations, such as Leroy Meyers and his father. When his weakened father could not work, Leroy convinced the Japanese to let him do both jobs so his father could rest. Leroy scrounged around the camp for extra food, and he gave part of his own meals so his father could recover faster.

Many held on to the most important items in their lives—family, country, religion—as incentive for surviving. Sgt. Jesse L. Stewart lost more than sixty pounds and suffered such cruel beatings that he coughed up blood, but he persevered for compelling reasons—what awaited him back home. "It would have been very easy for me to have given up the ghost at this time, but I knew my wife would be waiting for me at the end of the war and I wanted to go back to her and to my son, whom I had never seen and at this time did not even know I had, only knowing that my wife was pregnant at the time I left for duty on Wake Island. Also while still on Wake Island, I had been told by a Japanese Interpreter [sic] that I would never live out the war and I was determined to do so and see that this man was brought before Justice for the acts which he committed against both United States Civilians and servicemen on Wake Island. . . . We took these beatings, we took this humiliation, we took the persecution and the degradation, we stood by in our faith in the United States and what it stood for, we dreamed of Old Glory flying over us once more, of cleanliness, of good food, and good clothes, and we trusted in our God and in our Nation to come to deliver us from this hell."[32]

Men risked their lives to create handmade American flags, even though they had to keep them hidden until war's end. Gathering cloth from old uniforms or tattered sheets, men fashioned rude Stars and Stripes in an effort to keep morale high. Two men in one camp laboriously stitched together a flag by taking red cloth from a Japanese quilt, white cloth from sheets, and blue material from a pair of dungaree pants donated by an Australian officer. While the flags could not yet take their proper places atop a flagpole, the prisoners drew inspiration from knowing that the Stars and Stripes (a symbol that some individuals in less threatening times take for granted) existed amidst their misery.

Above all, maintaining a positive attitude helped pull men through the years of confinement. Some knew they would survive or adopted the approach that if only one man returned, it would be him. "I was just too ornery to die," claimed Lieutenant Hanna, an outlook made stronger by the men's faith that the United States would prevail and they would be freed. Corporal Holewinski divided his time in camp into phases. "You handled it by saying in the springtime, 'It [the end of the war] will happen this fall.' When fall came, you said, 'It will happen this spring.' " [33]

Murray Kidd never doubted he would survive, because he was determined to see Boise again. "I always thought if there was one guy who was gonna get home, I'm gonna be it," he explained years later. Corporal Marvin felt the same. "I always figured the will to live is a lot stronger than the will to die. There was no doubt in my mind that I was going to make it."[34]

Some men used laughter to endure each day. Joe Goicoechea joked with George Rosendick, with other Americans, and even with the Japanese. Pfc. Max Dana constantly teased Sgt. Stephen Fortuna, who had been his recruiting officer in the States, "Hey, how about those good things you told me about the Marine Corps? Is this part of it?"[35] When forced to salute the Japanese, many men saluted with their left hands instead of the right and made sure the middle finger was raised more than the other digits. If the Americans had to urinate while working outside, they purposely turned toward a monument erected in honor of Japanese soldiers. This lasted until the Japanese caught on and ordered it stopped, at which time the men turned toward the east—the direction of Japan—and pretended they aimed at the emperor.

Ishihara expressed to more than one man his surprise that they did not act like prisoners, that they lacked any sense of shame over surrendering. Goicoechea answered that they had never been prisoners before and did not know how to act.

Others turned to hatred to keep them alive. Private Laporte hated his

Japanese captors. Corporal Johnson hated an American isolationist politician, Sen. Burton K. Wheeler of Montana, because he always voted against the military. He vowed to survive prison camp, return to the United States, and kill the senator. "I thought, 'We are here with the Japanese all around us, and you're back there [in the United States] with the guns we wanted to buy.' He's the man who kept us from having the necessary equipment. I wanted to come back and kill him. That kept me alive in camp."[36]

Religion also contributed to some of the men pulling through. Pfc. LeRoy N. Schneider credited the weekly sessions conducted by Major Devereux where men said the rosary together with helping him, while Corporal Holewinski turned to prayer and confession as an aid.

Inevitably, though, others gave up. The first man to die at Woosung was a civilian who simply refused to eat the food dished out, lay in his bunk, and died. "Some guys didn't make it because they didn't want to take it anymore. You could tell when a guy got to that stage and that he didn't have long," said Joe Goicoechea. "You could try to stop it, but you could only tell him so much."[37]

"An Exercise in Survival"

J. O. Young claimed that in many ways, "Camp life was an exercise in survival"[38] that separated the boys from the men. In a classic example of Charles Darwin's theory, the fittest survived at the cost of the weak.

Some civilians believed that the military created an informal three-tiered hierarchy in camp—officers occupied the top, followed by the enlisted personnel, and finally the civilians. While the officers enjoyed a few amenities not shared by the others, most men in camp coexisted well. Sometimes a person from one group might create harsh feelings and do something to irritate individuals in another, such as behaving improperly or cooperating with the Japanese, but on the whole relations among the three groups went smoothly.

Enterprising prisoners opened up "businesses" catering to certain needs. One man cut hair; another repaired shoes or washed clothes. Behind these legitimate concerns stood the black market trades, where men bartered for more food, bootleg alcohol, medicines, and other items. They had to exercise extreme caution, however, to avoid detection. After catching one man involved in black market activities centering around food, the Japanese tied all his fingers together, then twisted the string until every digit broke.

The product that created the largest demand, and thus the most traffic, was cigarettes. Men who did not smoke used cigarettes as a medium of exchange to acquire food and other necessities. Since camp officials restricted the number of letters going to the United States, for instance, Private William B. Buckie, Jr., purchased the rights to another prisoner's letter home with a handful of cigarettes. Other men, suffering from nicotine withdrawal, were willing to part with almost anything for extra tobacco. Ten cigarettes, with the most value placed on Camels and Lucky Strikes, for instance, might buy a man someone else's bowl of rice, while chocolate bars from Canadian food parcels also brought a good yield. Many prisoners recalled those individuals who willingly gave up their sorely needed food to obtain a few cigarettes.

Bootleg alcohol also enjoyed a ready market. Some men operated illegal stills in which they brewed their own versions of beer or liquor. Medics with access to alcohol sometimes appropriated it for their own use, and prisoners who worked at the Kiangwan Racetrack smuggled in fuel consisting of ethanol.

One type of prisoner gained almost universal condemnation from his fellow captives—the individual who collaborated with the enemy. Every camp possessed a few men who, out of a desire for more food or because they could no longer bear the strain, turned in the names of prisoners who violated the rules. These men, labeled traitors by their cohorts, generally lived lonely lives from then on, except for the periodic nighttime visits by angry Americans who administered severe beatings.

Wake Islanders state that when compared with the camps they later encountered inside Japan, the Chinese prison camps offered a better existence. One reason was the opportunity they had to participate in sports or other activities. Following supper and on Sundays, the men had time to read, play softball, or become involved in a number of different hobbies.

Since Woosung and Kiangwan stood close to Shanghai, where a large and friendly international community offered help to the captives, the Americans enjoyed a three-thousand-volume library containing the works of Mark Twain, Charles Dickens, Sinclair Lewis, Erle Stanley Gardner, and back issues of magazines. Each evening J. O. Young read Charles Dickens's *David Copperfield* at Woosung, while other men leafed through magazines or newspapers the Japanese allowed into camp. Young recalled that the Gideons, a religious group, sent a box of Bibles, but few were read because "most were used as toilet paper as diarrhea swept through camp."[39]

Major Devereux established classes in subjects such as mathematics and foreign languages, but had to cancel them for low attendance. After tiring days working in a garden or on Mount Fuji, the last thing the men wanted to do was pay attention in a classroom. Instead, some of the men taught themselves. Lieutenant Kinney, who never gave up on the idea of escaping, learned the Chinese language on his own.

As was true on Wake, cardsharps prowled both Woosung and Kiang-wan. The Japanese banned card playing, but the men ignored it. Each night the men posted a lookout, then opened their poker matches. If a guard approached the barracks, the lookout yelled the signal, "Air the blankets!" which meant the men should remove all traces of gambling and move to their sleeping platforms. Eventually the Japanese figured out the scam, which forced the Americans to be more circumspect in their card playing.

The fiercest competition came with the Sunday sports contests. Barracks formed teams of their best athletes in softball and football, then challenged squads from other barracks. Over the course of time, heated rivalries built, and impassioned fans cheered on their favorites. Little quarter was given or asked.

"I went through the line one time in a football game," said Joe Goicoechea, "and this Marine got rough! He'd knock me on the ass. We played touch football, but it could get rough. We also played softball, and it was bitterly contested because we had some good ballplayers."[40]

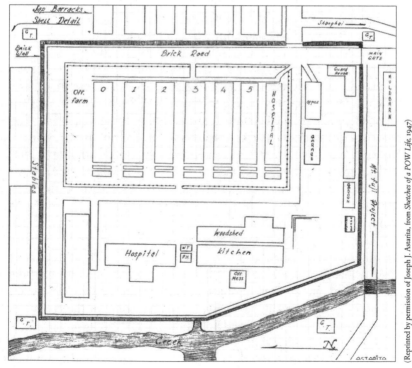

(Reprinted by permission of Joseph J. Astarita, from *Sketches of a POW Life*, 1947)

Kiangwan Prison Camp

"Remember Those Hamburgers?"

Books, sports, work, sleep—none of those compared to the one topic that dominated every man's mind. One thousand men, confined together and forced to go without it for so long, naturally thought about it, talked about it, and dreamed about it. Not girls—food.

"By far the most talked about, the most insistent, ever-present basically important element in our incarceration was food," wrote Hans Whitney. "We were hungry before and after meals. We were hungry all the time."[41]

Though the daily ration varied throughout the war, all men could basically expect to receive a cup of cooked rice, two cups of watery soup that the men labeled "Tojo water," and three cups of weak but hot tea. Men carried the food into each barracks in huge buckets; then a trusted prisoner selected for his fairness poured the food into each man's cup. After everyone had received their portion, the server handed out leftovers until no food remained. The men meticulously remembered where in line the server stopped with the leftovers, because that is where he had to start the next time.

The watery soup provided little nutrition. A few vegetables usually floated in the tepid concoction, and a man felt lucky if gristle or a tiny piece of meat happened to appear. The men had to be wary of biting too hard on the rice, which obviously consisted of floor sweepings, because it frequently contained pebbles and other hard substances.

For men in such terrible conditions, the diet hardly sufficed to keep meat on their bones. Private First Class Gatewood dropped from 200 pounds to 137, Forrest Read lost thirty pounds in one month, and Hans Whitney, despite eating a cat and sparrows, lost one hundred pounds. Tattoos on the bodies of men distorted into unrecognizable shapes because the bearer had lost so much weight. Joe Goicoechea did not have to visit the latrine for twelve days because he consumed such a small amount of food.

Not surprisingly, fights erupted over food. Men yelled at the server that he resumed leftovers in the wrong spot or that he failed to stir the soup often enough so the vegetables rose from the bottom. J. O. Young never thought he would be placed in such an awkward situation when enjoying all those hamburgers with Pearl Ann, but he was chosen in his barracks to dish out the food. Called the "King of the Ladle," Young stirred the soup for every man, and made sure that he packed and leveled off each bowl of rice. He encountered more problems if the rice burned and hardened on the bottom of the bucket, for everyone wanted some of the crunchy and chewy substance that was considered something of a delicacy.

The Wake Islanders quickly learned to eat anything, no matter how atrocious it looked. In the early days, a few men refused to eat, but they either changed their minds or they died.

Lieutenant Kessler joked with his friends about the stages through which a prisoner passed. "A short timer would turn away from the disgusting sight of dead weavils [sic] sprinkled like bits of cocoanut [sic] over the cereal; a man with more time as a P.O.W. would pick out the weavils and eat the cereal; but the longtime P.O.W. would eat it all and then reach for the weavils discarded by others—weavils were protein."[42]

Men supplemented their diets in different ways. Since tobacco alleviated hunger pangs, many took up smoking. Those who worked outside camp smuggled in vegetables or fruit by hiding it in their crotches as they passed by the guards. Joe Goicoechea ate caterpillars, which he thought tasted like bacon, as well as tangerine or orange peels lying on the ground for their vitamin C. Men traded with Chinese laborers for eggs whenever the guards were not looking.

Some stole extra food. Ellis Gordon endured beatings that distorted his face to the size of a basketball, yet he continued to commit the offense for which he was punished—stealing food. He stated that men readily accepted physical pain to relieve the pangs of hunger. "Hunger is a peculiar feeling," he wrote in a letter after the war, "and I've seen where food even came before 'God.' We would steal or try and deal with the Japs, in order to get something to eat. And when we were caught, this is the kind of treatment we received."[43]

Sgt. Jesse L. Stewart eased his hunger pangs by stealing, but suffered remorse afterwards. He admitted to stealing whatever he could from the Japanese, which was never very much, but he anguished about "going against all the teachings we had been given by our parents and by the schools that we had attended in the States . . ."[44]

Hunger made men appreciate what most people living in normal situations take for granted. Commander Cunningham relished what he called one of the best meals he ever tasted when he received a small bit of margarine to spread over his rice. Private First Class Gatewood dreamed one night that he feasted on a huge stack of hotcakes, then awoke to find himself licking the pillow as if it were covered in syrup. Men swapped recipes for actual dishes like young boys trade baseball cards, even though they knew they could not feast on any of the delectables until after the war. Maj. George H. Potter compiled a sixty-six-page book of recipes during his confinement. One page contained elaborate recipes for "Potato, onion, carrot burger," "Sweet sauce," "Spiced pickle vinegar," "Hasenpfeffer," "Mexican Guacamole," and "Yorkshire Pudding."[45]

One day, Corporal Johnson reminisced with a friend about a San Diego hamburger drive-in. They and many other young men frequented the place because of a beautiful carhop, who kept her blouse unbuttoned partway down for the benefit of her male customers. An ample bosom now took second place. "I said, 'Pappy, remember that drive-in down by the civic center?' He said, 'Yea, boy! Remember those hamburgers? They were a full inch thick!' Our mind was on food."[46]

Pfc. James King had dated an attractive young woman in Hawaii whose father owned an ice cream parlor. Instead of thinking of the girl, King had more immediate needs about which to fantasize. "I used to dream about that ice cream shop," he explained years later. "Malted milks, especially. I dreamed more about that than about her. Sex was on a low priority after the first few months. When you're hungry all the time, you think about steaks and lobsters."[47]

The men so constantly thought about food that Lieutenant Kahn worried about its medical effects. He spoke to the officers and begged them to do something to halt the conversations about food. "Talk to the men about sports, sex, anything to get their minds off food," Lieutenant Kahn implored. "They're thinking about food all day and that's causing them to salivate, and that's bad because saliva is strong in acid and that is going into their stomachs and eating their stomachs."[48]

With the assistance of a dentist, Private First Class King momentarily suspended his attention on food. He also learned that while thoughts of sex had receded, they still did not linger far from the surface. A Japanese officer discovered King carrying contraband around the camp, and as punishment smacked him in the jaw with a rifle butt. When the camp dentist worked without medication on two cracked teeth in King's mouth, a curvaceous Japanese dental assistant kept stroking one of his arms in an effort to distract him from the pain. The nearness of the female and the gentle touch of her hand made King realize that once back home, he would have little trouble readjusting to a more normal "social" regime, and for a few moments, that Hawaiian ice cream parlor took a back seat to lust. "That one incident taught me that I was still male. She sure distracted me from what that dentist was doing! She was young and very attractive, and could not have been over twenty or twenty-one. It was almost as good as Novocain."[49]

The International Red Cross helped out whenever possible, but the prisoners never knew when the Japanese would allow a shipment of food into camp and how much of the shipment would actually be handed out. In every camp, Japanese officers and guards stole large portions before giving the remainder to the Americans. Lieutenant Hanna estimated that of the two or three Red Cross shipments his camps received, the Japanese confiscated at least half the material.

A typical Red Cross package contained small portions of fifteen different items, ranging from eight ounces of cheese and twelve ounces of corned beef to four ounces of instant coffee and ten cigarettes. The material packed in tin containers stayed relatively fresh, but hundreds of small worms infested the rest, including the coveted chocolate bars. Even though the men fumed that the Japanese kept part of what was rightfully theirs, Red Cross parcels, sporadic though they were, dramatically boosted morale.

The first shipment arrived a few days before Christmas 1942. This reminder that someone outside camp had not forgotten them breathed new life into the weary Wake Islanders. Lieutenant Kinney saw it as evidence that people in the United States cared about them and were doing what they could to make a harsh situation easier, while the event confirmed Hans Whitney's faith in ultimately being rescued. Most men formed groups of four or five, pooled their contents, and slowly dished out the delicacies.

The men enjoyed a pleasant surprise that first Christmas from an American who lived in Shanghai and operated a successful restaurant that catered to Americans. Jimmy James, a retired American sailor, had not yet been placed in detention by the Japanese, and somehow he persuaded the authorities to let him send in a Christmas meal of turkey, sweet potatoes, coffee, and cigars. The men worshiped Jimmy James for what they considered a miracle, and counted that meal as one of the few highlights of their time in camp.

Death and Disease

Relatively few men in China and Japan died from beatings or torture. Improper diet and the diseases that accompanied it contributed the most to camp fatalities. Of the 1,593 men captured on Wake Island, 244 perished. A handful of men died from harsh treatment or electrocution, but the vast majority succumbed to illnesses they may have beaten had they been healthier.

The winter's bitter cold joined with the summer's sweltering temperatures and swarms of flies to produce a year-round life-threatening environment. Mosquitoes buzzed all around the men outside and in their screenless barracks, causing malaria, dysentery, and other debilitating illnesses. The situation so concerned the Japanese commander, Colonel Yuse, that he ordered each man to kill ten flies per day. When the Americans ignored the order, Yuse obtained their cooperation by offering one cigarette for every ten flies brought in. That incentive plan proved so successful that Yuse upped the quota to one cigarette for every one hundred flies killed, at which time the results again plummeted. One man, most likely caught in the throes of nicotine agony, fashioned a huge twelve-by-twelve-inch flyswatter and commenced a solitary killing spree.

With the flies, mosquitoes, and inadequate diet, a succession of ailing prisoners headed to the camp hospital felled by malaria, dysentery, fever, or beriberi, which the men feared because of the hideous swelling and subsequent scars it produced. Camp doctors, for instance, removed six quarts of water from Hans Whitney's body and an additional amount from his lungs because of beriberi. Other prisoners fell ill from consuming rats or other creatures that populated the camp. Few men, if any, escaped being sick at one time or another. Lieutenant Kahn designated the most serious with a red tag, indicating the man was to remain in bed all day, or a blue tag, allowing the prisoner to work at lighter chores around the camp.

Despite Lieutenant Kahn's efforts, some Wake Islanders inevitably succumbed in the harsh conditions. Mark Staten, a civilian employee, died on February 18, 1942, of beriberi, and S1c. Joseph Comers passed away the following August from tuberculosis. Sgt. Alton J. Bertels, the Marine who barely missed going home when his discharge from the service was delayed by the December 8 attack, never again saw the United States. He died in March 1945 from tuberculosis. More men died as the war unfolded, some to disease and some to accidents, but the work of Lieutenant Kahn and his staff prevented the tally from growing to inordinate numbers.

Lieutenant Kahn earned everyone's praise for his tireless efforts in treating ailments. With few medicines at hand, he administered bits of charcoal in water to ease dysentery and stomach troubles, sulfur for rashes and skin problems, and—as the men loved to joke—aspirin for everything else. When necessary, Lieutenant Kahn performed surgery without anesthetics.

Lieutenant Kahn's diagnoses often proved to be his most effective treatment. Whenever he feared that a weakened man would die from working, Lieutenant Kahn, frequently backed by a sympathetic Dr. Shindo, argued with Japanese officials that the man was too ill to work. He frequently had to be creative in his choice of maladies, for most camp commanders stipulated that no prisoner could be excused from work detail unless seriously injured or suffering from a temperature over 103 degrees.

"Lieutenant Kahn invented more diseases than anyone had ever heard of, and the Japanese had a fear of catching diseases," claimed Corporal Johnson. "When a man got too weak to work and looked like he might die, he invented a disease to get him on light duty."[50]

A few men perished accidentally. One Marine died when, in passing vegetables through to a friend, he touched the electrified fence. Joe Goicoechea and another civilian attempted to give him artificial respiration, but nothing revived the Marine. After surviving the fifteen-day battle at Wake, after enduring the hell that was the *Nitta Maru*, after coping with hunger and weariness and pain in camp, Navy S2c. Raymond K. Hodgkins Jr. died when he reached across the electric fence, not for food or in a vain attempt to escape, but because he participated in that all-

American activity—baseball. When the ball rolled through the fence, Hodgkins accidentally touched the fence and died.

No one knows if another death was accidental or deliberate. One day a young Japanese guard and a young civilian teased one another. The American pretended to be heading toward the fence to escape, and the Japanese soldier raised his rifle as if pretending to fire. This went on for ten minutes, when suddenly the guard's rifle discharged and killed the American. Other prisoners rushed to the scene, but since the bullet severed the youth's jugular vein, they could do nothing. Some claim the death was a tragic accident, while others swear the guard intended to kill the American.

The deaths, as well as the squalor and misery, affected a few men's minds. After witnessing the killing described above, one prisoner walked around the camp muttering the phrase, "Blood, blood, blood." Another could only pass through the gate of the electric fence to his outside work with his eyes covered, head down, helped by friends.

The Japanese gave a wide berth to these and other men they considered mentally ill. One man subject to sudden fits of anger once picked up a stick and began swinging it at a group of Japanese soldiers. The guards hurried away instead of confronting the man. During an inspection by the camp commander, another ill individual drew concentric circles on the floor with chalk and stood inside. When the commander walked up to him the man shouted, "You yellow bastard, you can come in the first circle but don't you come in the second one."[51] The officer quietly shuffled by to inspect other Americans.

As the war wound into its third and fourth years, conditions changed for the men in Chinese camps. Most headed to new camps inside Japan, and some moved to other locations in China, but all took heart that their lengthy ordeal might soon cease. Signs indicated that their nation, once so energized by the Wake Island defenders, was coming to their rescue.

CHAPTER 12

★

"You Go Home Soon"

"You People Are Supposed to Be Dead"

The worst psychological and emotional battle the Wake Island prisoners waged was the desire to learn something of home, first of their families and friends, and second of the war's progress. The men felt isolated and distant, for they could do little but wait by day or lie awake on their planks at night and hope all was well back home. Nothing was more frustrating for a father than the inability to be with his wife and children, or for a son to be far from parents.

In the absence, letters filled the void, but information from home was sporadic. One contact came in June 1942 when the Japanese repatriated a group of embassy personnel and guards to the United States in an exchange of diplomatic personnel. The freed Americans telephoned or telegraphed many of the men's families to let them know their relatives were alive.

That did not help the men stuck in Kiangwan or other prison camps, however, since only a trickle of letters from the United States reached their hands. Lieutenant Hanna sent a letter to Vera whenever the Japanese allowed him to, which was no more than once or twice each year, but he never received a note in return from his wife, even though she wrote many. He later learned that Vera received only two of his notes.

This lack of communication bothered Lieutenant Hanna, whose thoughts always seemed to be of Vera and Erlyne. "Not being able to know for sure what kind of shape Vera was in and hearing nothing about my daughter wore on my mind a lot. It is just something you had to get through like everything else."[1] Lieutenant Hanna had no way of knowing that Vera volunteered her services to the United Service Organizations (USO), providing a touch of comfort and friendliness to other servicemen far from home, or that Erlyne now spoke in complete sentences and tucked baby teeth under her pillow. He did not even have any photographs of his family—they had been destroyed during the bombing of Wake.

In 1942, the Japanese allowed some men to record radio messages to their families, which ham operators back in the United States relayed to the appropriate locations. Lieutenant Hanna, realizing the Japanese permitted the recordings as a propaganda move, said very little other than to let Vera know he was thinking of them and to give Vera power of attorney in his absence. Dan Teters informed Florence he was well, while other men inserted hidden messages to fool the Japanese. One civilian said that he weighed the same as Jimmie as a way of letting his parents know his weight had dropped to the same as his sister, Jimmie Sue, lighter by sixty pounds. Other men mentioned they loved the Japanese just as much as so-and-so back home, then named a person they despised.

In September 1942, the parents of Marine Pfc. Robert B. Murphy received a short note from Mrs. E. C. Coxon of Burlingame, California, that their son was alive. Mrs. Coxon heard his name among a list of prisoners broadcast by Tokyo and forwarded the information in case the Murphys had been unaware of the information. A second woman, Esther Culver, listened to the same broadcast and wrote the Murphys, "So many times the only notice from the Govt. is 'Missing in Action,' and that can mean so many things. Suspense is hard to bear, I know."[2]

Later in the war, a Tokyo radio station broadcast a new group of messages, including a greeting from Corporal Marvin to his parents which the local newspaper printed. "I am in good health and hope you are all in good health," stated Marvin. "I am praying for an early reunion so that I may see you again soon. Don't worry about me. Pray I will return in good mind and body."[3] In these ways, the Wake Islanders registered little triumphs that made life more bearable.

Mail provided the other main contact with home, but no one could count on that as a steady source of information since mail arrived so infrequently. The initial letters did not trickle in until the fall of 1942, almost one year after Wake's fall. Those fortunate few to obtain a letter read and reread the notes until the creased pages threatened to fall apart, passed them around to other men to read, and pinned them to the walls near their platform.

"My dear dear Boy," started a letter written to John Rogge from his mother in October 1942. "You can never know what a tremendous relief and thrill it was to get your first letter written June 2 but received Sept. 21. I read it out loud to grandpa [sic] and Charles and oh how happy they were!"[4] The letters, though sporadically delivered via embassies from neutral countries, brought a touch of home to the war-weary Wake Islanders.

Those who received no correspondence, such as Lieutenant Hanna, faced almost unendurable misery and anxiety. Major Devereux wrote that "Men who were brave in battle have cried in the dark because they didn't get a letter. Exhausted men have lain all night staring at the raw ceiling, trying to stop wondering what's happening at home."⁵

No matter the information, good or bad, civilian and military alike would have given their last rice bowl for letters from home. Cpl. Robert M. Brown had heard nothing from home until the spring of 1944, when his name finally appeared on a camp list to receive a letter. Ecstatic over the sudden good news, Brown could not figure out why the interpreter, Ishihara, wanted to see him and a few other men. When the group entered his office, Ishihara held several letters in his hand. After glaring at the Marines, Ishihara shouted, "You leave your cheap, common women at home and they dare to write you here. Your whores dare to speak of love. This is not a time for love; this is a time for war! Maybe you Marines think first of love and then of fighting. Maybe that's why you now live in this camp."

Ishihara slowly smiled after the tirade, then one by one ripped up the letters and threw the shreds at Brown and the others. "Here, take them and be ashamed." The Marines retrieved what they could, but they could never forgive the insult they felt at what Ishihara had done. "I doubt that I will ever recover from the hatred I felt and feel for Mr. Ishihara," Brown wrote in 2002. "He still lives on in my nightmares."⁶

The most painful news from home entailed either a sweetheart breaking off the relationship with her incarcerated boyfriend, or the shocking revelation concerning the death of a loved one. A handful of Marines and civilians received the dreaded "Dear John" letters from girlfriends who had found someone else or grown weary of waiting. The news usually plunged the prisoner into an emotional tailspin from which he escaped only through the encouragement and support of camp mates.

Death of a loved one offered its own form of cruel punishment, for the prisoner had to bear the loss alone while the rest of his family suffered thousands of miles outside his reach. Major Devereux's wife, Mary, succumbed to diabetes in the summer of 1942. The International Red Cross notified Devereux in August, but it was not until April 1943 that the Japanese permitted Devereux to write his nine-year-old son, Paddy. For eight months, Devereux not only had to grieve for the wife he no longer had, but also deal with the frustration of being unable to console his young son, thousands of miles away with his grandparents in California.

The emotional distress was evident from Devereux's opening words to his son. "Our loss must have indeed been a shock to you; it was to me. We both loved her so very much. I only wish that I could be with you, but you are indeed fortunate to have your grandparents to watch over you."

The rest of Devereux's letter offered advice any father might give a son:

Do well in school, keep active in sports, write whenever possible. He urged Paddy not to boast too much about his father and the Marines. "Your mother wrote that you were 'throwing your weight around' the post on account of the Wake Island Marines. They did quite well and I am proud of them, but remember that it just so happened that we were there. Anyone else would have done the same. You must remember that the work done behind the lines is often more vital than that at the front."[7]

The letter moved not only Paddy and family, but the entire nation, as copies of the missive appeared in newspapers and magazines. A HERO WRITES TO HIS SON,[8] proclaimed the headlines in the *Washington Post* for December 30, 1943. Though Devereux attempted to downplay Marine heroics at Wake, his letter only solidified public opinion that the men on Wake Island deserved noble status.

Devereux's letter was not typical of those sent from prison camp. Most men could use only one sheet, or a postcard, often restricted to no more than twenty-five words, which severely restricted the amount of information they could include. For instance, Edgar N. Langley wrote two letters home, one in 1943 and the other in 1944. Each consisted of one paragraph, mainly filled with words designed to comfort the parents. His October 22, 1944, letter mentioned his surprise that they had moved to a new home. "I am sure anxious to get back and see how I like my new home. I know I shall be happy as long as both of you are well and happy. I am so glad you have chickens and stock too." For some inexplicable reason, a Japanese censor clipped out the next sentence, leaving only the closing. "I am well and getting along fine so don't worry."[9]

J. O. Young proved to be one of the more fortunate men when three of his letters reached their Boise destination. "Hunting season is in full swing, sure would like to be out hunting those ducks and pheasants with you," he wrote in one letter to his parents. "With God's help and will we'll all be together soon enjoying those good times we use [sic] to have." A card to Pearl Ann, whom he called "Pear-l," told her he was "well and doing fine," and advised her that if she needed any money, she was to borrow it from his father. In another letter he referred to "that home I'm planning for us."[10]

A few officers tried to sneak military information by the Japanese. In late 1942, Devereux conveyed material to the Marine commandant explaining the defensive successes and failures at Wake via Lt. D. E. Kermode, Royal Naval Reserve, who had been in Woosung before being repatriated to England.

Lieutenant Kessler instituted a plan he established with his wife before leaving for Wake. He told her that in a crisis, if he could get a letter to her, he would include a secret message using the first letter of the second word in each line. In February 1942, Kessler noticed that the Japanese interrogated any Marine who had ever been stationed on Midway. Correctly figuring the Japanese planned an offensive at that location—the June naval battle of Midway proved to be a decisive action of the war—Kessler arranged his next note to spell out "WATCH MIDWAY." He never knew if this information helped anyone, but at the time he felt that he had contributed to the war in some small way.

Besides letters from home, the men had other ways of acquiring information of world events. Early in the captivity, the Japanese handed out one radio to each barracks, set to a Japanese-approved station in Shanghai that broadcast news with a pro-Japanese slant. Before long, though, Wake's mechanics and aviators adapted the radios so they picked up other stations that carried a more balanced assessment of the war news.

The Japanese learned what a few men had done, but did not bother to do anything as long as the war news remained positive for their nation. By late 1943, however, with the United States military gaining momentum and the fortunes of war reversing at Midway and Guadalcanal, camp officials removed the radios. Even that step did not prevent experienced mechanics, especially Lieutenant Kinney, from fashioning his own radio out of spare parts.

News of the Allied march across the Pacific heartened the Americans, but it also led to growing impatience. Month after month, the men waited for news indicating that the war's end drew near. They realized a difficult road lay ahead for their nation and tried to keep things in perspective, but under the extraordinary conditions in which they lived, patience often lost out. The men in James Allen's barracks started chanting in the spring of 1943 and each spring after, "Spring is sprung. The grass is riz. I wonder where the Allies is?"[11]

Radio provided one of the most emotional moments for the prisoners when on New Year's Eve 1944, the men picked up a familiar station. When an announcer said, "This is San Francisco," men at first cheered, then fell deathly silent as they absorbed names and songs from what seemed a distant past. For a moment, they had a viable connection with the United States, an unbreakable lifeline that burst through their isolation to remind them that something waited for them and someone was coming to their rescue.

News trickled in through other ways. As he walked to work on a canal project near Woosung in 1942, Joe Goicoechea spotted a ship clearly marked with an enormous red cross. Streams of wounded Japanese soldiers, some hobbling, others in a state of shock, poured down the gangway. Goicoechea and those with him welcomed the sight, for they figured the

United States or another Allied nation had inflicted punishment on the enemy.

Japanese guards handed out tidbits of information, but only if the news favored their side. The guards never tired of showing the Americans photographs of Pearl Harbor, which always demoralized the men, and one guard informed Cunningham of Roosevelt's death in 1945, boasting incorrectly that the president committed suicide because the burdens of conducting a losing war effort were too much for him to handle. Pro-Japanese English-language newspapers and magazines, such as the *Nippon Times*, continued to be provided by the captors until the war news turned sour.

Finally, newly arrived American prisoners provided another, more accurate source of news. They confirmed the bad—such as Pearl Harbor—but also brought good news with tales of victories at Midway and Guadalcanal, Tarawa, and the Marshall Islands. The Wake Islanders kept pace with Pacific developments, all the time trying to curb their growing impatience over when the conflict might end and allow them to go home.

The addition of recently captured Americans, however, also showed the men how ignorant people back home were about their condition. A crew member of one American bomber shot down reacted incredulously when he met Corporal Johnson and other men from Wake Island. He stared at Johnson as if he were a ghost and then exclaimed, "You people are supposed to be dead!"[12]

"He Saved My Life"

Most Americans captured after the defense of Wake wound up in either China or Japan. A smaller group of about four hundred, however, remained on the atoll until battle wounds healed or to work for their Japanese captors.

One civilian volunteered to stay on Wake rather than board the *Nitta Maru*. Since some of the wounded were military, the Japanese at first ordered the Navy surgeon, Lieutenant Kahn, to stay behind on the island. Dr. Shank admired the younger physician, but Kahn's inexperience bothered the more practiced doctor. He felt the wounded and ill had a better chance of survival if he remained to nurse the men back to health. He doubted the Japanese doctors would provide anything but a cursory glance at the men, so his presence would ensure that the Americans most in need of medical attention received it.

Dr. Shank recognized another factor that others overlooked. He learned in discussions with Japanese officers that they intended to eventually evacuate all American military personnel on Wake. If Kahn and a pair of pharmacists' mates stayed instead of him, they would leave as soon as all the military members were healthy enough to ship out. The civilians working on Wake, more than three hundred men, would then lack medical care other than what the Japanese provided. Dr. Shank arranged a switch with Lieutenant Kahn, an admirable choice that had tragic repercussions for the honorable man.

Every Wake Marine or civilian who encountered Dr. Shank describes him in reverent terms, similar to the manner in which people speak of an esteemed country doctor in whose hands residents had placed their lives for years. With limited resources and medicine, he labored tirelessly to bring care to the men, even if it meant defying the Japanese.

Marine Sgt. Jesse L. Stewart owed his life to Dr. Shank, whom he called "one of the finest men it has ever been my priviledge [sic] to know."[13] Wounded on December 9 when shrapnel from a Japanese bomb shattered his left leg, Stewart lay in the makeshift hospital while infection threatened his life. Dr. Shank implored the Japanese to allow him to operate with Japanese medical equipment and medicines, but each time an officer ignored his request. When Dr. Shank argued with a Japanese doctor, who wanted to amputate Stewart's leg, an officer named Seishi Katsumi slapped him for being arrogant.

Dr. Shank's obstinacy held off the Japanese long enough for him to take his own lifesaving measures. With time running out—Stewart's leg had even turned black from the infection—Dr. Shank scavenged through the ashes of the demolished American hospital until he located a pair of scissors and a pair of tweezers. He cleaned the instruments as much as possible under the circumstances, then without anesthesia to adminster, he removed the shell fragments from Stewart's leg while two nurses held the Marine down.

The rest of the Americans remained on Wake because of their construction skills. The civilians completed projects already started before December 8, such as the airfield and gun emplacements, plus worked on new projects assigned by the Japanese. The captors pushed the men so hard that by December 1942, forty-five men had perished because of exhaustion and insufficient diet.

Murray Kidd, who saw the irony of coming to Wake to construct American defenses, only to complete them for the Japanese, also worked in a warehouse holding the food supplies. The Japanese mess sergeant in charge, a man named Tada, assigned Kidd the task of making sure no Japanese soldier took more food than allotted, a chore he performed so well that the mess sergeant allowed Kidd to quietly sneak extra food for himself. That additional nutrition helped Kidd survive a period that felled other construction workers.

The Americans enjoyed the help of another benefactor on Wake, a Korean named Lee Bong Moon. Brought in to cook for the Japanese officers, Moon took pity on the overworked, beaten, and underfed Americans. He secretly passed out food to men who worked near the kitchen, and when eight civilians attempted to steal a boat and escape from the atoll on October 13, 1943, Moon hid four drums of gasoline near the beach for the men to use. While the Japanese watched a movie, the Americans paddled out to sea, disappeared from Moon's sight, and headed toward Midway. The men vanished, likely either drowned or recaptured by other Japanese forces and executed.

Two other civilians defied the Japanese, at least for a time. Fred J. Stevens and Logan Kay avoided capture for seventy-seven days after December 23. They hid in Wake's dense brush, hoping that an appearance by the United States Navy would save them. Finally, running out of food and water, the weary men surrendered and joined their comrades.

They were fortunate to avoid the fate suffered by another Wake civilian, a man named by Stewart as "Babe" Hoffmiester. Caught in May 1942 stealing food and cigarettes from a warehouse by the Japanese, and already singled out for being twice warned against violating rules, Hoffmiester stood trial and was sentenced to death. On May 10, Mothers' Day, in front of twenty Americans forced to witness the event, the Japanese tied Hoffmiester's hands behind his back, blindfolded him, and made him kneel beside a seven-foot-long pit along the lagoon with his head extending over the hole. After teasing him in an unsuccessful effort to unnerve the civilian, a guard beheaded the American. Katsumi ordered the witnesses to tell the other prisoners what they had seen and that this punishment awaited anyone who disobeyed orders.

Two groups of Americans departed Wake in late 1942. Twenty Marines, now healthy enough to travel, boarded the *Asamu Maru* in the fall and headed to prison camps in Japan. When two hundred civilians left Wake on September 20 on the *Tachibana Maru*, an all-civilian work force of ninety-eight remained—ninety-seven to complete work projects and Dr. Shank, who refused to abandon his fellow civilians.

Murray Kidd, originally scheduled to leave, almost became one of the ninety-eight when he agreed to change places with a man selected to stay. The other captive wanted to remain with his buddy, who was bound for Japan, so Kidd, who had no desire to be taken even farther from the United States, offered to trade places.

When Kidd informed Sergeant Tada, however, Tada told Kidd, "If you're supposed to go, you go." Kidd sensed that the sergeant knew something of which the American was totally unaware and canceled the deal with the young civilian.

Before Kidd boarded the *Tachibana Maru*, Sergeant Tada inspected the vessel, then offered more words of advice. "He told me to take a jug of water with me because he knew there wasn't much water on the ship. He was a decent man. He went with me to the ship and handed me a package of stuff, cigarettes and other things. He got me on that ship, and then I never saw him again."

With his kind gestures, Sergeant Tada saved Murray Kidd's life, something the American never forgot. "He saved my life. The kid ended up getting killed. I know Tada knew what was going to happen."[14]

As the war wound through 1943, the United States Navy targeted Wake for repeated bombing raids. Sometimes, American task forces bombarded the location on their way to other destinations, and carrier aircraft used Wake as bombing practice. Corporal Holewinski, recuperating from his December 23 wounds, recalled a February 1942 raid by American aircraft that rattled both the Japanese and the Americans. As Holewinski waited out the intense bombing in a dugout, a friendly Japanese interpreter inched over toward him, put his arm around Holewinski, and said, "Remember how nice I was?"[15] The enemy soldier feared that the raid preceded an American invasion that would end with his capture by hostile Marines.

The assault of October 1943, a particularly intense bombardment, so angered the Japanese commander, Rear Adm. Shigemitsu Sakaibara, that he exacted vengeance on the civilians. On October 6, ninety-eight Americans, including Dr. Shank and the young worker whose place Murray Kidd almost took, marched under guard to the beach.

From nearby, Lee Bong Moon watched the proceedings. The Japanese led the Americans to a three-foot-deep ditch meandering along the beach, blindfolded them, lined them up in three rows in front of the ditch, and machined-gunned the defenseless men. "All the prisoners, both dead and wounded, were bayoneted," explained Moon. "One of the prisoners only known to me as Mr. John, was one of my best friends. In the first burst of fire he was wounded in the left shoulder. There was an American water tank to the right, and because it was almost dark and the faces were barely to be seen, I recognized him because he had a red jacket on. He also recognized me and when he was wounded he ran for the protection of the water tank. I met him there, picked him up, and carried him into the jungle [brush]."

Moon bandaged the American's wound and promised to return with food. Two days later, however, a Japanese soldier searching for birds discovered the American. Four captors, one carrying a sword, led the wounded man to a depression near a road and forced him to kneel. When Moon spotted the proceedings, he hurried up to see what was happening. His gaze caught that of Mr. John. "He was kneeling with his hands tied behind his back. We again recognized each other, and again tears came to his eyes."[16] Shortly after, a sword thrust ended the civilian's life. Sakaibara later had the ninety-eight bodies exhumed and dispersed about the atoll in an effort to make it appear they had been randomly killed in different American bombing attacks.

"Wake Is a Dangerous Island"

No example better illustrates the ironies that surround Wake than the condition of the so-called "victors" on Wake after the December battle. While the Americans headed into dreary prison camps, Japanese soldiers manned the vacated defenses at Wake, prepared to repel any American counterattack. As the Japanese waited for an assault that never occurred, they became each day more like their imprisoned foes.

The diary of L.Cpl. Watanabe Mitsumasa, of the Mixed Independence Regiment No. 113, First Battalion, Anti-tank Gun Company, provides an illuminating glimpse into life for the Japanese on Wake. In the 268 days covered in the diary, from April 21, 1944, until March 11, 1945, Mitsumasa mentioned the presence of American aircraft on 243 days. The succession of blows affected both morale and performance. On May 5, 1944, for instance, Mitsumasa wrote that "Enemy planes come nearly every day as if on schedule. We are all very nervous."

In many ways, the tables had turned on the Japanese, who now found themselves in situations similar to those of the Americans in China and Japan. He repeatedly referred to the lack of rations and how often the men discussed food, just like the men languishing in Woosung and other camps. "All one hears about on Wake is food, we have to rely on substitution to fill our stomachs," he entered on May 11, 1944. He wrote of eating roasted rat, leaves, vines, and referred to frequent punishments of men who stole food from the warehouse. Superiors jailed a soldier named Private Ikeda for eating sixteen cans of meat, then gave him so little nourishment that he perished. "Exchanging a life for 16 cans of meat. Oh, God save our soul. He was one of the healthy fellows in our squad. Wake is a dangerous island."

An occasional submarine shuttled in food and other supplies, and fish from the lagoon helped—when U.S. bombs lambasted the lagoon on May 17 and produced hundreds of dead fish floating on the surface for their enjoyment, Mitsumasa called them "a gift from F. D. Roosevelt"—but as the successful American drive pushed westward and severed the supply line from Japan, the men on Wake became more isolated than ever. Without hope of returning to their homeland until after the war, they had to survive on their own efforts, forgotten, underequipped, and underfed.

Conditions so deteriorated that Mitsumasa finally lost hope. "If only I could get out of here,"[17] he added on February 1, 1945. Nothing changed, however, and the soldier penned his final entry on March 11. Mitsumasa died of malnutrition sometime between August 7 and September 4, 1945, never having returned to the homeland he loved.

"The Rats Were Just as Hungry as We Were"

Mitsumasa's passion for Japan would have escaped the American captives, for they experienced a different side. Most of the Wake prisoners lived in a Japanese camp at some time during the war, and those who endured Woosung and Kiangwan contended that the time they subsequently spent in Japan was far worse. In May 1945, J. O. Young and Forrest Read entered their new camp in northern Japan to shocking news—almost half the prisoners succumbed there the previous winter, which brought snow accumulations up to eighteen feet deep. Neither man, so weakened that they doubted they could survive such a fierce winter, expected to see the next spring.

George Rosendick took one look at the inhabitants of the Osaka steel mill and camp and realized he had made a terrible decision. Before leaving China, he and Joe Goicoechea argued whether the new camps in Japan would be worse than Kiangwan. Rosendick could have remained in China, for the Japanese had not chosen him to depart in the same group as Goicoechea, but he let his friend talk him into going to Japan with him. Now he doubted the wisdom of his selection, a conclusion reinforced by meeting the men who had languished in the camp for two or three years, including men captured in the Philippines. "We looked like Charles Atlas compared to some of them," claimed Goicoechea, "but you know, it did not take long for us to look like them, especially our older men."[18]

Harsher work assignments proved to be the main difference between Japanese and Chinese camps. Japan, sorely strapped for laborers because so many young men had been sent away to fight, used American prisoners of war as slave labor to produce war matériel. Some men disappeared into coal mines, where they braved cave-ins, explosions, and coal dust. J. O. Young toiled such long hours in the shipyards of Osaka, a large port town west of Tokyo, that he lost twenty-three pounds in twenty-four days. Bombarded by deafening factory noises, the men had to carry large beams of steel weighing over three hundred pounds.

Young witnessed men purposely break their bones to avoid the exhausting work, a trick a demoralized Young tried once by pulling a 250-pound casting down on his leg. He only skinned his leg, but the episode showed to what extent the men's morale had plunged after three years in confinement, away from loved ones, decent food, and fun.

The Japanese guards in the Home Islands made the soldiers in China seem friendly. One guard called the prisoners those "dirty sons of bitches Americans,"[19] then beat anyone who incurred his wrath. A group of soldiers smacked Joe Goicoechea so badly about the face and neck that he incurred headaches that bother him to this day. The only solace the men took from the increased punishment was the pattern that developed—whenever something bad for Japan happened in the war, more prisoners received beatings. Obviously, the war had soured for the enemy.

Murray Kidd purposely formed few friendships at Camp 18 near Hiroshima, one of the harshest camps, since he did not want to go through the anguish of watching a buddy die. So many men succumbed to the extreme cold and lack of food that the Japanese placed a coffin next to the man they thought would die next. Once he expired, they shoved the body into the wooden box and carted him off.

"There was no heat and no hospital, not a thing," Kidd mentioned years later. "We had many men from Wake die, at least, in camp, mainly from disease. You'd get a cold, then pneumonia. Guys younger than me got sick and died. The work schedule was rough, ten to twelve hours a day building a dam, and we didn't ever see a softball or anything all the time we were there. We just worked! There was no fun, no relaxation, no religious services, just work. Everything froze in the winter, so we didn't have water for baths and we couldn't keep our teeth clean. A lot of guys don't have any teeth anymore."[20]

According to Hans Whitney, 234 prisoners, some from Wake, perished during the war's last year at a Kawasaki camp near Osaka, where J. O. Young almost broke his leg. Up to five men died each day at the Yawata Iron Works Camp No. 3, and Joe Goicoechea had to eat his meals for two days in Osaka with the body of a dead American prisoner lying next to him.

"I still have nightmares over what happened in Japan," wrote Goicoechea. He claimed rats, lice, and fleas were constant companions, and that "all kinds of bugs eating on you was terrible." He added that "the damned rats running [across] our face at night, while you was trying to sleep" kept waking the tired men. Goicoechea harbored no ill will toward the rats, though, because "The rats were just as hungry as we were."[21]

Escape

When people today meet Wake Islanders, one question that usually arises is, "Did you try to escape?" Most readily admit they did not, for practical reasons. Incarcerated in a foreign land among people that looked dramatically different and spoke an alien language, any prisoner outside camp would quickly draw notice. Americans escaping from European camps could more readily blend into the general populace, but the men in China and Japan lacked that opportunity. The Wake Islanders languishing in Japan proper abandoned all hopes for escape; only in China did Americans consider such an adventure.

Commander Cunningham, Dan Teters, and three other men made the first escape attempt. On the night of March 11, 1942, the group burrowed under the electrified fence and dashed into the surrounding countryside outside Woosung, hoping to reach friendly Chinese forces. Within twenty-four hours, though, Japanese soldiers captured all five and took them to a local jail, where the Japanese secret police interrogated them. The Japanese eventually returned the men to Woosung, placed them on trial, and sentenced them to lengthy jail terms in Shanghai's notorious Ward Road Jail.

Cunningham tried again on October 6, 1944, this time by sawing through the bars in his cell window, sliding down a rope into a garden below, and fleeing through Shanghai's busy streets. In less than ten hours, though, the Japanese recaptured him and returned him to his cell. They later sentenced Cunningham to life in prison for this second attempt.

One escape involving Wake Island personnel succeeded. On May 9, 1945, Lieutenant Kinney and Lt. John McAlister, joined by two other non-Wake Marines, jumped off a train transporting them to another Chinese prison camp. That same night two Wake civilians, Bill Taylor and Jack Hernandez, followed suit. The men, separated from one another during the leap from the train, hid in fields by day and moved by night, hoping to meet friendly Chinese forces before the Japanese caught up to them. Kinney encountered a helpful Chinese guide, who took him to pro-American Chinese troops. They escorted Kinney to another location, where he was reunited with the other three Marines. After being flown to American forces in China, Kinney and his group boarded a plane bound for the United States, which they reached on July 9. Bill Taylor also fled to friendly forces and returned home, but Jack Hernandez broke a leg jumping from the train and was recaptured.

Other men mounted escape attempts, but none succeeded. Major Devereux believed that as the individual in charge of the Marines, he had a duty to remain and fight for their welfare, to keep as many men alive as possible, so he never considered escaping. Eventually, the Japanese forced every American to sign a pledge stating they would not try to escape, an action the Americans grudgingly carried out after making clear they signed under coercion and gave no legal credence to the document.

Beginning in the latter half of 1944, and especially as 1945 dawned, escape receded in the prisoners' minds, for the evidence of war's end became clearer. In fact, the weary prisoners from Wake Island received visual proof that forces from their homeland were drawing nearer.

"That Reassuring Sound"

Just when the Wake Island defenders seemed to be losing hope, events pointed to an end to their misery. For three years, captivity had kept the men from the active portion of the war, but now the war came to their doorsteps. Every prisoner remembered when he first sighted American bombers and fighters overhead in late 1944 and early 1945, a landmark episode that instantly reestablished the connection to their military brethren fighting the war. Corporal Marvin and his Marine buddies so enthusiastically cheered the event that angry Japanese guards beat them afterwards. This was one punishment they did not mind, however, for the appearance of aircraft meant the United States military could not be too far away.

In the subsequent weeks, Forrest Read felt like a newborn baby being lulled to sleep by the guttural, rhythmic drone of the B-29 bombers on their nightly bombing runs. "I can still hear that reassuring sound. It made us feel good that we were that close to something from home."[22] For the first time since they had left the United States, Marines, Navy, Army, and civilian personnel sensed the presence of friendly forces, especially when short-range American fighters sped into view. Since the smaller aircraft could not fly much farther than a few hundred miles, the prisoners knew rescue might be only weeks away.

The aviators piloting those aircraft purposely flew at lower altitudes for the prisoners' benefit. An officer aboard the aircraft carrier USS *Bennington*, briefing Marine aviators about their next mission over Japan, mentioned the presence of prisoner of war camps in the vicinity of the target area and reminded his men what their arrival meant. "In these camps are members of the Marine Corps, including undoubtedly some of the survivors of the garrison of Wake Island. They have been prisoners of the Japs for more than three years. When these men look up and see us we must be sure to be flying at a low enough altitude so that they will know who we are."[23]

The prisoners reacted like schoolchildren starting their first day of summer vacation. They jumped and hugged each other, yelled and cheered as tears coursed down their cheeks. Devereux waved excitedly to the pilots in a squadron of Army fighters that buzzed the camp, and when he turned back to look at the other Marines, he noticed that for the first time in three years, they whistled in glee. When American fighters shot down three Japanese planes, the men in Lieutenant Kessler's camp hollered as if their favorite team had just scored the winning touchdown in a college football game. "No gift in the world could have made us so happy as to know that our prison camp had been found, our dreams of relief from past hardships had come true,"[24] wrote Hans Whitney.

As soon as the jubilation subsided, a more appalling reality gripped the men. They now engaged in a life-or-death race that would be determined by events outside their control—what would arrive first, death at the hands of the Japanese, or liberation by fellow Americans? Freedom lay enticingly close, but would the Japanese simply hand them over to victorious troops, or would they massacre the prisoners beforehand? Logic dictated that the Japanese would not kindly accept defeat.

"Some Japanese told us the Americans were going to invade right where we were," said Murray Kidd. "They told us if that happened, we would be the first to go. That wasn't too good a thing to hear. We wanted the Americans to get there, but then that [the massacre] would happen."[25]

Their fears were not unfounded. A document unearthed after the war yielded evidence that the Japanese intended to institute a mass program of extermination. The document stated that if an American invasion attempt appeared likely and any camp seemed about to fall into American hands, a "final disposition" of the prisoners would be carried out. The document added in chilling words, "Whether they [prisoners] are destroyed individually or in groups, or however it is done, with mass bombing, poisonous smoke, poisons, drowning, decapitation, or what, dispose of them as the situation dictates." The order ended, "In any case it is the aim not to allow the escape of a single one, to annihilate them all, and not to leave any traces."[26]

The prisoners faced other dilemmas, as well. Since some of the camps existed in areas being bombed by American aircraft, the men could easily be harmed or killed by their own forces. The steel mill in which Private First Class Gatewood worked proved to be a popular target for American bombers. During one raid Gatewood heard the sickening screech of a bomb falling, hid behind a stack of wheels, then was rattled from the impact of a huge *"Thud!"* A five-hundred-pound bomb landed twenty feet from him without exploding. Had the bomb not been a dud, Gatewood would have been blown to pieces.

A loud crash startled Murray Kidd early one morning. When he and the others ran into the kitchen, an enormous unexploded bomb that had crashed through the ceiling protruded from the floor. During another raid, a huge boulder smashed directly onto a spot Joe Goicoechea had only moments before vacated.

Cpl. Robert M. Brown sat in a prison train heading toward Osaka and its steel mills when American aircraft attacked. "Our guards nearly panicked, but ordered us off the train and down the back side of the embankment," Brown wrote after the war. "Bombs were exploding on the other side as close as a couple of a hundred yards. I thought: 'Are we going to end our captivity by being clobbered by our own people?' Soon the bombs began moving away, and as we got back on top to reboard the train, we could see heavy flames in the near distance. 'Go get them, guys,' we said."[27] Brown's life may have been in danger, but he still wanted his country to mount a relentless attack, even if he had to perish in the process.

The prisoners could hardly believe the incredible devastation caused by American bombers. Having been confined to prison camps for three years, the Wake Islanders had been out of touch with military innovations, so the widespread damage awed them. In July 1945, Major Devereux peeked out the window of the train in which he rode. He viewed nothing but rubble on both sides of the track, caused by previous American raids. Though weary, Devereux and the other men with him grinned widely.

"Good God, the firebombs had just leveled the towns!" exclaimed Private Laporte when he looked out the window. "We were happy, and if the guards had not been around, we would have jumped up and cheered."[28]

Joe Goicoechea and George Rosendick witnessed the horrible Tokyo fire raid from their nearby prison camp on April 15, 1945. Women and children ran screaming through the city, while debris swirled upward in immense boiling columns. The massive fires so concerned the two Americans that Rosendick feared they would perish from weapons dropped by U.S. aircraft. "I thought how horrible it would be to survive this long, only to be killed by your own people,"[29] stated Rosendick after the war. On the other hand, they also saw the deadly cost of attacking Japan when enemy antiaircraft guns downed eight B-29s.

In retaliation for the bombings, mobs of angry Japanese civilians often attacked prisoners as they were being transported to work or to another camp. Corporal Brown's train had stopped in Tokyo on July 4, 1945, on its way to Hokkaido, when a mob rushed the prisoners. Japanese guards contained the crowd, but not before the civilians seriously injured one American by beating him with a baseball bat.

"Here's to That Atom Bomb, Whatever It Is!"

The end to their incarceration came in August 1945, when atom bombs leveled the Japanese cities of Hiroshima and Nagasaki and speedily led to the Japanese surrender. Few Wake Islanders knew of the atom bomb or of any other events that terminated the most destructive war in history, but they did not care. Liberation brought everything they desired right back into their lives—home, family, food, freedom.

Lieutenant Hanna awoke one morning to discover the guards had left. Most every day that Lieutenant Kessler and other prisoners marched to the mines, Japanese children lined up to spit and to toss rocks at them. One August morning, however, the children bowed instead.

Hans Whitney's friend, a man named Mack, understood a little Japanese. As he listened to a Japanese broadcast over a radio, he suddenly leapt and shouted that the war had ended. In plain view of the guards, who did nothing to halt him, Mack ran to every barracks to share the news.

"We were the only company working that day," stated Corporal Marvin.

> We went to lunch and the officers and guards, who usually ate at the end, they all left at 12:30. At 1:00 they usually got us up and back to work, but they never showed up until 1:30. They were very sullen. They just said don't go to work. I walked to the machine shop where I worked and asked my officer what was wrong, and he said the war was over and "You go home soon." About an hour later the guards took us back to camp, and we tried to tell the other guys the war was over but nobody would believe us.
>
> That night hardly anyone slept, and we said if we fall out for work the next day the war isn't over. Well, we fell out for work, and this Jap was giving us a big speech, and this interpreter said there had been a three-day halt in the war. Just about that time a torpedo bomber flew across the barracks and dropped cigarettes in a little parachute that said the war was over. I'm telling you, we really came unglued.[30]

On August 18, an English-speaking Japanese officer explained the cessation of hostilities to Devereux in a manner that must have made the major grin. "We have decided to stop fighting though our Army has not been beaten in the field," rationalized the Japanese. The same day Cunningham and five other Americans, all incarcerated for escape attempts, were taken to the commander's office. "The war is over," said the Japanese. "We hope the Americans and the Japanese will shake hands and become friends again. You will be taken from here tonight to another place."[31]

Corporal Johnson was so delighted with the news that he decided he would not, after all, return to the United States and kill Senator Wheeler. Instead, he joined other prisoners around a keg of beer the Japanese brought in to celebrate the end of fighting. A Japanese officer explained that because of the inhumanity of the atom bomb and because of his desire for peace, the emperor had decided to end the war. When the Japanese officer said that they would all now drink a toast to the future friendship of the United States and Japan, one of the Americans grabbed a container full of beer and shouted, "Take off buster! Here's to that atom bomb, whatever it is!"[32]

The men in Hans Whitney's camp butchered two pigs "liberated" from nearby farms for a camp feast. Corporal Johnson joined others in singing old college songs and other popular tunes, while the Americans in Japan's Hakodate Prison Camp No. 3, including Gunner Hamas and other Wake Island Marines, held an emotional ceremony. Fifteen men weaved together bits of red, white, and blue cloth into a crude Stars and Stripes, and as one man sounded Morning Colors on a bugle left by Japanese guards, the entire camp assembled. For the first time in almost four years, stilled servicemen watched their country's flag rise to the top of an improvised flagpole fashioned from a cut young tree. Men who had not lost their composure after the battle or during difficult moments in prison camp unabashedly stood at attention while tears streamed down their faces. The flag for which they had fought and for which some of their friends had died, was at last once again flying proudly over their heads.

On the other hand, some Americans sought vengeance on the men responsible for the cruelties of their prison ordeal. Pfc. Jacob Sanders hunted for a particularly cruel guard who had slashed his face with a cane. Sanders never found the guard, who had already fled, and claimed later that "I really scared myself thinking that I would want to kill someone, but his treatment was so brutal that I felt it was called for."[33]

In Pfc. James King's camp, a group of men created a hangman's noose out of some rope, stormed to the factory in which they had been forced to toil, and lynched the guard who administered cruel beatings with regularity. When the group threatened to drag out and hang the Japanese for whom Private First Class King worked, a decent man who had given the American extra food, King interceded in his behalf and prevented his death.

Even in weakened condition, many men headed into the nearest town for better food or to enjoy the companionship of women. Lieutenant Hanna's camp "sort of took over the town adjacent to us. For one thing, they had one of those community baths, and we all took a bath. That felt good. The Japanese citizens made themselves scarce. To get to this little town we had to go on a train. We stopped the train and got on. When we were ready to go back we stopped the train and went back."[34]

Corporal Marvin and a group of Americans grabbed bicycles from Japanese citizens, and told them to stay where they were until they returned. The Americans headed to town, where they took over the local movie theater and public bath, then returned hours later to find the Japanese still waiting quietly for the bicycles.

Private Laporte ignored advice from a British officer who claimed it might be too dangerous to meander through a city full of Japanese. "We went walking into the town and there was not one soul to be seen nowhere. They was all inside hiding. The Japs were scared to death of us because they had been told we would kill everyone."[35]

After being confined in a Shanghai jail for escaping, Commander Cunningham enjoyed the opportunity of taking a leisurely walk on his own. He mentioned later how liberating was this action. "It was something I had not been able to do for three years and eight months, and I reveled in the sight of the stars—not just a few as seen through a barred window, but all of them. For the first time I could walk as long as I liked and stay up as late as I chose. Glorying in this apparently trifling privilege, I found myself realizing at last that I was free."[36]

One thought nagged at Cunningham as he breathed fresh air and allowed the wind to caress his cheeks—had the people in the United States considered him a coward all these years for surrendering the garrison at Wake? As commanding officer on Wake, Cunningham took responsibility for the surrender, a fact that deeply bothered him. With plenty of time on his hands to think about it, Cunningham thought of the men who had died fighting, and of the men who faced years of pain and misery in prison camp, and debated whether he could have done something different. He assumed the American public had condemned him for not fighting to the last man. "Even thoughts of home and loved ones brought with them a sense of foreboding. Had they been shamed by my conduct of the defense? Already the thought that I might be court-martialed for surrendering the island haunted me."[37]

The thoughts so bothered Cunningham that he had once asked a group of men in prison camp how they could be playing cards and laughing after surrendering. The men replied that while they did not like losing the battle on Wake, they could not be fighting the war all the time.

Even the Japanese noticed Cunningham's quandary. One of the guards tried to reassure him by reminding him that Japan had never lost a war in its twenty-six centuries of existence.

"Acting Like a Damn Fool in General"

Cunningham would quickly have his answer, for relief operations started as soon as the war ended. Twenty-eight teams of four men each spread inside Japan to check on prison camps and to prepare the men for their journeys home. By September 2, less than one month after atomic bombs had destroyed Hiroshima (August 6) and Nagasaki (August 9) and only one day after Japanese representatives signed the document of surrender to officially end the war, the Army established a hospital ship and set up processing facilities in Yokohama.

Teams of Americans parachuted into camps farther inside Japan or in China. They told the men to remain in camp until they received further orders, and explained that aircraft would soon be dropping food, clothing, medical supplies, and other necessities.

People back home followed the proceedings with great interest, for the men of Wake had been heroes since the war's initial days. Headlines in the *Washington Daily News* for September 13, 1945, proclaimed DEVEREUX, WAKE HERO, IS FOUND and stated that "the gallant commander of the heroic U.S. Marine garrison on Wake Island, has been found safe and well in a prisoner of war camp on Hokkaido, northernmost of the Jap home islands, and is awaiting evacuation by plane."

According to the article, Devereux wanted to set one thing straight. "The first thing I'd like to get on the record is that we did not send that radio message saying, 'Send us more Japs.' We had all and more than we could handle right then and there."[38]

After American fighters buzzed their camp, the men with Forrest Read spelled out the word FOOD with bedsheets. The fighters departed, but shortly after returned with provisions and a note saying B-29 bombers would drop more material. Other men painted large PW [prisoner of war] on rooftops.

Bombers dropped fifty-gallon drums of canned goods and other items into most camps, which were eagerly snatched up by the famished prisoners. J. O. Young joined the others in cheering, crying, waving his hat, and "acting like a damn fool in general."[39] Since the men had been without decent food in so long, some became ill immediately after eating, but they did not let that stop them.

That natural craving for nourishment proved to be fatal for a handful of Wake Islanders. After huddling in dugouts on Wake that rattled from Japanese shells and bombs, after seeing men die and bleed, after stomaching the humiliating defeat and surrender, after enduring three and one-half years of prison camp and all its terrors, some men lived to witness war's end, only to die in an operation intended to bring them home when faulty parachutes failed to stop the plunges of the heavy drums. A food canister killed one civilian in Lieutenant Hanna's camp. The man standing next to Private First Class Sanders died in similar fashion, and a bag of food dropped by a fighter pilot appeared to be heading directly toward Forrest Read, who broke his foot jumping off a fence to avoid the missile. In Murray Kidd's camp, a case of food hit one civilian in the neck and killed him instantly, but since the man had cooperated with the Japanese by informing on fellow Americans, few shed any tears. When two men in Corporal Johnson's camp died the same way, the men cut up some of the parachutes and spelled out on a nearby hill, NO MORE DROPS.

The first group of ex-prisoners arrived on the hospital ship on September 4, followed by additional units throughout the remainder of September. By the end of the month, most men had been evacuated from their camps and flown to the Twenty-ninth Replacement Depot near Manila in the Philippines for medical examinations, back pay, uniforms, and a chance to send a message home. While in the Philippines, they had to complete a questionnaire about their time in camp that investigators hoped to use in war crimes trials against abusive Japanese officers and soldiers.

Touching scenes greeted the newly liberated Americans. When the men with Hans Whitney stepped into a naval craft for the ride to the hospital ship, the sailors manning the boat removed their shirts and carefully wrapped them around the shivering ex-prisoners, preferring to let them ride in relative comfort while they braved the trip without shirts. Nurses in fresh white uniforms welcomed Whitney as he boarded the hospital ship. The females, a welcome sight to every man, stepped forward to lend a hand, but broke down in tears when they realized how weak and thin the men were. Sailors helped Whitney to a room where he showered and donned a pair of pajamas, his first clean clothes since December 1941. After devouring two fried eggs, toast, bacon, and the item most demanded by the former prisoners—ice cream—Whitney climbed into a soft bed and fell into a sleep that was interrupted several times by nightmares.

While being evacuated from Japan, a few of the men encountered a sight they have never forgotten—the devastation at Nagasaki caused by the atom bomb. Along the route transporting Private First Class Gatewood and others from camp, the troop train traveled directly through what had once been a city. "It was about a month after they dropped the atom bomb," recalled Gatewood. "I just couldn't believe it. The only thing standing was a wall here or part of a wall there. This Japanese welder had told us about the bomb at Hiroshima, that one bomb did this, and then he showed us a picture. I thought, 'That's impossible!' I thought he meant one plane dropping all kinds of bombs, but he kept saying, 'No, one bomb!' "[40]

Civilian Rodney Kephart passed through Nagasaki on September 15 and stared, mouth open, at the hellish terrain. "I gasped, I swallowed hard, I tried to believe my own eyes," he wrote after the war. "I looked, rubbed my eyes and looked again—yes, it was true—the landscape was scorched of everything consumable by fire; to the ridge of the hills the vegetation was brown from the heat. All things were gone. Where dwellings, orchards, and gardens had been there were but bare terraces scorched with terrific heat. Where there had been factories there was but twisted steel."[41]

Any man who witnessed the rubble of Hiroshima or Nagasaki could not help being moved for the women, children, and elderly citizens who perished in the conflagration or would shortly expire from the bomb's effects. After all, many had been innocent victims who had little to do with causing the war and the hatred endemic to it. To a man, however, they believed then, and still contend today, that the atom bomb saved their lives. They would either have died in camp, overworked and undernourished, or the Japanese would have executed them before the American military could assault the Home Islands and free them. The weapon terminated a war that had only one of two alternatives for the prisoners—they would either die in prison camp, or they would live and return to the United States. While feeling compassion for the Japanese victims lost at the two cities, they have never doubted the propriety of their nation using the bomb.

"It Was Here the Marines Showed Us How"

Two thousand miles across the Pacific, on September 4, a Marine unit aboard the destroyer escort USS *Levy* strained to catch a glimpse of their destination—Wake. They had certainly heard of the location, and one passenger—Col. Walter L. Bayler, who became the famous "last man off Wake Island" when he left the atoll on the final flight out—had once fought there, so they were anxious to land and retake the atoll for the United States. No one expected resistance from the large garrison of Japanese, but every Marine maintained extra vigilance just in case.

Rear Adm. Shigemitsu Sakaibara, Wake's commander, and five aides led the Japanese surrender party out to the ship in a small whaleboat. The United States military representative designated to receive their surrender, Marine Brig. Gen. Lawton H. Sanderson, curtly refused to acknowledge a Japanese offer to shake hands. This was Wake, the place where the country commenced its four-year-long march to victory, and he was not about to be friendly with the men responsible for the deaths of Wake military and civilian personnel.

When Sanderson cautioned Sakaibara about Japanese sabotage, the admiral assured him he need not worry. Almost 1,900 of his men had already died from bombings or disease, and the survivors were too weak from malnutrition to mount any effective resistance. Sakaibara then affixed his signature to the surrender document and to eleven copies.

A landing party of about twenty-five Marines, including Colonel Bayler, headed to Wake Island. Fittingly, Colonel Bayler stepped off the craft first, then took the Americans on a quick tour of the place. When they asked a Japanese officer for the location of graves of Wake military or civilian personnel, he pointed to two large mounds. The Americans had yet to learn about the mass execution ordered by Sakaibara, so they headed on their way.

The American contingent then gathered for the flag-raising ceremony. Everyone, including a color guard, stood at attention as a Marine sounded colors, then watched the Stars and Stripes once again fly over Wake. "The flag raising was a very emotional event," said Marine combat correspondent Sgt. Ernie Harwell, later the longtime voice of the Detroit Tigers baseball team. "Getting this outpost was the culmination of the war because of what Wake meant to everyone."[42]

General Sanderson ended the brief ceremony by officially handing over control of Wake to Navy Comdr. William Masek. Masek summed up the emotions of everyone, both those on the atoll and the American population back home, when he said, "I accept this island proudly. Because this is Wake Island. Not just any island. It was here the Marines showed us how."[43]

★

CHAPTER 13

"I Was Doing What I Was Trained to Do"

Now that the war had ended, thousands of American prisoners of war, including Lieutenant Hanna and Joe Goicoechea, waited impatiently for orders to head back to the United States and their families. Most had to remain in Japan until their records could be checked and transportation could be arranged, or until their health improved sufficiently for them to make the transpacific voyage. As a result, instead of the Wake Island defenders steaming triumphantly into San Francisco harbor as a group, they filtered home at varying times. No matter when they returned, though, the men experienced one of the most powerful moments of their still-young lives.

"A Very Warm Greeting"

Major Devereux arrived home before most of his men. On September 15, he flew to the escort carrier *Hoggatt Bay*, where he rejoined fellow Wake officers for their first American cooked meal. After a brief layover in Hawaii, Devereux landed in Washington, D.C., on September 26, where he was reunited with his son, Paddy, who hoped to ride horses and attend baseball and football games with the father he had not seen in so long and whom the nation had adopted as its own.

Devereux's hometown of Chevy Chase, Maryland, honored him with an enthusiastic parade. Twenty thousand people lined the streets to welcome their hero, a man the *Washington Times-Herald* called "the smiling little guy who bought time for America when time was the most precious commodity on earth." The Marine Corps Band played patriotic tunes for the throng, which fought back tears when the band started the notes of the Marine Hymn. Gen. Alexander Vandegrift, the Marine commandant, addressed the crowd about the significance of what the Marines accomplished on Wake. "Throughout the war the slogan of the marine corps [sic] always was remember Pearl Harbor and remember Wake."[1]

The reaction for Commander Cunningham stood in stark contrast to that of Devereux. He arrived in New York City on September 7, then immediately headed to Washington, D.C., for a reunion with his wife and daughter. His wife, though delighted to hold her husband in her arms once again, choked back tears at the sight of the gaunt Cunningham.

Along his route home, Cunningham, still concerned about being considered a failure, realized that few in the public recognized his name. Since most bulletins issued by the Navy Department during the battle emphasized the Marine role in the fighting, Devereux's name, not Cunningham's, gained all the publicity. Few people knew that Cunningham had even served on the atoll, let alone acted as its commanding officer. Contrary to the emotional parade held to honor Devereux, Cunningham returned to empty streets. "My reputation, where it existed at all, was that of a commander who did not command," he wrote in his memoirs. "To a fighting man, there can be no worse dishonor short of treason itself." Adding insult to injury, when people who met Cunningham learned that he had been on Wake, they invariably asked the officer, "You were on Wake? Then you were with Devereux?"[2]

After being freed from prison camp, Lieutenant Hanna boarded a ship in Tokyo Bay, where he enjoyed his first clean uniform and decent food. Like most Wake Islanders, he asked for ice cream when given the option of any food he could have. Hanna settled in on the ship and then sent a message to Vera in Louisiana that he was all right.

Hanna had to remain in Hawaii for two days of official business before flying to San Francisco. He called Vera once he landed in California and arranged a meeting in Wichita, Kansas, the destination of Hanna's next set of hospital tests, then hopped an airplane for the trip eastward.

Hanna arrived in Wichita around 2:00 A.M., three hours before Vera and Erlyne pulled in by car. Lieutenant Hanna, whose once-haggard appearance had been improved by a better diet and extra rest, enjoyed what he described as a "very warm greeting"[3] with his wife at the entrance to the terminal. Though he guessed that Erlyne would not remember him, his daughter's affectionate welcome seemed to wash away the previous three years. After more than two weeks of fighting on Wake, a month of captivity on the atoll, a few grueling weeks on the hell that was the *Nitta Maru*, and the years in confinement, the hero of Hanna's guns was once again where he belonged—in the arms of loved ones.

Other military personnel, many still younger than most college graduates, gradually headed home to their families. In other conditions, other times, a twenty- or twenty-one-year-old might have been called a young adult or novice worker, yet even the youngest of Wake's defenders—one Marine, having lied about his age to enlist, was still only a teenager—had seen more, experienced more, and endured more than 99 percent of the nation they defended.

"There Wasn't No Fanfare"

Just emerging from three and one-half years in prison camp, each man inevitably passed through a period of adjustments to peacetime living. When some former prisoners first slipped into comfortable hospital beds, they waited for the nurses to leave the room, then slid out from the covers and slept on the hard floor because the softer mattresses bothered them. On the ship that transported them to Guam, Pfc. Jacob Sanders and other Marines complained that the ship's doctor would not allow the men to eat anything they wanted. The physician correctly predicted that the richer food would seriously affect their digestive systems, but his words meant nothing to men possessing an enormous craving for the very thing of which they had been deprived.

When the ship docked at Guam, the Marines took their grievance to another doctor on the island, who readily gave permission for them to consume to their hearts' desire, an assent that signaled a feeding frenzy. Some of Sanders's buddies grabbed entire loaves of fresh bread, smeared them with butter, and stuffed them down their throats as quickly as they could. Not surprisingly, they became ill as the first doctor had predicted.

"We ate everything. We'd eat and then go to the end of the chow line and eat again, until we left Guam," said Corporal Marvin. "Then they gave us tiddlywinks so we could only eat one meal. You had to show that color tiddlywink for each meal and without it you couldn't even get through the line. They didn't want us to overdo it because some of the fellows ate so much they got sick. Some of the guys were gaining one pound a day."4 Marvin, who had dropped to 115 pounds from his prewar weight of 180, regained most of the weight loss before reaching the United States.

When Private First Class Gatewood arrived in the United States and telephoned his sister, he spent thirty minutes trying to convince her who he was. "They had heard nothing of me since the first part of 1945, when they received a card. They thought I was dead. My sister kept telling me, 'I don't know what you are trying to pull, but you're not my brother.' I said, 'If I'm not, you haven't got another brother named George.' She said, 'I don't know who you're trying to kid, but you're not Martin.' She didn't recognize my voice. I had just turned eighteen when I went into the service, and here I was five years later calling and talking to her."[5]

The first returnees from Wake enjoyed festive celebrations. When Private First Class Sanders's ship, for instance, steamed under the Golden Gate Bridge in San Francisco, boats filled the harbor and cars lined the bay, all with horns tooting a welcome for the ship bearing prisoners of war. Huge signs reading WELL DONE, BOYS and GRATEFUL NATION WELCOMES YOU greeted others.

Conditions changed for those who followed the first wave. Delayed in a hospital along the route or held up by a slow-moving troop transport, the men pulled into quiet harbors and empty docks. By then the nation, weary of war and reminders of all things military, had turned its attention from parades to the more civilian pastimes of rebuilding careers and raising families. Private Laporte steamed under the same bridge as Sanders, yet found no one waiting. "The great expectations kind of mellowed by the time we got home. The country wasn't throwing out any ceremonies at the time. There wasn't no fanfare. We just went to military hospitals. There was no crowd waiting at the docks yelling and cheering."[6] Sadly, many of the men who played such prominent roles in raising the country's morale in the war's bleak early days, when the country most needed a lift, received a lukewarm welcome from that same nation upon returning.

"The Most Wonderful Day of My Life"

A gangrenous leg and other maladies kept Joe Goicoechea from returning to Boise immediately. Physicians in Okinawa briefly considered amputating the leg, but heavy doses of penicillin over several weeks cleared the problem. As soon as his leg permitted, the Idahoan roamed the hospital halls, visiting other men and exploring the building. Finally, after receiving an avalanche of complaints from nurses that their patient refused to follow orders, doctors told Goicoechea that if he were healthy enough to be that much of a problem, he was well enough to go home.

When Goicoechea landed in San Francisco, he and George Rosendick shared a large suite arranged by Morrison-Knudsen. The company handed each man the same package that every construction worker eventually received—a check to cover immediate expenses and ration coupons to purchase clothes and food. He and Rosendick took time from their fun to visit a local military hospital for amputees, where the brother of one of their friends was being treated for serious wounds suffered at the February 1945 battle of Iwo Jima. Goicoechea had always made the best of every situation in which he found himself, whether as a student in school, a worker on Wake, or a prisoner in camp, but this trip deeply affected him. The young Marines, each one missing an arm or leg, looked at Goicoechea and Rosendick without speaking. The pair left feeling that while they had suffered their own share of hardships, others faced tribulations on a grander scale.

Clutching a bottle of bourbon to help pass the time, Goicoechea hopped a train in April 1946 for the ride home to Boise. Back in familiar surroundings, he joined Rosendick and Kidd in their usual prewar activities, now usually accompanied by a fair amount of alcohol. For the next few months, the trio made the rounds of bars and nightclubs in the Boise area, three happy-go-lucky young men out to enjoy a life denied them for too long. None was eager to return to work; fun and games dominated the agenda. Murray Kidd claimed that after he returned to Boise and settled in with his parents, "We got our back pay and laid around and drank for two or three months."[7]

Family members guaranteed that the homecomings for the other Idahoans, J. O. Young and Forrest Read, would long be remembered. Young, still unsure of how Pearl Ann might feel after all these years and after leaving in such abrupt fashion, telephoned his family from Hawaii so they could meet him when he arrived in California. As the ship pulled into San Francisco, Young scanned the faces lining the docks for signs of Pearl Ann. Young broke into a wide grin when he saw a little blonde in a red dress. Recognizing Pearl Ann standing beside his mother, Young rushed off the ship.

As Young barreled through the passengers to reach Pearl Ann, she waited to see whom he would first greet. Pearl Ann concluded that if Young hugged her before his mother, it meant he still loved her, but if he hugged his mother first, that would be a telltale sign that he no longer wanted to marry her. Her heart raced as Young descended the gangway toward them, rushed up, and threw himself into the arms of his fiancée. One month later, the pair married in Salt Lake City, a union that produced nine children, thirty-six grandchildren, and six great grandchildren. The two still live in Idaho, fifty-eight years after their marriage.

Because of his injuries, Forrest Read did not return until later. He flew into San Francisco and entered a hospital with other wounded men, who peppered him with questions about the fight for Wake and his time in prison camp. Read figured that once he recovered, he could go back home and resume his life, but in the meantime he knew his family would do what it could to travel west and see him. With limited funds, however, he did not expect anything soon.

One day as he chatted in his room with other patients, four people walked in. Read fell silent as he gazed at his mother, wife, sister, and brother-in-law. Sensing that Read wanted to be alone with his family, the other patients left, at which time the five engaged in a warm welcome. "[It was] the most wonderful day of my life to be back in their arms and knowing I would soon be going back with them to good old Idaho and our home and see my old dad."[8]

Once home, Read feasted on pies, milk shakes, and hamburgers. Within three months, his weight soared from 128 to a more normal 198, in part because of the graciousness of his neighbors. The local newspaper ran a feature story on Read which included a photograph, but since the picture was of Read during his stay in the hospital, he appeared gaunt. A torrent of neighbors and friends came by, mostly to drop off food for Read.

Unfortunately, not every family celebrated the return of loved ones, since so many men had been killed during the battle or in captivity. Especially devastating was the tragic confusion involving the two McDonald families, both of whom had boys named Joseph on Wake. In 1942 the government notified the Reno, Nevada, family of one Joseph McDonald that their son had been killed in the 1941 battle. The Reno McDonalds held a memorial service for their son, then began the ordeal of coping with the loss of a loved one.

Much to their shock, in 1945 the government informed them of a terrible mistake in identification. Their son had been found alive in prison camp and was headed home, while the other worker with a similar name, Joseph Thomas McDonald from Cody, Wyoming, was actually the man killed. The Reno McDonalds greeted a son they believed had died long ago, while the Cody McDonalds mourned the loss of someone they assumed had been alive.

Controversy over Command

A minor controversy erupted following the war over who should receive credit for guiding the 1941 Wake defense. Every war bulletin issued by the Navy Department during the battle stressed the presence of Major Devereux and the Marines while ignoring Commander Cunningham. Possibly the Navy, embarrassed over its poor showing at Pearl Harbor, did not want a Navy officer associated with what then appeared to be a second defeat in the Pacific. When the garrison surprisingly held on for two weeks and gained the admiration of the nation, the Navy could not then reverse course and credit Cunningham for something for which they did not want to blame him. Possibly the Navy Department, occupied with bringing order out of the chaos that existed after Pearl Harbor, simply either did not know

Cunningham had arrived at Wake—he reached the atoll only a few days before the battle—or forgot he had been stationed there.

From the battle's earliest days, Major Devereux and the Marines received the lion's share of praise, in the national publications, from President Roosevelt, and throughout the military. When Lieutenants Kinney and McAlister returned from their successful escape attempt and read the accounts of the battle, they could hardly believe the descriptions. Where, they wondered, was mention of Commander Cunningham? The Marines deserved the praise they received, but so did Cunningham. "Although I certainly did not intend to take any well-deserved credit away from Major Devereux, I remained baffled by the apparent neglect of Cunningham's role,"[9] Kinney wrote in his autobiography. When Kinney asked a group of reporters why that happened, they explained that when they inquired at the Navy Department in 1941 about the identity of the superior commander at Wake, they were told that a navy commander had been assigned, but that they did not know if he had yet arrived. Major Devereux's name was then mentioned as commander of the defense battalion, and from that time on his name, for lack of any other, occupied top position.

Even President Roosevelt, who loved the Navy as much as anyone, unwittingly lent credence to the belief that Wake was strictly a Marine show with his presidential unit citation of January 1942. He praised the Marines in general, and Devereux and Putnam specifically, in the proclamation, while never once referring to Commander Cunningham. If ever a president would fight to preserve the honor of the Navy, that man would be President Roosevelt, but his omission produced more adulation for the Marines.

Hollywood's production, *Wake Island*, added more luster to the Marine legend. While the film included a naval commander at Wake, the character played no prominent part in the battle and was wounded in the first air raid, opening the door for the Marine commander to take charge over the entire atoll.

The controversy heightened with the 1946 publication of Major Devereux's account of the battle, first in a four-part series in the *Saturday Evening Post* and then the next year with the appearance of his book. Devereux took credit for running Wake's defenses, which was accurate, but also downplayed Cunningham's role. Since Devereux beat everyone else to the market, his version of events registered first with readers, while subsequent volumes, including Cunningham's own in 1961, had to contend with the rendition already established by Devereux.

The top civilian leader at Wake, Dan Teters, rushed to Cunningham's defense. Already angry that Devereux had not given much credit to the civilian volunteers in his book, Teters wrote to Cunningham, saying that he knew the naval officer commanded the atoll and he did not understand why

Devereux basked in the limelight while Cunningham wallowed in the background.

Every man who served at Wake, civilian and military, can recite the chain of command—as superior officer Cunningham commanded the atoll, and Major Devereux, his subordinate, handled the defense battalion. As top officer in the defense battalion, however, Devereux called the shots on most military matters, including issuing the December 11 order to hold fire until the Japanese ships had drawn in. The Marines rarely, if ever, saw Cunningham or waited for his orders—they had no need to, for Major Devereux handled their affairs.

Both Cunningham and Devereux deserve praise for the outstanding performance at Wake, but must bear blame for the miserable manner in which they demeaned the memory of Wake with their postwar bickering. Instead of sharing accolades, each tried to claim the greater portion for himself. Cunningham insisted he thought of drawing in the Japanese on December 11, yet no Marine stationed inside Deverux's command post remembered Cunningham contacting the Marine. Pfc. James King, who manned the switchboard in Devereux's command post that day, stated that any communication from Cunningham to Devereux would have come through him, and he never received a call from the naval officer concerning the tactic—Devereux alone handled that responsibility. On the other hand, on December 23, Devereux smoothly attempted to sidestep the question of surrender by nudging Cunningham into issuing the order. The Wake defenders, as well as the families of both officers, deserved better than this.

"Absolutely Foreign to Me"

The Wake defenders faced assimilation into a society they had not experienced in four years. Adjustments to postwar conditions, in the nation as well as with their families, took time.

"I am making every effort to bring myself back to the life that now presents itself before me," wrote civilian Rodney Kephart to his mother on September 17, 1945, shortly after he had been liberated from camp. "After the three years and nine months of slavery, torture, and starvation one is a little slow of thought and ignorant of the up-to-date things of life. I have found in the last 24 hours, from listening to the radio, many things mentioned that are absolutely foreign to me."[10] New world figures replaced deposed or deceased leaders; new songs, movies, and books occupied spots once held by old familiars; new automobiles and household appliances offered luxuries unheard of in 1941.

No two men experienced the process in similar fashion. Corporal Marvin could not accept that people could be so nice to him; he half expected someone to suddenly start shouting at him or beating him. Private First Class Sanders realized the country had changed more than he thought when he boarded a bus with a female driver at the helm, a position once the exclusive domain of males. Just before Christmas, Private First Class Gatewood traveled to his brother-in-law's home for a celebration. As he talked to relatives, a loud series of explosions produced panic in the Marine. "The kids were firing firecrackers, and I was about ready to crawl under every car in town."[11] Gatewood needed almost a year before daily noises, which reminded him of the barrages and bombings at Wake, failed to bother him.

Corporal Johnson had to become accustomed to again hearing everyone speak English instead of Chinese or Japanese. After years of being fenced in, Johnson also took frequent walks about his old neighborhood, enjoying the freedom of movement as much as the reminiscing the treks caused.

Many prisoners worried that either they had so changed, or that their nation, occupations, and families had been so altered that they could not successfully readjust to civilian life. In the peacefulness at home, could the former prisoners rapidly shift gears and drop the defenses accumulated during captivity?

Guilt hounded some men. Though society recognized survivors of Japanese prison camps as heroes, the men themselves often did not. Some ex–prisoners of war hated to admit that they had surrendered to the enemy, even if it had been unavoidable, or suffered remorse that they had survived when other prisoners succumbed.

Many of the men thus kept their emotions tightly bottled inside. Family and friends could not hope to understand what the men had endured, so the men did not talk much about their ordeal, at least in the early years.

Even popular books and movies about prison camps, such as *Stalag 17*, *The Bridge on the River Kwai*, and *The Great Escape*, tossed an additional burden at the men. Most cast the American captives as fun-loving, brash soldiers who constantly harassed the enemy and continually tried to escape. While truth existed in this image, it was far from reality. The majority of men had simply tried to remain alive and outlast the war. When people at home asked what camp was like, though, they expected an answer similar to what they read in books or saw at the movies.

A sizable number showed the symptoms of what is now called post-traumatic stress disorder—frequent nightmares, flashbacks to prison camp, depression, and anger. Government studies indicated that while 25 percent of all veterans suffered from the disorder, almost 90 percent of ex-POWs battled the malady. Wake Island defenders were no exception.

While government programs assist service personnel today, none existed in 1945. Former prisoners of war were questioned, given food and clothing, and then sent on their way. Instead of sharing their burdens with psychiatrists, World War II prisoners had to handle the situation on their own and with the support of loved ones.

One prisoner recalled, "Nobody helped us with our transition to civilian life. The U.S. Army retrained its guard dogs, but there were no programs for us POWs. I guess your family was supposed to be your psychiatrist."[12]

Rather than offer support, the government adopted a hard stance. Most ex-POWs, especially those from Japanese camps, suffered from heart and liver problems, diminished eyesight, and nervous disorders, but the Veterans Administration (VA) would not pay for treatment unless the men could prove a service-related connection. Since no records existed from prison camp, the men faced a difficult task.

Gradually, assistance trickled in. By 1949, the government agreed to pay ex-POWs two dollars for each day of confinement in prison camps. After the Vietnam War, when many POWs wrote accounts and spoke out about their suffering, the government's views softened. In 1985, Congress created the Prisoner of War Medal to honor that forgotten group.

While the assistance that the military and civilians received from their government proved erratic, the help they gained from one another more than compensated. They formed an organization, the Defenders of Wake Island, which holds annual reunions and publishes a newsletter, the *Wake Island Wig-Wag*. At the reunions, the veterans, accompanied by family and friends, share war stories, laughs, and a few drinks, and in the process help make a traumatic experience bearable. Some at first scoffed at the notion that they might have been affected by the war, but they came to the reunions and gradually learned that every man had, in some way, been changed.

Lieutenant Hanna, subsequently promoted to colonel, wanted to forget all about the war and move on with his life. He did not start talking about the era until he attended his first reunion of the Wake Island Marines in the 1970s. There, again amidst fellow soldiers who endured the same tribulations and thus could empathize with him, Hanna opened up. "After talking to the boys who had been in prison with me, that did more good than anything else. Eventually I told my family everything."[13]

Joe Goicoechea mentioned little to his family, but attended reunions of the civilians for the comradeship and feelings of solidarity. Reunions helped John Rogge discuss his experiences because he knew "that they understood you. I have talked to neighbors and my children, but I'm wasting my breath"[14] because they cannot possibly understand his ordeal.

Corporal Marvin remained silent until his children entered high school, when they started asking him about World War II, and for many years Private First Class Gatewood shared his thoughts only with his brother. He agreed to talk to the rest of his family only after his youngest son viewed the Steven Spielberg movie, *Saving Private Ryan*, and told his father, "I know that you went through more than Private Ryan did."[15] Father and son started chatting, and gradually Gatewood related the entire story.

After viewing the same movie, one of Murray Kidd's grandchildren called him and cried, "Oh, Papa, you were in that kind of war!" When another of Kidd's grandchildren celebrated his eighteenth birthday, Kidd's daughter mentioned to Mrs. Kidd that the grandson was the same age as her father when he traveled to Wake. "It makes you think of what Murray experienced at such a young age," said Mrs. Kidd. "They were young kids."[16]

While Murray Kidd discussed the Wake story with few family members, he realized the impact the Japanese had had on his family, both good and bad. He lost some of the finest years in his life; he tolerated hunger and illness and pain; he watched fellow Americans die. Yet he also saw how the nobler side, in this case from an enemy soldier named Tada who warned Kidd to leave Wake, allowed him to return and start his family. "Tada saved my life. Because he did that," Kidd asserted as he swept his hand in the direction of photos adorning his family room, "all these pictures are here."[17] A small friendship struck in hard times led to images of five grandchildren and three great-grandchildren adorning an Idaho wall.

Many family and friends assumed they already knew some of what their relative had experienced, for they had seen Hollywood's popular wartime movie about Wake a few years previous. When Wake Island veterans attended screenings of the film, though, they did not know whether to laugh about the movie's absurdities or cry over its inaccuracies. Lieutenant Hanna felt it had no bearing with reality, and Private Laporte saw so many discrepancies in the uniforms, vehicles, and actions that he branded the version "far out in left field." Major Devereux believed the movie cast Dan Teters in a poor manner by having his character feud with the Marines, something he never did on Wake, and Corporal Holewinski thought the film was "far-fetched and far from the truth."[18]

After a brief period during which they regained their strength, the men returned to jobs and more normal living. Lieutenant Hanna remained in the Marine Corps until 1958 when, after spending most of his life in the military, he retired with the rank of colonel, attended trade school, and opened an electronics repair shop. Joe Goicoechea, Murray Kidd, and

George Rosendick continued to perform construction work around the world, including stops in Africa and Afghanistan, until their retirements in the 1980s. Corporal Holewinski returned to Gaylord, Michigan, and entered a long career in law enforcement.

Some, six years after leaving prison camp, received orders back to the Far East when war erupted in Korea. Private First Class Gatewood, Captain Godbold, Lieutenant Kessler, and Captain Platt were a few of those who saw action during the conflict. While inspecting the front lines on September 27, 1951, Captain Platt, the courageous leader who rallied his men at Wilkes Island, died when a mortar shell exploded near him. Private Laporte not only fought in Korea for over a year, but the career Marine also served with an infantry company in Vietnam, his third war in less than twenty-five years.

Gatewood's family had been promised that no man from Wake would ever have to serve in Asia again, but when he received orders sending him back, they unsuccessfully lobbied to have the destination changed. Gatewood subsequently suffered wounds in battle, from which he recovered enough to be sent back to the front lines, but an officer in the hospital that treated Gatewood checked the Wake Marine's record and instead ordered him home. "He's had enough of this crap in World War II,"[19] the officer concluded.

Commander Cunningham retired a rear admiral from the Navy in 1950 and lived in Memphis, Tennessee, until his death on March 3, 1986. Major Devereux remained on active duty with the Marine Corps until 1948, rising to the rank of general. He subsequently served as a Republican member in the House of Representatives from Maryland (1951 to 1959) and lived in Ruxton, Maryland, until his death in Baltimore on August 5, 1988. Devereux is buried in Arlington National Cemetery.

The military showered honors on the servicemen from Wake. A total of sixty-six decorations for bravery went to the Wake defenders, including a posthumous Medal of Honor, the nation's highest award for valor, to Capt. Henry T. Elrod, in 1946. Ten men received Navy Crosses, the second-highest medal for courage under fire, including Lieutenant Hanna, Corporal Holewinski, Major Putnam, Commander Cunningham, Major Devereux, and the civilian physician, Dr. Lawton E. Shank. In addition, six Silver Stars, four Gold Stars, thirty-four Bronze Stars, four Air Medals, and seven Legion of Merit awards were given to various men. Gunner McKinstry, Lieutenant Poindexter, Sgt. Johnalson Wright, the civilian father-son duo of Fred and George Gibbons, and Dan Teters all received one or more honors.

While these men resumed their lives, authorities brought to justice the Japanese war criminals involved with Wake. The main tormentor of the

Wake Islanders, Ishihara, the Beast of the East, received a twenty-year sentence for torturing prisoners. The Japanese soldiers who beheaded the five Americans aboard the *Nitta Maru* received life sentences, while their commander, Lt. Toshio Saito, committed suicide before his trial ended. Admiral Sakaibara, the man responsible for ordering the executions of ninety-eight civilians on Wake, walked to the gallows on June 18, 1947, after being found guilty of war crimes, while two subordinates received life sentences for their roles in the massacre.

Other Japanese involved in the Wake Islanders' incarcerations, such as junior officers and guards, either disappeared into Japanese society and avoided retribution, or received relatively minor sentences. Other than a handful of high-ranking officers sentenced to death, like Admiral Sakaibara, no Japanese soldier or official who supervised the Americans from Wake spent more than thirteen years in prison. Many rejoined their families long before that. Seishi Katsumi, for instance, received an initial sentence of five years in prison for his role in the beheading of Babe Hoffmiester on Wake in May 1942, but served only three years and one month before being set free.

While the returning ex-prisoners entered what in many cases proved to be awkward readjustment periods back home, most of their captors quickly resumed their former lives. While Wake servicemen and civilians battled nightmares, contended with the effects of malaria and malnutrition, and endured constant pain from repeated beatings, the Japanese officials responsible for those torments moved on to new futures and fresh challenges.

The final insult, as far as Wake Islanders were concerned, occurred in December 1958, when U.S. authorities freed the last group of war criminals a scant thirteen years after the war. The effects of what the captors inflicted on the men from Wake lingered far beyond that date—in some cases to the present day—but the culpable Japanese had their debt marked, "Paid in Full," long before.

"I Had Japs Stickin' a Bayonet in My Chest"

While the defenders gained their greatest glory engaging in the totally adult action of fighting in combat, they afterwards suffered, in many cases for years, from an ailment commonly associated with childhood. "You damn right I had nightmares!" stated Private Laporte in 2001. "I'd wake up at night and I had Japs stickin' a bayonet in my chest. They lasted several months. They slacked off for so long, then about nine years ago I had another nightmare, and I woke up and I was kicking my wife. There were these hand grenades flying at me and I was kicking them down into a hole."[20]

Until about ten years ago, Lieutenant Hanna experienced horrendous nightmares in which he relived the fight around his gun, and Corporal Johnson dreamed that Japanese planes flew through the driveway to his home. For the first few years, in his sleep Pvt. William Buckie kept reenlisting in the military and reliving the entire Wake experience. Finally, the night terrors eased, until his son grew old enough to join the service, at which time Buckie's nightmares returned. One of Johnson's friends in the Marines still screams in his sleep every night, and Private First Class Gatewood has such vivid dreams about a group of Japanese soldiers slowly closing in on him that his wife has to wake him to stop the squirming and shouting. "He starts jerking a little bit, and his feet start going," explained Mrs. Grace Gatewood. "He doesn't need to go through all that again."[21]

Franklin Gross experienced the same: "My God, for twenty-five years I had nightmares. I was dreaming of killing Japs. Nobody could go through that and come out the same. We're all a little jumpy, a little more nervous than most people. Most all our guys—and you could probably get a better answer from our wives—most all of us are damn hard to get along with."[22] Dreams hound Joe Goicoechea, who claims that maybe if he did not have such a clear memory of the war years, he could sleep better at night.

The nightmares are only one way in which Wake Island has affected the men. After four years of near-starvation in prison camp, most of the men make sure that food is always nearby. Corporal Marvin and Murray Kidd both wanted a full refrigerator at home, and for years following the war, Lieutenant Kessler hoarded food, candy, soap, crackers, and other items. When his wife asked him what he was doing, he always replied, "Just in case."[23]

Physical maladies affect the men. Lieutenant Hanna and his wife were unable to have any additional children, a fact Hanna attributes to the beatings and ordeals of prison camp. On one of Corporal Johnson's first visits to a military hospital, a physician checked his feet, which were knotted and hardened by wearing the same boots and socks during the battle, and wondered how Johnson ever made it into the Marine Corps. Johnson replied that first he entered the Corps, then got the poor feet.

In a sworn statement after the war, Sgt. Jesse L. Stewart attempted to explain the difficulties he faced each day of his life as a result of his war experiences:

> Our health was ruined, we were suffering from various diseases, prominent amoung [sic] them was malnutrition and Beri-Beri. We have this cleared up to a certain extent but it may return at any time. Many of [us] have sicknesses that may snatch us from this world at any time, others are faced with years of suffering and worrying, not

knowing when we will be stricken with something resulting from this hell we went through.

In my own case I have been unable to gain my weight back even though I have been given the best food that money can buy and have been given the best medical attention available, I do not have any strength nor endurance; I am in a run-down condition and have frequent stomack [sic] spells during which times it is hard for me to eat the best of food. . . . Although I am still a young man, I have not the strength and endurance of a man twice my age.[24]

Private First Class Gatewood has had both knees replaced, has suffered two strokes, and is bothered by sleep deprivation, all caused by the conditions of prison camp. Lung problems that developed in Japanese foundries afflict Corporal Marvin, and many men still have shrapnel lodged somewhere in their bodies—Marvin in his head, Hanna in his leg. Hanna contended that the harshness of prison camp so weakened him that he became more susceptible to a stroke about five years ago, and his eyesight has drastically deteriorated. John Valov lost twenty-two teeth to nutritional deficiencies and took so much medication for various war-related ailments that he claimed his dresser looked like a drugstore.

From his brutal beatings in prison camp, Joe Goicoechea still suffers from such intense headaches that he constructed his own room in the basement of his house to which he can retreat. "Two, three times a week I get headaches. Bad headaches. I go downstairs. I don't bother nobody down there. If I got a headache, I lie down there and I sleep down there at night. Hell, if I slept with my wife I'd drive her crazy! I might get up at two A.M. and walk around." If Goicoechea has to go somewhere or be at his best, he takes medication to combat the headaches. Despite the malady, Goicoechea refuses to slow down because of a few medical problems he may have acquired along the way. "Guys tell me they can't do this and they can't do that. I just go and do it. The heck with it."[25]

John Rogge's wife, Virginia, said her husband and many other Wake Islanders have trouble curbing their anger. The men lost control of their lives for four years, and now when anyone poses an obstacle, they resent it. "I don't take orders very well," said Virginia, "and that's frustrating because he likes to be in charge. That's typical of the men on Wake Island. From being out of control for so many years, they have to feel they're in control for the rest of their lives."

Mrs. Rogge claimed another group of people have been affected by Wake—the wives. She once mentioned to another that she did not deserve as much in disability as other Wake wives because she had not been married to John that long. The woman replied, "Oh, we've all been through a lot. You deserve anything you get."[26]

Cece Schneider, the wife of Marine Pfc. LeRoy Schneider, claimed that since her husband's return in 1945, Wake Island has never been far from their lives. In those early years, she frequently caught LeRoy staring into space, lost in his own thoughts. Whenever she asked him what he was thinking about, LeRoy dropped his head toward the floor and shook his head, as if to tell her not to probe too deeply. As a result, Cece felt estranged from her husband at a time he most needed her.

Then his nightmares grew more intense, causing Schneider to groan so loudly that the sounds awakened the children in another room. They sat in their beds, afraid to move but hoping that something could help their father. Schneider gradually overcame the worst of the nightmares, but the thoughts still linger.

The filthy conditions in which the men lived and worked caused Harry Jeffries, a civilian worker, to insist on a spotless apartment after returning to the United States. He hired a cleaning crew to come in once each week to meticulously dust, sweep, and polish every inch. Jeffries also stockpiled a year's supply of essential items, such as toilet paper, canned goods, and soap, and he slept with a gun under his pillow because of the graphic nightmares that assailed him about Japanese chasing after him.

Corporal Marvin remembers the weather. "I've been cold ever since, or it sure seems like it. It doesn't bother me now, the cold. You forget about it—well, you don't really forget about it."[27]

On the other hand, some of the defenders point to their years as a character-fashioning era, a time from which they emerged stronger and more resolute. Corporal Holewinski, for instance, believes he successfully ran for county sheriff in part because of the war. "I had a different outlook on things," he says. "I like people who work at things instead of expecting things to be handed to them."[28]

All groups at Wake experienced the effects of the war, but the Morrison-Knudsen workers faced additional woes. They not only endured the same conditions as the military, but they also suffered from a lack of recognition and, at first, few government benefits. Their company provided help in the form of monetary advances, free physical examinations, and a ticket home, but for a time that was about all the men received. The government did not grant them veterans' benefits because, even though they were on Wake, they had not been in the military.

For a man like Joe Goicoechea, who stood side by side with the Marines, suffered wounds, and was prepared to die for his nation, being ignored by the government hurt. "Them bombs don't know friends from foe when they come down," said Goicoechea, who believes he contributed just as much as any serviceman on the atoll. "You bet I did! I did everything they asked me to do and told me to do. And sometimes I did it on my own without them knowing about it. I'd go and get stuff, like food, and bring it back. I had night watches."29

John Valov wrote a 1946 letter to then Colonel Devereux expressing his astonishment over the shabby treatment he felt the civilians received. He stated the Marine Corps hardly seemed to care about their plight. "I could certainly cry for shame," he movingly informed Devereux. "The self respect which comes from participation in a vital task, the opertunity [sic] to receive the thanks of a grateful nation, which all G.I.'s are receiving is not for us."30 Valov explained that he knew veterans who had never been near the front lines who enjoyed full benefits, yet he, who had actually been in the fray, helping the military repel the enemy, had none.

The government finally granted veterans' benefits to the construction workers in January 1981. Once they completed the paperwork showing evidence of injuries that were connected to the defense of Wake, which in some cases took months or even years because of lack of documentation, they enjoyed equal benefits with the military.

The civilians, however, were not the only ones finding it difficult to gain compensation from the government. At first the government only granted Corporal Holewinski a 10 percent disability, despite his being wounded four times. Over the years, with help from friends who knew how to use the system, Holewinski earned a 100 percent disability.

Private First Class Gatewood labored until 2001 to receive full disability. Doctors repeatedly rejected his requests, and a bureaucrat once told him he should be happy with the 10 percent benefit he did enjoy. Now, after a grueling fight which gained him the proper compensation, Gatewood states that "Anyone who was on Wake should receive 100 percent just for being in prison camp."31

"Never Have They Apologized for What They Did to Us"

A current issue that has once again brought Wake Islanders together is that of obtaining compensation from the Japanese government for the flagrant wartime abuses, including being used as slave labor. Germany has awarded compensation to Holocaust victims, the United States government has granted money to Japanese-Americans harmed by the forced relocations during the war, and American dollars rebuilt the nation's former enemies, Germany and Japan. After all they endured, the men feel justified in seeking remuneration.

So far, none of the large Japanese companies that utilized the men in their wartime factories, mines, and shipyards has paid the former prisoners a single penny, even though the companies constructed a profitable business during that time. Any American can drive the highways of the country today and see evidence of Japanese corporate successes. Mitsubishi, which produces automobiles, built the *Nitta Maru* that transported the Americans across the Pacific. The company emerged relatively healthy from World War II, in part because of slave labor. Kawasaki, Nippon Steel, and Mitsui all registered profits from the sweat of the Wake defenders.

It galls men like Colonel Hanna, Joe Goicoechea, and Corporal Holewinski that Mitsubishi-made vehicles dot the American countryside, or that Kawasaki produced some of New York City's subway cars. The men do not hate the Japanese. They only want fair retribution from companies who survived a horrible war on the backs of prisoners.

"*Never* have they apologized for what they did to us," exclaimed Corporal Gross. "We lived with them for four years. There's not a barbarian who lived—Attila the Hun, Ghengis Khan, or anyone—who was any worse than our captors. I don't hate the Japanese. I have Japanese friends today. It's the ones who captured us."[32]

The War Claims Acts of 1948 and 1952 provided some compensation. Funded by Japanese assets frozen by the Roosevelt administration at the start of the war, prisoners of war received about $2.50 per day for their captivity, hardly fair recompense for the suffering involved. Critics of the paltry amount claim the United States government did not want to antagonize Japan at a time when both the Soviet Union and North Korea threatened Asia's stability. A democratic, economically sound Japan served as a buttress against communism, and thus bolstered United States interests in the area.

Ex-prisoners, buoyed by a 1999 California Superior Court ruling that any foreign-based company doing business in California could be held responsible for claims dating back to the war, have begun to sue Japanese industries. They are often assisted by the Center for Internee Rights, Inc., a nonprofit organization established to help former prisoners and to obtain an apology from the Japanese government. More than thirty Japanese companies that used slave labor have been sued in recent years, although no decision has yet been reached.

By 2002, Pfc. James King had a class action lawsuit against Nippon Steel. "They profited off us," explained King. "It bothers me to see they are still making money when we may have saved them during the war."[33] King and his attorneys are determined to pursue the matter for as long as it takes, despite any legal obstacles they may face.

Though the efforts continue, Joe Goicoechea is also not holding his breath for any large settlement. "Aw, I don't think they'll ever get anything.

They [the U.S. government] sold us down the river in 1948 and 1952. They were scared the Russians would take over Japan."[34]

"I Don't Feel Like a Hero"

When people learn what Colonel Hanna, Corporal Holewinski, and the others did at Wake, they invariably label the men heroes. The facts certainly justify that appellation, but it is one word you will never hear the Wake Islanders use. They believe they did nothing more than what any other group of Americans would have done—their duty. "I was doing what I was trained to do and trying to stay alive while I done it,"[35] explained Corporal Johnson.

Corporal Gross expressed what most of the military will tell you, that being considered a hero exaggerates their importance. "People always say you're a hero, and to most Wake Islanders it's embarrassing. You know, any other group of Marines with the same amount of experience would have done the same thing. It's no small thing what we did, because we probably delayed the Japanese going to Midway about thirty days. They had to go back and regroup, and it took them sixteen days to take Wake, so it slowed their timetable. It was quite a feat, but any other bunch of experienced Marines would have done the same."[36]

Colonel Hanna is more emphatic about the topic. He remained at his gun, despite the belief that he would soon die, because that was what he was supposed to do, but the label of hero fits uncomfortably. "That day [at the gun]," he said as tears welled in his eyes, "I didn't think any more about it [killing men], but I have since. It's bothered me a lot. I killed four men myself with my .45. I don't know how many I killed shooting at the ship. You see their faces, their expressions when they get hit. I think about it even up to now. I don't feel like a hero."[37]

Instead of being labeled supermen, Wake Islanders hope that people simply do not forget what happened at Wake. They fear that elementary and secondary schools fail to teach World War II, or that the nation cares little for what unfolded so many years ago. If they are correct and that tendency persists, they contend it would negate everything they accomplished. Civilian John Rogge claims that the men of Wake Island are already "like the line of the 'Whiffenpoof Song' that says, 'And we shall pass and be forgotten with the rest.' All of us."[38]

That is why many of the men have, in slowly increasing numbers, returned to Wake. They walk the atoll, retrace their wartime steps, visit their gun positions, and reminisce about events that so altered their lives— drawn to a location as if a continuing sense of duty so compelled them. In reconnecting with the atoll, the men gain a sense of satisfaction, a completion that had been missing.

Murray Kidd, George Rosendick, and Joe Goicoechea remained close friends all their lives. They saw each other almost every day in Boise, sharing a cup of coffee at a local doughnut shop or helping one another with chores. Each August 6, the day the United States dropped the first atom bomb in 1945, the three gather in a restaurant to hoist a few drinks and celebrate over dinner. Ironically, the waitress who usually serves them and with whom they have developed a friendship is a Japanese woman whose family came to the country after the war.

In the summer of 2002, shortly after he was interviewed for this book, Murray Kidd passed away from heart complications. Goicoechea and Rosendick still reside near Boise, enjoying family and life, but they sense they are a part of a rapidly dwindling group. The youngest of the men, military and civilian, have reached their early eighties, so news of another death, though difficult, hardly surprises them anymore. With each passing, another link to a remarkable epic has disappeared.

After a happy marriage that lasted almost sixty-two years, Colonel Hanna's wife, Vera, died in November 1999. His love for her has never abated, even though he can no longer talk to her or hand her the little gifts he used to bring home. A stroke has slowed the Marine, but neighbors and a group of retired Marines who live close by check in every day. Colonel Hanna does not have to wander far from home, anyway, for he maintains a wide correspondence with people through e-mail.

He would not want to stray, for his residence contains every reminder of the two things he most loved in his life—Vera and the Marine Corps. Mementos of their life together, and pictures of Vera, rest in most rooms. Hanna's cleaning lady knows that she can move every item in the home except two magnetized photographs of Vera on the kitchen refrigerator near where Hanna reads and works. The colonel never wants Vera out of his sight.

Every day he wears one of the Marine shirts he proudly owns—the T-shirt he wore for our interview bore the inscription, MARINES NEVER DIE, THEY JUST GO TO HELL TO REGROUP—and Corps memorabilia adorn his walls, next to the medals and awards he has received. He states that his being a part of the Wake Island story was the highlight of his career and has "made me special to other Marines." When informed of the incident where other military personnel stood and saluted the Wake Island Marine who entered the lounge during a conference, Hanna allows a few more tears to course down his cheek. "I would rejoin the Marines in an instant if I could," he asserts without bravado. "It's sort of hard to explain, but it's a feeling you have about the Marines—once a Marine, always a Marine. I know they wouldn't take me now, but if I had a chance to go back in, I would."[39]

Colonel Hanna appreciates the manner in which the Marine Corps has honored the Wake Island Marines. The unit has received invitations to the commandant's house, and most current Marines are familiar with the epic defense. "Everyone learned about the Wake Island story during training," explains Mark Cruz of Michigan, a former Marine who still holds Colonel Hanna and the other defenders in high esteem. "They told us about all the big World War Two Marine battles—Wake, Tarawa, Iwo Jima. You admired those guys and what they did."[40]

Were Colonel Hanna to fly out to Wake, he would undoubtedly experience another emotional moment. The atoll holds a memorial to the Wake Island Marines that includes bronze plaques informing the reader of the heroic battle. The monument's cleanliness impressed one Wake Island Marine who visited the spot, Charles A. Holmes—the plaques sparkled as if new. When he later asked a government worker stationed on the atoll who took care of the memorial, the worker replied that every time a group of Marines lands at Wake—which is often, as Wake is still used as a refueling stop for transpacific flights—someone from the group heads out to the site and polishes the plaques.

The simple action is fitting. Wake's defenders want no big fuss, no wild celebrations. They want to be remembered. They could ask for no better way than by having fellow Marines polishing small plaques on a tiny plot of Pacific coral sand.

Notes

INTRODUCTION—"Wake Island Marine on Deck!"

1. Author's interview with Commander Michael P. O'Connor, March 22, 1997.

CHAPTER 1—"An Ordinary Group of Americans"

1. Grace Tully, *F.D.R.: My Boss* (Chicago: Peoples Book Club, 1949), p. 262.
2. Tully, *F.D.R.*, p. 255.
3. Joseph P. Lash, *Roosevelt and Churchill, 1939–1941* (New York: W. W. Norton & Company, Inc., 1976), p. 488.
4. Gordon W. Prange, *At Dawn We Slept: The Untold Story of Pearl Harbor* (New York: Penguin Books, 1981), p. 559.
5. "Tragedy at Honolulu," *Time*, December 15, 1941, p. 19.
6. James MacGregor Burns, *Roosevelt: The Soldier of Freedom* (New York: Harcourt Brace Jovanovich, Inc., 1970), p. 165.
7. Robert E. Sherwood, *Roosevelt and Hopkins: An Intimate History* (New York: Harper & Brothers, 1948), p. 436.
8. Burns, *Roosevelt*, p. 172.
9. Author's interview with Franklin Gross, March 13, 2001.
10. Author's interview with Ewing Laporte, March 14, 2001.
11. Author's interview with Joseph Goicoechea, April 12, 2002.
12. Goicoechea interview, April 12, 2002.
13. Goicoechea interview, April 12, 2002.
14. Goicoechea interview, April 12, 2002.
15. Author's interview with Murray Kidd, April 13, 2002.
16. Author's interview with J. O. Young, June 11, 2002.
17. Author's interview with Pearl Ann Young, June 11, 2002.
18. J. O. Young, *Reminiscences*, privately published, undated, the J. O. Young Collection, p. 1.

19. Pearl Ann Young interview, June 11, 2002.
20. Hans Whitney, *Guest of the Fallen Sun* (New York: Exposition Press, 1951), p. 15.
21. James P. S. Devereux, *The Story of Wake Island* (New York: J. B. Lippincott, 1947), p. 20.
22. Goicoechea interview, April 12, 2002.
23. Whitney, *Guest of the Fallen Sun*, p. 15.
24. L. A. Magnino, *Jim's Journey: A Wake Island Civilian POW's Story* (Central Point, Oregon: Hellgate Press, 2001), p. 32.
25. Whitney, *Guest of the Fallen Sun*, p. 16; Reba Wilkerson, "Wake's Forgotten Survivors," *American History Illustrated*, December 1987, p. 41.
26. Gregory J. W. Urwin, *Facing Fearful Odds: The Siege of Wake Island* (Lincoln: University of Nebraska Press, 1997), pp. 71–72.
27. Laporte interview, March 13, 2001.
28. Author's interview with John S. Johnson, March 19, 2002.
29. Brig. Gen. Woodrow M. Kessler, USMC (Ret.), *To Wake Island and Beyond: Reminiscences* (Washington, D.C.: History and Museums Division, 1988), p. 19.
30. Gross interview, March 5, 2001.
31. Laporte interview, March 14, 2001.

CHAPTER 2—"It Would Be Nice to Have Six Months More"

1. Author's interview with John Rogge, April 11, 2002.
2. John Rogge interview, April 11, 2002.
3. Magnino, *Jim's Journey*, p. 35.
4. Joseph Goicoechea, *Memoir*, p. 2.
5. Laporte interview, March 14, 2001.
6. Gross interview, March 13, 2001.
7. Author's interview with Kenneth Marvin, February 5, 2002.
8. Author's interview with John S. Johnson, March 26, 2002.
9. Kessler, *To Wake Island and Beyond*, p. 21.
10. Kessler, *To Wake Island and Beyond*, p. 24.
11. Marvin interview, February 5, 2002.
12. Devereux, *The Story of Wake Island*, p. 39.
13. Devereux, *The Story of Wake Island*, p. 41.
14. Devereux, *The Story of Wake Island*, p. 28.
15. Duane Schultz, *Wake Island: The Heroic, Gallant Fight* (New York: St. Martin's Press, 1978), p. 26.
16. Gross interview, March 13, 2001.
17. Gross interview, March 13, 2001.
18. Robert J. Cressman, *"A Magnificent Fight": The Battle for Wake Island* (Annapolis, Maryland: Naval Institute Press, 1995), p. 34.
19. Goicoechea interview, April 12, 2002.
20. Devereux, *The Story of Wake Island*, pp. 28–29.
21. Urwin, *Facing Fearful Odds*, pp. 164–165.
22. W. Scott Cunningham with Lydel Sims, *Wake Island Command* (Boston: Little, Brown and Company, 1961), p. 20.
23. Cressman, *"A Magnificent Fight,"* p. 62.
24. Maj. Paul A. Putnam File, Putnam personal biography, Marine Historical Center.

25. Maj. Paul A. Putnam File, letter to Col. Claude A. Larkin, December 3, 1941, Marine Historical Center.
26. Cressman, *"A Magnificent Fight,"* p. 68.
27. Author's interview with Brig. Gen. John F. Kinney, USMC (Ret.), October 30, 2002.
28. Col. Arthur Poindexter, "The Battle of Wake Island," in 1942: *"Issue in Doubt"* (Austin, Texas: Eakin Press, 1994), p. 110
29. Brig. Gen. John F. Kinney, USMC (Ret.), with James M. McCaffrey, *Wake Island Pilot: A World War II Memoir* (Washington: Brassey's, 1995), p. 53.
30. Marvin interview, February 5, 2002.
31. Author's interview with Ralph Holewinski, June 28, 2002.
32. Ted Morgan, *FDR: A Biography* (New York: Simon and Schuster, 1985), pp. 614–615.
33. Kinney and McCaffrey, *Wake Island Pilot*, p. 54.
34. Marvin interview, February 5, 2002.
35. "Navy Is Superior to Any, Says Knox," *New York Times*, December 7, 1941, p. 1.
36. Kinney and McCaffrey, *Wake Island Pilot*, p. 49.
37. Goicoechea interviews, March 5, 2002; April 12, 2002.
38. Devereux, *The Story of Wake Island*, p. 31.

CHAPTER 3—"The Marines Will Show Them a Thing or Two"

1. Urwin, *Facing Fearful Odds*, p. 227.
2. Devereux, *The Story of Wake Island*, p. 43.
3. Marvin interview, February 5, 2002
4. Author's interview with Martin Gatewood, February 20, 2002.
5. Cressman, *"A Magnificent Fight,"* p. 85.
6. Whitney, *Guest of the Fallen Sun*, p. 18.
7. Devereux, *The Story of Wake Island*, p. 45.
8. Whitney, *Guest of the Fallen Sun*, p. 20.
9. Devereux, *The Story of Wake Island*, p. 50.
10. Forrest Read, *Reminiscences*, in the Forrest Read Collection, privately published, undated, p. 1.
11. Martin Gatewood interview, March 20, 2002.
12. Whitney, *Guest of the Fallen Sun*, p. 20.
13. Author's interview with James O. King, March 21, 2002.
14. Laporte interview, March 14, 2001.
15. Gross interview, March 13, 2001.
16. John Toland, *But Not in Shame: The Six Months After Pearl Harbor* (New York: Random House, 1961), pp. 40–41.
17. Cressman, *"A Magnificent Fight,"* p. 88.
18. Author's interview with Col. Robert M. Hanna, USMC (Ret.), February 6, 2002.
19. Urwin, *Facing Fearful Odds*, p. 248.
20. John F. Wukovits, "The Fight for Wake," *WWII History*, May 2002, p. 40.
21. Kinney and McCaffrey, *Wake Island Pilot*, p. 57.
22. Kinney and McCaffrey, *Wake Island Pilot*, p. 57.
23. Kinney and McCaffrey, *Wake Island Pilot*, p. 59.
24. John Costello, *The Pacific War, 1941–1945* (New York: Quill Books, 1982), p. 144.

25. Cunningham and Sims, *Wake Island Command*, p. 72.
26. Cunningham and Sims, *Wake Island Command*, p. 60.
27. Urwin, *Facing Fearful Odds*, p. 265.
28. Murray Kidd interview, April 13, 2002.
29. Cunningham and Sims, *Wake Island Command*, p. 63.
30. Young, *Reminiscences*, pp. 3–4.
31. King interview, March 21, 2002.
32. Kessler, *To Wake Island and Beyond*, p. 47.
33. Richard Wheeler, *A Special Valor: The U.S. Marines and the Pacific War* (New York: New American Library, 1983), p. 8.

CHAPTER 4—"I Used to Hear a Lot of Guys Pray"

1. Major C. A. Barninger to Lt. Colonel James P. S. Devereux, informal report, October 8, 1945, National Archives.
2. Read, *Reminiscences*, p. 3.
3. Goicoechea interview, April 12, 2002.
4. Devereux, *The Story of Wake Island*, p. 69.
5. Murray Kidd interview, April 13, 2002.
6. Cressman, *"A Magnificent Fight,"* p. 289.
7. Johnson interview, March 26, 2002.
8. Urwin, *Facing Fearful Odds*, p. 304.
9. Goicoechea interview, April 12, 2002.
10. Goicoechea interview, April 10, 2002.
11. Goicoechea interview, March 5, 2002.
12. Goicoechea interview, April 12, 2002.
13. Goicoechea interview, April 12, 2002.
14. Read, *Reminiscences*, p. 2.
15. Robert J. Casey, *Torpedo Junction: With the Pacific Fleet from Pearl Harbor to Midway* (Indianapolis: The Bobbs-Merrill Company, 1942), p. 25.
16. Sherwood, *Roosevelt and Hopkins*, p. 436.
17. "U.S. Radio at War," *Time*, December 15, 1941, p. 48.
18. "Full Blast," *Time*, December 22, 1941, p. 9.

CHAPTER 5—"The Island Was to Be a Cake Walk"

1. Interview of Sub-Lt. Shigeyoshi Ozeki, in the Dan King Collection, Marine Corps Research Center, Quantico, Virginia (hereafter cited as Ozeki interview).
2. Ozeki interview.
3. Ozeki reminiscence in Gregory J. W. Urwin Web site, astro.temple.edu/~gurwin/ffoozeki.htm.
4. Devereux, *The Story of Wake Island*, p. 81.
5. John R. Burroughs, "The Siege of Wake Island," *American Heritage*, June 1959, p. 69.
6. Ozeki interview.
7. Whitney, *Guest of the Fallen Sun*, p. 22.
8. Toland, *But Not in Shame*, p. 82.

9. Johnson interview, March 19, 2002.
10. Martin Gatewood interview, February 20, 2002.
11. Holewinski interview, June 28, 2002.
12. King interview, March 21, 2002.
13. Burroughs, "The Siege of Wake Island," p. 70.
14. Ozeki interview.
15. Urwin, *Facing Fearful Odds*, p. 328
16. King interview, March 21, 2002.
17. Hanna interview, February 6, 2002.
18. Wheeler, *A Special Valor*, p. 14.
19. Kessler, *To Wake Island and Beyond: Reminiscences*, p. 53.
20. Toland, *But Not in Shame*, p. 83.
21. Ozeki interview.
22. Devereux, *The Story of Wake Island*, p. 90.
23. Samuel Eliot Morison, *History of United States Naval Operations in World War II, Volume III: The Rising Sun in the Pacific, 1931–April 1942* (Boston: Little, Brown and Company, 1965), p. 234.
24. Blaine Taylor, "Fight Left Unfinished," *Military History*, December 1987, p. 37.
25. Urwin, *Facing Fearful Odds*, p. 334.
26. King interview, March 21, 2002.
27. Cunningham and Sims, *Wake Island Command*, p. 92.
28. Cunningham and Sims, *Wake Island Command*, p.93.
29. Cunningham and Sims, *Wake Island Command*, p. 83.
30. Toland, *But Not in Shame*, p. 83.
31. Cressman, *"A Magnificent Fight,"* p. 139.
32. Wheeler, *A Special Valor*, p. 15.
33. "Fort by Fort, Port by Port," *Time*, December 15, 1941, p. 23.
34. Winston S. Churchill, *The Second World War: The Grand Alliance* (Boston: Houghton Mifflin Company, 1950), p. 620.
35. Urwin, *Facing Fearful Odds*, p. 7; "Still Under American Flag," *The Idaho Daily Statesman*, December 13, 1941.
36. Cressman, *"A Magnificent Fight,"* p. 138.
37. Schultz, *Wake Island*, p. 11; "Stand at Wake," *Time*, December 22, 1941, p. 19.
38. "Tiny Garrison Holds Out Against Attacks," *The Honolulu Advertiser*, December 12, 1941; "Marines Hold Off Wake Assault," *Detroit Evening Times*, December 12, 1941, p. 37.
39. Casey, *Torpedo Junction*, p. 34.
40. "Islands," *Newsweek*, December 22, 1941, p. 19.
41. "Helpmate," *Time*, December 22, 1941, p. 12.
42. Cunningham and Sims, *Wake Island Command*, pp. 96–97.

CHAPTER 6—"Our Flag Is Still There"

1. Marvin interview, February 5, 2002.
2. Murray Kidd interview, April 13, 2002.
3. Jacob R. Sanders, *Autobiography of Jacob R. Sanders*, as Told to and Written by his Daughter, Cathy M. Sanders, undated, in the Jacob R. Sanders Collection, pp. 5–6.

4. Marvin interview, February 5, 2002.

5. Laporte interview, March 14, 2001.

6. King interview, March 21, 2002.

7. John Rogge interview, April 10, 2002.

8. Hanna interview, June 21, 2002.

9. J. O. Young interview, June 11, 2002.

10. Devereux, *The Story of Wake Island*, p. 102.

11. Devereux, *The Story of Wake Island*, p. 103.

12. King interview, March 21, 2002.

13. Devereux, *The Story of Wake Island*, p. 103.

14. Author's interview with William F. Buehler, November 30, 2002.

15. Goicoechea interview, April 12, 2002.

16. Devereux, *The Story of Wake Island*, p. 120.

17. Lt. Col. Walter L. J. Bayler, *Last Man Off Wake Island* (Indianapolis: The Bobbs-Merrill Company, 1943), p. 109; Lt. Col. Paul A. Putnam, "Report of VMF-211 on Wake Island," October 18, 1945, pp. 15–16.

18. Gross interview, March 13, 2001.

19. Murray Kidd interview, April 13, 2002.

20. Cunningham and Sims, *Wake Island Command*, p. 101.

21. Johnson interview, March 19, 2002.

22. Urwin, *Facing Fearful Odds*, p. 279.

23. Hanna interviews, February 6, 2002; February 20, 2002.

24. Martin Gatewood interview, February 20, 2002.

25. Kessler, *To Wake Island and Beyond*, p. 62.

26. Martin Gatewood interview, February 20, 2002.

27. Whitney, *Guest of the Fallen Sun*, p. 22.

28. Author's interview with Max J. Dana, November 25, 2002.

29. "Message from Wake," *Time*, December 29, 1941, p. 14.

30. Marvin interview, February 5, 2002.

31. "Wake and Guam Reported Taken," *New York Times*, December 9, 1941, p. 12.

32. "Tiny Band of Marines, Facing Sure Death, Hold Wake Island with No Idea of Surrender," *Detroit Free Press*, December 12, 1941, pp. 1, 12.

33. Charles Hurd, "Marines Keep Wake," *New York Times*, December 12, pp. 1, 18; Edward T. Folliard, "Marines Gallantly Hold Wake, Sink 2 Japanese Warships," *Washington Post*, December 12, 1941.

34. Charles Hurd, "Wake and Midway Hold Out, U.S. Communiques Reveal," *New York Times*, December 13, 1941, p. 1, December 15, 1941, p. 1; "Japs Again Rain Bombs On Island," *Idaho Daily Statesman*, December 15, 1941, p. 1; "U.S. Marines Still Fighting to Save Wake," *Detroit Free Press*, December 15, 1941, p. 1.

35. "Marines Are Still There," *New York Times*, December 16, 1941, p. 6.

36. " 'Send Us Some More Japs,' Wake Marines Ask Navy," *New York Times*, December 17, 1941, p. 7; "In the Pacific, 'Our Flag Is Still There'; The Marines Hold Midway and Wake," *Quantico Sentry*, December 19, 1941, p. 1.

37. Urwin, *Facing Fearful Odds*, p. 10.

38. "Stand at Wake," *Time*, December 12, 1941, p. 19.

39. Lt. Col. R. D. Heinl, Jr., "We're Headed for Wake," *Marine Corps Gazette*, June 1946, p. 37.

40. Schultz, *Wake Island*, p. 98.

CHAPTER 7—"They Don't Guarantee You're Coming Back"

1. Diary of John R. Himelrick, in the John R. Himelrick Collection, Personal Papers Collection, Marine Corps Research Center, Quantico, Virginia (hereafter cited as Himelrick diary.)
2. Devereux, *The Story of Wake Island*, pp. 104–105.
3. Hanna interview, February 6, 2002.
4. Johnson interview, March 26, 2002.
5. Marvin interview, February 14, 2002.
6. Johnson interview, March 26, 2002.
7. Goicoechea interviews, March 5, 2002; April 12, 2002.
8. Burroughs, "The Siege of Wake Island," p. 71.
9. Schultz, *Wake Island: The Heroic, Gallant Fight*, p. 81.
10. Burroughs, "The Siege of Wake Island," p. 71.
11. Cressman, "A Magnificent Fight," p. 164.
12. Himelrick diary.
13. Devereux, *The Story of Wake Island*, p. 133.
14. Devereux, *The Story of Wake Island*, p. 134.
15. Hanna interview, February 6, 2002.
16. Laporte interview, March 14, 2001.
17. Cressman, "A Magnificent Fight," pp. 172–173; Urwin, *Facing Fearful Odds*, p. 398.
18. David O. Woodbury, *Builders for Battle: How the Pacific Naval Air Bases Were Constructed*, (New York: E. P. Dutton and Company Inc., 1946), p. 323.
19. Cressman, "A Magnificent Fight," p. 173.
20. Cunningham and Sims, *Wake Island Command*, p. 115.
21. Letters from Henry T. Elrod to Elizabeth Elrod, December 20, 1941, in the Henry T. Elrod Collection, Marine Corps Research Center, Quantico, Virginia.
22. Martin Gatewood interview, February 20, 2002.
23. Johnson interview, March 26, 2002.
24. Marvin interview, February 5, 2002.
25. Devereux, *The Story of Wake Island*, p. 127; Marvin interview, February 5, 2002.
26. Author's interview with Henry Frietas, April 8, 1992.
27. Peter Andrews, "The Defense of Wake," *American Heritage*, July–August 1987, p. 78; Toland, *But Not in Shame*, p. 103.
28. Johnson interview, March 26, 2002.
29. King interview, March 21, 2002.
30. Martin Gatewood interview, February 20, 2002.
31. Marvin interview, February 5, 2002.
32. Martin Gatewood interview, February 20, 2002.
33. Urwin, *Facing Fearful Odds*, p. 438.
34. Burroughs, "The Siege of Wake Island," p. 72.
35. Urwin, *Facing Fearful Odds*, p. 439.
36. "To the Marines on Wake Island," *Washington Post*, December 24, 1941.

CHAPTER 8—"I Was Surprised at Some of the Younger Ones"

1. Devereux, *The Story of Wake Island*, p. 143.
2. Johnson interview, March 26, 2002.
3. Toland, *But Not in Shame*, p. 98.
4. Ozeki interview.
5. Wheeler, *A Special Valor*, p. 21.
6. Andrews, "The Defense of Wake," p. 76.
7. Read, *Reminiscences*, p. 4.
8. Dana interview, November 25, 2002.
9. Bernard E. Richardson memoir, "Wake Island: End of Combat," in Gregory J. W. Urwin Web site, astro.temple.edu/~gurwin/fforich.htm, (hereafter cited as Richardson memoir), p. 3.
10. Richardson memoir, p. 5.
11. Richardson memoir, p. 5.
12. Buehler interview, November 30, 2002.
13. Johnson interviews, March 19, 2002; March 26, 2002.
14. Johnson interview, March 26, 2002.
15. Johnson interview, March 26, 2002.
16. Johnson interviews, March 19, 2002; March 26, 2002.
17. Johnson interview, March 26, 2002.
18. Richardson memoir, p. 6.
19. Richardson memoir, p. 7.
20. Richardson memoir, p. 7.
21. Toland, *But Not in Shame*, p. 105.
22. Toland, *But Not in Shame*, p. 106.
23. Johnson interview, March 26, 2002.
24. Richardson memoir, pp. 10–11.
25. Young, *Reminiscences*, p. 5.
26. Richardson memoir, p. 12.
27. Toland, *But Not in Shame*, p. 109.

CHAPTER 9—"We'll Make Our Stand Here"

1. John Goette, *Japan Fights for Asia* (New York: Harcourt, Brace and Company, 1943), p. 93.
2. Toland, *But Not in Shame*, p. 97.
3. Goette, *Japan Fights for Asia*, p. 93.
4. Ozeki interview, p. 4.
5. Ozeki interview, p. 4.
6. Laporte interview, March 14, 2001.
7. Toland, *But Not in Shame*, p. 102.
8. Hanna interview, June 21, 2002.
9. Ozeki interview, p. 4.
10. Cressman, *"A Magnificent Fight,"* p. 216.
11. Toland, *But Not in Shame*, p. 101; Hanna interview, July 30, 2002.
12. Toland, *But Not in Shame*, p. 99; Putnam to Commandant of the Marine Corps, "Report of VMF-211 on Wake Island," p. 4.

13. S. E. Smith, ed., *The United States Marine Corps in World War II* (New York: Random House, 1969), p. 50.
14. Devereux, *The Story of Wake Island*, p. 160.
15. Gross interview, March 13, 2001.
16. Toland, *But Not in Shame*, p. 102.
17. Urwin, *Facing Fearful Odds*, p. 504.
18. Lt. Col. Arthur A. Poindexter, "An Informal Report of the Operations of the Machine Gun Battery and the Mobile Reserve During the Defense of Wake, December 1941," March 25, 1947, Marine Historical Center, p. 6; Toland, *But Not in Shame*, p. 106.
19. Author's interview with William O. Plate, October 28, 2002.
20. Ozeki interview, pp. 6–7.
21. Hanna interview, June 21, 2002.
22. Toland, *But Not in Shame*, p. 104.
23. Goette, *Japan Fights for Asia*, p. 94.
24. Hanna interviews, February 13, 2002; June 21, 2002.
25. Holewinski interviews, May 16, 2001; June 28, 2002.
26. Holewinski interview, June 28, 2002.
27. Hanna interview, June 20, 2002.
28. Holewinski interview, June 28, 2002.
29. Cunningham and Sims, *Wake Island Command*, p. 123.
30. Cunningham and Sims, *Wake Island Command*, p. 133.
31. Devereux, *The Story of Wake Island*, p. 173.
32. Devereux, *The Story of Wake Island*, pp. 161–162.
33. Col. George H. Potter to the Director, Division of Public Information, "Defense of Wake," March 27, 1947, National Archives, p. 7.
34. Devereux, *The Story of Wake Island*, pp. 173–175.
35. 2nd Lt. John Hamas to Lt. Col. James P. S. Devereux, informal report, October 12, 1945, National Archives, p. 8.

CHAPTER 10—"Remember Wake Island"

1. Hamas, informal report, p. 8; Devereux, *The Story of Wake Island*, pp. 175–176.
2. Devereux, *The Story of Wake Island*, p. 178.
3. Theodore A. Abraham, Jr., *"Do You Understand, Huh?": A POW's Lament, 1941–1945* (Manhattan, Kansas: Sunflower University Press, 1992), p. 19.
4. Martin Gatewood interview, February 20, 2002.
5. Laporte interview, March 14, 2001.
6. Devereux, *The Story of Wake Island*, p. 180.
7. Devereux, *The Story of Wake Island*, p. 181.
8. Marvin interview, February 12, 2002.
9. Hanna interviews, February 13, 2002; June 21, 2002.
10. Devereux, *The Story of Wake Island*, p. 182.
11. David D. Kliewer, Personal Diary of First Lieutenant David D. Kliewer, in the National Archives Collections, p. 4.
12. Devereux, *The Story of Wake Island*, p. 185.
13. Richardson memoir, p. 13.
14. Johnson interview, March 26, 2002.

15. Johnson interview, March 26, 2002.

16. Buehler interview, November 30, 2002.

17. Richardson memoir, pp. 13–14.

18. Read, *Reminiscences*, p. 5; Johnson interviews, March 26, 2002; April 2, 2002.

19. Devereux, *The Story of Wake Island*, p. 196.

20. Rodney Kephart, *Wake, War and Waiting . . .* (New York: Exposition Press, 1950), p. 21.

21. Devereux, *The Story of Wake Island*, p. 198.

22. Holewinski interview, June 28, 2002.

23. Gross interviews, March 5, 2001; March 29, 2002.

24. Joseph Goicoechea, *Memoirs*, p. 20.

25. Martin Gatewood interview, February 13, 2002.

26. Robert M. Brown, *Memoir*, www.azcentral.com/news/specials/veterans/brown.html (hereafter cited as Brown, *Memoir*).

27. Cressman, *"A Magnificent Fight,"* p. 240.

28. Cunningham and Sims, *Wake Island Command*, pp. 144–145.

29. Hanna interview, February 20, 2002.

30. Cressman, *"A Magnificent Fight,"* p. 253; Urwin, *Facing Fearful Odds*, p. 471; Goette, *Japan Fights for Asia*, p. 93.

31. "Wake Island Epic," *Washington Post*, December 24, 1941.

32. Andrews, "The Defense of Wake," p. 78.

33. Burns, *Roosevelt*, p. 223.

34. Arthur A. Poindexter Collection, Marine Corps Research Center, Quantico, Virginia.

35. "Wake Island Epic," *Washington Post*, December 24, 1941; "The 'Issue' On Wake Island," *New York Times*, December 30, 1941, p. 18.

36. Radio broadcast, January 12, 1942, in the William P. McCahill Collection, Marine Corps Research Center, Quantico, Virginia; "WAKE!" comic book in the William F. Delaney Collection, Marine Corps Research Center, Quantico, Virginia.

37. Letter from 1st Lt. C. P. Lancaster, U. S. Marine Corps, to Mrs. Nellie Marvin, May 18, 1942, in the Kenneth L. Marvin Collection.

38. Ted Shane, *Heroes of the Pacific* (New York: Julian Messner, Inc., 1944), pp. 21–22.

39. "Wake's Stand," *Newsweek*, August 11, 1942, p. 60; *Los Angeles Times*, September 24, 1942; *The Saturday Evening Post*, 1942.

40. Cunningham and Sims, *Wake Island Command*, p. 144.

41. Young, *Reminiscences*, p. 5.

42. Cunningham and Sims, *Wake Island Command*, p. 146.

43. John Rogge interview, April 11, 2002.

44. John Rogge interview, April 10, 2002.

45. Johnson interviews, March 19, 2002; April 2, 2002.

46. John Rogge interview, April 11, 2002.

CHAPTER 11—"I Was Torn from Everything I Knew"

1. Murray Kidd interview, April 13, 2002.
2. Johnson interview, April 2, 2002.
3. Laporte interview, March 14, 2001.
4. Edgar N. Langley Collection, Marine Corps Research Center, Quantico, Virginia.
5. Kinney and McCaffrey, *Wake Island Pilot*, p. 91.
6. Cunningham and Sims, *Wake Island Command*, p. 152.
7. Kinney and McCaffrey, *Wake Island Pilot*, p. 92.
8. Marvin interview, February 12, 2002.
9. Whitney, *Guest of the Fallen Sun*, p. 32.
10. Sanders, *Autobiography of Jacob R. Sanders*, pp. 8–9.
11. Johnson interview, April 2, 2002.
12. Cunningham and Sims, *Wake Island Command*, p. 154.
13. Cunningham and Sims, *Wake Island Command*, p. 155.
14. Cunningham and Sims, *Wake Island Command*, p. 159.
15. Marvin interview, February 12, 2002.
16. Whitney, *Guest of the Fallen Sun*, pp. 33-34.
17. Goicoechea, *Memoirs*, p. 25.
18. Devereux, *The Story of Wake Island*, p. 222.
19. Kessler, *To Wake Island and Beyond*, p. 88.
20. Goicoechea interview, April 12, 2002.
21. Martin Gatewood interview, February 28, 2002.
22. Sanders, *Autobiography of Jacob R. Sanders*, p. 7.
23. Hanna interview, February 13, 2002.
24. Whitney, *Guest of the Fallen Sun*, p. 45.
25. Whitney, *Guest of the Fallen Sun*, p. 43.
26. Gross interview, March 13, 2001.
27. Goicoechea interview, April 12, 2002.
28. Johnson interview, April 2, 2002.
29. Laporte interview, March 14, 2001.
30. Urwin, *Facing Fearful Odds*, p. 550.
31. Laporte interview, March 14, 2001.
32. Master Technical Sergeant Jesse L. Stewart, legal deposition, January 24, 1947, National Archives.
33. Hanna interview, February 13, 2002; Holewinski interview, May 16, 2001.
34. Murray Kidd interview, April 13, 2002; Marvin interview, February 12, 2002.
35. Dana interview, November 25, 2002.
36. Johnson interview, March 26, 2002.
37. Goicoechea interview, April 12, 2002.
38. Young, *Reminiscences*, p. 8.
39. Young, *Reminiscences*, p. 7.
40. Goicoechea interview, April 12, 2002.
41. Whitney, *Guest of the Fallen Sun*, pp. 48-49.
42. Kessler, *To Wake Island and Beyond: Reminiscences*, pp. 112–113.
43. Ellis Gordon letter to Provost Marshall, October 30, 1945, National Archives.
44. Stewart, legal deposition.
45. George H. Potter, recipe in the George H. Potter Collection, p. XX, Marine Corps Research Center, Quantico, Virginia.

46. Johnson interview, April 2, 2002.
47. King interview, March 21, 2002.
48. Johnson interview, April 2, 2002.
49. King interview, March 21, 2002.
50. Johnson interview, April 2, 2002.
51. Kessler, *To Wake Island and Beyond*, p. 124.

CHAPTER 12—"You Go Home Soon"

1. Hanna interview, February 20, 2002.
2. Letters from Mrs. E. C. Coxon and Esther Culver to the parents of Robert Murphy, September 1942, in the Robert Murphy Collection, Marine Corps Research Center, Quantico, Virginia.
3. "War Prisoner Heard on Radio," undated newspaper article in the Kenneth L. Marvin Collection.
4. Letter from Margery L. Rogge to John Rogge, October 27, 1942, in the John Rogge Collection.
5. Devereux, *The Story of Wake Island*, pp. 224-225.
6. Brown, *Memoir*.
7. Brig. Gen. James P. S. Devereux Personnel File, Marine Historical Center.
8. "A Hero Writes to His Son," *Washington Post*, December 30, 1943.
9. Letter from Edgar N. Langley to his parents, October 22, 1944, in the Edgar N. Langley File, Marine Corps Research Center, Quantico, Virginia.
10. Letters in the J. O. Young Collection.
11. Magnino, *Jim's Journey*, p. 139.
12. Johnson interview, March 26, 2002.
13. Stewart, legal deposition.
14. Murray Kidd interview, April 13, 2002.
15. Holewinski interview, June 28, 2002.
16. Statement of Lee Bong Moon regarding war crimes, August 11, 1948, National Archives.
17. Watanabe Mitsumasa diary, from the James P. S. Devereux Collection in the Special Collections at Boston University.
18. Goicoechea, *Memoirs*, p. 49.
19. Thomas J. Elliott, "Perpetuation of Testimony," April 23, 1947, National Archives.
20. Murray Kidd interview, April 13, 2002.
21. Goicoechea, *Memoirs*, p. 49; Goicoechea interview, April 12, 2002.
22. Read, *Reminiscences*, pp. 12–13.
23. Devereux, *The Story of Wake Island*, p. 14.
24. Whitney, *Guest of the Fallen Sun*, p. 63.
25. Murray Kidd interview, April 13, 2002.
26. Linda Goetz Holmes, *Unjust Enrichment: How Japan's Companies Built Postwar Fortunes Using American POWs* (Mechanicsburg, PA: Stackpole Books, 2001), p. 116.
27. Brown, *Memoir*.
28. Laporte interview, March 14, 2001.
29. Author's interview with George Rosendick, April 12, 2002.
30. Marvin interview, February 12, 2002.

31. Devereux, *The Story of Wake Island*, p. 238; Cunningham and Sims, *Wake Island Command*, pp. 239–240.
32. Johnson interview, April 2, 2002.
33. Sanders, *Autobiography of Jacob R. Sanders*, p. 10.
34. Hanna interview, February 13, 2002.
35. Laporte interview, March 14, 2001.
36. Cunningham and Sims, *Wake Island Command*, p. 241.
37. Cunningham and Sims, *Wake Island Command*, p. 168.
38. Don Caswell, "Devereux, Wake Hero, Is Found," *Washington Daily News*, September 13, 1945, p. 1.
39. Young, *Reminiscences*, p. 14.
40. Martin Gatewood interview, February 28, 2002.
41. Kephart, *Wake, War and Waiting . . .* , pp. 80–81.
42. Author's interview with Ernie Harwell, January 21, 1989.
43. Sgt. Ernie Harwell, "The Wake Story," *Leatherneck*, November 15, 1945, pp. 6–7.

CHAPTER 13—"I Was Doing What I Was Trained to Do"

1. Roland Nicholson, "Bethesda Greets Devereux On Homecoming," *Washington Times-Herald*, September 30, 1945.
2. Cunningham and Sims, *Wake Island Command*, pp. 246, 277.
3. Hanna interview, June 20, 2002.
4. Marvin interview, February 14, 2002.
5. Martin Gatewood interview, February 27, 2002.
6. Laporte interview, March 14, 2001.
7. Murray Kidd interview, April 13, 2003.
8. Read, *Reminiscences*, p. 18.
9. Kinney and McCaffrey, *Wake Island Pilot*, pp. 162–163.
10. Kephart, *Wake, War and Waiting . . .* , p. 78.
11. Martin Gatewood interview, February 28, 2002.
12. Lewis H. Carlson, *We Were Each Other's Prisoners* (New York: Basic Books, 1997), p. 225.
13. Hanna interview, February 20, 2002.
14. John Rogge interview, April 11, 2002.
15. Martin Gatewood interview, February 28, 2002.
16. Author's interview with Lena Kidd, April 13, 2003.
17. Murray Kidd interview, April 13, 2003.
18. Laporte interview, March 14, 2001; Holewinski interview, May 16, 2001.
19. Martin Gatewood interview, February 28, 2002.
20. Laporte interview, March 14, 2001.
21. Grace Gatewood interview, February 28, 2002.
22. Gross interview, March 13, 2001.
23. Kessler, *To Wake Island and Beyond*, p. 144.
24. Stewart, legal deposition.
25. Goicoechea interview, April 12, 2002.
26. Virginia Rogge interview, April 11, 2002.
27. Marvin interview, February 12, 2002.
28. Holewinski interview, May 16, 2001.

29. Goicoechea interview, April 12, 2002.

30. Letter of John Valov to Colonel Devereux, April 18, 1946, from the James P. S. Devereux Collection in the Special Collections at Boston University.

31. Martin Gatewood interview, February 28, 2002.

32. Gross interview, March 5, 2001.

33. King interview, March 26, 2002.

34. Goicoechea interview, April 12, 2002.

35. Johnson interview, April 2, 2002.

36. Gross interview, March 13, 2001.

37. Hanna interview, June 20, 2002.

38. John Rogge interview, April 10, 2002.

39. Hanna interviews, June 20, 2002; June 21, 2002.

40. Author's interview with Mark Cruz, October 30, 2002.

Bibliography

PRIMARY SOURCES

AT THE NATIONAL ARCHIVES

The National Archives is where the researcher will locate most of the official military records. Especially pertinent are the:

> Records of the Bureau of Naval Personnel, Casualty Branch, Records Relating to POWs in Japanese Camps, Box 6
> Records of the Office of the Chief of Naval Operations, World War II and Operational Reports, Individual Personnel, Boxes 1730, 1723
> Records of the Office of the Judge Advocate General (Navy), War Crimes Branch, Correspondence, 1944–1949, Boxes 2, 3, 9
> Records of the United States Marine Corps, USMC Geographic Files, Boxes 359, 360
> Records of the United States Marine Corps, Marine Garrison Forces Correspondence, Box 2

The most helpful documents were:

Barninger, Major C. A. To Lt. Col. James P. S. Devereux, informal report, October 8, 1945.

Barninger, Lt. Col. Clarence A. Official reply to Historical Section questionnaire, February 18, 1947.

Bayler, Maj. Walter L. J. To the Commanding Officer, Marine Aviation Detachment, Marine Aircraft Group 21, "Report on Wake Island, Period of the 7th to 20th December, 1941," February 18, 1942.

Borth, WO Harold C. To Lt. Col. James P. S. Devereux, informal report, October 23, 1945.

Campbell, Francis C. "Perpetuation of Testimony," October 11, 1946.

Cunningham, Captain W. S. To Commandant of the Marine Corps, "Report of VMF-211 on Wake Island," November 1, 1945.

Cunningham, Comdr. W. S. To Commandant, 14th Naval District, "Report on Conditions at Wake Island," December 20, 1941.

Elliott, Thomas J. "Perpetuation of Testimony," April 23, 1947.

Freuler, Herbert. To Lt. Col. James P. S. Devereux, informal report, October 9, 1945.

Godbold, Lt. Col. Bryghte D. To Lt. Col. James P. S. Devereux, informal report, October 9, 1945.

Goodman, Capt. W. H., and Mr. Joel D. Thacker. "An interview with 1st Lt. John F. Kinney," July 23, 1945.

Gordon, Ellis. "Perpetuation of Testimony," November 19, 1945.

Greeley, 1st Lt. Robert W. To Lt. Col. James P. S. Devereux, informal report, October 9, 1945.

Hamas, 2nd Lt. John. To Lt. Col. James P. S. Devereux, informal report, October 12, 1945.

Hanna, 1st Lt. Robert M. To Lt. Col. James P. S. Devereux, informal report, October 11, 1945.

Heinl, Lt. Col. "Notes on Interview with Lieutenant Colonel John F. Kinney," March 13, 1947.

Hevenor, H. P. Letter to Colonel Clark, December 20, 1941.

Keene, Capt. Campbell. To the Secretary of the Navy, "Activities of Task Group 9.2 at Wake Island, November 29–December 23, 1941," December 20, 1945.

Kessler, Capt. Woodrow M. To Lt. Col. James P. S. Devereux, informal report, October 11, 1945.

Ketner, WO Bernard O. Legal deposition, February 24, 1948.

Kinney, 1st Lieutenant John F. To Lt. Col. James P. S. Devereux, informal report, October 12, 1945.

Kliewer, 1st Lt. David D. To Lt. Col. James P. S. Devereux, informal report, October 23, 1945.

Lewis, Maj. William W. To Lt. Col. James P. S. Devereux, informal report, October 9, 1945.

Lewis, Lt. Col. William W. Official reply to Historical Section questionnaire, February 28, 1947.

McAlister, 1st Lt. John A. "Perpetuation of Testimony," September 11, 1945.

McAlister, 1st Lt. John A. To Lt. Col. James P. S. Devereux, informal report, October 12, 1945.

McAlister, Lt. Col. John A. Official reply to Historical Section questionnaire, June 18, 1947.

McKinstry, MGUN Clarence B. To Lt. Col. James P. S. Devereux, informal report, undated [1945].

Platt, Lt. Col. Wesley M. To Lt. Col. James P. S. Devereux, informal report, undated [1945].

Platt, Lt. Col. Wesley M. Official reply to Historical Section questionnaire, March 10, 1947.

Potter, Col. George H. To Lt. Col. James P. S. Devereux, informal report, October 13, 1945.

Potter, Col. George H. To the Director, Division of Public Information, "Defense of Wake," March 27, 1947.

Potter, Lt. Col. George H. Legal deposition, May 5, 1947.

Putnam, Lt. Col. Paul A. To Secretary of the Navy, "Recommendation for the Navy Cross, case of Second Lieutenant Robert Melton Hanna," October 25, 1945.

Putnam, Lt. Col. Paul A. To Lt. Col. James P. S. Devereux, informal report, October 9, 1945.

Putnam, Lt. Col. Paul A. To Commandant of the Marine Corps, "Report of VMF-211 on Wake Island," October 18, 1945.

Putnam, Lt. Col. Paul A. "Prisoner of War Report," October 17, 1945.

Stewart, MTSgt Jesse L. Legal deposition, January 24, 1947.

Tharin, Maj. Frank C. To Lt. Col. James P. S. Devereux, informal report, October 16, 1945.

What, Wong Sen. "Perpetuation of Testimony," January 18, 1947.

THE MARINE HISTORICAL CENTER

The Marine Historical Center in Washington, D.C., holds the personnel files of most Marines, as well as official papers and interviews with prominent individuals. The facility is indispensable for any serious research on World War II.

Bayler, Maj. Walter L. J. To the Commander-in-Chief, U.S. Pacific Fleet,"Report on Wake Island, Period of the 7th to 20th December, 1941," January 7, 1942.

Devereux, Brig. Gen. James P. S. Personnel files.

Devereux, Col. James P. S. Historical Section interview, February 12, 1945.

Devereux, Col. James P. S. To Commandant of the Marine Corps, "Discrepancies in a Report on the Defense of Wake Island," November 19, 1947.

Elrod, Maj. Henry T. Personnel files.

Hamas, John. Letter to Commandant of the Marine Corps, October 11, 1946.

McAlister, Colonel John A. Personnel files.

Poindexter, Lt. Col. Arthur A. "An Informal Report of the Operations of the Machine Gun Battery and the Mobile Reserve During the Defense of Wake, December 1941," March 25, 1947.

Poindexter, 2nd Lt. Arthur A. Personnel files.

Putnam, Major Paul A. Personnel files.

Putnam, Major Paul A. To the Commanding Officer, Marine Aircraft Group 21, "Report of Operations, December 4-20, 1941," December 20, 1941.

MARINE CORPS RESEARCH CENTER

This beautiful facility on the grounds of the Marine base at Quantico, Virginia, holds the personal papers of thousands of Marines. The names of the collections used for this book are:

William F. Delaney
Lester A. Dessez
Henry T. Elrod
Neal Hanley
John R. Himelrick
W. H. Kerr

Dan King
John F. Kinney
Frederick A. Knight
Edgar N. Langley
William P. McCahill
Frances M. McKinstry
Robert Murphy
John E. Pearsall
Arthur A. Poindexter
George H. Potter
William Rossiter
Vilmer W. Skavdahl
John G. Workman

BOSTON UNIVERSITY LIBRARY

This library contains two key collections, the papers of Brig. Gen. James P. S. Devereux and of RADM Winfield S. Cunningham. Among the items in these collections were the Dan Teters Affidavit, dated November 24, 1945, and a moving letter from John Valov to General Devereux, dated April 18, 1946.

PERSONAL PAPERS

Fortunately, numerous Marines and civilians made their personal recollections, memorabilia, and photographs available to me. I obtained many fascinating pieces of information from these remarkable collections.

Martin Gatewood Collection
Joseph Goicoechea Collection
Robert M. Hanna Collection
Ralph Holewinski Collection
Kenneth L. Marvin Collection
Forrest Read Collection
John Rogge Collection
Jacob R. Sanders Collection
J. O. Young Collection

PERSONAL RECOLLECTIONS, DIARIES

Brown, Robert M. Memoir, www.azcentral.com/news/specials/veterans/brown.html.
Goicoechea, Joseph. *Memoirs*, June 14, 2001.
Gordon, Ellis. Radio interview, October 8, 1945.
Himelrick, John R. Diary, in the John R. Himelrick Collection, Marine Corps Research Center, Quantico, Virginia.

Katsumi, Seishi. Diary, in the Lester A. Dessez Collection, Marine Corps Research Center, Quantico, Virginia.

Kinney, John F. Diary, in the John F. Kinney Collection, Marine Corps Research Center, Quantico, Virginia.

Kliewer, David D. Personal Diary of First Lieutenant David D. Kliewer, National Archives.

Knight, Frederick A. Diary, in the Frederick A. Knight Collection, Marine Corps Research Center, Quantico, Virginia.

Ozeki, Dr. Shigeyoshi. "Wake Island in Sight," interview with Dan King, in the Dan King Collection, Marine Corps Research Center, Quantico, Virginia.

Ozeki, Dr. Shigeyoshi. Reminiscence in Gregory J. W. Urwin Web site, astro.temple.edu/~gurwin/ffoozeki.htm.

Pearsall, John E. Diary, in the John E. Pearsall Collection, Marine Corps Research Center, Quantico, Virginia.

Potter, George H. Recipes, in the George H. Potter Collection, Marine Corps Research Center, Quantico, Virginia.

Read, Forrest. *Reminiscences*, in the Forrest Read Collection, privately published, undated.

Richardson, Bernard E. "Wake Island: End of Combat," in Gregory J. W. Urwin Web site, astro.temple.edu/~gurwin/ffoozeki.htm

Sanders, Jacob R. *Autobiography of Jacob R. Sanders*, as Told to and Written by his Daughter, Cathy M. Sanders, undated, in the Jacob R. Sanders Collection.

Young, J. O. *Reminiscences*, undated, in the J. O. Young Collection.

INTERVIEWS

All interviews conducted by me, whether in person or by telephone, were tape recorded with permission. I cannot thank these individuals enough for sharing their time and information with me.

Marines

BUCKIE, WILLIAM B. Telephone interview on November 20, 2002.

BUEHLER, WILLIAM F. Telephone interview on November 30, 2002.

BYER, LAWRENCE. Personal interview on March 14, 2002.

DANA, MAX J. Telephone interview on November 25, 2002.

GATEWOOD, GRACE, wife of Martin Gatewood. Telephone interview on February 28, 2002.

GATEWOOD, MARTIN. Telephone interviews on February 13, 2002; February 20, 2002; February 27, 2002; February 28, 2002.

GROSS, FRANKLIN. Telephone interviews on March 5, 2001; March 13, 2001; March 29, 2002.

HANNA, ROBERT M. Telephone interviews on February 6, 2002; February 13, 2002; February 20, 2002; July 30, 2002. Personal interviews on June 20, 2002; June 21, 2002.

HARTUNG, ARVEL. Telephone interview on December 10, 2002.

HARWELL, ERNIE. Personal interview on January 21, 1989.

HASSIG, EDWIN F. Telephone interview on November 18, 2002.

HOLEWINSKI, RALPH. Telephone interview on May 16, 2001. Personal interview on June 28, 2002.

JOHNSON, JOHN S. Telephone interviews on March 19, 2002; March 26, 2002; April 2, 2002.

KING, JAMES O. Telephone interviews on March 21, 2002; March 26, 2002.

KINNEY, GEN. JOHN F. Telephone interview on October 30, 2002.

LAPORTE, EWING. Telephone interviews on March 13, 2001; March 14, 2001.

MARVIN, KENNETH. Telephone interviews on February 5, 2002; February 12, 2002; February 14, 2002.

SCHNEIDER, LEROY. Personal interview on September 17, 1989.

Navy

BALHORN, MARVIN. Telephone interview on March 18, 2002.

CHAMBLESS, ORBAN R., *Tangier* crew member. Telephone interview on April 8, 1992.

FRIETAS, HENRY, *Tangier* crew member. Telephone interview on April 8, 1992.

FRUIN, RICHARD, *Tangier* crew member. Telephone interview on April 25, 1992.

GERBERDING, OLIVER. Telephone interview on November 18, 2002.

LARSON, WESLEY, *Tangier* crew member. Telephone interview on April 15, 1992.

PLATE, WILLIAM O. Telephone interview on October 28, 2002.

UNGER, JOHN. Telephone interview on October 29, 2002.

WILKINSON, C. A., Jr., *Tangier* crew member. Telephone interviews on April 7, 1992; April 20, 1992.

Civilians

COMSTOCK, BENJAMIN F., Jr. Telephone interview on November 20, 2002.

GOICOECHEA, JOSEPH. Telephone interviews on February 26, 2002; March 5, 2002. Personal interviews on April 10, 2002; April 12, 2002.

KIDD, LENA, wife of Murray Kidd. Personal interview on April 13, 2002.

KIDD, MURRAY. Personal interview on April 13, 2002.

ROGGE, JOHN. Telephone interview on March 19, 2002. Personal interviews on April 10, 2002; April 11, 2002; April 12, 2002.

ROGGE, VIRGINIA, wife of John Rogge. Personal interview on April 11, 2002.

ROSENDICK, GEORGE. Personal interview on April 12, 2002.

YOUNG, J. O. Telephone interviews on June 11, 2002, June 18, 2002.

YOUNG, PEARL ANN, wife of J. O. Young. Telephone interview on June 11, 2002.

Others

CRUZ, MARK, former Marine. Personal interview on October 30, 2002.

FARRELL, NANCY, Wake Island researcher. Telephone interview on March 6, 2001.

O'CONNOR, COMDR. MICHAEL P., USN. Personal interview on March 22, 1997.

SANDERS, CATHY, daughter of Pfc. Jacob R. Sanders. Telephone interviews on February 20, 2002; March 12, 2002.

NEWSPAPERS

The Atlanta Constitution
Boston Globe

Chattanooga Evening Times
Detroit Free Press
Detroit News
Detroit Times
The Honolulu Advertiser
Honolulu Star Bulletin
Idaho Daily Statesman
The Jersey Journal
Los Angeles Examiner
Mesabi Daily News
Minneapolis Times
Montgomery Journal
New York Times
Quantico Sentry
Washington Daily News
Washington Evening Star
Washington Post
Washington Times-Herald

BOOKS

Abraham, Theodore A., Jr. *"Do You Understand, Huh?": A POW's Lament, 1941–1945*. Manhattan, Kansas: Sunflower University Press, 1992.

Agawa, Hiroyuki. *The Reluctant Admiral: Yamamoto and the Imperial Navy*. Tokyo: Kodansha International Ltd., 1979.

Astarita, Joseph J. *Sketches of P.O.W. Life*. Brooklyn: Rollo Press, 1947.

Bateson, Charles. *The War with Japan*. East Lansing: Michigan State University Press, 1968.

Bayler, Lt. Col. Walter L. J. *Last Man off Wake Island*. Indianapolis: The Bobbs-Merrill Company, 1943.

Berry, Henry. *Semper Fi, Mac: Living Memories of the U. S. Marines in World War II*. New York: Arbor House, 1982.

Biggs, Chester M. *Behind the Barbed Wire*. Jefferson, North Carolina: McFarland & Company, Inc., 1995.

Brinkley, David. *Washington Goes to War*. New York: Alfred A. Knopf, 1988.

Buell, Thomas B. *Master of Sea Power: A Biography of Fleet Admiral Ernest J. King*. Boston: Little, Brown and Company, 1980.

Burns, James MacGregor. *Roosevelt: The Soldier of Freedom*. New York: Harcourt Brace Jovanovich, Inc., 1970.

Carlson, Lewis H. *We Were Each Other's Prisoners*. New York: Basic Books, 1997.

Casey, Robert J. *Torpedo Junction: With the Pacific Fleet from Pearl Harbor to Midway*. Indianapolis: The Bobbs-Merrill Company, 1942.

Center for Internee Rights, Inc. *Newsletter*. May–July 2002.

Churchill, Winston S. *The Second World War: The Grand Alliance*. Boston: Houghton Mifflin Company, 1950.

Cohen, Stan. *Enemy on Island. Issue in Doubt: The Capture of Wake Island, December 1941*. Missoula, Montana: Pictorial Histories Publishing Company, 1983.

Collier, Basil. *The War in the Far East, 1941–1945*. New York: William Morrow & Company, Inc., 1969.

Commager, Henry Steele. *The Story of the Second World War*. Washington: Brassey's, 1991.

Costello, John. *The Pacific War, 1941–1945*. New York: Quill Books, 1982.

Cressman, Robert J. *"A Magnificent Fight": The Battle for Wake Island*. Annapolis, Maryland: Naval Institute Press, 1995.

Cunningham, W. Scott, with Lydel Sims. *Wake Island Command*. Boston: Little, Brown and Company, 1961.

Darden, James B., III. *Guests of the Emperor: The Story of Dick Darden*. Clinton, North Carolina: The Greenhouse Press, 1990.

Daws, Gavan. *Prisoners of the Japanese: POWs of World War II in the Pacific*. New York: William Morrow and Company, Inc., 1994.

DeNevi, Donald. *The West Coast Goes to War, 1941–1942*. Missoula, Montana: Pictorial Histories Publishing Company, Inc., 1998.

Devereux, James P. S. *The Story of Wake Island*. New York: J. B. Lippincott, 1947.

Dower, John W. *War Without Mercy: Race and Power in the Pacific War*. New York: Pantheon Books, 1986.

Edwards, Jack, with Jimmy Walter. *Banzai, You Bastards!* Hong Kong: Corporate Communications, undated.

Funke, Teresa R. *Remember Wake*. Bloomington, Indiana: 1st Books Library, 2001.

Gailey, Harry A. *The War in the Pacific*. Novato, California: Presidio Press, 1995.

Giles, Rear Admiral Donald T., USN. *Captive of the Rising Sun*. Annapolis, Maryland: Naval Institute Press, 1994.

Goette, John. *Japan Fights for Asia*. New York: Harcourt, Brace and Company, 1943.

Goodwin, Doris Kearns. *No Ordinary Time*. New York: Simon & Schuster, 1994.

Hagan, Kenneth J. *This People's Navy*. New York: The Free Press, 1991.

Halsey, Fleet Admiral William F., USN, and Lt. Cmdr. J. Bryan III, USNR. *Admiral Halsey's Story*. New York: McGraw-Hill Book Company, Inc., 1947.

Harries, Meirion and Susie. *Soldiers of the Sun: The Rise and Fall of the Imperial Japanese Army*. New York: Random House, 1991.

Heinl, Lt. Col. R. D., Jr. *The Defense of Wake*. Washington, D. C.: Historical Section, Division of Public Information, Headquarters, U. S. Marine Corps, 1947.

Hill, Maj. Richard Vernon, Ret. *My War with Imperial Japan: Escape and Evasion*. New York: Vantage Press, 1989.

Holmes, Linda Goetz. *Unjust Enrichment: How Japan's Companies Built Postwar Fortunes Using American POWs*. Mechanicsburg, PA: Stackpole Books, 2001.

Holmes, W. J. *Double-Edged Secrets: U. S. Naval Intelligence Operations in the Pacific during World War II*. Annapolis, Maryland: Naval Institute Press, 1979.

Hough, Lt. Col. Frank O., Maj. Verle E. Ludwig, and Henry I. Shaw, Jr. *History of U. S. Marine Corps Operations in World War II: Volume I, Pearl Harbor to Guadalcanal*. Washington, D.C.: Historical Branch, Headquarters, U. S. Marine Corps, 1958.

Howarth, Stephen. *To Shining Sea: A History of the United States Navy, 1775–1991*. New York: Random House, 1991.

Hoyt, Edwin P. *Yamamoto*. New York: McGraw-Hill Publishing Company, 1990.

Hull, Cordell. *The Memoirs of Cordell Hull*. New York: The Macmillan Company, 1948.

Ienaga, Saburo. *The Pacific War: World War II and the Japanese, 1931–1945*. New York: Pantheon Books, 1978.

Jones, Wilbur D., Jr., and Carroll Robbins Jones. *Hawaii Goes to War: The Aftermath of Pearl Harbor*. Shippensburg, Pennsylvania: White Mane Books, 2001.

Karig, Cmdr. Walter, and Lt. Welbourn Kelley. *Battle Report: Pearl Harbor to Coral Sea*. New York: Farrar & Rinehart, Inc., 1944.

Kauffman, William F., producer and writer. "Those Who Also Served: The Civilian Construction Men of Wake Island." Videotape, Aviator Pictures, 2002.

Keegan, John. *The Second World War*. New York: Penguin Books, 1989.

Kelnhofer, Guy J. Jr., Ph.D. *Life After Liberation: Understanding the Former Prisoner of War*. St. Paul, Minnesota: Banfil Street Press, 1992.

Kephart, Rodney. *Wake, War and Waiting . . .* New York: Exposition Press, 1950.

Kerr, E. Bartlett. *Surrender and Survival: The Experience of American POWs in the Pacific, 1941–1945*. New York: William Morrow and Company, Inc., 1985.

Kessler, Brig. Gen. Woodrow M., USMC (Ret.). *To Wake Island and Beyond: Reminiscences*. Washington, D.C.: History and Museums Division, Headquarters, U.S. Marine Corps, 1988.

Kinney, Brig. Gen. John F., USMC (Ret.), with James M. McCaffrey. *Wake Island Pilot: A World War II Memoir*. Washington: Brassey's, 1995.

Kirk, Terence S. *The Secret Camera*. Redwood Valley, CA: Owl Wise Publishing, 1982.

Koppes, Clayton R., and Gregory D. Black. *Hollywood Goes to War*. New York: The Free Press, 1987.

Larrabee, Eric. *Commander in Chief: Franklin Delano Roosevelt, His Lieutenants, and Their War*. New York: Harper & Row, Publishers, 1987.

Lash, Joseph P. *Roosevelt and Churchill, 1939–1941*. New York: W. W. Norton & Company, Inc., 1976.

Layton, Rear Admiral Edwin T., USN (Ret.), with Capt. Roger Pineau, USNR (Ret.), and John Costello. *"And I Was There": Pearl Harbor and Midway— Breaking the Secrets*. New York: William Morrow and Company, Inc., 1985.

Leahy, Fleet Admiral William D. *I Was There*. New York: McGraw-Hill Book Company, Inc., 1950.

Leckie, Robert. *Strong Men Armed: The United States Marines Against Japan*. New York: Da Capo Press, 1962.

——. *The Wars of America*. Edison, New Jersey: Castle Books, 1966.

——. *Delivered from Evil: The Saga of World War II*. New York; Harper & Row, Publishers, 1987.

Lee, Clark. *They Call It Pacific*. New York: The Viking Press, 1943.

Lewin, Ronald. *The American Magic: Codes, Ciphers and the Defeat of Japan*. New York: Farrar Straus Giroux, 1982.

Lingeman, Richard R. *Don't You Know There's a War On?: The American Home Front, 1941–1945*. New York: G. P. Putnam's Sons, 1970.

Magnino, L. A. *Jim's Journey: A Wake Island Civilian POW's Story*. Central Point, Oregon: Hellgate Press, 2001.

Marolda, Edward J., ed. *FDR and the U.S. Navy*. New York: St. Martin's Press, 1998.

McBrayer, James D., Jr. *Escape!* Jefferson, North Carolina: McFarland & Company, Inc., 1995.

Millett, Alan R. *Semper Fidelis: The History of the United States Marine Corps*. New York: Macmillan Publishing Co., Inc., 1980.

Millett, Allan R., and Peter Maslowski. *For the Common Defense: A Military History of the United States of America*. New York: The Free Press, 1984.

Morella, Joe, Edward Z. Epstein, and John Griggs. *The Films of World War II*. Secaucus, New Jersey: The Citadel Press, 1973.

Morgan, Ted. *FDR: A Biography*. New York: Simon and Schuster, 1985.

Morison, Samuel Eliot. *History of United States Naval Operations in World War II, Volume III: The Rising Sun in the Pacific, 1931–April 1942*. Boston: Little, Brown and Company, 1965.

Mullins, Wayman C., ed. *1942—"Issue in Doubt": Symposium on the War in the Pacific by the Admiral Nimitz Museum*. Austin, Texas: Eakin Press, 1994.

Murray, Williamson, and Allan R. Millett. *A War to Be Won*. Cambridge, Massachusetts: The Belknap Press, 2000.

Nordin, Carl S. *We Were Next to Nothing*. Jefferson, North Carolina: McFarland & Company, Inc., 1997.

Pacific Island Employees Foundation, Inc. *A Report to Returned CPNAB Prisoner of War Heroes and Their Dependents*. Boise, Idaho: The Pacific Island Employees Foundation, Inc., 1945.

Perkins, Frances. *The Roosevelt I Knew*. New York: The Viking Press, 1946.

Perrett, Bryan. *Last Stand!: Famous Battles Against the Odds*. London: Arms and Armour, 1991.

Perrett, Geoffrey. *Days of Sadness, Years of Triumph: The American People, 1939–1945*. New York: Coward, McCann & Geoghegan Inc., 1973.

Potter, E. B. *Nimitz*. Annapolis, Maryland: Naval Institute Press, 1976.

——. *Bull Halsey*. Annapolis, Maryland: Naval Institute Press, 1985.

Prados, John. *Combined Fleet Decoded: The Secret History of American Intelligence and the Japanese Navy in World War II*. New York: Random House, 1995.

Prange, Gordon W., in collaboration with Donald M. Goldstein and Katherine V. Dillon. *At Dawn We Slept: The Untold Story of Pearl Harbor*. New York: Penguin Books, 1981.

Pratt, Fletcher. *The Marines' War*. New York: William Sloane Associates, Inc., 1948.

Roosevelt, Eleanor. *This I Remember*. New York: Harper & Brothers, 1949.

Roosevelt, Elliott. *As He Saw It*. New York: Duell, Sloan and Pearce, 1946.

Rottman, Gordon. *US Marine Corps 1941–1945*. Oxford, England: Osprey Publishing, 1995.

Russell, Lord Edward. *The Knights of Bushido*. Bath, England: Chivers Press, 1958.

Schultz, Duane. *Wake Island: The Heroic, Gallant Fight*. New York: St. Martin's Press, 1978.

Shane, Ted. *Heroes of the Pacific*. New York: Julian Messner, Inc., 1944.

Sherrod, Robert. *History of Marine Corps Aviation in World War II*. Washington, D.C.: Combat Forces Press, 1952.

Sherwood, Robert E. *Roosevelt and Hopkins: An Intimate History*. New York: Harper & Brothers, 1948.

Shindler, Colin. *Hollywood Goes to War*. London: Routledge & Kegan Paul, 1979.

Simmons, Brig. Gen. Edwin H. USMC (Ret.). *The United States Marines, 1775–1975*. New York: The Viking Press, 1976.

Smith, S. E., ed. *The United States Marine Corps in World War II*. New York: Random House, 1969.

Spector, Ronald H. *Eagle Against the Sun: The American War with Japan*. New York: The Free Press, 1985.

Spiller, Henry. *From Wake Island to Berlin*. Paducah, Kentucky: Turner Publishing Company, 1997.

Stimson, Henry L., and McGeorge Bundy. *On Active Service in Peace and War*. New York: Harper & Brothers, 1948.

Survivors of Wake, Guam, and Cavite, Inc. *"How the Newspapers Told It . . . "* Boise, Idaho: Survivors of Wake, Guam, and Cavite, Inc., 1979.

Thomas, Lowell. *These Men Shall Never Die*. Philadelphia: The John C. Winston Company, 1943.

Toland, John. *But Not in Shame: The Six Months After Pearl Harbor*. New York: Random House, 1961.

——. *The Rising Sun*. New York: Random House, 1970.

Tully, Grace. *F.D.R.: My Boss*. Chicago: Peoples Book Club, 1949.

Urwin, Gregory J. W. *Facing Fearful Odds: The Siege of Wake Island*. Lincoln: University of Nebraska Press, 1997.

Van der Vat, Dan. *The Pacific Campaign*. New York: Simon & Schuster, 1991.

Wake Island Wig-Wag, various dates.

Weinberg, Gerhard L. *A World at Arms*. Cambridge, England: Cambridge University Press, 1994.

Wheeler, Richard. *A Special Valor: The U.S. Marines and the Pacific War*. New York: New American Library, 1983.

Whitney, Hans. *Guests of the Fallen Sun*. New York: Exposition Press, 1951.

Winton, John. *Ultra in the Pacific*. Annapolis, Maryland: Naval Institute Press, 1993.

Woodbury, David O. *Builders for Battle: How the Pacific Naval Air Bases Were Constructed*. New York: E. P. Dutton and Company Inc., 1946.

Wukovits, John F. *Devotion to Duty: A Biography of Admiral Clifton A. F. Sprague*. Annapolis, Maryland: Naval Institute Press, 1995.

Young, Donald J. *First 24 Hours of War in the Pacific*. Shippensburg, PA: Burd Street Press, 1998.

Zich, Arthur. *The Rising Sun*. Alexandria, Virginia: Time-Life Books, 1977.

ARTICLES

Andrews, Peter. "The Defense of Wake." *American Heritage*, July–August 1987, pp. 65–80.

Baldwin, Hanson W. "The Saga of Wake." *The Virginia Quarterly Review*, Summer 1942, pp. 321–335.

Bartlett, Tom. "Wake Island Diary." *Leatherneck*, March 1985, pp. 40–47, 60.

——. "Wake Island Marine: Still in Love with the Corps." *Leatherneck*, December 1988, pp. 38–43.

——. "Wake Island Reunion." *Leatherneck*, December 1995, pp. 34–36.

Bayler, Lt. Col. Walter L. J., as Told to Cecil Carnes. "Last Man Off Wake Island." *The Saturday Evening Post*, April 17, 1943, pp. 26–27, 39, 41, 44.

Burroughs, John R. "The Siege of Wake Island." *American Heritage*, June 1959, pp. 65–76.

Butcher, Lt. Comdr. M. E., USN. "Admiral Frank Jack Fletcher, Pioneer Warrior or Gross Sinner?" *Naval War College Review*, Winter 1987, pp. 69–79.

"Congressional Medal." *Yale Alumni Magazine*, January 1947, p. 25.

Cunningham, Rear Admiral Winfield Scott, USN (Ret.). "The Truth Behind the Wake Island Marine Hero Hoax." *Cavalier*, May 1961, pp. 11–15, 70–82.

Devereux, Lt. Col. James P. S., as told to Lt. Comdr. J. Bryan, III, USNR. "This Is How It Was: Part One." *The Saturday Evening Post*, February 23, 1946, pp. 10–11, 84, 87, 89–90.

———. "This Is How It Was: Part Two." *The Saturday Evening Post*, March 2, 1946, pp. 28–29, 52–54, 56.

———. "This Is How It Was: Part Three." *The Saturday Evening Post*, March 9, 1946, pp. 28–29, 83–84, 86.

———. "This Is How It Was: Part Four." *The Saturday Evening Post*, March 16, 1946, pp. 20, 98, 101, 104, 106.

"Enlistments." *Time*, January 5, 1942, pp. 44–45.

"First Jitters." *Time*, December 22, 1941, pp. 11–12.

"Flame of Glory." *Time*, January 19, 1942, pp. 22–23.

"Fort by Fort, Port by Port." *Time*, December 15, 1941, pp. 23–24.

"Full Blast." *Time*, December 22, 1941, pp. 9–10.

Harwell, Sgt. Ernie. "The Wake Story." *Leatherneck*, November 15, 1945, p. 7.

Heinl, Lt. Col. R. D., Jr. "We're Headed for Wake." *Marine Corps Gazette*, June 1946, pp. 35–38.

"Helpmate." *Time*, December 22, 1941, p. 12.

Holmes, Charles A. "A Sky Gunner's Battle for Wake." *Naval History*, April 1987, pp. 49–54.

"Islands." *Newsweek*, December 22, 1941, p. 19.

Jenks, Sgt. Chuck. "Wake Island: Then and Now." *Leatherneck*, December 1984, pp. 46–47.

Junghans, Earl A. "Wake's POWs." *Naval Institute Proceedings*, February 1983, pp. 43–50.

Keene, R. R. "Wake Island." *Leatherneck*, December 2001, pp. 24–31.

Lundstrom, John B. "Frank Jack Fletcher Got A Bum Rap." *Naval History*, Summer 1992, pp. 22–27.

"Message from Wake." *Time*, December 29, 1941, p. 14.

Nihart, Col. Brooke, USMC (Ret.). "The Abortive Expedition to Relieve Wake." Speech given to Wake Island Defenders, October 11, 1991, pp. 1–13.

O'Brien, Cyril J. O. "Wake's Defender." *VFW: Veterans of Foreign Wars Magazine*, January 1980, pp. 32–33.

Poindexter, Arthur A. "Our Last Hurrah on Wake." *American History Illustrated*, February 1992, pp. 64–67, 74.

"The President Addresses the Congress on the State of the Nation, January 6, 1942." *Time*, January 12, 1942, p. 12.

Schneider, Cece. "Pilgrimage to Wake Island." *Leatherneck*, January 1992, pp. 36–41.

"Stand at Wake." *Time*, December 22, 1941, p. 19.

Taylor, Blaine. "Fight Left Unfinished." *Military History*, December 1987, pp. 35–41.

"Tragedy at Honolulu." *Time*, December 15, 1941, pp. 19–23.

Urwin, Gregory J. W. "The Road Back From Wake Island, Part I." *American History Illustrated*, December 1980, pp. 16–23.

———. "The Road Back From Wake Island, Part II." *American History Illustrated*, January 1981, pp. 43–49.

——. " 'An Epic That Should Give Every American Hope:' The Media and the Birth of the Wake Island Legend." *Marine Corps Gazette*, December 1996, pp. 64–69.

"U.S. Radio at War." *Time*, December 15, 1941, pp. 48–50.

"Wake." *Newsweek*, December 29, 1941, p. 17; January 5, 1942, p. 14.

"Wake Island: Americans Retake Pacific Outpost from a Starving Jap Garrison." *Life*, September 24, 1945, pp. 49–50.

"Wake's 378." *Time*, January 5, 1942, pp. 20–21.

"Wake's Stand." *Newsweek*, August 11, 1942, p. 60.

Wensyel, James W. "Odyssey of the Wake Island Prisoners." *World War II*, November 2000, pp. 34–40, 86.

Wharton, Don. "Wake Island." *Look*, September 22, 1942, pp. 39–41.

Wilkerson, Reba. "Return to Wake." *American History Illustrated*, December 1987, pp. 46–48.

——. "Wake's Forgotten Survivors." *American History Illustrated*, December 1987, pp. 40–45.

Wukovits, John F. "A Nation's Inspiration." *World War II*, September 1992, pp. 30–37.

——. "Ernie Harwell for *Leatherneck*." *Naval History*, July/August 1996, pp. 42–44.

——. "The Fight for Wake." *WWII History*, May 2002, pp. 36–47.

Index